A GENERAL HISTORY OF EUROPE

EDITED BY DENYS HAY

EUROPE IN THE
NINETEENTH CENTURY
1830-1880

H. HEARDER

LONGMAN
London and New York

940·28

LONGMAN GROUP LIMITED
London

*Associated companies, branches and representatives
throughout the world*

*Published in the United States of America
by Longman Inc., New York*

First published 1966
Second impression and first paperback edition 1970
Fourth impression 1976

**Library of Congress Cataloging in Publication
Data**

Hearder, Harry.
Europe in the nineteenth century, 1830–1880.

(A General history of Europe)
Bibliography: p.
Includes index.
1. Europe—History—1815–1871. I. Title.
D359.H34   1976   940.2'8   75-37539
ISBN 0-582-48212-7
ISBN 0-582-48344-1 pbk.

For Anna

Printed in Hong Kong by
Sheck Wah Tong Printing Press

Contents

CONTENTS

CONTENTS

CONTENTS

CONTENTS

CARYSFORT COLLEGE
LIBRARY

Page

CONTENTS

Maps

xiii

Acknowledgments

We are indebted to the copyright owners for permission to reproduce copyright material from the following:

Germany 1815–1890 by G. B. Smith (Edward Arnold (Publishers) Ltd); *Everyman's Atlas of Asia* (John Bartholomew & Son Ltd); *Handbook on Italy Part 2* (H.M.S.O.); *The Age of Revolution in Europe* by E. J. Hobsbawn (Weidenfeld & Nicolson Ltd); and *Economic Geography of Europe* by Blanshard and Visher (McGraw-Hill Book Company).

Preface

I am glad to be able to use this opportunity to thank Professor W. N. Medlicott for having introduced me, a good many years ago now, to the history of nineteenth-century Europe, and for all the kindness and encouragement which he has given me ever since. I would like, too, to recall my debt to the late Dame Lillian Penson, who first guided my attempts in original historical writing, and whose formidable personality never completely concealed a great warmth and generosity of spirit. In the writing of this volume itself I have depended a good deal on the advice and suggestions of Professor Denys Hay, who read the typescript. My colleague, Mr W. M. Stern, was kind enough to read chapter IV and to make meticulous and invaluable comments. My colleagues in the department of International History at the London School of Economics have often helped me in conversation, often without realizing that they were doing so, and Dr M. S. Anderson deserves a special word of thanks both for the example which he has provided for me in writing his own volume in the series, and for discussing the common problems presented in the writing of such studies. For specific suggestions of useful books or articles I would like to thank Mr R. C. Perkins, Dr W. B. Stephens of *The Victoria County History* and Professor Michael Wolff of *Victorian Studies*. My wife typed a draft of the greater part of the volume, and her comments did much to improve the style. But, obviously, for any remaining imperfections of style, errors of fact, or inadequacies of interpretation, I am alone responsible.

I have tried to follow the pattern suggested by Professor Denys Hay for the series, in the sense that I have attempted to present the Europe of these years in the round. I have mentioned not only the monarchs, politicians and diplomats, but also the writers and engineers, the artists and farmers, the workers and bankers. I make no apology for the longish sections on social conditions and education, since I believe that those two considerable sections of the community—the poor and the children —have too often been forgotten in histories of Europe. On the other hand I have not wanted to play down the more traditional themes of constitutional or diplomatic history, since I believe that the struggle for power between political groups or nations, the preservation of peace and the causes of wars must remain central themes of the historian. With regard to the sections devoted to the histories of the various European countries a word of explanation may be offered on the grouping within chapters. A natural grouping might have been of Germany and Austria together, rather than of Germany and Italy in one chapter, and Austria, Russia and Turkey in another. The civilizations of Germany and Austria were certainly closer in every sense than were those of Russia and Austria. I decided, however, to group together Germany and Italy, since this enabled me to compare and contrast two emerging nation states. In grouping Austria with Czarist Russia and the Ottoman Empire I did not intend a slight on that much maligned institution, the Habsburg Monarchy.

I

The Sources

The historian of nineteenth-century Europe is faced with so vast a quantity of source material, most of it relatively accessible, that he must either restrict his research to a very small field of study, or else be extremely selective, not merely in the sources which he employs, but in those which he consults. Thus the historian studying a mere six months of the foreign policy of one Great Power in the second half of the century would find relevant material in the archives of many countries— material contained in a great many bound volumes, files or boxes of despatches. If he then decided that it was necessary to consider public opinion with regard to his theme, he might feel obliged to consult the European press for the period, and could thus give himself an almost endless task. Historians of earlier centuries may find that their sources

BIBLIOGRAPHY. Some of the larger European archives publish lists or introductions to their material, but there is no single compilation or summary of all such publications for nineteenth-century sources. One short guide to the sources of diplomatic history in western European archives has been prepared for American scholars, and is useful as a very brief introduction: D. H. Thomas and L. M. Case, editors, *Guide to the Diplomatic Archives of Western Europe* (Philadelphia, 1959). A valuable work of reference for the diplomatic historian is H. Temperley and L. M. Penson, *A Century of Diplomatic Blue Books, 1814–1914* (Cambridge, 1938), which lists those British Parliamentary Papers which emanated from the Foreign Office, and has short essays on the policies of the various foreign secretaries of the period with regard to the publication of Blue Books. There is no similar publication for the enormous number of British Parliamentary Papers which deal with domestic issues. The technical origins of the diplomatic Blue Book are discussed in an article by Valerie Cromwell—'The Administrative Background to the Presentation to Parliament of Parliamentary Papers on Foreign Affairs in the Mid-Nineteenth Century', in the *Journal of the Society of Archivists*, vol. II, No. 7 (April, 1963). A great deal has been written on the history of the Press, though much of it, not surprisingly, of a journalistic nature. Two scholarly works on the British press deserve mention: A. Aspinall, *Politics and the Press, c. 1780–1850* (London, 1949) and the official and anonymous *History of 'The Times': The Thunderer in the Making, 1785–1841* and *The*

I

are too few: the medievalist, with a limited number of relevant documents, will spend much time and energy in considering the precise
validity and significance of each precious piece of evidence. The nineteenth-century historian must, obviously, also be sure of the authenticity and importance of the smallest document, but, because of his
nearness in time to his sources, this will usually prove a comparatively
easy task. His more difficult task will certainly be that of selection—of
deciding which piece of evidence to use, and which to discard, which
factors to consider and which to omit.

The diplomatic history of the nineteenth century has now been
studied with considerable thoroughness, though there will always be
new questions to answer and unexamined sources to explore. More,
perhaps, than any other aspect of nineteenth-century history, the diplomatic one has a number of well ordered archives at its disposal, archives
containing a wealth of public and private despatches, notes, telegrams
and memoranda. Some European governments have maintained a fifty-
year rule, by which they have refrained from making diplomatic documents available to the public for the first fifty years after they have been
written, but the rule has not, of course, applied to the period 1830–80 for
some years. In nearly every country of western and central Europe the
diplomatic archives are now readily open to the interested and qualified
public—in other words, to historians—who can search at leisure
through the papers of the various foreign ministries. In one sense, then,
the diplomatic historian has a straightforward task. But he has other,
less straightforward, ones. In the papers of the foreign ministries he
will find only very rarely general statements of the principles on which
governments based their policies, or even what the ultimate aims and
objectives of policy were. More often he will find only day-to-day
accounts of negotiations in which there are few, if any, general state-

Tradition Established, 1841–1884. A study of the French press in the special
context of a history of censorship and government control is Irene Collins, *The
Government and the Newspaper Press in France, 1814–1881* (Oxford, 1959). A
recent series of little books, called *Collection Kiosque* and published by Armand
Colin, deals with the press in a popular but well documented fashion. Several of
them cover periods of the nineteenth century, and one in particular contains
useful material: Charles Ledré, *La Presse à l'Assaut de la Monarchie 1815–1848*
(Paris, 1960). René de Livois, *Histoire de la Presse Française* (2 vols., Lausanne,
1965), is informative and attractively illustrated. An excellent quick survey of
the European press for the greater part of the period is contained in: John
Roach, 'Education and the Press', in *The New Cambridge Modern History*, vol. x,
edited by J. P. T. Bury (Cambridge, 1960).

ments. It remains for the historian to reduce such records of negotiations to a coherent summary, and to provide an interpretation which will be valid for his readers. Diplomatic archives do, however, occasionally contain generalized statements of interest to the historian. In the archives of the Quai d'Orsay for the period of the Second Empire there are, for example, occasional memoranda, drawn up by a foreign ministry official for the information of the emperor himself, and making statements on the general situation. In a similar manner the permanent under-secretary in the British Foreign Office would sometimes draw up a memorandum on the diplomatic scene in Europe for the benefit of a secretary of state who had just been appointed to the Foreign Office. And occasionally, of course, even a foreign minister himself, in the midst of negotiations, will make a general statement of his policy. Harold Temperley and Dame Lillian Penson extracted a number of such generalized comments on the principles of British foreign policy during the period 1815 to 1914 from the Foreign Office papers in the Public Record Office, and published them with brief editorial essays under the heading *The Foundations of British Foreign Policy* (Cambridge, 1938).

Another difficulty faced by the diplomatic historian is the habit some political leaders had of conducting negotiations through unofficial channels, so that a record of the negotiations did not appear in the foreign ministry papers. Napoleon III preferred secret, personal diplomacy, and often left his foreign ministry and regular diplomats in the dark regarding his intentions. Often he did not even inform them of negotiations which he had already conducted. Thus the secret pact of Plombières,[1] which Napoleon drew up, verbally, with Cavour in 1858, left no traces in the French foreign ministry, and Count Walewski, the foreign minister, was not even told of its existence. The only records left of Plombières are the letters which Cavour wrote back to Turin. It did not, however, follow that because a government was autocratic or authoritarian it would necessarily conduct secret, personal diplomacy. Although after 1870 Bismarck's diplomacy became increasingly tortuous, and although as Chancellor he was responsible to no one except the emperor, he nevertheless worked through the regular diplomatic channels. His ambassadors were carefully trained and selected, and could be trusted as well—perhaps better—than any unofficial agent. Cavour and Palmerston, on the other hand, though fully responsible constitutional ministers, preferred on occasions to by-pass the official

[1] See below, pp. 146–7 and 235.

diplomatic routes. Cavour kept an unofficial agent, Costantino Nigra, in Paris from the summer of 1858 until the war of 1859, and it was through Nigra, not the accredited minister, that negotiations with Napoleon were conducted. Palmerston developed the habit of writing private letters to his two or three most important ambassadors, in addition to the official despatches. Such private letters did not have to be numbered or filed among the official despatches in the Foreign Office; they would never be published as parliamentary blue books, and so could be less inhibited and more personal in their approach. After Palmerston's resignation from the Foreign Office in 1851 the practice of keeping up a private correspondence, parallel to the official one, between foreign secretary and principal ambassadors, was continued. In the cases of Cavour and Palmerston, however, the historian has been fortunate: both Cavour's correspondence with Nigra, and Palmerston's correspondence with his ambassadors have survived as invaluable sources. But Napoleon's habit of conducting diplomacy in a very personal and secretive manner has been more serious for the historian, all the more so as Paris was without doubt the centre of European diplomacy for by far the greater part of the life of the Second Empire. For the two years 1858 and 1859, for example, the correspondence of the British Foreign Office with Paris filled twelve bound volumes; with Constantinople for the same period it filled ten volumes, with Vienna seven volumes, and with Berlin only five.

As regards primary printed sources there are now many series of published documents available to the diplomatic historian for the period. But however massive in bulk, and however impartial and scholarly the editing, such printed series are inevitably only selections, and can never be completely a substitute for research in the archives. Nevertheless they can be of immense use for reference. Among the many collections of treaties which have been published, one, in particular, is of use to British historians: even before the end of the period Sir Edward Hertslet, the librarian of the Foreign Office, had started publishing his collection of treaties and accompanying maps—*Map of Europe by Treaty* (London, 4 vols., 1875–91). But the first large collections of printed despatches were produced not for historians at all, but for the British Parliament. By 1830 it was already established that no government could refuse to print and circulate a selection of despatches on a given question if a motion to the effect had been passed in parliament. Any individual M.P. or peer could bring forward a motion that 'papers be laid on the table of the House', and since Castlereagh's time no such motion has ever been refused. Once the motion was passed, the permanent under-secretary at the Foreign Office would select the despatches or other documents which he felt might safely and profitably be made public, and the foreign secretary, and sometimes also the prime minister, would then revise the selection for printing and publication. Bound in blue paper, and so called a 'Blue Book', copies of the final product were sent to each member of parliament and put on sale for the public. A Blue Book could consist of a single sheet or several hundred pages, but in most cases it gave a surprisingly full and fair account of the negotiations about which questions had been asked. The volume of Blue Books published increased steadily and reached peak numbers in the 1850s. Thereafter the numbers declined, so that the twentieth-century public is much less well informed on foreign policy than the early Victorians were. The great spate of Blue Books in the mid-nineteenth century thus constitute an impressive source for the diplomatic historian, and the comparison of the Blue Books with the original manuscripts one of his more pleasing pastimes. Before 1880 no other European power produced anything to compare with the British diplomatic Blue Book.

Some of the earliest selections of diplomatic documents prepared to satisfy historical interest—as opposed to the British parliamentary papers which, of course, played a part in the political history of their day— came from Germany. In 1902 Heinrich von Poschinger edited a series of despatches on Prussian policy in the last years of Frederick William IV's reign, before the King's madness necessitated the Regency of Prince William: *Preussens Auswärtige Politik, 1850 bis 1858* (Berlin, 3 vols., 1902). After the first world war a sequel to the series was produced when in both Germany and France ambitious publications illustrated the origins of the Franco-Prussian War, from the two opposing standpoints: *Auswärtige Politik Preussens, 1858 bis 1871*, edited by E. Brandenburg, O. Hoetzsch, H. Oncken (Oldenburg, 8 vols., 1933), and *Les origines diplomatiques de la guerre de 1870–1871* (Paris, 29 vols., 1910–32). Many secret German documents dealing with the war of 1870, and lacking from these two series, have recently been published, edited by Georges Bonnin under the title *Bismarck and the Hohenzollern Candidature for the Spanish Throne* (London, 1957), a publication which made it clear that Bismarck had been conspiring for the Hohenzollern Candidature earlier and more deliberately than had previously been realized.[1] Another recent series of printed documents relating to the

[1] See below, p. 150.

5

causes and consequences of the Franco-Prussian War, and to much else beside, are *The Holstein Papers*, edited by Norman Rich and M. H. Fisher (Cambridge, 1955–63)[1]—the memoirs, diaries and correspondence of the man who managed Bismarck's foreign ministry and who subsequently helped to force the chancellor into reluctant retirement. Between the two world wars most of the great powers who had fought in 1914 were obsessed with the question of 'war guilt', and with this in mind large series of documents were commissioned. Both the French and German series went back to 1871 and so have material which is relevant to the last decade covered by this book: *Documents diplomatiques françaises, 1871–1914* (Paris, 36 vols., 1929 *et seq.*), and *Die grosse Politik der europäischen Kabinette, 1871–1914,* edited by Johannes Lepsius, Albrecht Mendelssohn Bartholdy and Friedrich Thimme (40 vols. in 54, Berlin, 1922–27). Since the second world war Italy has been foremost in the publication of series of diplomatic documents. An immense undertaking in the charge of a commission of the Italian Foreign Ministry has been started, under the title of *I documenti diplomatici italiani*, to cover the whole period of Italy's existence as an independent state. A series starting in 1861 has been edited by Walter Maturi, and another series relevant here, starting at 1870, has been edited by Federico Chabod, but both of these distinguished editors have died before the project is complete. Other series of diplomatic documents, dealing with more limited themes, have been started in Italy since the war. They are too numerous to list here, but examples are a series dealing with Anglo-Sardinian relations, edited by Federico Curato, and another with Austro-Sardinian relations, edited by Angelo Filipuzzi; both start in 1848. Professor Curato's publications contain many hitherto unpublished despatches from the Public Record Office in London, and Professor Filipuzzi's many from the *Haus-, Hof- und Staatsarchiv* in Vienna. Thus are the contents of the great European archives slowly being laid before the interested scholars.

The public archives, however, are by no means the only important source for the student of international history. Collections of private papers now exist in archives all over western Europe, often well organized and readily available to historians. The correspondence of secondary figures are often carefully preserved by their heirs, and though not permanently open to the researcher can be examined by private arrangement. Private letters, whether consulted in manuscript or in pub-

[1] Published also in the original German: *Die geheimen Papiere Friedrich von Holsteins* (Gottingen, 4 vols., 1956–62).

lished form, constitute a primary source quite as much as do the official despatches. The published memoirs or autobiographies of diplomats are clearly not a primary source in quite the same sense, since they have often been written long after the events they discuss and are inevitably coloured by subjective factors—faulty memory or personal vanity. Nor are they merely secondary sources in the sense that the writings of professional historians are. The diplomats of the nineteenth century were prolific in their memoirs. Since their main function in life was to pass messages or record their conversations with foreign ministers, or sometimes monarchs, it is not surprising that they found it easy and tempting to write their memoirs after they had retired. So numerous are they, that only a sample, drawn at random, can be given here: those of an Austrian, Comte de Hübner, *Neuf Ans de Souvenirs d'un Ambassadeur d'Autriche à Paris, 1851–1859* (Paris, 2 vols., 1904), of an Englishman, Lord Augustus Loftus, *The Diplomatic Reminiscences of Lord Augustus Loftus, 1837–1862* (London, 2 vols., 1892), of a Saxon, whose writings were rather more pungent than the common run of diplomatic memoirs, Count C. F. Vitzthum von Eckstaedt, *St Petersburg and London, 1852–1864*, edited by Henry Reeve and translated by E. F. Taylor (London, 2 vols., 1887), and of a Frenchman from the post-1870 period, Vicomte de Gontaut-Biron, *Mon Ambassade en Allemagne, 1872–1873* (Paris, 1906).

For the internal political histories of European countries the sources are inevitably more varied, though one general rule holds: constitutional régimes leave fuller records than autocratic ones. There is, in the first place, more to record about a régime in which an elected assembly is active—more legislation and more political change; and, in the second place, the records themselves are more explicit and more generous. Great Britain, with her long reports of parliamentary debates in *Hansard* and her vast collections of parliamentary papers on a great variety of domestic topics, has far more records for the period 1830 to 1880 than any of the other great powers. More authoritarian countries depend for their internal history on private papers, administrative correspondence and police reports. It is safe to say that the more dynamic the political life of a country, the better the historical sources which it leaves. So far as legislative and parliamentary activity is concerned, the régime which approached, perhaps, most closely to Britain in the extent of its records was the July Monarchy in France, with its *Bulletin des Lois du Royaume de France, Règne de Louis-Philippe Ier, roi des français* (31 vols., 1831–1847), and its series under the general headings *Chambre des Députés, Chambre des Pairs* and *Annales du Parlement français*. The diminutive assembly of the Second Empire was a less lively and important, if, in theory, more representative, place, and its documentation is correspondingly insignificant. The records of all other European parliaments during the period are meagre when compared with *Hansard*. Many French ministers have made up for the lack of parliamentary sources by leaving full memoirs, but the central figure of French history for the period—Napoleon III—has left comparatively few papers.[1] Valuable records of the Second Empire were destroyed in the burning down of the Tuileries by the Commune. On the other hand the efficient administration of nineteenth-century France has left comparatively full records, though they have perhaps been inadequately used by historians as yet. Portions of Theodore Zeldin, *The Political System of Napoleon III* (London, 1958), show to what use the reports of the prefects can be put.

For the history of Italy before unification private papers are also more revealing than any public documents. In the twentieth century Italian governments have administered the publication of great national editions of the writings of the three traditional heroes of the *Risorgimento*, Mazzini, Garibaldi and Cavour. Inevitably the least impressive of the three is the six-volumed collection of the writings of Garibaldi, including his strange, naïve autobiography. The National Commission charged with the publication of Mazzini's collected writings started its work in 1905, on the centenary of his birth. Half a century later they had published one hundred volumes, and the work is not yet complete. It has been calculated that Mazzini wrote some fifty thousand letters, of which over ten thousand have been found. The national edition of Cavour's writings is in a much less advanced stage. It will eventually replace, among other things, the old Piedmontese work, *Lettere edite ed inedite di Camillo Cavour*, edited by Luigi Chiala (Turin, 6 vols., 1882–87), whose complete historical integrity is in some doubt. Among the many documents published in Italy in recent years is an interesting series to illustrate how the various institutions of Italy were integrated and standardized after the political unification of 1859–61. The series, under the direction of Alberto M. Ghisalberti and Alberto Caracciolo, is called *L'Organizzazione dello Stato* and includes volumes on parliament, the administration, the ministry of foreign affairs, the educational system, the relations between Church and State, the fiscal system and the armed forces.[2]

---

[1] They are listed and briefly discussed in Appendix I, pp. 359–60, of T. A. B. Corley, *Democratic Despot* (London, 1961).
[2] See also below, p. 208.

Among the many sources for the history of the unification of Germany one document, published in many editions and translations, is of unique interest and importance—Bismarck's reminiscences: *Gedanken und Erinnerungen* (Stuttgart, 2 vols., 1898), of which an English version is *Bismarck, the Man and the Statesman, being the Reflections and Reminiscences of Otto Prince von Bismarck*, translated and edited by A. J. Butler (London, 2 vols., 1898). The first draft of the work was dictated to Lothar Bucher, the historian and diplomat, and Bismarck himself then wrote several other drafts, taking great pains not only to convey a precise impression of his own ability, but also to perfect the literary style. The historian may no longer accept Bismarck's implication that every step of his policy before 1870 was part of a master-plan for the unification of Germany, but he must still regret that so few of the great figures of history have taken such pains to give so interesting an account of their acts and ideas.

Of the men who ruled Austria in the period only Count Beust left memoirs—*Aus drei Viertel-Jahrhunderten* (Vienna, 2 vols., 1887)—which are in any way comparable in interest to those of Bismarck. Of the men who ruled Russia only Prince Nesselrode has had a collection of letters published and these, of course, relate in large part to the earlier period. There is nothing on his successor as chancellor, Gorchakov, who is in a sense the central figure of Russian history from 1856 until his death in 1883. The sources for Russian history available to western scholars are of course comparatively thin.

While the written sources for political historians multiplied in the nineteenth century, the statistical sources, in which economic historians are particularly interested, also became at once more numerous and more reliable. The first censuses conducted in Europe, completed in the eighteenth century, are discussed in an earlier volume of this history.[1] In 1801 both France and Britain had their first censuses, though they consisted merely of an enumeration of the population, without the collecting of names. They were probably very inaccurate, but are, of course, better than nothing. Since 1801 a census has been held in Britain every ten years, and since 1841 all the names of inhabitants have been listed. In 1851 an exceptionally thorough census was made, with the occupations and professed religion of everyone being recorded. Only the statistical results were published, but the original manuscripts of this remarkable investigation into the social structure of Britain are openly available in

[1] M. S. Anderson, *Europe in the Eighteenth Century 1713–1783* (London, 1961), pp. 77–8.

the Public Record Office, and the social historian could still extract much from them. By the mid-nineteenth century many more statistics were being accumulated than ever before, and many of these have as yet been imperfectly used by historians. The British consular reports, for example, contain a great deal of statistical and economic information which has rarely been used. Already in the 1820s George Canning at the Foreign Office and William Huskisson at the Board of Trade had decided that the consuls should be asked to supply economic information, and throughout the period the consuls sent back many statistics to the Foreign Office on the population, finances, industry, agriculture, and, above all, trade of the countries in which they were residing.

For social, as opposed to strictly economic, history, the kind of source which can be most profitably used has been the subject of spirited and important polemics in recent years. To obtain knowledge of the social conditions prevailing in mid-nineteenth-century Europe is surprisingly difficult. The surviving statistics are by no means conclusive: in some vital respects they are very fragmentary, and anyhow are usually open to more than one interpretation. At the other extreme are the novels of the period, which provide a full interpretation in human terms, but cannot, of course, by their very nature as fiction, be accepted as untarnished truth. In between these two groups of sources are other contemporary verbal impressions, usually of a more or less prejudiced nature, including political pamphlets and, on a higher level, reports of parliamentary commissions. With regard to the evidence of creative writings the help of scholars of literature must be sought. A novelist whose work is considered excellent in a literary sense is also more likely to write with the kind of integrity and authenticity which will make his descriptions of life and conditions more valid for the historian. The permanent literary value of the novels of George Eliot, Balzac, Tolstoy or Zola is an indication that they are more reliable as historical evidence than are the sentimental stories of only temporarily popular writers. And the literary value set upon novelists who are not in the first rank—Charles Kingsley, Mrs Gaskell, Benjamin Disraeli—is also relevant to the historian.

The first set of statistics to be considered in determining social conditions in Britain at the time of the Industrial Revolution related to the death rate. M. C. Buer, *Health, Wealth and Population in the Early Days of the Industrial Revolution* (London, 1926), showed that the death rate in Britain was declining over the period 1750 to 1850, and concluded, a little rashly perhaps, that living conditions must have been rising. But when the death rate is considered for shorter periods it is seen to fluctuate considerably, and in the 1830s it was actually rising. More significant statistics are those regarding wages and prices which Sir John Clapham, *Economic History of Modern Britain*, vol. 1 (Cambridge, 1926), used to suggest that workers were improving their position from 1785 to 1850. Since Clapham wrote, the statistical pursuit of 'real wages' is a source which has attracted several economic historians. The 'real wage' is estimated quite simply by a correlation of actual earnings in cash with actual retail prices, but any decision as to which retail prices should be included has inevitably been an arbitrary one.

In establishing a cost-of-living index historians, like governments, have experienced difficulties, and even some of Clapham's figures have subsequently been shown to be misleading. Economic historians of the Industrial Revolution have therefore more recently shifted their attention to what evidence there is of the amount of food actually consumed per head of population. As regards the basic food—bread and potatoes—there is little reliable statistical evidence, but as regards the consumption of meat, the returns made by the Collector of Beasts Tolls at Smithfield Market have provided interesting evidence. Broadly speaking the returns show that the average man's consumption of meat fell in the first decade of the period, as it had done since the beginning of the century, but that after 1840 it rose again. But even the returns from Smithfield Market have their shortcomings: they give the numbers of sheep and cattle slaughtered, but not the weight of meat provided. Nor are even these figures comprehensive, since pigs are not included. It is logically possible, though not probable, that the decline in the consumption of lamb, mutton and beef from 1800 to 1840 was accompanied by an increase in the consumption of pork. Furthermore the Smithfield returns relate only to London, so that, to regard them as conclusive, the historian must first make the assumption that the same proportion of wealth and poverty existed in London as elsewhere.

Social historians are thus inclined, at some stage in their arguments, to fall back upon population figures, of which so far only the death rate has been mentioned. The undeniable fact of an enormous increase in population all over Europe in the period may have been due to a rising birth rate, a falling death rate, or varying combinations of the two. But a rising birth rate could be explained by a variety of arguments, and demographers are by no means in agreement as to the valid ones in this case. Nor is a declining death rate necessarily evidence of improving conditions. If the birth rate continues to rise for half a century or longer, as it probably did in most of Europe in the period, the average age of the population will decline, and the death rate can be expected to decline also. On the other hand, if the birth rate after rising for some decades then falls or remains constant, as was the case in France in the nineteenth century, the average age will increase, and the death rate could well increase without implying deteriorating conditions.

Statistical sources, then, give no easy answers to general questions. They must be used in conjunction with all other sources, not least the literary ones. Of the novels dealing with what Disraeli called 'the condition of the people', those by Mrs Gaskell are cited in chapter VI, and among them in particular *Mary Barton*. Her novels are important because of their deep sincerity. She had no political axe to grind, but was eager only to present a true picture. In *Cranford* she showed that she had the literary integrity of a Jane Austen, and if in *Mary Barton* there are stronger signs of the influence of Dickens and a consequent sentimentality, there are no indications of distortion in the descriptive passages. Such novels—and those of Zola also deserve particular mention—are perhaps less misleading as a historical source than are the political pamphlets of the day. But the pamphlet literature must not be neglected. For Germany there are, for example, the pamphlets of Alexander Schneer, *Ueber die Zustaende der arbeitenden Klassen in Breslau* (Berlin, 1845) and *Ueber die Not der Leinenarbeiter in Schlesien und die Mittel, ihr abzuhelfen* (Berlin, 1844); and for England there is the longer and better documented work by Friedrich Engels, *The Condition of the Working Class in England* (original edition, 1844; translated and edited by W. O. Henderson and W. H. Chaloner, Oxford, 1958). They paint a grim picture of working conditions before 1850,[1] but not grimmer than that painted by most of the English press, from *The Times* to the *Northern Star*, nor than that presented by the numerous reports of British Parliamentary commissions. Such sources were the ones favoured by the socialist historians, the Webbs, the Hammonds and the Coles. By adding the evidence of the statistical sources, subsequent academic historians have tended rather to obscure than to reverse the picture. The question regarding social conditions in mid-nineteenth-century Europe remains an open one.

The press of western Europe expanded very considerably in the period covered by this book, and presents the historian with a large and fascinating source for almost every department of his work. Its expansion was due partly to the growth of population and the spread of literacy, but more perhaps to the building of the railways, which carried

[1] See chapter VI.

newspapers much further and more quickly than had ever been possible before. Political factors were also, of course, relevant. As the censorship or government control, and 'taxes on knowledge', were reduced, the press became a significant and influential part of public life. Britain was the first country in the world to have a free and responsible press, though France inherited a tradition of dynamic and influential journalism from the Revolution. The British press of the eighteenth century had been a disreputable institution run by rakes and eccentrics, though with the occasional touch of genius. *The Times* was the first English paper to make great efforts to appeal to the respectable and sober middle class. It became a national institution under Thomas Barnes, who was editor from 1817 to 1841. Barnes was a well-educated man with legal training and experience as a political and literary critic: in a sense, the first modern type of editor of a serious newspaper. In the crisis over the Reform Bill he took a forceful liberal stand, and *The Times* became known as the 'Thunderer'. Perhaps more than any other Englishman Barnes established the right of an editor not only to report news without official restraints, but to add independent political comment. His quarrel with the Whigs soon after the passing of the Reform Act encouraged him to adopt a policy which *The Times* has often followed since—that of supporting the Tories, but trying to keep them as liberal as possible. Thus Barnes encouraged and helped Peel in the preparation of the Tamworth Manifesto.[1] Barnes was succeeded as editor by J. T. Delane who directed *The Times* for nearly forty years—from 1841 to 1877. Conditions for a free press in England were improving steadily. From 1825 the size of a newspaper was no longer limited by law; a tax on advertisements was lowered in 1833; and the value of the stamp which had to be affixed to a newspaper was reduced to a penny in 1836.

John Thadeus Delane, who took *The Times* to the peak of its power, was only twenty-three when he was made editor. Unlike the volatile and bohemian Barnes, Delane was an austere figure, who changed the character of *The Times* from the outspoken 'Thunderer' to the respectable and responsible organ it has since been. By its independence and its hold on the opinions of the English upper and middle classes *The Times* became a political force greater perhaps than any other European newspaper of the nineteenth century. The reports of William Howard Russell, *The Times* war correspondent in the Crimea, and Delane's use of them, were mainly responsible for the resignation of Aberdeen's

[1] See below, p. 182.

13

government in 1855. Throughout the period *The Times* is thus a major primary source.

The reduction of the taxes in the 1830s led to new departures in British journalism. *Punch* was founded in 1841 and the *Illustrated London News* in 1842, both in their different ways providing sources for the social historian. An important London paper, the *Daily News*, was founded in 1846, and for its first seventeen numbers was edited by Dickens. But while these publications were aiming at the middle class, a robust working-class press had developed. The *Northern Star*, one of the most radical of newspapers, was for some years a rallying place of Chartist sympathies. In 1853 the advertisement tax, and in 1855 the newspaper stamp tax, were at last abolished, enabling the foundation of the *Daily Telegraph* in 1855, the first paper to sell for one penny. In 1861 the paper duty was abolished, and *The Times* now faced stiffer competition. The *Daily Telegraph* and the *Standard* took away some of *The Times*'s middle-class readers, and the *Morning Post* some of her more aristocratic ones. The circulation of *The Times* had risen from 10,000 in 1834 to 70,000 in 1861. No other morning paper came anywhere near this figure, but the *Telegraph* and *Standard*, which both had evening editions, could claim circulations of 150,000 and 130,000 respectively in 1861, and whereas *The Times* failed to increase her circulation for the remainder of the period, the *Telegraph* continued to expand.

Though the provincial press in Britain had been far from negligible, no morning paper was published outside London until 1855, because the taxes made the cost too great. The *Manchester Guardian* had been founded in 1830, as a sevenpenny weekly. The reduction of the stamp duty in 1836 enabled the *Manchester Guardian* to be sold twice a week at fourpence, and eventually the abolition of the stamp duty in 1855 changed the *Guardian* into a daily. In the same year the *Liverpool Daily Post* was founded, and in the next few years the *Birmingham Daily Post* appeared, and the *Scotsman* and the *Glasgow Herald* became dailies.

In the rest of Europe the press—where it existed on a comparable scale—was not so closely centred on the capital city, but was spread more widely throughout the different regions. While the French press was as varied as the British and had quite as dramatic an influence on political life, no single newspaper in France acquired the prestige or sustained power held by *The Times* in England. Sudden changes of régimes and of the laws relating to censorship prevented the smooth

THE PRESS

emergence of a free press in France, but the opening of the period happens to correspond with a phase of great activity. In 1829 were founded two periodical publications which in their different ways were to be valuable historical sources—the authoritative *Revue des Deux Mondes*, and the *Revue de Paris*, which had the first serialized French novels, including works by Dumas and Balzac. After the July Revolution several newspapers which had distinguished careers ahead of them were founded: *Le Siècle*, *L'Avenir*, *L'Epoque* and *La Presse*.

The newly found—and as it proved, short-lived—freedom of the press allowed the publication of more extreme organs. The Saint-Simonian, Enfantin, bought the *Globe*, and preached socialism in its columns for the next sixteen months. The paper with the largest circulation in France in 1830 was the *Constitutionnel*, which had pursued a moderate liberal policy under the restoration governments, and had prepared the way for the July Monarchy. It expressed the ideas of Thiers and had fluctuating fortunes, its circulation falling from about 23,000 in 1830 to 6,000 in 1840, and then rising again to 23,000 in 1845. To the right of the *Constitutionnel* was the *Journal des Débats*, which put across Guizot's doctrine of the *juste milieu*, but the *Journal des Débats* fell in circulation also from some 15,000 in 1830 to less than 10,000 in 1845. Two cheaper papers pulled ahead in the 1840s—*Le Siècle* and *La Presse*, the former reaching a circulation of 34,000 by 1845 and the latter 22,000.[1] Emile de Girardin, the founder editor of *La Presse*, depended partly on advertisements for his profits, at that time a practice commoner in London than Paris. By 1838 the fourth page of *La Presse* was containing advertisements worth 150,000 francs. Girardin supported Louis Napoleon's election campaign in 1848, and was a major factor in the sweeping victory.

Having got into power by the help of the press, Napoleon called a halt to journalistic activity. In his first years of power he suppressed nine-tenths of the French press, but after the relaxation of the censorship in 1868 new and revolutionary newspapers appeared. With the Third Republic the era of the very cheap press began when *Le Petit Journal* was founded, and sold for a sou. By 1872 it had a circulation of 212,500, and so anticipated the popular press in England by some years.

The German press was slower to develop than either the British or French, partly because of the more authoritarian censorship, and partly because there was no great political or cultural capital to equal

[1] Charles Ledré, *La Presse à l'assaut de la monarchie 1815-1848* (Paris, 1960), p. 244.

15

London or Paris. A radical newspaper like the *Rheinische Zeitung*, of Cologne, rarely had a long life in Germany. Founded by the rich, liberal industrialists, David Hansemann and Ludolf Camphausen, the *Rheinische Zeitung* was edited by the young Marx from October 1842, until March 1843. Marx then resigned rather than submit to the Prussian government's censorship, and the paper was subsequently suppressed. Perhaps the most important German newspaper of the period was the *Allgemeine Zeitung* of Augsburg, but it, too, was censored by the Bavarian government, and had to drop the services of Heine, its correspondent in Paris, at the request of the authorities. The largest Berlin paper, the *Vossische Zeitung*, had a circulation of less than 20,000 in 1847, while the next two largest German papers, the *Allgemeine Zeitung* and the *Kölnische Zeitung*, had only some 8,000 readers.

The revolutions of 1848 brought a great proliferation of newspapers all over western and central Europe, and especially in Italy. Few of them survived to the end of 1849, but in united Italy the tradition of a large number of small, and often short-lived, papers was to be re-established. In the Habsburg monarchy there was little independent journalistic activity before 1848, and, what little there was, was in Budapest rather than Vienna. After the revolutions a press was allowed to exist, but was closely supervised. The official Habsburg paper, the *Wiener Zeitung*, which had been founded as long ago as 1703, printed the news, but no comment. One liberal paper founded in 1848, *Die Presse*, continued to exist, and even retained its motto, '*Gleiche Recht für Alle!*', but expressed the opinion merely of the rich Viennese bourgeoisie. A Viennese paper in Italian, *Il Corriere Italiano*, was more polemical than the others, but was concerned to justify Austrian policy in Italy, and to attack Piedmont.

In Russia the press developed even more slowly. In 1843 there were only some 12,000 subscribers to all the chief Russian periodicals. The censorship was very savage, but there was no great eagerness on the part of the Russian reading public to foster a press. In the absence of a free independent press in Russia the official journals often voiced demands for limited reform, rather as they have continued to do from time to time under the Communists. In Alexander II's reforming period, his brother, the liberal-minded Grand-Duke Constantine, was Minister of Marine, and under Constantine the ministry's journal, the 'Naval Almanack', was edited by the radical Golovnin. It recommended not only reforms in the administration of the navy, but legal and educational reforms for the whole of Russian society.

Important new sources of information for the press were established by the birth of the news agencies, four of which became big concerns. The first was the Havas agency, centred in Paris and connected to Brussels and London by pigeon from 1840 until the development of the telegraph. A few years later Havas could switch to the telegraph, and Paul Julius Reuter, a Jewish bank clerk, founded the agency which has made his name famous, in 1847 in Aachen, as a small private project. Reuter soon moved to London, where his agency had no competition until 1870, when the Press Association was founded. Meanwhile another German, Bernhard Wolff, had founded in 1849 in Berlin another news agency which was to have a great future.

As a historical source, the press can, of course, be used only with extreme caution. Even when reporters and editors have no political axe to grind, nor any wish to embellish their stories, they must work in great haste, and cannot afford to be over-scrupulous in checking their own sources of information. But very often a news item which has previously escaped the attention of the historian altogether will form at least a good starting point for further research into other, more official or more reliable, sources. And as a source for the history of opinion the press has no substitute.

The main distinction between history and prehistory is that the former depends chiefly on written evidence while the latter depends upon archaeological findings. But besides its verbal profusion the nineteenth century has also left its architecture—to be scathingly discussed by a later age—and its art and music, much of which has earned rather more respect.[1] In addition it has left a type of record unknown to earlier ages: the photograph. From the initial discoveries of Louis-Jacques Daguerre (1789–1851) in 1829, photography developed so quickly that by the 1840s a good photographic record was being left of people and the world. The historian of the mid- and late nineteenth century can consequently feel a greater intimacy with his period than scholars of earlier ages have ever been able to feel. While the Napoleonic wars seem a remote historical event, the Crimean War—which is in fact much nearer in time to Waterloo than to 1914—seems recent and familiar, when considered with the aid of the many existing photographs. In the same way Napoleon I and Stein, when considered in contrast to Napoleon III and Bismarck, have a remoteness out of all proportion to the few decades which separated them. Only a very few portrait painters of genius have been able to reveal the subtle traits of personality which even a mediocre

[1] See chapter XIV.

photograph often shows. A study of Bismarck in 1870 by the photo-grapher Blanc[1] conveys a combination of intelligence and hardness, perhaps cruelty, which few paintings would be likely to capture. Court painters have usually flattered their models, but for the photographer flattery is less easy to attain. The painter Winterhalter portrayed the young Victoria as a pretty and seductive girl; the photographer Mayall, in a study of Victoria and Albert now in Windsor Castle, shows that the Queen, while still young, was a plain woman without a chin.[2] The physical and moral breakdown of Napoleon III in the late 1860s is revealed by more than one sad photograph, where he appears tired, shabby, listless and with his hair in need of a wash. Of all the vast accumulation of evidence left by the nineteenth century for the historian, the photographs are the most entertaining to handle, and not the least important.

[1] In the Gernsheim collection, reproduced in T. A. B. Corley, *Democratic Despot* (London, 1961).
[2] Reproduced in Elizabeth Longford, *Victoria R.I.* (London, 1964).

II

Europe in 1830

In 1830 the population of Europe was about 230 million—probably almost double that of a century earlier.[1] Europeans had changed in many ways over the years before 1830, but no single change was of equal significance to this simple numerical one. Improved means of production, the cultivation of new land and the survival of more infants had increased the number of Europeans without appreciably improving the conditions in which they lived. The vast majority of them were peasants, whose lives were spent in tiny geographical areas, and for whom the changes of the seasons were still more important than any national or international event. In southern and eastern Europe only a very few people could read and even in the more advanced north-west the standard of literacy was too low to justify a popular press. Not only did no morning paper arrive in the villages, but many people outside the capital would be unfamiliar with the personal appearance of the sovereign or his ministers. Before the invention of photography, only cheap woodcuts, litho prints, china figures or commemorative crockery would convey to the majority of people any impression of the faces of their rulers, and such impressions would be stylized and often misleading. Only in Great Britain had any degree of industrialization taken place by 1830, and even in Britain the process was in an early stage. Above all, effective communication from place to place was still lacking. The horse was still the basic unit of land transport. The development of the railways was to alter European modes of transport more in the fifty years from 1830 to 1880 than they had been altered in the previous five hundred years.

The enormous growth in population was not without a political significance. New ideas, formulated by the middle classes, or by visionaries of any class, were by 1830 being accepted by ever larger numbers of the

[1] W. Ashworth, *A Short History of the International Economy* (London, 1952), p. 14.

urban population. Popular ideas, prejudices and allegiances began to have potential importance for politicians and diplomats. The ideas of a Mazzini would reach a wider public than the ideas of a Voltaire had ever done. The vast numbers of European subjects who had grown to maturity even during the one generation before 1830 were making some form of representative government not only necessary for their own welfare but vital for the very survival of government itself. It might have been imagined from this that the individual political leader would no longer command the same power and influence that he had commanded in earlier centuries, but leaders like Cavour, Bismarck and Disraeli utilized popular movements of thought and sentiment, and exploited constitutional systems, to secure quicker and perhaps greater triumphs than a Louis XIV or a Frederick the Great had ever secured through inherited authority. The successful leaders of the post-1830 world may have been idealists or ruthless careerists, and were more often both at once, but they had this in common: they all recognized the growing significance of the liberal and nationalist ideas which had survived the defeat of Napoleon. These ideas, coupled to the growth in population, gave a few individuals of exceptional ability great potentialities of power.

The extraordinary growth of population had been a basic factor in the French Revolution, as it was to be in the unification of Germany and Italy. Napoleon had taken the ideas of the Enlightenment as far afield as Egypt and Poland, and he had done so by means of enormous armies. Ever since 1793 modern methods of mass conscription had made the 'nation in arms' a new and formidable unit of power. Napoleon's god had been on the side of the big battalions, and had remained on their side at Leipzig and Waterloo. Another factor behind Napoleon's success had been the growth in numbers of an educated, well-trained and efficient professional class. That old historical cliché, 'the rising middle class', is perhaps present in every age. Inevitably there are always groups or individuals in the middle class who are growing richer, and will soon seize political influence and power proportionate to their economic strength, just as there are other members of the same class who are growing poorer and will soon drop out of the bottom of political history. The future usually lies with 'the rising middle class', and when they are patronized by a ruler with the power of Napoleon I the whole process is accelerated.

In 1815 the fall of the bourgeois Napoleonic régimes in France, Italy, Spain, the Low Countries, Switzerland, west and central Germany and Poland had been permanently confirmed, and the old dynasties with

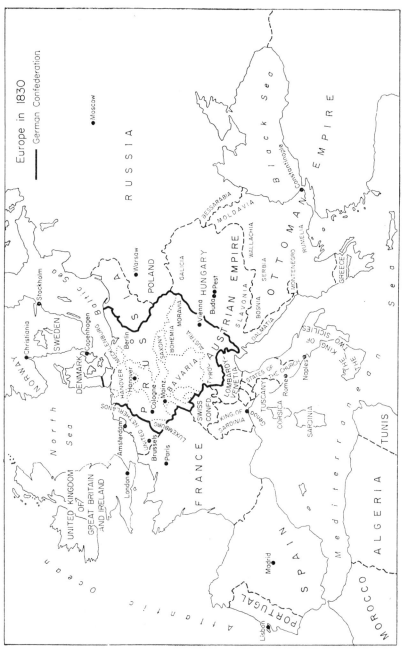

Europe in 1830

— German Confederation

Moscow

RUSSIA

Black Sea

OTTOMAN EMPIRE

Constantinople

BESSARABIA

MOLDAVIA

WALLACHIA

GALICIA

HUNGARY

Vienna Budo Pest

RUMELIA

SERBIA

MONTENEGRO

GREECE

AUSTRIAN EMPIRE

SLAVONIA

BOSNIA

DALMATIA

Warsaw

POLAND

Baltic Sea

Stockholm

SWEDEN

Christiania

NORWAY

Copenhagen

DENMARK

MECKLENBURG

Berlin

HANOVER

Hanover

Cologne

Mainz

SAXON

BOHEMIA

MORAVIA

AUSTRIA

TYROL

LOMBARDY-VENETIA

Genoa

SWISS CONFED.

KING. OF SARDINIA

TUSCANY

STATES OF THE CHURCH

Rome

CORSICA

SARDINIA

Naples

THE KING OF THE TWO SICILIES

P R U S S I A

BAVARIA

LUXEMBURG

UNITED NETHERLANDS

Amsterdam

Brussels

Paris

FRANCE

North Sea

UNITED KINGDOM OF GREAT BRITAIN AND IRELAND

London

Atlantic Ocean

SPAIN

Madrid

PORTUGAL

Lisbon

Mediterranean Sea

MOROCCO

ALGERIA

TUNIS

I. EUROPE IN 1830

only a few exceptions had been restored. But in some cases the old dynasties had been restored with a difference. It had been necessary for the conquerors to make some concessions to the new ideas, which in France, Italy and West Germany the professional classes had tested and found to be, for the most part, practicable.

In the defeated country, Louis XVIII was obliged to issue his Charter, giving France a very limited constitution. For the government which had the thankless task of ruling France after Napoleon's defeat there can be said to have been two great problems. The first was the constitutional one: should the absolutism of the *ancien régime* be restored? The second was a social one: should property, titles, government posts, wealth be returned to the old ruling class, or should the eminently respectable marshals, administrators and peasant proprietors of the Empire be left in possession of their rich acquisitions? The reply to the first of these problems did not necessarily condition the reply to the second. In theory four permutations were possible. An absolute or a constitutional monarchy could be superimposed, on either the Napoleonic administration and social order or on a restored landed aristocracy of returning emigrants. Left to himself Louis XVIII would probably have preferred to rule as an absolute monarch, but to leave the social revolution little disturbed. In 1815 the restored Bourbon king of France was an elderly invalid, who had enjoyed a quiet life in exile, had scarcely expected to be restored by the allies, and hoped he could live his remaining years in comparative peace. He was not averse to retaining Napoleon's advisers and marshals, who were more stable men than the inexperienced and embittered emigrants. But Louis was quite unconvinced of the benefits of a constitution, and issued his charter only to satisfy the wishes of the allies, and above all of the Czar Alexander I. The emigrants, on the other hand, and especially the brother of Louis XVIII, the comte d'Artois, believed that the social changes which France had introduced since 1789 must be reversed. For the aristocrats the institutions and the men of the Revolution and of the Empire had a whiff of the guillotine about them. It is probably true to say that the Ultras, as the emigrants were called once they had returned to political life, were less offended by Louis XVIII's charter than they were by the retention of ministers who had served Napoleon. In practice it would have been impossible for the Church and the emigrants to retrieve their former lands and posts. More than two decades had passed since they had left France. Men comparatively young in the years 1789–93 had grown old in exile, and France had changed in the meanwhile beyond recall. But some, at least, of the emigrants were given posts in the restored régime, whence they could agitate and struggle for a complete return to the system of Louis XV. It was under these auspices that the restored Bourbon monarchy had been established; it was to survive until the middle of 1830. Constitutionally, anyhow, Louis was obliged to follow the wishes of the allies. Napoleon had always retained a constitutional façade, and when he abdicated in 1814 a senate survived him and could negotiate with the enemy. Issued in June 1814, Louis XVIII's charter in practice kept the social organization of the Revolution, and the administrative organization of Napoleon, while attempting to introduce a political system which was strangely alien to French ideas and owed much to English political tradition. The declared principles behind the charter were representative government, ministerial responsibility, freedom of religion, of the press and 'of persons'. Existing titles and ranks were guaranteed. The ruling class and bureaucracy in France under the Empire had been chosen purely for its talent. The principle of equality of opportunity had been observed as it had never been in any society before. Government had been centralized, and members of the civil service had developed a strong public spirit and sense of duty to the community. These features of the social revolution were retained by Louis XVIII. In its social organization, as opposed to its political régime, France after the restoration was still so democratic as to be a splendid anachronism in post-1815 Europe. The very first point in the charter had declared: 'Frenchmen are equal before the law, whatever may be their titles and their ranks.'[1] Only a central governmental system was lacking. The charter was the first of many unsuccessful attempts to solve the problem of effectively controlling the high seat of political power without preventing it from functioning altogether. A satisfactory constitution has been evading the political skill of Frenchmen ever since 1789.

The charter of 1814 declared: 'All justice emanates from the king',[2] but: 'The Civil Code and laws actually existing which are not contrary to the present Charter remain in force.'[3] In other words, the Code Napoleon was retained, and with it other imperial institutions: the University, the Bank, the Legion of Honour, the imperial titled hierarchy. They had become part of the life of France and were not to be

[1] *Les Lois Françaises de 1815 à 1914*, ed. by L. Cahen and A. Mathiez (Paris, 1933), p. 14.
[2] *ibid.*, p. 18, Clause 57.　　　　　　　　[3] *ibid.*, p. 19, Clause 68.

discarded. But the constitution introduced by the charter was wholly un-French in conception. To the extent that it was copied from England it was bound to be an artificial creation. The English constitution had developed organically from roots deep in English history and tradition. To transplant such a growth in an underdeveloped country may be possible; to transplant it in the soil of a France rich with her own traditions, remote and recent, was impossible. There were to be three powers: the hereditary crown, the Chamber of Peers and the Chamber of Deputies. The Chamber of Deputies was to be elected by those Frenchmen who paid 300 francs in taxes, numbering only from 88,000 to 110,000 until 1830; about one in 320 of the population. But the lower house, once elected, was responsible for the budget. The king retained those powers which he had in England only in theory, and which he had long ceased to have in practice. He could appoint his own ministers, veto laws, convoke, adjourn and dissolve the Chamber of Deputies. The chambers could criticize ministers, but it was never clear to what extent the ministers were really responsible to the chambers. There were, then, certain important points of contrast with English parliamentary precedent, but these were less striking than the similarities. Even some of the more ceremonial features of English political life were introduced, like the speech from the throne at the opening of a new session, and the address of the house in reply. The charter did not allow for any future revision of the constitution. The English constitution being an unwritten and historical one contains no formal regulations for its own revision, but this has never mattered in practice. It has merely given each Reform Bill a somewhat revolutionary nature, or made it, at least, a big jump in the evolutionary process. But for a written constitution like that of Louis XVIII, the omission was disastrous. In the event no important reform was introduced to the constitution, whose main features were still intact at the opening of 1830.

The chambers were dominated throughout the period 1815–30 by two distinct upper-class groups: the owners of industry in the east and in Normandy—an industry which had developed under Napoleon's Continental System, with British products largely excluded from the French home market, and which was still protected by the economic policy of the governments of the restoration; and an aristocracy of the land, which, like the aristocracy of industry, had for the most part emerged from the middle class of pre-revolutionary France. The Continental System and the emigration had thus created powerful new classes whose interests dictated that they should cooperate with the Bourbons so long as the Bourbons could preserve internal peace. But if the Bourbons abandoned a moderate policy, the new moneyed classes would quickly look elsewhere.

Political life in restoration France was certainly not stagnant. The chambers played an active role; ministries were frequently formed and dismissed; the Ultras quarrelled with the Moderates; there was much debate, struggle and bitterness. But in this considerable political vitality only a small part of the nation could join. The peasants, urban workers, the lower clergy, most tradesmen and civil servants, in a word, all the working class and most of the middle class, were excluded. But, in spite of the high promises of the Revolution, most of these people had never experienced regular political representation. So long as the government could retain the support of the rich, the narrowness of French political life was no great danger. Louis XVIII had managed to preserve the balance. He had chosen his ministers wisely. Decazes and Richelieu had been moderate and able men, and even Villèle had kept the wheels of government turning. Only towards the end of Louis's reign had the extremists of the right tightened their hold on affairs. His death in 1824 revealed how much France had owed to the sense of compromise of her ridiculous old monarch. The new king, the duc d'Artois, now Charles X, in many ways an intelligent man, lacked that most necessary of all gifts of statecraft—a sense of what was politically possible. The great Catholic revival which had developed since 1815 had heightened the political struggle, encouraging both its supporters and its opponents to act fanatically. The extreme right-wing assembly which was sitting when Charles came to the throne proceeded to champion the two buttresses of the *ancien régime*—the old aristocracy and the Church. In the few years before 1830 laws were passed granting large sums to the dispossessed emigrants, making sacrilege punishable by death, muzzling the press. Finally in 1828, Charles appointed as chief minister Polignac, a superstitious and rash man, wholly out of touch with the opinions of Paris and the real forces in France. Louis XVIII had appointed ministers of his own choice, but his choice had usually been a good one, and conditions had been different. By 1828, Charles had already lost the good will of the middle classes. When the year 1830 opened, the rich and powerful in Paris—men like the banker, Laffitte—had already tired of the Bourbons, and were wondering where their interests now lay.

Across the channel, Great Britain, too, was on the eve of great political and social change in 1830. In spite of a striking increase since 1750, the population of Great Britain was still very much less than that of

France. Without the seven or eight million in Ireland, the inhabitants of Great Britain numbered only 16 or 17 million, compared with over 32 million in France.[1] But the English constitution, archaic and badly in need of revision as it was, permitted a greater percentage of the population to be represented in the central government than did the newly created constitution in France.[2] Whereas in France ability to vote depended only upon sex, age and income, in England it depended also upon the type of constituency one lived in. In the older towns of southern England a surprisingly democratic system had prevailed, with most householders having the vote, and sending two members per borough to parliament. Where these older towns were still well populated this led to a healthy political life, but more often the southern boroughs had decayed to a point where corruption became easy. In the more extreme examples—the rotten boroughs—the rich landowner or patron had so firm a control of the voter that he could buy or sell parliamentary seats as pieces of property. In the north the opposite situation prevailed. There large cities had appeared since 1750 and were not taken into account by the electoral system. Manchester and Birmingham sent no member to parliament.

Out of this electoral chaos a strangely homogeneous group of men emerged to sit as members of the House of Commons—the great majority of them landed gentry, with very similar interests and educational background to those of their cousins of the nobility who sat in the House of Lords. The powerful new manufacturing interests were very inadequately represented in parliament, and the large working class which had drifted into the towns and there multiplied itself was not represented at all. Already before the end of the eighteenth century parliamentary reform had been a current political issue. But in the interval between the loss of the American colonies and 1830 a strange listlessness had fallen upon party politics in England. The wars with Napoleon had led to the longest era of uninterrupted Tory rule in English history. The Whig opposition had dissipated its strength in

[1] J. H. Clapham, *Economic History of Modern Britain. The Early Railway Age 1820–1850* (Cambridge, 1930), p. 54; M. C. Buer, *Health, Wealth and Population in the Early Days of the Industrial Revolution* (London, 1926), p. 272.

[2] To arrive at a precise figure for the English electorate in 1830 is impossible in view of the heterogeneous nature of the electoral arrangements in the various constituencies. But if Sir Llewellyn Woodward's figure of 435,000 in *The Age of Reform* (Oxford, 1938), p. 84, is taken, it can be assumed that something like one in forty of the population had the vote, which compares very favourably with France's one in 320.

internal disputes, and had lost heart over the years. It was identified with no strong new influence in the country. Its leaders owed their wealth to land, and had few links with the manufacturing classes. On the contrary, in the 1820s industry and commerce was represented in the country's political life by the Canningite wing of the Tory party, rather than by the Whig opposition.

1815 had found Lord Liverpool in office at the head of a Tory government whose main aim had been to prevent the spread of new political or social ideas. The negative and repressive nature of its policy had given the Tory party a reputation which was to require many years of positive administration to modify. But with the admission into the government of Canning and Peel in 1822, and Huskisson in 1823, Tory policy began to thaw. While Peel, as home secretary, reformed the criminal code, Huskisson as president of the Board of Trade conducted an onslaught on mercantilism. Meanwhile the Whigs, unable to agree on parliamentary reform, had agitated for a great cause of abstract justice—Catholic emancipation. Wellington's government, in 1829, was at least obliged to grant this measure, causing dissension in the Tory party as the bill was passed. Only then did the Whigs turn their full attention to parliamentary reform, to find that the world of industry and labour was only awaiting political leadership to force upon parliament the greatest legislative measure of the century. In the opening of 1830 the Tory régime which had held power for a quarter of a century was losing its grasp, while the middle classes, as in France, were looking elsewhere for the defence of their interests.

Only in France and England had modern industrialization started by 1830, and even in France it had reached a merely primitive stage. In the rest of Europe the pattern of life had changed very little since the eighteenth century. In the Catholic countries on the western fringe of Europe—Ireland, Spain and Portugal—social conditions were much as they had been for decades. Only in the realm of political ideas had there been changes. In Ireland the British government's decision to unite the Irish and English parliaments in 1800 had been bitterly resented. Any attempt to integrate Ireland completely with Great Britain was doomed to failure. Once the Irish Catholics had secured a right to share in the public life of the country, by the Act of 1829, their position was less hopeless. The Ireland of 1830, though desperately poor and with civic disturbances evidently endemic, was not the tragic, depopulated country of 1850. She was the victim of economic misfortune and administrative indifference: not yet of overwhelming social disaster.

Spain had been one of the cockpits of Europe in the Napoleonic era, both in a military and ideological sense. The politically conscious in Spain, especially the officer class, had dedicated themselves to the ideas of the French Revolution. The constitution of 1812 had allowed for a single legislative chamber elected by universal manhood suffrage—a recognition of the principle of popular sovereignty in a recklessly pure form. From this extreme of democracy, never, of course, fully put into practice, Spain had been dragged back to the beliefs and atmosphere of the counter-reformation by the restored Bourbon King Ferdinand VII in 1815. The constitution had been abolished, and the nobility given back their privileges and even local feudal jurisdiction. Not surprisingly, it was in Spain that the first revolution against the 1815 restoration took place. In 1820 a military revolt in Cadiz was organized by officers who disapproved of the king's decision to reconquer his lost colonies in South America. The revolt quickly became identified with the broader issue of the repression in Spain herself, and Ferdinand was forced to accept the 1812 constitution. For three years the revolution survived in Spain, until, in 1823, Ferdinand's absolutism was restored by a French invasion to which the governments of Russia, Austria and Prussia had given their blessing. In 1830 he still ruled without institutional restraints, but surrounded by ceaseless court intrigues.

In Portugal, too, a constitution had been introduced as the result of revolution in 1820. Here the situation had been complicated by a succession rivalry, and by British naval intervention in support of the constitutionalists in 1826. Three years later the absolutist claimant to the throne, Miguel, had succeeded in having himself proclaimed king. In 1830 Portugal, no less than Spain, was in the hands of an unscrupulous autocrat, whose power was uncertainly based on armed force, a numerous priesthood and the ignorance of the peasant.

The despots who ruled the Italian states in 1830 appeared at first view more firmly entrenched than their counterparts in the Iberian countries. But there were reasons for supposing that Italian revolutionary movements would one day sweep away the old order in the Peninsula. Italian liberalism was a more sophisticated creed than that of the Spanish democrats. The Napoleonic régimes had been more fully appreciated by the Italian professional classes than they had ever been in Spain. The ideas of the eighteenth-century Enlightenment had, anyhow, been familiar to educated Italians before Napoleon had descended from the Alps in 1796. Tuscany and the Austrian provinces had experienced the reforms of the Grand Duke Leopold and his brother,

Joseph II, respectively. In some respects the Code Napoleon appeared primitive to the citizens of Florence, whose own civilized legal codes had been based on the ideas of the philosopher, Beccaria.

To the limited class of the politically conscious the 1815 restoration was a huge anachronism. Absolutist régimes were established under the House of Savoy in the kingdom of Sardinia, which included Piedmont, the island of Sardinia and Genoa, once a proud republic; in the independent duchies of Tuscany, Parma and Modena; in the Papal States, occupying central Italy, and with an even longer eastern than western coastline; in the kingdom of the Two Sicilies under the restored House of Bourbon. Lombardy and Venice were ruled directly from Vienna. The monarchs themselves were in every case less cruel and less stupid than Ferdinand of Spain, but the régimes were not less archaic. Only Tuscany, always an oasis of civilization, retained much of the enlightened administration of the Napoleonic eras. The professional classes as a whole accepted the restoration as inevitable, and would not have risked their careers in revolutionary plottings. But if a revolution should once succeed, they would be willing to accept posts in the new government, or at the least, to acquiesce in the change. Conspiracy was left to a few desperate men, who were prepared to join secret societies, of which the most active were the 'Carbonari'.

Originating in Naples before the fall of Napoleon, the Carbonari had been used by the English agent, Lord William Bentinck, and by King Ferdinand himself against the Napoleonic régime of Murat. Believing that England and Ferdinand had betrayed them in 1815 when the autocratic kingdom of the restoration emerged, the Carbonari now depended upon an insurrection of their own to secure the constitution of which they had been cheated. The Carbonari have usually been associated with Italy, and with good reason for it was there that they secured their greatest successes. But it was essentially an international organization. The 1820 rising in Spain had owed something to the Carbonari, and there were members in Ireland, England, Greece and America. Filippo Buonarotti, in Paris, was the head of the cosmopolitan movement, if anyone was; but he could never secure the loyalty or obedience of all branches. Later in 1820 insurrections, planned almost entirely by the Carbonari on the spot, broke out in Naples and Piedmont. In Naples Ferdinand proclaimed a constitution, and appointed a government of liberals. But the revolutionary government found the rest of Europe opposed to it, and eventually succumbed in 1821 to an Austrian invasion. In Piedmont and in Austrian Lombardy the leaders of the

Carbonari were aristocrats and intellectuals, like Federico Confalonieri or Silvio Pellico. Many of the members, as in Naples, were less worthy men—discontented army officers, or even men wanted for non-political crimes—but on the whole the organization was an upper or middle class one. The entrance fee of 25 francs and monthly subscription of 5 francs would have been enough to keep out the poor.[1]

The 1821 rising in Piedmont was not more successful than that in Naples. The king, Victor Emmanuel I, abdicated, and his successor, Charles Felix, suppressed the revolution with Austrian help. The Carbonari had taken on an insuperable task: to impose constitutions upon reluctant monarchs, who could secure the military support of Austria and the moral support of all the other Powers. The importance of the society for the history of Italy lies in its ultimate aims, rather than in its short-lived triumphs. Although the oath of allegiance was strangely obscure, and mentioned no aims, the Carbonari made no secret of their nationalism. They hoped one day to create a united Italy, even though this was clearly not a political possibility at the moment. The Papal States had been undisturbed by revolution in 1820–21. The Pope's army consisted of foreign mercenaries—Swiss, Irish, anything but Italian—and was not yet influenced by 'Carbonari' ideas. But by 1830 misgovernment of the Papal States had grown unbearable. Leo XII, who ruled from 1823 to 1829, had been a rigid individualist. Opposed to the influence of Metternich in Italy, he was equally averse to liberal or secular ideas. He had given all important ministerial posts to cardinals, and had placed education entirely in the hands of the priests. On his death in 1829 a pro-Austrian Pope was elected as Pius VIII. The professional classes, already antagonized by clerical government and a corrupt judicial system, began to feel the first tremblings of national sentiment.

Another area of western Europe on the eve of revolution in January 1830 was the south-western half of the United Netherlands. In 1815 Holland and Belgium had been united under the crown of the House of Orange, mainly to satisfy Castlereagh's conceptions of the strategic needs of Great Britain. By a coincidence, the union had proved satisfactory from an economic point of view. The maritime trade and colonial possessions of the North had formed a good complement to the agriculture and industry of the South. The Dutch king, William I, had taken great pains to ensure the prosperity of Belgium and had granted a comparatively generous constitution. But from the first moment of

[1] E. E. Y. Hales, *Mazzini and the Secret Societies* (London, 1956), p. 40.

union, it was apparent that differences of religion, language and temperament prevented the two races from living together politically. By 1830 the liberals and Catholics of Belgium were making common cause against an authority which had remained, in their eyes, an alien one. The greater part of Germany had been less directly influenced than had western Europe by the ideas of the French Revolution. In the years 1815 to 1830 the great and small princes of Germany maintained their authority with less difficulty than did the rulers of Italy and Spain. The patriotic students' societies, which constituted the only opposition to the governments of Germany, were much less of a threat than were the Carbonari in the west. Napoleon had destroyed the archaic pattern of Germany and the quaint fiction of the German Empire. Some three hundred states had been reduced to thirty-eight, including thirty-four princes and four surviving free towns. On 18 June 1815 the thirty-eight states declared themselves united in the German Confederation or 'Bund', with the object of 'maintaining the external and internal security and the independence and integrity of the individual states'. In other words, the Confederation of 1815, which was to survive until Bismarck's day, was an alliance of states for the specific purpose of preserving their independence. It was concerned not with uniting Germany, but with blocking the formation of an integrated state. It was a confederation to prevent a federation. The sole constitutional organ, the Assembly of the Confederation, was a permanent conference of plenipotentiaries, sitting at Frankfurt, under the presidency of the Austrian representative. The plenipotentiaries were diplomats rather than delegates. They were not elected, but simply appointed by their governments and sent with definite instructions. Each of the German states retained its own sovereign government, its own foreign policy, its own army. The Assembly met for the first time late in 1816. At first some members tried to introduce political proposals, but it soon became apparent that nothing would come out of the Confederation. The assent of each individual German government was necessary for any measure. The great solemnity of the Assembly could not conceal its impotence. Article 13 of the constitution of the Confederation had laid down that in some unspecified future each German prince should give his subjects a constitution, or more precisely, a *Landständische Verfassung*, or 'Constitution of regional estates'—an expression which looked backward to medieval institutions, rather than forward to representative government. The Austrian and Prussian governments ignored the article. The elector of Hesse was busy after 1816 in establishing a new despotism. The only 'elector' left, he no longer elected anyone, nor was he elected by anyone. When the Assembly of the Confederation remonstrated with him, he ignored it. But the majority of the states of northern Germany permitted the ancient estates to meet. South Germany had been more fully exposed to the radical simplification of frontiers by Napoleon, but in the north many tiny states survived. Not only many of these, but also a few of the larger states—Hanover, Mecklenburg and Saxony—preserved the estates, traditional bodies, consisting mainly of the nobility. Some German states, especially in the south, had written constitutions, with elected houses of representatives, having the power to vote financial measures and to legislate. But even in these there was no ministerial responsibility: the prince appointed his own ministers. Most liberal of the German princes was the grand-duke of Saxe-Weimar, whose assembly of deputies really represented the towns and the peasantry. In the years 1818–20, Bavaria, Baden, Württemberg and Hesse-Darmstadt introduced constitutions of the French type.

With few exceptions there was no political vitality in Germany. The great majority of Germans in the years 1815–30 were supremely uninterested in public affairs. They were not actively in favour of or in opposition to absolutism. The majority of German princes, their ministers and their priests, on the other hand, believed in absolutism as a positive political creed, and accepted the teaching of the Swiss writer, Haller, who had refuted Rousseau's 'Social Contract' with his own theory of the state as the private property of the Crown. The only active opponents in Germany to the absolutist creed were the universities. The 1813 War of Liberation had produced a patriotic movement among students—a great, vague, ill-founded hope of German unity after the war. The students' societies remained francophobe and incredibly naive in their political ideas. They burned the Code Napoleon with as much enthusiasm as they burned the works of Haller. But it was from these children and cranks that the mystique of German nationalism, with its flag of red, black and gold, emerged.

Unintentionally, the diplomats of 1815 had given the potential leadership of north and central Germany to Prussia. By giving her the northern Rhinelands, the Treaty of Vienna had made Prussia the chief guardian of Germany against the West. The steady growth of Prussia during the eighteenth century had been crowned in 1815 by the acquisition of lands around the Rhine and in Saxony, increasing the population by about 1,400,000 and 800,000 respectively. Prussia had not come under direct French influence as west Germany had. In her most desperate and humiliated moments, Prussia had preserved her independence and refused to join Napoleon's Confederation of the Rhine. Changes brought about in Prussia during the Napoleonic wars were inspired by the need to fight, not to copy, the French. A traditional characteristic had become intensified during the wars—an absurd respect for authority, whether it was the authority of the absolute monarch, of the landowner over the peasants, or of the nobility who held all high military and civil commissions. Frederick William III ruled as an absolute monarch from 1797 to 1840. The one good feature of his reign was the high quality of his civil servants, who, although still mostly noblemen in 1830, had to pass examinations to obtain their posts, and had high standards of industry and duty to the community. Only in the Rhinelands was a commercial middle class appearing in any numbers. The government was firmly seated in 1830. There was only the faintest reflection of the unrest simmering in the west.

The Austrian monarchy in 1830 had a stronger grip upon Germany than did the Prussian, but was faced by far graver basic problems. The Austrian emperor, Francis II, had reigned since 1792, had dissolved the Holy Roman Empire in 1806, but had survived the troublesome period of revolution and wars. A man with a certain dignity, and not unpopular, he yet had a small mind and was very much the intellectual inferior of his three predecessors, Leopold II, Joseph II and Maria Theresa. The ideas both of the Enlightenment and of the revolutionary era had meant nothing to him.

The empire over which Francis reigned was a colourful cross-section of central and eastern Europe. It embraced both historic units and provinces which had never experienced national unity. The former included the hereditary lands of the Habsburgs; the lands of the Crown of Bohemia: the provinces of Bohemia and Moravia, and that portion of Silesia which had not been stolen for Prussia by Frederick the Great; the Polish kingdom of Galicia; the lands of the Crown of St Stephen: the kingdom of Hungary, the principality of Transylvania, Croatia and Slavonia, and a Serbian province. Outside these four groups were the Italian provinces of Lombardy and Venetia, ethnically and linguistically homogeneous, but with no precedent of historic unity. The four historic kingdoms were occupied by many races, speaking many tongues: Germans, Italians, Magyars, Rumanians and several Slav peoples— Czechs, Slovaks, Poles, Ruthenians, Slovenes, Croats and Serbs. Not, as yet, very conscious of their racial, linguistic and religious differences, the peoples of the Empire had their lives lightly administered by a

33

largely German-speaking civil service. Since the imperial servants themselves were not particularly proud of their German nationality, it was
fitting that the highest official, the imperial chancellor, should view life
from an essentially international standpoint. Prince Clement von Metternich had controlled the foreign policy of Austria since 1809, and had
been principally responsible for the complete lack of a domestic policy.
By temperament and conviction he was opposed to the idea of change,
and determined to preserve monarchical absolutism throughout the
Empire, and, where possible, throughout Europe. In the days of his rise
to power he had been regarded as a lazy sceptic, but in the 1820s a
subtle change had come over his personality. The deaths of two
daughters, a son and two wives in one decade had hardened him, and
made him more devoted to his work. His power had reached its peak in
1819, when he had obliged the German princes to accept the Carlsbad
Decrees, which dissolved the student societies in Germany and established a thorough press censorship. After 1830 his personal hold on the
emperor was to weaken, but he retained a greater influence in Germany
than any other man, and until 1848 was to control the foreign policy of
the immense baronial estate which was the Habsburg empire.

On the other side of Germany the little kingdom of Denmark was
ruled, like Prussia and Austria, by a despot, though a rather more enlightened one. Frederick VI (1808–39) had been deprived of Norway in
1814, but in 1830 still retained the duchies of Schleswig and Holstein.
Norway had passed to Bernadotte, who ruled Sweden as Charles XIV.

In spite of the arrival on the Swedish throne of a French marshal with
a revolutionary background, the traditions of Swedish political life had
not been broken. Like Britain, Sweden had retained her historic constitution. A royal council of state was the real governing body, but
legislation was controlled by the ancient Diet of four estates—nobility,
clergy, bourgeoisie and peasants. In 1840 the council of state was to be
transformed into a modern cabinet and administratively organized into
seven ministries.

Norway had the most egalitarian society in Europe. The Danish
ruling class had departed in 1814, leaving a population of peasant
proprietors, merchants, fishermen and sailors. Although they had fought
unsuccessfully to resist the imposition of Swedish sovereignty, Nor-
wegians afterwards found themselves under a surprisingly lenient
régime. The constitution of 1814 had created an Assembly with wide
powers. A council of state separate from that in Sweden was chosen by
the king and sat in Christiana. But so long as Bernadotte lived, the Nor-

wegians did not happily accept his sovereignty, and had to fight to preserve what was, after all, a virtual autonomy. Only with the succession of Oscar I in 1844 was the Norwegian Assembly partly pacified by the recognition of a separate national flag.

If political life in most of western and central Europe was at a low ebb in 1830, in eastern Europe an already dark scene was becoming darker. With the death of Alexander I in 1825 the last hopes of a liberal future for Russia and Poland faded. Already before 1820, Alexander had renounced the radical influences of his youth, and, in true Russian style, had made rhetorical confessions of past errors to foreign diplomats. But at least as long as he lived the 1815 experiment of an autonomous, constitutional kingdom of Poland was not completely abandoned. With the accession of his brother, Nicholas I, Russia returned to that part of the policy of Catherine the Great which was tyrannical and imperialistic, and forgot that part of her policy which was enlightened and cosmopolitan. No less autocratic than the governments of Prussia or Austria, Russian administration under Nicholas differed from that of the other Powers in being far more corrupt. The Polish Diet had met very rarely in Alexander's reign. Since 1825 it had not met at all. By 1830 the Polish nationalist movement, which Alexander had encouraged in his ambiguous way, was suffering from a biting sense of frustration.

Even further gone than the Russian in the slow process of decay was the Turkish Empire. Only by an extraordinary display of energy had the Sultan Mahmoud II (1808-39) prevented its final collapse. A privileged military caste, the Janissaries, had become a cancer in the Ottoman Empire, terrorizing the capital and preventing either reform or sound government. Mahmoud's greatest achievement was the building up of an alternative military force and the massacre of the Janissaries in 1826. If this ruthless but necessary act prevented the complete paralysis of government in Constantinople, it came only after successful revolts in the Christian provinces of European Turkey. The Serbs under their illiterate peasant chief, Kara George, had secured autonomy before the end of the Napoleonic wars, while remaining under the sultan's suzerainty. Nor did the sultan have more than a nominal authority in Egypt, where Mehemet Ali, a much greater political leader than Mahmoud, had been laying the foundations of a modern state since 1805. European Turkey differed from the rest of the Continent in one significant respect. Whereas Christian governments in the rest of Europe had permitted no Muslim communities to survive, in the Ottoman Empire the Christian communities had been officially tolerated. In some parts of the Empire, notably in the Danubian principalities, which were one day to become Rumania, the Greek Orthodox Christian Church formed a supplementary authority to the secular government of the sultan. Only in Greece did the Church become a revolutionary body.

In 1820 serious revolts had broken out at several points throughout the Greek world. For eight years victory and defeat alternated for the Greeks, while both sides inflicted foul atrocities upon each other. The educated classes of western Europe showed greater sympathy for the Greek insurrection than they had shown for the more civilized revolutionaries of Italy. Byron, at the peak of his fabulous reputation, travelled to Greece and died there. Finally, in 1827-28 the powers had intervened, British and French fleets destroying the Ottoman fleet at Navarino, and a Russian army invading the Rumanian principalities of Moldavia and Wallachia. From the intervention of the powers, and from the long years of Greek resistance, the Ottoman Empire survived, but with real power in the Balkans slipping from it. By the Russo-Turkish peace of 1829 the Danubian principalities were to be temporarily occupied by Russian troops, although remaining under the sultan's suzerainty. In the event, Turkish troops were never to return and the Russians were to stay for five years, radically influencing the future of the principalities. Early in 1830 Greek independence was at last recognized by the powers, though the boundaries of Greece were still unsettled, and no king had yet been found for the new state.

The Greek question had caused much dissension among the powers, and had furnished final proof that the regular meetings of great congresses could not solve every international problem. In terms of diplomatic history the period 1815 to 1830 is one of great interest. To few periods has more detailed research been devoted, and few periods have aroused such heated academic debate. About the 1815 settlement itself opinion is still divided. Liberal historians of the last century overlooked the constructive characteristics of the settlement—the ruling on international rivers, the declaration against the slave trade; but whether the peaceful nature of the period covered by this volume owes anything to the terms of the Treaty of Vienna is open to argument. It is true that the bigger mistakes of the settlement—the unification of Holland and Belgium, and the restoration of ancient but undeserving dynasties in Spain and Italy—dealt with secondary questions. In primary questions—the French and German settlements—a certain amount of wisdom and moderation was shown. But when all the positive points in favour of the settlement have been made, a basic argument remains: in 1815 the opportunities for reform in Europe were immense. Developments have taken place in times of flux which had seemed Utopian a few years before, and would have seemed Utopian again a few years after, once settled days had returned. In 1848 Europe was narrowly to miss achievements which, by 1858, had taken on once again the appearance of mad dreams. Spanish South America came nearer to unity at the moment of achieving its independence than it has ever been since. And who can say when the thirteen United States of America would have become a nation if they had not done so at the moment of birth? The apologists of the 1815 settlement have tended to forget that much would then have been possible to men of vision which was to become unthinkable by 1830. The nineteenth century was never again to furnish such an opportunity. The story of the years 1830 to 1880 is one of slow reform and isolated revolutions, of the gradual improvement of institutions and occasional increase of human welfare.

The negotiators of 1815 had understandably been obsessed with the need to establish a permanent peace, and they had decided on the broad policy of establishing agreement between the powers rather than resorting to independent action. As Metternich put it:

> All I ask is a moral understanding between the five great powers whose strength and prestige make them the natural arbiters of European destiny. I ask that they take no important step, do nothing which might endanger the general peace, without a previous joint understanding.[1]

In practice the mystical phrases of Alexander's Holy Alliance amounted to the same policy. Castlereagh, too, had been enthusiastic about the wisdom of frequent personal contacts and frank discussions between the rulers of the powers. For the first five or six years after the Congress of Vienna international cooperation worked. Each of the powers refrained from military actions before they had obtained the consent or at least the acquiescence of the other powers. But by 1822 the attempt to govern Europe by congressional judgments was meeting obstacles, and by 1830 the state of international anarchy more usual in Europe had returned. The immediate reasons for the failure of the congress policy included the growing distaste of the British government for international intervention in the affairs of sovereign states; the death of Castlereagh and the arrival at the Foreign Office of Canning, with his strictly individual national policy; British independent recognition of the new

---

[1] C. de Grunwald, *Metternich* (English translation, London, 1953), p. 201.

states in South America; the revolt of the Greeks who were fighting for the czar's religion, but who were simply a Levantine breed of Carbonari in Metternich's eyes; and the death of Alexander and succession of Nicholas I, who distrusted western ideas, and, like Canning, preferred to pursue an individual national policy. The deeper reason for the failure of government by congress lay in the narrowness of vision of the men in power, and especially of Metternich. The Austrian Chancellor regarded the congresses simply as a means of maintaining the *status quo*. He could not conceive of them regulating European affairs in a positive sense. The Congresses of Troppau and Laibach did not consider the validity of the new Neapolitan régime of 1820 objectively. They merely considered how the old order could be re-established. Metternich was too intelligent to suppose that all change could be resisted for ever. He merely believed that it should be resisted for as long as possible. His was a policy of despair.

While the autocratic governments of Europe shared a common fear of humanity, romantic conspirators were erecting unsophisticated, unrealistic, revolutionary philosophies, based on an unbounded faith in humanity. The optimistic revolutionaries took their basic ideas from three writers who had all worked in the eighteenth century, and who were all dead by 1830: Rousseau, Herder and Saint-Simon, the forerunners of nineteenth-century liberalism, nationalism and socialism respectively.

From Rousseau they had learned that sovereignty should rest in the people. By his stress on the beauty of a simple life and of direct human community, Rousseau's most important message had been an egalitarian one. From Herder the nationalist revolutionaries of the nineteenth century learned that all true culture sprang from the *mores* and language of the common people, the *Volk*. Artificially imported, cosmopolitan culture could do nothing but harm. National character was the most important quality in the world. From Saint-Simon the men of 1830 acquired their first nebulous socialist ideas. They learned to respect the working classes as the source of wealth, and to affirm that capital should be in the hands of the state.

The influence of these three political creeds was radically to change the character of European civilization over the next decades. But in 1830 they were the property of a few, small, exceptional groups of Europeans: French demagogues, English radicals, German students and professors, Italian conspirators or Slav poets. On the surface, the Europe of 1830 was little different from the Europe of 1815. The same dynasties were at the head of the same governmental systems. But the great increase in population which was accompanying industrial development meant that the new ideas would have a more sudden and a more overwhelming effect than fresh ideas had had in the past. The new creeds were about to manifest themselves in revolutionary movements in France, Belgium, Italy, Germany, Poland and Great Britain. At first only the cause of the liberals was to triumph. The nationalists had to wait some years for fresh leaders, and the socialists had to wait still longer. But the middle classes of the 1820s were preparing to become the ruling classes of the 1830s, and in western Europe they were not everywhere to prepare in vain. Men who had been too young to share the sentiments of 1815 were waiting to come into their political inheritance.

III

Political Ideas

The relationship between thought and action in history is a subtle and seldom obvious one. On the question of which precedes the other the men with whose ideas this chapter is concerned would have disagreed, as they disagreed about almost everything else. Mazzini was convinced that thought was basic, and must be prior to action, and the English radicals would not have questioned the claim. Marx, on the other hand, would have disapproved of a book in which a chapter on political ideas preceded the chapters on economic and political developments. For Marx ideas were simply the product of environment, of economic interests and material developments. A man's thought would throw more light on the society which had produced him than on the society for

BIBLIOGRAPHY. For a study of the political ideas of the period there is, of course, no substitute for reading the original works of the theorists themselves. Their most important writings are referred to in the text of this chapter; in nearly every case they have run into many editions and been translated into several languages. Commentaries, analyses and criticisms of the various theories form a considerable literature in themselves. A good lively introduction is provided by John Bowle, *Politics and Opinion in the Nineteenth Century* (London, 1954). There are two accounts of nineteenth-century French political thought, both of which keep quite close to actual political developments in France. The more detailed is R. H. Soltau, *French Political Thought in the Nineteenth Century* (London, 1931), but J. P. Mayer, *Political Thought in France from the Revolution to the Fourth Republic* (London, 1949), is more recent. A short, lucid study of British political thought at the end of the period is contained in Sir Ernest Barker, *Political Thought in England, 1848–1914* (Oxford, 1928). Italian thought is dealt with, more fully, in Luigi Salvatorelli, *Il pensiero politico italiano dal 1700–1870* (Turin, 1949). A single theme, vital for the period, is considered in a refreshing manner in J. L. Talmon, *Political Messianism* (London, 1960). Much has been written on nationalism, though less on the nineteenth-century species than might have been expected, considering its central importance. However an essay which deals well with the nineteenth century and contains reflections from a lifetime of scholarship is Carlton J. Hayes, *Nationalism: a Religion* (New York, 1960). A defence of the ideas of Hegel is made by H. Marcuse, *Reason and* which he was planning. Yet even Marx might have paused before applying the theory to his own place in history.

Much of the thought of the period 1830 to 1880 was to have a greater influence on the post-1880 period than on its own. Only with the success of the Russian Revolution of 1917 was the doctrine of Marx to have a direct influence on the formation and policy of an important government. But the thought of the French socialists influenced the central theme of French history from 1830 onwards, and for two moments prior to 1880—in 1848 and in 1871—socialists gained power in Paris. The nationalists of mid-nineteenth-century Europe could trace their beliefs to Herder, Rousseau and Fichte, who were all dead by 1830, but they owed perhaps still more to Hegel, who died in the cholera epidemic of 1831 at the early age of sixty-one, and to Mazzini, who was still a young man at that time. Nationalism, as a more spontaneous, less intellectual and less logical movement than socialism, owed far less to its theorists. The direct influence of the teaching of Hegel's doctrines in German universities and schools was great, but united Germany had less reason to worship Hegel than communist Russia has to worship Marx. Treitschke's writings are interesting as explicit statements of the basic ideas

Revolution: Hegel and the Rise of Social Theory (Oxford, 1941), and an excellent short assessment of the ideas of Mazzini is Gaetano Salvemini's *Mazzini* (original Italian edition, 1905; English translation, 1956). A good survey of liberalism with a strong stress on nineteenth-century developments is G. de Ruggiero, *History of European Liberalism* (Oxford, 1927). A full and vivid account of the Benthamites is given by E. Halévy, *Growth of Philosophic Radicalism* (original edition, Paris, 3 vols., 1901–4; English translation, London, 1928). For the intellectual development of John Stuart Mill no account will ever improve upon his own in his *Autobiography*, which has been published in numerous editions. For De Tocqueville there is a recent short study: Jack Lively, *The Social and Political Thought of Alexis de Tocqueville* (Oxford, 1962), and a sympathetic study of the conservative tradition, with a heavy slant towards American writers, but with interesting pages on Macaulay, Tocqueville, Disraeli and John Stuart Mill, is Russell Kirk, *The Conservative Mind* (London, 1954). For socialist thought, generally, in the period, the best account is G. D. H. Cole, *A History of Socialist Thought* (London, 5 vols., 1953–60), vols. I and II being the relevant ones. A hostile commentary, necessary to adjust the balance, is Alexander Gray, *The Socialist Tradition* (London, 1948). An admirable recent work of scholarship, which avoids both doctrinaire support of Marxism and the carping note often present in English studies of Marxism, is George Lichtheim, *Marxism* (London, 1961). Harold Laski's edition of the *Communist Manifesto* (London, 1948) has a good introductory essay. Roger Morgan, *The German Social Democrats and the First International 1864–1872* (Cambridge, 1965), is a lucid and scholarly account.

behind Bismarck's Germany; yet no one would suggest that without Treitschke Bismarck would have failed in his task. It is impossible to understand political developments in England in the 1830s and 1840s without an appreciation of the thought of Bentham, but for English history of the 1850s and 1860s, John Stuart Mill, like Treitschke in Germany, is more significant as a symptom than an influence. This does not mean that it is less important to study Mill or Treitschke than Bentham in considering the history of the nineteenth century. On the contrary, political ideas are equally relevant to a study of political action whether they were a reflection or cause of that action.

The migration of ideas follows no fixed rules. Theories may have their greatest effect immediately they have been formulated, or at a surprisingly remote period. A Mazzini or a Louis Blanc may play an important active role in political events. A Bentham or a Marx may have a more fundamental influence, in a later age. A Treitschke or a T. H. Green may have a direct influence on the sons of the ruling class because of their university appointments. A Guizot or a Disraeli may contribute creative political ideas while regarding his main task as the administration of public affairs.

The two most striking events of the period in Europe were the creation of Germany and Italy as modern nation states. Diplomacy, war and revolution were all needed in unifying Germany and Italy, but underlying all three was a movement of ideas, incoherent and even contradictory ideas, but passionately held by steadily growing minorities of the people. The movement can best be defined as an awakening of a sense of national identity. The idea of belonging to a tribe, a very large family, with its own individual customs and way of life, and to a region or *pays*, had always been present among the peoples of Europe. Another concept, that of the independent, integrated state with fixed geographical limits, had emerged with the growth of strong monarchy in the late medieval and Renaissance periods. It was for the nineteenth century to identify the two concepts—to demand that a single tribe or nation should correspond to an independent and united state in a limited geographical area. Primitive manifestations of nationalism are recognizable in the period between the Middle Ages and the nineteenth century. St Joan had appealed to a French, and Luther to a German nation. The maritime boundaries of England had encouraged her inhabitants to think of themselves as a nation since, at latest, Tudor days. But on the continent the seventeenth and eighteenth centuries had experienced something of a reaction against the growth of national self-consciousness. The Enlightenment had been a cosmopolitan movement, and the educated classes had tended to lose any strong sense of national identity. Eighteenth-century wars in Europe, if not overseas, were dynastic wars, and in the intervening periods of peace the European aristocracy mixed as they had never done before. Styles in art and architecture became standardized throughout western and central Europe. Only with the French Revolution did the change come.

Any organic doctrine of the state could give rise to a nationalist movement. Thus Rousseau and Burke unwittingly prepared the way for Fichte and Hegel. But for a nationalist movement to be coherent, the vague concept of the 'nation' must be based upon some element held in common, whether that element be racial consciousness or illusions, language, culture, religion, geography or a mixing of any two or more of these. Where all five elements coincided—as in Italy, Ireland and Poland —very strong and ultimately successful nationalist movements developed. In Germany there was no religious unity and no very clearly defined geographical limits, but the elements of language and culture held in common, and with them a mystique of 'race', proved sufficient. Most tangible and most potent of the elements making up a nation was perhaps a common language—on which a common culture to some extent depended. The Panslav movement, as well as having no religion in common, lacked a common language; no Panslav state emerged. In contrast, the Rumanians, possessing a very individual language and living in a reasonably compact area, formed a nation-state in the teeth of opposition from their old sovereign, the Ottoman sultan, and from two of the Great Powers. Herder had based his concept of nationality on language and culture, and Fichte, too, wrote of language rather than of race. In this sense, they were the ancestors of Mazzini's Italian nationalism, rather than of later German nationalists who became obsessed with the unscientific and unverifiable idea of race. But Fichte had this in common with later nationalists in Germany—he brought a wholly unjustifiable and puerile value judgment into his study of language nationalism. He naively believed that Greek, Latin and German were 'purer' languages than French or Italian, and that German culture was therefore more vital. He had the good sense to recognize that French, Spaniards and Italians were all partly Teutonic, and that Germans were partly Slav, but having closed the front door to racial prejudice, he opened the back door to it by claiming the superiority of German culture.

Having a stronger influence on German thought than either Herder or Fichte, Georg Wilhelm Friedrich Hegel (1770–1831) owed much to both of them, though more, perhaps, to the idealism of Kant. If Herder's ideas were to be over-simplified, but turned to good use, by Mazzini, Hegel's philosophy was to form the more sterile aspect of the system of Marx. After a university education in theology, Hegel had spent his earlier years teaching and writing, until publishing his *System of Philosophy* over the years 1812 to 1816. In 1821 he had followed Fichte as Rector of Berlin University, and in the same year had published his *Fundamentals of the Philosophy of Right*. For the last decade of his life he lectured in Berlin, earning a great reputation throughout Germany. After his death his ideas permeated from the universities to the German schools, often in a dangerously simplified form. His most original contribution to European thought lay in his concept of the historical nature of truth. He believed, as Giambattista Vico (1668–1744) had already suggested, that values depended upon their historical context. For Hegel there was, certainly, an Absolute, but it was an Absolute emerging in the working of history. Ideas were always changing. Institutions were always changing. Only in the eternal swinging of the pendulum from thesis to antithesis to synthesis was ultimate truth revealed.

Like Rousseau, Hegel conceived of the community as organic and unitary, in contrast to the eighteenth-century idea of a free association of people living according to the terms of a contract. The state was as much an organ of nature as the individual, and since the state was manifestly stronger than the individual, freedom could only be achieved through it. Like Burke's political philosophy, Hegel's had no place for paper constitutions or artificial contracts. Government must be a natural, organic growth. The wills of the individuals in society added up to a general will, but a general will which, unlike Rousseau's, would be a developing and creative one. The individual will itself had no significance, and the individual had no rights except through the state. Apologists for Hegel have taken this doctrine of the general will as a justification for considering him one of the earliest supporters of constitutionalism. Certainly as a boy of nineteen Hegel had welcomed the French Revolution, but his mature writings show an increasing respect for authoritarianism. He sees the sovereign power as the embodiment of the state, and it is not surprising that totalitarian régimes have taken their inspiration from him, whereas no pluralist society has ever acknowledged him. He was not concerned to safeguard individual freedom, because he believed that the individual could reach a higher freedom by letting his will play through the nation. The doctrine of Will played an enormous part in Hegel's theories. The Will of God was experienced through the nation and through history.

A disastrous limitation of Hegel's thought was his failure to conceive a higher unit of power than the nation, or a higher authority than the state. Not only did he not try to wrestle with international problems, but he did not see them as needing solution. He believed that war was a splendid manifestation of national vitality. Partly this was because he had shared in the Prussian humiliations under Napoleon, and enjoyed the final triumph of the War of Liberation and the victories of Leipzig and Waterloo, without experiencing the sufferings of the battlefield. He did not hope—as Mazzini was to hope—that the creation of nation states would be but one step to a greater unity, that a higher authority would one day be established. For Hegel the force which moved history, being a divine force, was above any human moral code. Standards of good and evil were valid in everyday life; they were not valid in history: above all, they were not valid in the working of the state.

The nation had but to fulfil its mission. Each nation had its appointed hour when it could dominate world history. Herder had imagined each nation making its own individual contribution to history, but he had thought in terms of cultural contributions. Mazzini, too, was obsessed with the concept of national 'mission', but whereas he imagined these 'missions' to be complementary and contemporary with each other, Hegel imagined them to be conflicting and to succeed each other in a series of master races. Hegel's scheme of the past is contained in his *Philosophy of History*, a published version of lectures given at Berlin. Of great erudition and powerful synthesis, the work is based on a somewhat naive patriotism, as its division into four parts—the oriental world, the Greek world, the Roman world, and the German world—indicates. The German era, which had not then reached its culmination, was to be one of real freedom—freedom through the nation. Throughout Hegel's nationalism there is a lack of any sense of political reality. His is an academic construction which lacks the sharp edge, the shrewdness and the human wisdom of many contemporary works. By contrast, Burke's *Thoughts on the Causes of the Present Discontents* had been grounded firmly in the politics of George III's early days, but for that very reason its doctrine of party was at once a universal and an immediately applicable one. Bentham's *Fragment on Government* was equally a *pièce d'occasion* and a work whose practical insight was to inspire men then unborn. Outrage at human sufferings was to call forth the inspired writings of Fourier and Proudhon and the crystal-clear doctrine of the

Communist Manifesto. Or again, an urgent sense of apprehension at new developments in society was to encourage the deep warnings of de Tocqueville and John Stuart Mill. Hegel's work on the other hand was obscure and remote from life. Like T. H. Green's *Principles of Political Obligation*, it had an intellectual consistency and unity, but was dangerously removed from problems of practical politics. Hegel had no constructive message for Europe; at his worst he was merely juggling with abstract ideas. Schopenhauer, writing, certainly in a spirit of professional jealousy, but also with some sense, asked:

> How should the minds that in the freshness of youth have been strained and ruined by the nonsense of Hegelianism, be still capable of following Kant's profound Investigations? They are easily accustomed to take the hollowest jingle of words for philosophical thoughts, the most miserable sophisms for acuteness, and silly conceits for dialectic, and their minds are disorganized through the admission of mad combinations of words to which the mind torments and exhausts itself in vain to attach some thought.[1]

It was a misfortune for Europe that a generation of Germans grew up under the influence of Hegelian nationalism. If Mazzini's mind was less powerful and less original than Hegel's, his influence on history was more beneficial. Mazzini's nationalism was only a part, if the most important part, of his religion. He believed, too, in republican institutions; and—more important still—he believed that man's ultimate loyalty was to humanity itself, where Hegel could envisage no higher cause than that of the nation.

Giuseppe Mazzini (1805–72), the son of a professor of anatomy, lived the life of a conspirator and exile, with only one brief period of political power in 1849 while the Roman republic survived. Almost the prototype of the romantic revolutionary, he shared the characteristic associated with the English poets of the Romantic school—an excessive, effeminate sensibility. Surrounded by his canaries and cigar smoke, dressed always in black as a mourner for Italy, he had more taste for tragedy than for pleasure or humour. Yet his political philosophy was a profoundly optimistic one. He trusted the innate goodness and intelligence of man, and believed only that society must be given freedom and a sense of religious duty for it to reach perfection. His nationalism came from a natural sympathy with the martyrs and conspirators of the Italy of his youth and from readings of Herder. His social democracy

---

[1] Schopenhauer, *The World as Will and Idea*, preface to second edition (English edition, translated by R. B. Haldane and J. Kemp), 1891, vol. i, p. xxvi.

came from Saint-Simon. His original contribution lay in his complete reconciliation of liberalism and nationalism: his conviction that the individual and the nation were equally sacred. He praised religion as the ennobling element in man, but his religion was really a glorification of the principle of social service. Some later Russian socialists, in the religious nature of their belief in service to society, showed that they had more in common with Mazzini than with Marx. Mazzini believed that vital political thought had to be imbued with a religious sense. He could never appreciate English empiricism, and from his long years in London learned nothing from the English radicals. Benthamite ideas he despised. Religion was to supply the common purpose to society. A religious spirit, working through democratic principles, like the principle of universal suffrage, would lead to human progress. Universal suffrage, without a common faith, would lead only to instability and a new form of coercion—coercion by the majority. There was a need, then, for a new faith. Historical religions, and especially Christianity, had all helped man to know God, but their role had been played out. Mazzini's preoccupations with the religious idea, while providing a tremendous motive force to the movement of Italian nationalism, rendered him and his followers ineffective when the task of organization began.

The part of his message which had most influence on the Italians of his day, and on groups of intellectuals throughout Europe, was the appeal to nationality. He felt a passionate sympathy not only for the cause of Italy, but for the aims of all nationalist groups in Europe—Poles, Hungarians and south Slavs. At a time when only the smallest minorities wanted to redraw the map of Europe along lines suggested by nationality, Mazzini believed that the dream of 'the People' was for national self-expression. He did not pass judgment on the wisdom or unwisdom of this dream. His belief in democracy was so complete that, having once decided what was the desire of the People, he did not go on to consider whether this desire could possibly lead to anything but unqualified good. If the People wished for nationality, then nationality, as he declared in the 'Principles of Belief' of his society, Young Europe, was 'sacred'.

In most of his writings Mazzini was declaring his dogma to eager disciples. But occasionally he answered charges, and on one occasion he gave an answer, in less nebulous terms than usual, to critics of his doctrine of nationality. This was in an article in the *Jeune Suisse* in January 1836,[1] an article which has been strangely neglected by Mazzinian

---

[1] 'Humanité et Patrie', *Jeune Suisse*, 13 and 23 January 1836. Vol. VII of *Scritti editi ed inediti*, national edition.

scholars. The charge was that nationalism as a creed was 'incomplete', 'egoistic' and even 'reactionary', that it contrasted with the need for 'fusion', 'harmony' and 'union', that the very word 'nationality' was too small for the nineteenth century, that it was an anachronism, 'a manifestation of the past, a formula of the middle ages which has made so much blood run'. Having stated the charge he was to answer, Mazzini argued, surprisingly, that his own attitude was a realistic one. Ideas alone could not bear fruit unless they were in tune with the spirit of the age. Political philosophers could not choose their own ground. 'We do not believe in the eternity of races', he wrote; 'we believe in Unity—Unity in Humanity.' But a united humanity could not be achieved in one epoch. The desire of the peoples for nationality was the motive force of the nineteenth century; it could only later be utilized for creating a united Europe. Mazzini's conviction that states based on national divisions and free institutions would not go to war with each other, but would grow into a higher unity, was an example of his excessive optimism. But it was an optimism no less justified than Marx's claim that governments of the proletariat would never experience the sense of national rivalry.

Mazzini's *Duties of Man* provided Italian nationalists with a simple but complete philosophy. No political theorist performed the same function for German nationalists. Hegel's philosophy could be used to justify the creation of a great and glorious Germany, but Hegel himself had been thinking of the Prussian state rather than of any new political unit. It was for Heinrich von Treitschke (1834–94) to provide the more immediate theory for united Germany, though his work was in no sense a parallel to that of Mazzini. The son of a general, Treitschke was a liberal in his early days. While still a boy, he played an active role in the demonstrations which brought about the 1848 revolution in Saxony. Even after the defeat of the revolution in Germany, Treitschke grew up as a typical patriotic German liberal. But the frustrations of 1848, added to the personal frustration of his deafness, ultimately had their effect. The cult of the nation came to predominate over respect for individual freedom. In 1861 Treitschke published a reply to John Stuart Mill's *On Liberty*, with its plea for the individual. In the 1860s Treitschke entered enthusiastically into work of propaganda for Bismarck, but his chief activity remained his academic profession, and in 1874 he secured Ranke's chair of history at Berlin. Ranke, the embodiment of historical impartiality, opposed the appointment. Treitschke's *History of Germany in the Nineteenth Century* started to appear in 1879, but his most important work of political philosophy, the *Politics*, was published only posthumously, from lecture notes. His influence for the period prior to 1880 was thus exerted through his lectures and his lesser works. From 1862, the year when Bismarck seized power in Prussia, Treitschke recommended Prussian leadership in Germany. He despised the smaller German states, believed that Frederick II had been the greatest monarch in history and looked to Bismarck to make a Prussian empire, based on the incomparable virtues of the German race. His Prussian mystique owed much to his historical researches into the medieval order of the Teutonic Knights, who had possessed that simple nobility which Fichte had long before considered almost as the feature by which a German could be recognized. Treitschke's belief in the destiny of Prussia and Bismarck's astonishing political achievements over the years 1862 to 1870 acted and reacted on each other. Treitschke's nationalism was thus grounded not so much on an intellectual theory about language or race as on a respect for force—for the strength of the larger nation. Unlike Mazzini, he felt no sympathy for other nationalities, whether triumphant or suppressed. He is less moved by the abstract concept of German nationality than by the crude fact of German strength. 'An army organized on a really national foundation is the sole political institution which binds citizen to citizen', he wrote; 'it is not the German parliament, as was formerly hoped, which has become the real and effective bond of national union, but the German army.'[1] He carried glorification of war a stage further than Hegel had done. He saw it as a clash between 'the great collective personalities of history'. 'The state', he said, was 'the most supremely real person that exists.'[2] Hegel's idea of the national will, taken out of its philosophical context, had run wild and become the monstrous 'statism' of Treitschke.

His racialism was as extreme as his 'statism'. German virtues were equalled only by the decadence of neighbouring races. The English preserved a certain manly quality only because they were occasionally involved in colonial wars, but their main characteristics were their materialism and their absorption in business. Above all the Jews were a disruptive force in national life. Some Jews, he agreed, had 'succeeded in really adopting the nationality of the people among whom they live', but there were others 'for whom the language they speak has no inward meaning'. He hoped that with time Jews would acquire a real sense of German nationality, but until then it was for Germans to reject any

[1] *Politics* (English edition, 1916), vol. II, p. 390.
[2] *Politics*, vol. I, p. 17.

alien element from their culture. 'Whenever he finds his life sullied by the filth of Judaism the German must turn from it, and learn to speak the truth boldly about it.'[1]

Thus European nationalism had moved from Mazzini to Treitschke, from the days of 1848 when the different nationalities could see a common purpose in revolution, to the 1870s when new nation states faced each other in a spirit of racial rivalry, pride and growing hatred. Nationalism had been an illogical creed from the first. In terms of utility, it is perhaps convenient to be ruled by a government which speak one's own language; but this alone would scarcely justify all the violence, martyrdom and warfare which went into the making of nation states. The revolutionaries of the period 1815 to 1848 had identified nationalism with their struggle against the old autocracies, and if, in so doing, they had been illogical, their failing had been an understandable one. The enemies of liberalism and nationalism had been the same governments and the same system—the governments of Austria and the German and Italian petty states, and the conservative system of Metternich.

If the people is identified with the nation, the concept of popular sovereignty can be seen as the aim of both liberals and nationalists. Once a group has recognized itself to be a nation, it can demand self-determination either on liberal or nationalist grounds. In the years 1789–92 the doctrine of Rousseau had been put into practice in France, when the people or nation had taken over sovereignty from the weak hands of a dynastic king. The liberal-nationalist movements of the years 1815 to 1848 were in a sense simply a continuation of the European movement which had started in 1789. For a statement of this pure type of classical liberalism Victor Cousin's Introduction to his *Political Speeches*, published in 1851, serves well. Cousin declared that his principles could be summed up as 'an understanding and love of the French Revolution'. Just as Descartes had abolished classical authority in philosophy and substituted for it freedom of speculation and thought, so must the human conscience be regarded as the only moral authority or dogma in life. 'The only foundation of legitimate authority is the interest and consent of the people.'[2] In philosophy, reason was sovereign; in politics, the nation had been proclaimed sovereign by the French Revolution. In both philosophy and politics there were two basic schools of thought: the one which started with authority and fashioned humanity to fit it, the other which started with humanity and derived all authority from it. In other words, the struggle of the day could be

[1] *Politics*, vol. I, p. 302.   [2] *Discours Politiques*, 1851, p. iii.

resolved into a simple struggle between authority and freedom. The French Revolution had done for the world what Descartes had done for the mind—it had freed it from an outmoded authority. Opponents of the French Revolution protested that man was incapable of governing himself, yet they provided as a substitute for the government of man by man—the government of men by other men.

If most liberals accepted Cousin's definition of the basic constitutional principle of the French Revolution, they disagreed profoundly on the question of how the common aim of representative government was to be attained. The French had inherited the tradition of revolution, but even the most radical of English thinkers preferred an evolution to the total destruction of the existing government. John Stuart Mill in his famous essay *On Liberty* defined as a weakness of many continental reformers that they were incapable of reshaping their institutions. They felt that either the government was good, in which case it could be trusted with full power and it would inevitably carry out the will of the people; or the government was bad and should be destroyed completely. They could never believe that it was precisely absolutism which had corrupted the government, and it merely had to have its powers limited for it to become a good government. Writing at the time of the Second Empire, Mill was probably thinking of the French, and of republican revolutionaries like Mazzini. Had he thought further, he would have realized that the revolutions of 1848 in Germany, Austro–Hungary and Italy had, in most cases, merely limited the power of the governments, and subsequent events had shown that this was not enough. By the middle of the century all parts of western and central Europe had experienced brief experiments in constitutionalism, but only in a few cases had the experiment been allowed to succeed. One aspect of the liberalism of the period was this simple revolt against autocratic government, an attempt first to secure some form of constitution and then to widen its basis. But another no less important aspect was the economic one: the demand that industry, agriculture and trade be freed from governmental supervision and regulation. Originating in Adam Smith and the French economic philosophers of the eighteenth century, the classical doctrine of free trade was developed by a group of English radicals. A new way of thinking about legal and constitutional issues combined with a belief in the virtues of uncontrolled trade and industrial development to give dynamic originality to the thought of the Utilitarians or Benthamites.

Jeremy Bentham (1748–1832) had followed his father into the legal profession. His little masterpiece, *A Fragment on Government*, was

POLITICAL IDEAS

published in 1776, but when the French Revolution broke out and Bentham was already fifty-one, he had not acquired a great reputation. His work, in translation, reached France, Russia, Spain and South America before its worth was recognized in England. Although he died at the age of eighty, in the year of the great Reform Act, it was in early Victorian England, in the age of Melbourne and Peel, that Bentham's influence was to be greatest. Paradoxically the materialist and atheist Bentham was virtually ignored in the sceptical days of the eighteenth century, and yet was the inspiration for much legislation in the England of the Oxford Movement. Bentham's appeal to the Victorians lay in his belief in progress, in 'improvement', in responsible government, and in the adaptability of his doctrine to justify the more ruthless and self-righteous aspects of *laissez-faire* industrialism. The fundamental part of his creed, the 'principle of utility', is already fully developed in *A Fragment on Government*. The principle declared that arguments about historic rights or constitutional precedents were irrelevant. 'I cannot help persuading myself', wrote Bentham, 'that the disputes between contending parties —between the defenders of a law and the opposers of it, would stand a much better chance of being adjusted than at present, were they but explicitly and at once referred to the principle of UTILITY . . . All else is but womanish scolding and childish altercation.'[1] In a few words the whole cumbersome theory of the historic contract was ridiculed, and in its place was erected a political habit of thought based on what Bentham called his 'fundamental axiom': 'It is the greatest happiness of the greatest number that is the measure of right and wrong.'[2] The belief in human improvement based on utilitarian considerations was further supported by the conviction that the pursuit of happiness by each individual contributed to the good of all. The idea, with all its naive optimism, was readily accepted by such wise men as Cobden, Guizot and Peel. It enabled respectable and otherwise virtuous manufacturers to close their eyes to the grim conditions in which their employees worked and lived. Blown into the pompous and verbose system of Herbert Spencer, it served, later in the century, to postpone the organization of elementary social services in England.

Bentham himself has come into an unfair portion of the blame for the more brutal results of *laissez-faire*. The term 'Benthamite' has been applied to people who more closely influenced by the classical economics of Malthus and Ricardo. Distaste for governmental, or even legislative, intervention between employer and workers has been con-

[1] *Fragment on Government*, p. 170 of the 1776 edition.   [2] *idem*, p. ii.

52

sidered a Benthamite characteristic, though it was derived from, rather than stated by, Bentham himself. Thus Bertrand Russell talks of the 1848 Public Health Act as being opposed by 'the Benthamites', because the newspaper, *The Economist*, attacked the Act. Yet the Act was largely the work of Edwin Chadwick, a close friend and faithful disciple of Bentham. It was, of course, opposed to the classical economics, but it was at the same time a triumph of Benthamite rationalism in its disregard for traditional rights and its concern for immediate human welfare.

Like the nationalism of Mazzini, Utilitarianism and *laissez-faire* were optimistic doctrines. There seemed no reason to suppose that progress would not continue. The nineteenth century would inevitably be rewarded for all its industry. But already in 1830 a few lonely voices were beginning to express doubts about the supposed blessings of industrialism. By 1860 the liberal advance in politics and economics had stimulated great movements of protest. On the one hand, the bases of the Utilitarian creed had been challenged, and a few liberal thinkers themselves, John Stuart Mill in England and de Tocqueville in France, had indicated dangers which would have to be avoided in the progress to complete democracy. On the other hand, socialists all over western Europe had refuted even the claim that the Industrial Revolution had added to man's wellbeing. Where Bentham had seen European history in terms of 'improvement', de Tocqueville could see it in terms of an ever present peril of declining standards, and Marx could see it in terms of the creation of a monstrous new society which would have to be destroyed by class war.

A new conservatism offering a positive alternative to liberalism developed only towards the end of the period. Bismarck in Germany turned for support away from the liberals in 1879. Disraeli in England identified the old Tory party in 1867 with democratic constitutional ideas and in 1874–80 with social reform—one of the most brilliant political achievements of the century. The party of the right in Italy captured Cavour's political inheritance after his death in 1861, but had lost it again before the end of the period. From 1830 to 1860 European conservatism was very much on the defensive. No positive feature can be found in the policy and creed of Metternich, in spite of imaginative attempts by recent apologists. Guizot, who started his career by supporting a revolution of the vigorous moneyed class in France against the clericalism and would-be absolutism of Charles X, ended it as negatively as Metternich by resorting to an empty dynasticism: he believed that an alliance of the July Monarchy with moderately reformed Bourbon governments in Spain and Naples could be made the basis of a stable Europe. Only in England did the conservative tradition remain a continuously creative one throughout the period, and even in England the thread wore thin at times until the revival under Disraeli. The empirical nature of English conservative thought has prevented the emergence of original theorists since Burke, and it is significant that Burke was a Whig in origin. Only Samuel Taylor Coleridge, who lived until 1834, may be said to have carried Burke's concept of the English constitution as an organism and sacred growth into the age of the great Reform Act. But the influence of Coleridge was an intangible and short-lived one. His most valuable contribution was his insistence that the sanctity of human life is more important than any political idea. In this he was in line with the best trends of English empirical thought. The same humanism is apparent in the writings of the two cautious liberals, de Tocqueville and John Stuart Mill, who, like the conservatives, accepted the framework of society as it was, and pointed out the drawbacks which might accompany democracy.

Alexis de Tocqueville (1805–59) was born in the same year as Mazzini, but in a family of the nobility. Appointed a judge as a young man in the last years of Charles X's reign, he was granted permission to study the penal system in the U.S.A. by Louis Philippe's government in 1831. The result of his research was the brilliant *Democracy in America*, published in 1835. After a short political career under the July Monarchy and Second Republic, he retired from public life at the time of Napoleon III's *coup d'état* in 1851. Towards the end of his short life he wrote *L'Ancien Régime*, which was published in 1856. The completely scientific and objective nature of his enquiry into political and social problems gave his message a unique character which defies classification. The French right wing under the July Monarchy claimed that he was an aristocrat pointing out the evils of democracy; the left wing could claim that he predicted the inevitable advance of democracy. De Tocqueville himself remained unimpressed by the attempts made by political parties to exploit his work. He certainly did not believe that the development towards democracy would inevitably bring evil with it. He feared that it could lead to an abuse of freedom, but the solution was to prevent this by educational reform. He identified 'democracy' with the passing of political power from the middle class to the workers. There would be danger only if the working class secured power before the middle class had come to terms with democracy and educated the masses. The responsibility lay with the ruling class. That the new society would be different from the old could not be denied. With his experience of America, de Tocqueville showed that the old colourful culture of an aristocratic society must give place to the new democratic society with its strong, sober, mature and disciplined sense of social responsibility. If the old vistas of limitless individual freedom for the few were to be lost, they would be replaced by voluntary associations where all individuals would be, at least, respected. Provincial liberties would have to act as a safeguard against central tyranny. De Tocqueville's great fear was that democracies would accept excessive centralization, and so would establish an administrative despotism insufficiently controlled by the electoral system. So did this extraordinary young man, writing in the 1830s, see far and clearly into the future. His warnings were serious and timely, never interested, never aggressive, never hysterical.

John Stuart Mill (1806-73) was no less realistic than de Tocqueville, and, like the Frenchman, was preoccupied with the relationship between individual human values and central political power. The eldest son of Bentham's friend, James Mill, John Stuart is perhaps best known for his extraordinary education, which included Greek at the age of three. Launched on the world very young, he was already a mature thinker in the 1820s. By 1824, at the age of eighteen, he was contributing to the *Westminster Review* as an orthodox Benthamite. Two years later he experienced that crisis of conscience which was not uncommon among nineteenth-century intellectuals; he found that he doubted the whole purpose of his existence and the sincerity of his political creed. The crisis passed, but Mill remained a deeply introspective man, whose doubts were always stronger than his convictions. For thirty years he had a regular job with the East India Company where he proved a successful administrator. His *Principles of Political Economy* was published in 1848—the same year as the *Communist Manifesto*; and his *Essay on Liberty* in 1859—the same year as the *Origin of Species*. Unlike many political philosophers he had a brief taste of active political life. He was elected to Parliament in 1865, and in the short period before his defeat in the general election of 1868 witnessed the passing of Disraeli's Reform Bill, to which Mill proposed an amendment giving the vote to women. The amendment was defeated and ridiculed.

All the finest qualities of Victorian liberalism were exemplified in the thought of Mill. Gladstone called him the 'saint of rationalism'. While the theorizing of Treitschke, and even of Mazzini, owed much to the instincts and the blood, the thought of Mill, as of de Tocqueville or Marx, owed everything to the mind, even though it was a mind stirred, sometimes, to a passionate intensity. In Mill respect for freedom and respect for equality seem, for once, to balance each other. While his *Essay on Liberty* is one of the most eloquent pleas for individual freedom in the English language, the work of his last years—his concern for female emancipation—showed his Benthamite love for the principle of equality. His belief in freedom was no apologetic or negative one. He believed that the freedom of the individual, besides being a good in itself, was also necessary for the vitality of society. In mid-Victorian England freedom was threatened not by any would-be despot, but by the growing power of majority government, by the emergence of a democracy where the wishes of the minority would be ignored, where unusual opinions or tastes would not be tolerated, and where intellectual standards would be irretrievably lowered. A growing bureaucracy would absorb, waste and dehumanize men of talent. Thus, while Mill had inherited the radical Benthamite tradition, he combined it with a new sense of the dangers of a levelling democracy and of unrestrained *laissez-faire*. In measured and careful, but urgent terms he gave his warning for the future: 'There is a limit to the legitimate interference of collective opinion with individual independence: and to find that limit and maintain it against encroachment, is as indispensable to a good condition of human affairs as protection against political despotism.'[1]

A more complete reaction against utilitarianism was apparent in the thought of T. H. Green (1836–82), who was teaching at Oxford from 1860. Green believed that the state could perform a more creative function than Bentham or even John Stuart Mill would ever have admitted. Although Green himself belongs undeniably to the period covered by this book, his influence was felt only after 1906 when his student, Asquith, as prime minister, was laying the foundation of a welfare state in England. Green succeeded in reconciling historicism with a concept of progress, but in this he had been anticipated by a strangely contrasted figure, working in a very different atmosphere. The Italian revolutionary, Carlo Cattaneo (1801–69), whose work Green had almost certainly never read, had already by 1839 adapted the historicism of Vico to the optimism of the nineteenth century. In doing so, he discarded the romanticism of Rousseau and classical liberalism. He laughed at the idea of ever reaching the perfect kind of society envisaged by Mazzini—'those ideal republics, which must flourish, peaceful and intelligent, in the breast of static institutions'.[2] Instead he believed in progress not

[1] *On Liberty*, p. 6 of the 1929 edition, Watts, London.
[2] *Opere*, vol. v, p. 346, Bertani's 1882 edition.

by radical change, but by the utilization of whatever was worth inheriting from the past, and the discarding of those laws and institutions which were barbarous or anachronistic.

The radicals who looked beyond the triumph of democracy to its dangers and possible degeneration were a few individual prophets, who did not deny their own liberal pedigree and did not recommend a violent break with the liberal traditions. A more important reaction against *laissez-faire* liberalism and middle-class democracy was represented by a new creed, the creed of socialism. In January 1848 de Tocqueville, addressing the Assembly of the July Monarchy in the last days of its life, had pointed out a significant fact: that in recent times in Paris a large number of writings had appeared attacking the right of property. Less than six months later Europe witnessed the first major socialist rising in the June Days in Paris. The idea of social equality which had gathered appreciable support under the July Monarchy was not an entirely new one in 1830. Babeuf, the follower of Robespierre in the 1790s, had worked for his idea of a dictatorship of the poor. But the creation of an industrial proletariat provided a more clearly distinguishable class, not synonymous with 'the poor', but large enough to justify a new political faith, and to provide the fighting columns to support such a faith. The terrible conditions of the industrial workers in England and France, to be discussed in a later chapter, attracted in the first place the attention of philanthropists or agitators, who had no complete politico-economic philosophy with which to conduct the onslaught on the capitalist exploiters. But slowly it began to be realized by small groups of thinkers that the rights of the individual as they had been defined by the English, American and French revolutions did not protect the great majority of men in the new industrialized society from an unreasonable amount of suffering and what was in practice only a modified form of slavery. A real continuity of social justice could not be obtained merely by legislating in favour of a free economy. The free play of the laws of supply and demand did not protect the weak from the strong. Mazzini had learnt from Saint-Simon that the old concept of individual liberty was not enough to create a sound society, but Mazzini's energies were diverted away from the social issue into the struggle for Italian national independence. French followers of Saint-Simon could concentrate upon the central theme of his message, and one of them, Pierre Leroux, named the theme 'socialism'.

Nineteenth-century socialists are conventionally divided into the two groups, 'Utopians' and Marxists. The label 'Utopian' was given by

Marx himself to his predecessors, and subsequent political scientists have been perhaps too ready to accept it as a valid one. Marx and his followers claimed for themselves the title of 'scientific socialists', but in analysing what was wrong with industrial society the so-called 'Utopians' were no less scientific than Marx himself. It is enough to compare V. P. Considérant's *Principles of Socialism* with the *Communist Manifesto* to realize that this is true. It was in their proposed solution to the evils that Marx and Engels were perhaps more 'scientific' than their forerunners, though even here rather less so than has been claimed by Marxists. The immediate importance in the 1840s of socialists of all brands lay in their uninhibited denunciation of what the rest of the world was regarding as the splendid creation of an industrial society. Louis Blanc wrote in his *Organization of Labour*: 'Labour, under the empire of the principle of competition, is preparing for the future a decrepit, crippled, diseased and unwholesome generation.' Marx added to this the concept of the wage-slave:

> Masses of labourers, crowded into the factory, are organized like soldiers. As privates of the industrial army they are placed under the command of a perfect hierarchy of officers and sergeants. Not only are they slaves of the bourgeois state; they are daily and hourly enslaved by the machine, by the foreman, and, above all, by the individual manufacturer himself.[1]

The Comte de Saint-Simon, the earliest of the so-called 'Utopians', was already dead in 1830, but his influence on the development of socialist thought before 1848 was greater than that of anyone else. His great contribution had been to underline the two real evils in the world: war and poverty. If the idea is a commonplace today, it had a note of originality about it in the early nineteenth century. Saint-Simon had condemned private property, inheritance and unearned income. He had defined the proletariat as a successor of the serf, just as the serf had been successor to the slave. The institution of employment, like that of serfdom or slavery, would one day have to be abolished. Already the main lines of socialist thought were being traced, but the men who considered themselves Saint-Simon's disciples, Rodrigues and Enfantin, were scarcely worthy to continue his teaching.

More important than the Saint-Simonians in those early days of socialism was the Englishman, Robert Owen (1771–1858), who believed that a cooperative community and a thorough education for the workers

[1] *The Communist Manifesto*, edited by Harold Laski (London, 1948), p. 128.

could at once eliminate unemployment and increase human virtue and happiness. The cooperative idea, a positive alternative to economic competition, was also preached by an eccentric but inspired Frenchman, François Fourier (1772–1837). In an unhappy and often impoverished life, spent as a commercial traveller, clerk, and even, for a while, soldier, Fourier poured out the alternately mad and brilliant products of a vivid and chaotic imagination. As a young man at Marseilles he had been obliged to assist in the destruction of stores of rice, which were thrown into the sea to keep up prices, and he later traced his socialist revelation to this experience. His political beliefs owed more to his own painful personal history than to any academic education. He was not well read in the classic works of political philosophy. When his extraordinary writings are analysed, his doctrine is seen to be less extreme, on many points, than was that of Saint-Simon. He denounced neither property nor social inequality. He believed in a benevolent God, and saw himself as one of his more important prophets. Much of his writings have more in common with the visions of Blake than with the argument of political theorists. In some respects he seemed to recommend a return to the methods before the Industrial Revolution. He believed that artisans should again replace industrial labour, since industrialism had merely increased the number of the poor. His most original idea was the *phalanstères*, a cooperative group, which should be joint-owned by workers in the cooperative and by consumers. The *phalanstère* was to be wholly self-supporting, so that the institution of employment would be abolished. Both agriculture and industry were to be organized in this way, but the system was to depend upon a division of labour, which Fourier believed psychologically necessary for individual happiness. Work must be made attractive, and hostility between different groups in society eliminated. In his psychological approach to the question of labour, Fourier often showed a more sympathetic understanding of the human situation than Marx did.

A follower of Fourier with a far more systematic mind was Victor Prosper Considérant (1808–93). The clear and brief system contained in his *Principles of Socialism*, published in 1847, anticipates Marx on several points, and shows a real understanding of the social changes which had preceded the revolution of 1848. Considérant repeats the historical generalization that societies of classical antiquity were based on slavery, while feudal society was based on serfdom, already less hard and less brutal as a type of exploitation of man by man. Christianity brought the concept of fraternity, but a fraternity practised only between social

59

equals in the feudal hierarchy. The French Revolution brought equality of all before the law, but not a truly new social order. Individuals take their rank in the industrial order, in the social order and in the political order only by money, education or favour. In spite of the 'metaphysical liberalism' of the new laws and the legal destruction of privilege 'the present social order is still an aristocratic order, no longer, it is true, in principle and in law, but in fact'. There were exceptional individuals who rose above their social position, but as a general rule 'generations who are born in want, poverty or destitution, live their lives in want, poverty or destitution, and transmit this fatal heritage to their descendants'. In the same way the leisured classes bequeathed their ease and wealth to their children. Writing about life under Louis-Philippe, Considérant was expressing a simple truth about all capitalist society.

Fourier influenced only a small group of followers, of whom Considérant was the most intelligent. A contemporary who was to have a wider ultimate influence was Pierre Joseph Proudhon (1809–65) whose book *What is Property?* created a stir in Paris when it was published in 1840. Proudhon's reply to his own rhetorical question, 'It is theft', suggested an extreme position, but many points of his belief, as in the case of Fourier, surprise the reader with their moderation in comparison with Saint-Simon on the one hand or with Marx on the other. Proudhon believed that the principles of private property and communism were equally harmful, and that some synthesis should be evolved from them, a synthesis which would make possible a really free and just society. He pointed out that pure communism, like that enjoyed by Plato's guardians, needed slavery at its base, and he went on to give a vivid picture of the kind of society now associated with Stalinism:

> The irrevocability of its injustice, the violence which it does to individual sympathies and antipathies, the yoke of iron which it imposes on the will, the moral torture in which it holds the conscience, the apathy into which it plunges society, and finally the sanctimonious and stupid uniformity by which it enchains the free, active, reasoning, defiant personality of man have revolted general common sense, and irrevocably condemn communism.[1]

Proudhon accepted many of the economic institutions of capitalism, but wanted to reform them in a socialist sense. He believed that the secret lay in the method by which the products of society were distributed. He wanted the formation of a central bank which would record the credit

[1] *Qu'est-ce que la Propriété?* (Paris, 1873), p. 203.

value of labour performed. A central bank and a central workshop would ultimately replace the central political government. Governmental laws would be replaced by free contracts. So appeared a concept which was to become familiar to socialist thought—the concept of the withering away of the state.

The idea of a communal workshop to provide labour and to drive privately owned concerns out of business was the central theme of another French socialist under the July Monarchy, Louis Blanc (1811–1882). Blanc believed that competition was the great evil in capitalist society—competition between producers for markets, competition between workers for jobs, competition between men and machines. Out of this competition only the large capitalists gained. The solution was for the state to organize national workshops and national banks, and so to plan production according to the real needs of society. The moderate element in Blanc's scheme lay in his belief that private industry should not be eliminated by legislation, but by competition with the national workshops. In the spring of 1848 Blanc became a minister of the Second Republic, and for a short while was allowed to experiment with his idea of a national workshop. In view of its originality, of the grave economic situation in which it was tried, and of the hostility of most of Blanc's colleagues, it is not surprising that the experiment ended in disaster.[1]

The great age of early socialist speculation was the period from 1830 to 1848. It culminated in the publication in February 1848 of the *Communist Manifesto*, the work of Marx and Engels. Karl Marx (1818–83) was the son of a Jewish German lawyer, who had in 1818 recently been converted to protestant Christianity. Young Karl was a student of law, history and philosophy at a time when Hegel was dominating German thought, and the first considerable intellectual influence upon him was exerted by Hegel. As a Hegelian of the left, Marx was to be barred from teaching in a Prussian university. He took up journalism, but in 1843 was obliged to leave Germany for Paris. For the next five years, wanted by more than one government, Marx lived the life of a revolutionary exile in France and Belgium. Finally in 1848 he settled in England, where he remained, except for short absences, until his death. The first volume of *Das Kapital*, the result of many years' research, appeared in 1867.

Marx's colleague and benefactor, Friedrich Engels (1820–95), a son of rich German parents, had been sent to England to have experience in business. Working in the cotton industry in Manchester, Engels

[1] See below, pp. 172–3.

acquired his socialist ideas in direct contact with the new urban society. In 1844 he published his *Condition of the Working Classes in England*. He had met Marx in Paris, and in the years 1845 to 1847 the two men were together in Brussels where they evolved the theory of dialectical materialism. In these early days they tried to attract Proudhon to their opinions, but without success. Proudhon was afraid that Marx intended to indoctrinate the people with fresh dogmas, after all the old ones had been overthrown. Marx and Engels did not really need Proudhon. The two men performed complementary functions: Engels with his personal experience and great interest in the actual situation in England, and Marx with his more powerful and tenacious intellect and his concern for the future of Germany. In Brussels, they adopted the name 'communist' to distinguish themselves from 'Utopian' or Christian socialism or from a nebulous egalitarianism. Already Marx was devoting as much time to discrediting the deviationists as he was to the propagation of the socialist doctrine which they all had in common.

In 1847 the Communist party was officially founded in London as an underground organization. Late in the year the second meeting of the party formally adopted as their programme the abolition of the old bourgeois society and the foundation of a new community without classes or property. The main lines of Marxist thought had already crystallized, and some weeks later were written into the pungent, clear pages of the *Communist Manifesto*, which in the years before 1914 were to stir the few and horrify the many.

Not one of Marx's ideas was entirely original. His concept of historical developments stimulating their negatives, which in turn led to a synthesis of both, came from Hegel. His materialist modification of Hegel came from Feuerbach. His basic economic ideas were a development from Ricardo, and his theory of surplus value was similar to that of obscure, early English socialists like Hodgkin. His concept of the class struggle came from the French socialists of the July Monarchy. Marx's triumph lay in synthesizing all these ideas. Hegel and Ricardo would have been equally surprised at the use Marx made of their theories. He discarded the idealism of Hegel, and retained only his dialectical method. For the first time a socialist thesis was based squarely on a materialist philosophy. Marx could see in history only the clash between contending material forces, the never-ending struggle between the classes. Industrialism had had the effect of accentuating and aggravating the class struggle, which was in the nineteenth century becoming a straight fight between the middle and working classes. The course and result of the struggle were already determined by economic conditions. First causes were economic. Ideologies, morality, religion and metaphysics were by-products of the economic life of man.

With these convictions, it is not surprising that Marx was at his more original and effective when analysing trends in economic history. He claimed that the right of property justified itself by, and could conceal itself behind, the doctrine of the division of labour preached by the English classical economists. Division of labour implied division of tools and materials, and, ultimately, private property and capitalism; it was at the bottom of all class struggles. In recent times the concentration of the means of production had made it easy for a small number of capitalists to seize economic power. The previous middle class—small industrialists, tradesmen, artisans and peasants—had become part of the proletariat. The worker himself had become a machine with his life regularized as never before. He had no leisure, only sleep, food and work. He was a mere producer of other people's wealth, 'physically broken, spiritually bestialized'. But industrialism had had—and would have increasingly—another effect. By bringing the workers together in great numbers, it was giving them a sense of political and social identity. The proletariat was destined to be the revolutionary class of the future. Socialism, the abolition of employment, would be the creation of the triumphant proletariat revolution. A period of dictatorship would be necessary, but would give way to a democratic and classless society. Ultimately central committees of producers, subject to collective control, would replace the state.

Marx had seen far beyond his socialist predecessors and contemporaries, as a contrast of some of his ideas with those of Bakunin indicates. Michael Bakunin (1814–76), a Russian anarchist, owed much to Proudhon. When Bakunin spoke of abolishing inheritance, Marx retorted that it would require a social revolution to abolish inheritance, and when the revolution succeeded landed property and capital could at once be abolished: there would be no need to bother with 'the right of inheritance'. When Bakunin looked forward to achieving 'equality of the different classes', Marx pointed out the paradoxical nature of the idea: to 'equate' classes meant nothing; class itself must be abolished. When Bakunin advised the working class not to join in bourgeois politics, but only trade union activity, Marx declared that the distinction was irrelevant. All methods of attack on existing society, whether they were legal or illegal, constitutional or unconstitutional, must be employed. The end justified the means.

Already in the 1860s international links between socialists were being forged. In 1863 a group of English trade unionists organized a meeting in London to protest against Russian action in Poland. The meeting was attended by a few French delegates and the decision was reached to form an international socialist association. It was not intended to be a revolutionary society, but merely to put into practice Proudhon's ideas on cooperation among the workers. The first formal meeting of the new society, which assumed the title of the International Workingmen's Association, or, more familiarly, the First International, met in London in September 1864. Fifty members were charged with the task of drawing up a statute and of deciding between proposals presented by the revolutionary leaders—by Bakunin and his anarchist programme, by Mazzini who wanted the organization to be mainly political and firmly centralized, and by Marx who preferred a looser, federal organization and was less interested in nationalist revolutionary causes. The delegates accepted the ideas of Marx, and Mazzini, disillusioned with what he considered to be the 'materialism' of the International, subsequently broke all connections with it. The 1864 meeting produced a statute declaring the aim of the First International to be the association of the working classes to secure their own progress and emancipation. Subsequent meetings were held—in Geneva in 1866, in Lausanne in 1867, in Brussels in 1868 and in Basle in 1869. Marx's idea of the class struggle remained the central theme, but the International had no immediate practical plans, and since its members did not pay the subscriptions asked of them, it could do nothing but speculate.

On a national basis, however, Marxist groups had appeared in most European countries by 1880, and socialism was already becoming respectable with the formation of social democrat parties. Marx and Engels themselves were no longer young, though they still wrote with the same fire as in the 1840s. Even the bloody civil war of the Commune in Paris in 1871 was receding into the memory. The creed of socialism was already a familiar one, though its more striking achievements still lay in the future.

In the history of political thought the period 1830 to 1880 may be defined as the rise and decline of *laissez-faire* liberalism accompanied by a growing enthusiasm for the principle of nationality. One thing almost all the political philosophers of the period had in common—a firm belief in human progress. There was no Hobbes in the nineteenth century, no despair, no fear of life. There were monstrously wrong-headed ideas, like those of Treitschke, and there were angry, intolerant ideas, like those of Marx, but all thinking men of the period were preparing and expecting a better future. De Tocqueville and John Stuart Mill may have sounded warnings that the coming blessings need not be wholly unmixed ones, but theirs were still optimistic warnings, warnings given in due time. Seldom in history had man shown such confidence in his future.

IV

The Growth of Industry

The astonishing rise in population in Europe in the eighteenth and nineteenth centuries preceded the movement of industrialization. The former seemed to be a stimulant rather than a result of the latter. That the growth of industry cannot be regarded as an initial cause of the rapid increase in population in the nineteenth century is suggested by the simple fact that the number of Russians increased more rapidly than the number of western Europeans, and had been doing so throughout the eighteenth century. From 1722 to 1897 the population of Russia increased from 14 million to 129 million. For the purpose of the present argument these figures must be modified, as they are partly accounted for by the vast conquests of Russia in the period. But the population even of the original territory of Russia increased from 14 million to 65

BIBLIOGRAPHY. An admirable introduction to the history of the world economy as a whole in the latter part of the period is provided by W. Ashworth, *A Short History of the International Economy 1850–1950* (London, 1951). Of the many economic histories of Europe with a more conventional approach H. Heaton, *Economic History of Europe* (revised edition, London, 1948) is among the best. The most recent and most authoritative work on population is D. V. Glass and D. E. C. Eversley, editors, *Population in History: Essays in Historical Demography* (London, 1965), of which several chapters are relevant to the earlier part of the period. H. J. Habakkuk and M. Postan, editors, *The Industrial Revolutions and After* (Cambridge, 1965), which is volume VI, in 2 parts, of the *Cambridge Economic History of Europe*, also provides some new approaches to themes covered in this chapter. An excellent recent survey of British economic history since the middle of the eighteenth century is Walter M. Stern, *Britain Yesterday and Today* (London, 1962). For a more detailed study no substitute has yet appeared for J. H. Clapham, *Economic History of Modern Britain* (Cambridge, 1926); volumes I and II are the relevant ones for the period. British influences on the industrial revolution in Europe are considered in W. O. Henderson, *Britain and Industrial Europe, 1750–1850* (Liverpool, 1954), and the same author's *The Industrial Revolution on the Continent* (London, 1960) has much basic information. For industrial growth in France and Germany there are J. H. Clapham, *Economic Development of France and Germany, 1815–1914* (Cambridge, 1921); A. L.

million, in spite of considerable migration of Russians from the original territory to the newly annexed lands. In Britain, France and Germany the great increase in population was accompanied by industrialization and a drift of people to the towns and cities. In Russia a yet greater increase of population was a characteristic of the whole country, and was not accompanied by industrialization until the end of the nineteenth century. Economic historians have discussed the original causes of the rise in population at great length, but have come to no firm conclusion beyond deciding that a declining death rate rather than a rising birth rate is the predominant factor. Some respite from the terrible epidemics that decimated the population in earlier centuries—epidemics of plague, typhoid, cholera and so on—gave the human race in the small continent of Europe a chance to multiply in the eighteenth and nineteenth centuries. This respite owed little to medical knowledge or hygienic habits, which were still in a primitive state, though improved quarantine measures, in Britain at least, probably had some effect.

The large rise in population could be met by one of two reactions: the people could move to unused land, or they could utilize the land and resources they already possessed more intensively. Both methods were adopted in the nineteenth century. In the first place, over great tracts of Europe more land immediately adjacent to already cultivated areas was taken over for further cultivation. In the second place, land in remoter parts of the world was cultivated by Europeans who migrated from the home continent. During the period 1830–80 more Europeans moved farther in search of a livelihood than in any previous era, since they could now move for the first time comparatively easily and quickly to the other side of the world—to America or Australia. But far the most important reaction to the problem of over-population was to industrialize—to use new technical processes for creating wealth in urban communities. Technological advances were, of course, a prerequisite of industrialization, but to be effective they needed also the right

Dunham, *The Industrial Revolution in France, 1815–1848* (New York, 1955); and W. O. Henderson, *The State and the Industrial Revolution in Prussia, 1740–1870* (Liverpool, 1958). Of the many histories of specific industries only a few examples can be cited here: D. L. Burn, *Economic History of Steelmaking, 1867–1939* (London, 1940); L. F. Haber, *The Chemical Industry during the Nineteenth Century* (Oxford, 1958); D. C. Coleman, *The British Paper Industry, 1495–1860* (Oxford, 1962); G. Quazza, *L'industria laniera e cotoniera in Piemonte dal 1831 al 1861* (Turin, 1961). An authoritative and comprehensive history of the railways has still to be written.

demographic, economic, political and psychological conditions—all of which reacted and interacted on each other.

Industrialization in western Europe was one of the most striking features of the half-century from 1830 to 1880. The process was already well under way in Great Britain before 1830, but in the subsequent decades it spread on a big scale first to Belgium and France, and then to Germany. It would be a mistake, however, to imagine that industrial superiority came to western Europe only as a result of the classical Industrial Revolution which started about 1780. On the contrary, western Europe had been technically superior to the rest of the world, as regards the tools and instruments produced by her inhabitants, as early as the seventeenth century. Methods of production in the seventeenth century had not changed and industry was still on a tiny scale compared with what was to come, but already Europeans had the ideas in physics, provided by Newton and others, and a high sophistication of craftsmanship in such traditional instruments as clocks, water- or windmills, or spinning-wheels. In England there was in addition a special stimulant—the need to find a substitute for the diminishing supply of timber. Even by 1730 Europe had a considerable industrial lead over the rest of the world, and by 1830 fresh technological developments of immense importance had taken place.

One major development of the nineteenth century was to be the emergence of the process of mass production. Of industrial products of the eighteenth century, with a very few exceptions, no two were exactly alike, and no two could be made simultaneously by the same workman. Yet already by the start of the nineteenth century some of the conditions for mass production were already present. Sufficient power to operate many machines at once had been discovered in the steam engine, which was already in use in industry but had not been put on wheels to create a form of horseless transport. Already there were a few factories in which several power-operated machines were at work, especially in England. Yet even by 1850 the modern type of factory was the exception rather than the rule.

Only in Britain and Belgium was an industrial society in the new sense in existence in 1850, and it was, of course, in Britain that the industrial revolution had originated in the mid-eighteenth century. Certain industries had proved particularly adaptable to the use of steam power: cotton, iron, pottery and the brewery industry, and all these had found ever expanding markets. Yet change to the new techniques had by no means fully taken place in these British industries by 1830.

Economic historians today are inclined to date the important changes rather later than they have been dated previously. If cotton was already being spun in the factory by the end of the eighteenth century, it was only after 1815 that the factory system was applied, to any extent, to the weaving process. In 1830 the cotton industry was still in the transitional phase: hand looms were still twice as numerous as power looms; water power was still being used in the industry as well as steam, though steam was now more common. It was from 1830 to 1850 that British industry made perhaps its biggest advances compared with industry elsewhere. By 1850 the cotton industry had become completely modernized, and the number of people employed in the metallurgical and engineering industries had increased considerably. A large railway network already covered England, and everywhere from Newcastle to Plymouth more lines were under construction. Nothing on this scale had yet happened on the continent.

Second to Britain, but a long way behind, was the yet smaller country of Belgium. Though her independence was young in 1850, Belgium had been the first country to profit from the British example, and use British industrial skill and management on a large scale. Even before her independence, Belgium's mines were supplying much of the coal needed by the few factories elsewhere on the continent which were already operated by steam power.

After Britain and Belgium, France experienced industrialization, but it was very much later and never so complete as in Britain. In France the skill shown by a few individuals in evolving new techniques for industry did not compensate for the conservatism of most producers. The steam engine, already a familiar object in Britain, had scarcely appeared in France by 1830. Only in the 1840s were steam engines constructed, and even then they were usually very small ones. This comparative slowness in France can be explained partly by the shortage of raw materials, but partly also by the lack of initiative in manufacturers. Where private producers were cautious, governments had to pursue a more active economic policy. In both France and Germany the government played a much bigger role in encouraging economic development than in England, where private individuals and companies had raised the capital for, and administered the construction and growth of mines, mills, canals, railways and banks. Only in Ireland did the British government play a more active role, and even there only because of famine, and even then a far less active role than the circumstances really demanded. But on the continent governments were prepared to build railways, roads, factories, banks, technical schools and so on. It is significant that the first period of rapid industrial growth in France was that of the paternalistic Second Empire. Industrialization in France can be dated approximately from the peace of 1815 to 1870, but if the more important qualitative change came before 1848, the more important quantitative change came in the 1850s and 1860s. In 1870 French industry was using five times as much horse power as it had used in 1851, and three times as much coal was being consumed. The iron works in Le Creusot, which was producing 5,000 tons a year in 1836, had raised its output to 133,000 tons by 1867. From the 1830s to the 1860s French foreign commerce was trebled.

Germany developed later as an industrial power than Britain or France for several reasons. First, she lacked political unity, and so suffered from a great confusion of currencies, customs, weights and measures. Even when the Customs Union, the *Zollverein*,[1] had started to operate, it was no substitute for complete politico-economic unity. Secondly, communications between the various potentially industrial areas were poor. Thirdly, these areas—where there were mineral deposits—were on the edges of the country, and too remote from the centres of population. The Ruhr and Silesian coalfields were far from densely populated areas, and Silesia especially was very far from the sea. Fourthly, Germany was rich neither as a trading nor as an agricultural country: British industry had been based to a great extent on capital accumulated from trading; much of the capital for investment in German industry had to come in the early period from France. Finally Germany's North Sea ports were too far from the Atlantic to compete successfully with British and Dutch commerce, until the steamship reduced the importance of this factor.

All Germany's economic difficulties were overcome during the period covered by this book. Political unity was achieved, capital for investment in industry was accumulated and the transport system was transformed. The Prussians had started to build good roads in the 1820s, and increasingly after 1830 the bad communications of the country became a thing of the past. 8,000 miles of roads in 1837 had become 18,000 by 1862. River transport, especially on the Rhine, was also greatly improved after 1830. But for the big growth of industry railways were needed. The systematic and determined railway building in Germany started in the 1840s, and was at its most intense from 1850 to 1870. By the time of the establishment of the Empire in 1871 the last brake had been released

[1] See below, pp. 97–100.

on German economic development, and the acquisition of the rich lands of Alsace and Lorraine in that year completed the story. From 1871 to 1914 economic factors alone would ensure that Germany was the most powerful state in Europe. She already produced more coal than France in 1850. Both countries almost doubled their coal production from 1850 to 1860, but if the figures for the thirty years from 1850 to 1880 are taken, the contrast is striking: in that period France multiplied her production by little more than four, Germany by nearly ten. Coal production in Germany was dependent on the building of railways, which in their turn needed greater coal production. The use of the steam engine to accelerate transport on land and sea had been of enormous significance in Britain; it was perhaps even more important for Germany.

In other countries—Sweden, Italy, Switzerland and Austria—there were small industrial areas, but the changes from 1830 to 1880 could not compare in scale with those in Britain, Belgium, France and Germany. In Piedmont the wool and cotton industries moved from the world of the artisan into the new world of the factory in the period 1830–60. By the nineteenth century Russia had, comparatively speaking, declined as an industrial power. In the mid-eighteenth century Russia had produced more cast iron than England and France, and twice as much as Germany. Yet Russia's production of cast iron was surpassed by Britain's in 1805, by France's in 1828, and Germany's and even Austria's in 1855. By a marked paradox, when Russian diplomatic prestige and influence was at its highest in central and western Europe —from 1815 to 1854—her economic life was in many respects as primitive as it ever had been. Before the Crimean War the great majority of Russians never handled money, but gave services and received payment in kind. At the village markets trade was mostly carried on by barter. A money economy developed in Russia after the Crimean War partly because of the emancipation of the serfs,[1] which meant that labour had more often to be hired for cash, partly because of the export of wheat abroad, and partly because of the building of the railways. Until the 1860s industries remained merely unimportant supplements to agriculture, and industrial workers often worked in factories only in the winter and returned to the land for more productive work in the summer.

In addition to her primitive social and political institutions, Russia was handicapped, even more than Germany, by the awkward location of her mineral wealth. The iron ore of the Urals was very far from the

[1] See below, pp. 93, 109, 277–8.

71

areas of dense population and from the coal needed for smelting the iron ore. To take the products of the Urals to Moscow and St Petersburg canals and rivers had to be used, and only when the weather conditions were very favourable could the journey be done in less than six months. The iron ore of the Krivoi Rog region and the coal of the Donetz region were equally remote from Moscow and St Petersburg, and the great rivers flowed in the wrong direction. The building of railways was thus of vital importance for the economy of Russia, as it was for the economy of Germany. But unlike the countries of western Europe, Russia began to acquire a railway network before industrialization had started. By 1861 there were already a thousand miles of track; in 1880 there were 14,000 miles. While rapid industrialization in Russia did not start until after 1880, railways cannot exist without some attendant heavy industry. From a completely unindustrialized society in 1860, production of coal and iron was building up in the period to 1880. From 1860 to 1876 coal production multiplied itself by sixteen, and steel production by ten. Like Venus, Russian industry was born fully grown —created immediately on a scale as large, if not larger than industry in the west. A few large factories, rather than many small ones, was the pattern. Already in 1879, when intense industrialization was only just starting, some 40 per cent of the industrial workers were in factories employing more than a thousand men. This was partly due—again, as in Germany—to the very large role played by the state in the industrial revolution in Russia, following a long tradition of state intervention in the economic life of the country. In 1860 the State Bank was founded, and from then onwards not only made capital available for industry, but ran its own industrial enterprises. In 1857 the Russian government founded a railway by decree.

In economic terms Poland was the most modern part of the Russian empire. Polish industry developed quickly from small beginnings in the 1870s, exporting its products mainly to Russia. The textile industry, as in the west, was the first to be modernized, and Poland began training her own engineers and technicians. Coal and iron industries developed in the south-west, using modern industrial methods appreciably earlier than in Russia proper.

The most significant development in the economic history of Europe from 1830 to 1880 was a revolution of transport—the introduction of the railway. More than any other single factor, the railway altered the character and intensity of industrial life. Another factor, second in importance only to the coming of the railways, was the development of cheap steel. For over a century of rapid economic development railways and steel were to play a predominant role in European industry. Only in the second half of the twentieth century were the railways to be replaced by other forms of transport, and substitutes for steel to be found. First in time of the two economic developments was the building of the railways. Before 1830 there had been a great improvement in the roads, many of which were now macadamized, and canals had been developed as a cheap form of transport, especially in England, the Netherlands and France. But the invention of the steam locomotive, running over iron rails, and later steel rails, brought a dramatic increase in the speed of land transport. For his size, man is one of the slower of the animals. Before the nineteenth century he could move faster than his own slow pace only by attaching himself to another animal, usually the horse. But by the mid-nineteenth century he could move very much more quickly than any other animal solely by the use of a creature of his own brain. The dramatic nature of the development of the railway was fully appreciated by Europeans of the nineteenth century. Indeed, speculation was over-dramatic. In Britain the railway booms of 1835-37 and 1845-47 were followed by a crash in which many were ruined.

The first tentative railway lines in Europe were built in the 1830s, sometimes as experiments, sometimes as curiosities, but increasingly as serious—if not always successful—economic enterprises. Before 1830 railways had been built only for horse-drawn trucks, usually on coal fields. The one exception was the Stockton–Darlington line, the first railway triumph of George Stephenson. Constructed from 1821 to 1825, the Stockton–Darlington railway was the first public line in the world to use the steam locomotive, alongside horse traction. But Stephenson's reputation reached its peak in 1830 when the famous Liverpool–Manchester railway was opened—perhaps the most important single event to take place in the year which marks the opening of the period covered in this book. The ceremony was attended by the prime minister, the Duke of Wellington, and greeted with keen interest by the British public. It was marred only by the tragic death of the talented president of the Board of Trade, William Huskisson, who was also present for the occasion. Stepping across the track to speak to Wellington, Huskisson was struck by the open door of one of the coaches drawn by Stephenson's locomotive. Wellington subsequently remarked that Huskisson had always been clumsy. The comment was not a charitable one, but to be killed by one of the very few steam-drawn railway trains in existence may well be considered carelessness on a historic scale.

By 1830 there were thus two railways employing steam locomotives in England, and no other in the world. A railway using horse-drawn freight had been built in France in 1823. It covered a length of 18 kilometres and connected the mining town of Saint-Etienne with Andrézieux, a small port on the upper Loire. It was built against the resistance of landowners and carters, and was not a great financial success. A more serious concern, using a steam locomotive over flat stretches, was built in 1832 over a distance of 58 kilometres, connecting Saint-Etienne to Lyons. It was the work of a Jewish family of five brothers, the Séguins, one of whom had been to England to study the Stockton–Darlington railway. Intended simply as a freight line for the transportation of coal, the Saint-Etienne–Lyons railway later carried passengers, as with coal alone it did not pay its way. In these early days the railways in France had to fight competition from the financiers with canal concessions, and the French governments, who saw the railways as being always supplementary to the canals. The third railway in France, connecting Andrézieux to Roanne, further down the Loire, a distance of 68 kilometres, was opened in 1834. It was a financial failure, the company going bankrupt in 1836, mainly because the canal which was to connect Roanne and the railway to Digoin by 1830 was not completed in the event until 1839. For five years the Andrézieux–Roanne railway company was in liquidation, until Louis Philippe's government finally came to its aid with a loan. The three first railways in France—all of them in the small mining region of the Loire—were thus not a spectacular success. Like the Stockton–Darlington railway they were built to transport coal. The English line accepted passengers from the beginning; the French lines later did so also. The government and the public in France regarded the Loire railways with far less interest than was attracted by the Liverpool–Manchester railway in England.

By 1834 railways existed only in England and France, but in 1835 a line was opened in Germany from Nuremberg to Fuerth—a distance of only two or three miles. In 1836 the Belgians started an impressive plan of railway building with the opening of a line from Brussels to Antwerp. In two years there were some 150 miles of track—a more ambitious system than anywhere else on the continent. The first German railway of any length was built in Saxony in 1837. It linked Dresden and Leipzig, a distance of some seventy miles. In the same year Paris had her first railway, a short line to Saint-Germain, constructed by Emile Péreire, the follower of Saint-Simon, for James Rothschild. The next year the first railway line in Russia was built, from St Petersburg to the Czar's palace at Tsarskoe Selo. It had mainly a curiosity value, and was untypical of subsequent Russian railway building in that it was a product of private enterprise. In 1839 the second short line from Paris, this time to Versailles, was opened, while Italy was given her first railway, in—rather surprisingly—the kingdom of the Two Sicilies, from Naples to Portici.

The man who had set the example for the epidemic of railway building in the 1830s was George Stephenson. Born in 1781, Stephenson had grown up on a coalfield. His father worked one of the stationary steam engines on a pit near Newcastle-upon-Tyne. George's first job in the coalmine was to dig the stone and earth from the coal after it had been mined. At fourteen he was made assistant to his father on the steam engine at a shilling a day. At eighteen he could neither read nor write. In the year when Napoleon Bonaparte was made First Consul of the French Republic, George Stephenson started attending a village evening school to learn the Three Rs. He was married in 1802 and his son Robert was born in 1803. During the later stages of the Napoleonic wars the considerable British army maintained in Spain created a shortage of horses and fodder. The shortage encouraged the collieries and their engineers to search for a substitute for the horse. Already familiar with stationery steam engines, the engineers tried mounting the engine on wheels, and so invented the locomotive. No fewer than six men built steam locomotives before Stephenson, but his 'Blucher', built in 1814, was the first to run on an edge rail instead of in a slotted track. His very first railway, built from 1819 to 1821, was exclusively for the use of the Hetton colliery, but it was his public railways, from Stockton to Darlington, and from Liverpool to Manchester, which gave him national fame. His locomotive, the 'Rocket', was the fastest and most efficient in existence in 1830.

After the opening of the Liverpool–Manchester railway, Stephenson's services as a railway consultant were in big demand. In 1845 he went to Belgium to advise Leopold I on the Belgian railways. He did not share, and was not involved, in the railway mania of 1843–47 when so many Englishmen speculated frantically on railway building and were ultimately ruined. His reputation was untarnished at his death in 1848. His son, Robert Stephenson, was deliberately educated as an engineer to continue the impressive work of his father. Robert's construction of

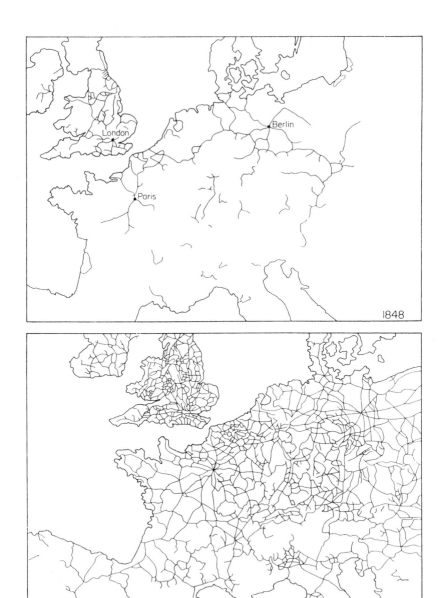

2. THE RAILWAYS OF EUROPE IN 1848 AND 1877

the London to Birmingham railway in 1838 established him as a great railway builder, and unlike his father he continued building railways through the extravagant years of the boom. But he did not restrict his engineering to railways alone. In bridge building his record was an impressive one. In 1847 his Royal Border Bridge at Berwick was built—the dramatic railway viaduct which Stephenson called the 'last act of union'. The Tyne bridge was completed in 1849 and the bridge over the Menai Straits in 1850. Most striking of all was the Victoria Bridge over the St Lawrence in Canada, completed in 1859. Unlike his father, Robert used his wealth for self-indulgence, drink probably contributing to his early death in 1859.

In Britain the railways were financed entirely by private investment. On the other hand the Belgian government decided as early as 1834 on state railways, while the French system from 1842 onwards combined state and private ownership. By 1840 Europe had 1,800 miles of railway, and by 1870, 65,000 miles. Railways were, of course, spreading elsewhere in the world, and especially in America, but in 1870 Europe possessed a half of all the lines in the world. As has been seen, Britain, Belgium, France, Germany, Italy and Russia had started railway building in the 1830s. Austria, Holland and Switzerland soon followed. But Britain retained her very considerable lead. By the end of 1850 some £240,000,000 had been invested in British railways, 6,084 miles of track had been opened, and 67,400,000 passengers carried. By 1870 the figures had risen impressively to £502,700,000; 13,562 miles; and 322,200,000 passengers. It was now possible to go from Edinburgh to London in twelve hours. The whole concept of speed and distance was being altered.

In France the railways were developed by small private companies, which eventually amalgamated to form six companies. After 1848 and under the Second Empire they were actively encouraged by the state. Péreire and Rothschild had together built the *Chemin de fer du Nord* which was opened in 1845, and they later constructed the line from Paris to Lyons. But Péreire subsequently gave his services to Napoleon III in founding the state bank, the *Crédit Mobilier*. If the state acquired a hold on railways in France, and retained a firm control in Belgium and Germany, in Austria it sold railways for revenue. The Habsburg government in 1856 sold lines from Trieste through Venice to Milan, and from Florence through Parma to Modena, to a company controlled by the Paris branch of the Rothschilds. Just before the war of 1859 the Austrian government sold the line from Vienna to the south to the *Südbahngesellschaft*, whose director was the Viennese Rothschild. The sales were to prove a false economy during the Franco-Austrian War, when France was better served than Austria by the railways of north Italy. After the first short railway line in Russia, from St Petersburg to Tsarskoe Selo, which was built by a private company, the Czar's government took over subsequent railway expansion. In 1843 the government built a line from Warsaw to the Polish-Austrian frontier, on the way to Vienna. In 1851 the line made familiar to the world by Anna Karenina's journeys, from St Petersburg to Moscow, was completed. By 1855 there were still only 660 miles of railway track in Russia, but under Alexander II the encouragement given to investment in the railways by Reutern, the minister of finance, eventually bore fruit.

The most important use of the steam engine was undoubtedly its application to the railway, but it was significant also for sea and ocean transport. A man whose career strikingly links the development of the railways with the development of the steamship was Isambard Kingdom Brunel. Given the job, in 1832, when a young man of twenty-six, of planning the Great Western Railway, which was to link the West of England with London, Brunel was brilliantly successful not only as an engineer, but also in getting the necessary capital from business men. He worked invariably on a scale substantially too large for sound economics. He overspent so much on the G.W.R. that the railway had not recovered from its large capital costs at the time of its nationalization in 1947. One misfortune for the G.W.R. was Brunel's choice of gauge. George Stephenson had built the Stockton–Darlington railway to a gauge of 4 feet 8½ inches for the simple reason that this was the existing gauge on the horse-operated railways of the mines. Brunel argued that much greater power could be exerted on the railways if a wider gauge was employed, and he built the G.W.R. to a gauge of no less than seven feet. Later the unfortunate G.W.R. had to change its entire layout, to link with other lines, at considerable expense. Yet by a strange irony Brunel may well have been right, and the rest of the world wrong. Most engineers today believe that the railways could have been run more efficiently with a wider gauge.

Brunel started his engineering career at the age of twenty, when he was entrusted by his father, Sir Marc Brunel, also an engineer, with the construction of the Rotherhithe Tunnel under the Thames. Most of the bridges of the G.W.R.—masterpieces like the Saltash Bridge connecting

Devon and Cornwall—were the work of I. K. Brunel. Architecturally, it is more generous to judge the Victorian age by Brunel's bridges than by the railway stations disguised as medieval cathedrals or the ministry offices posing as Renaissance palaces. Brunel's designs were daring and original. When he built the bridge over the Thames at Maidenhead, other engineers declared that the arches were far too flat, and that the bridge would not hold. Yet after well over a century of heavy use the bridge shows no sign of strain. Clifton suspension bridge and Bristol Docks were designed by Brunel, who also built railways in Italy, Australia and India.

Steamships were already functioning in 1830, but in limited conditions—only on rivers, lakes or narrow channels. The sailing ship remained for long supreme on the high seas, and sailing-ships like all other human equipment were being multiplied and improved. The first two steamships to cross the Atlantic arrived in New York on the same day—23 April 1838. But thoughout the 1840's the steamship was still less safe than the sailing ship. Steamships were faster, but needed more crew, and their machinery and stocks of coal took up valuable space, which, in sailing ships, made profits. Not surprisingly, it was Brunel who constructed the largest ship of the period—the fantastic *Great Eastern*. If the planning of the Great Western Railway was over-ambitious, the steamship *Great Eastern* was an immense and splendid folly. It was preceded by Brunel's *Great Britain*, which was 322 feet long and made of iron. The *Great Britain* was launched in 1845, and was the largest ship of her day. The *Great Eastern* had a displacement almost ten times as great. Whereas the *Great Britain* had been a success, the *Great Eastern* was built half a century too soon. No waterfront was equipped to deal with her, and she proved an economic disaster. Only in the 1850s did steamships generally become safer and more economical. Iron steadily replaced timber for the hull, and the paddle-wheel was soon replaced by a submerged propeller, but in the 1870s sailing ships were still being used to carry heavy freight cargoes.

For the steamships, the railways and engineering generally, iron was increasingly in demand. The production of iron multiplied itself many times between 1830 and 1880 in Britain, France and Germany, though the growth of output was greater in Germany than in the rest of Europe. Britain, however, maintained her lead as the world's greatest producer of iron throughout the period. In 1880 she was still producing more than three times as much pig iron as Germany, and more than five times as much as France. Britain was still providing about half the pig iron

79

in the world. Although France fell behind Germany in the 1860s, by any previous standards the French iron industry was expanding quickly. The biggest iron works in France, at Le Creusot, run by the Schneider brothers, increased production steadily under the July Monarchy, and more impressively under the Second Empire.

Perhaps the most important technological event of the period was Bessemer's discovery in 1856 of a much quicker and cheaper means of producing steel. Henry Bessemer (1813–98), the son of a Frenchman who had settled in Hertfordshire, had received an informal education from his father. An inspired inventor, he had already brilliant ideas to his credit before he turned to steel. The Royal Society of Arts awarded him a medal for a sugar cane press, and his invention of a process for making a powder for producing gilt paint earned him a fortune in an age when gilt was much in fashion. In the London suburb of St Pancras he set up the machinery for manufacturing his gilt paint in great secrecy, and so earned the financial independence which enabled him later to work on steel.

The need for stronger iron in the manufacture of cannon in the Crimean War drew Bessemer's attention into the field in which his name was to become a famous one. The processes then in use in the production of wrought iron and steel were slow and required many highly skilled men. In 1854 Britain produced only 100,000 tons of steel, and production elsewhere in the world was still more negligible. Costing about £50 a ton, steel was not likely to find a large market. At the start of the Crimean War Bessemer's fortune seemed at a low ebb. His attempts to interest the British War Office and Napoleon III in an invention of a ribbed shell that could be fired from a smooth-bored cannon failed, and he then turned to metallurgy. In 1855 he took out a patent for a new process for making cast steel, and, by way of three further patents, by March 1856 had evolved the famous process which earned him a second fortune. Ironmasters eagerly bought licences to use the Bessemer process, but at this stage the system was not a success. The ironmasters who used it lost money and the steelmakers refused to have anything to do with it. It was left to a Swedish ironmaster, G. F. Goränsson, to discover in 1857 that when the Bessemer process failed—as it so often did—the failure was due to phosphorus and sulphur impurities in the iron ore. Goränsson's experiments with very pure charcoal iron invariably succeeded. Bessemer promptly changed to the Swedish pig iron, set up his own firm, Henry Bessemer and

Company of Sheffield, in 1858, and produced steel which earned him his third and greatest fortune. In the 1860s other steelmakers adopted the Bessemer process. From 1866 to 1868 Bessemer and his partner, Robert Longsdon, had an average annual income of £200,000 from royalties alone. From 1870 onwards steel rapidly began replacing wrought iron for railway lines and the boilers of railway engines. In 1859 the first ship made of Bessemer steel was launched on the Thames, and by 1865 eighteen steel ships had been built. In the 1860s the Bessemer process spread to Belgium, France, Germany and Austria.

An anglicized Frenchman had made the first break-through in the production of cheap steel. A German living in England, Friedrich Siemens (1826–1904) in 1867 perfected a more satisfactory process. Siemens played a hot stream of air and a jet of burning gas on liquid iron in an open hearth. The process had the advantage over Bessemer's that it could be more closely controlled, it could utilize scrap iron, and produced steel of a more consistently high quality. But Siemens's process shared the drawback of Bessemer's that only iron ore which contained no phosphorus could be used. Already by 1870 sources of the purer iron ore in Britain were running out. In that year 400,000 tons had to be imported, and by 1880, 3 million tons were being imported annually to Britain. The next step in the production of cheap, strong steel would inevitably be some process for removing the major impurity of phosphorus from the iron ore.

Sidney Gilchrist Thomas, a clerk in London, had studied metallurgy at evening classes in Birkbeck College. A young man of twenty-six, in poor health, he worked out in 1876 a method of removing the phosphorus from molten pig iron, so that phosphoric ore could be used for the making of steel. The practical stages of the process were perfected with the help of his cousin, Percy Carlyle Gilchrist, an analytical chemist in the ironworks of Blaenavon in South Wales. The phosphoric ore was plentiful in Britain, France and Germany, but the British ironmasters had already set up their expensive plant for the original Bessemer process, and were not inclined to change. Consequently the Gilchrist-Thomas method was adopted on a bigger scale in France and Germany than in Britain, at least until the 1920s. But for Europe as a whole Thomas's discovery had an importance comparable with those of Bessemer and Siemens. When Bessemer himself died in 1898 he was an immensely rich and renowned figure, but the world's production of steel by his original process had begun to decline in face of competition from the more widely applicable Gilchrist-Thomas process.

Nevertheless it was Bessemer who had taken the first steps in converting steel from a rarely used and over-expensive metal into being a commonplace in industrial civilization. In his own way Bessemer had as great an influence on history as Bismarck. And when Bismarck, in 1862, spoke of 'blood and iron', he was already, in metallurgical terms, a little out of date.

Besides revolutionizing all industry, the Industrial Revolution created an entirely new industry of its own—the machine industry. London, Birmingham, Manchester, Newcastle and Glasgow all developed machine industries early, and in 1843 the export of machinery from Britain was at last permitted. Much had, in fact, already been exported illegally. The most important plant producing machinery outside Britain was the Cockerill plant at Seraing in Belgium. A French machine industry on a smaller scale developed at Le Creusot.

The textile industry had been the first to use machines and factories. Textiles had helped to make the wealth of Britain in the eighteenth century, and continued to do so after 1830. In the 1850s textiles—principally cotton—accounted for about 60 per cent of the value of British exports. At least one-eighth of all the workers in England and Wales in 1851 were employed in the textile industry, though this must still be compared with those employed in agriculture, which accounted for more than a fifth of the total working population. Wool was following cotton into the factory in 1850. In France, too, it was to the cotton industry that the factory system was first applied on a big scale. The cotton industry in Alsace was founded only at the beginning of the nineteenth century, and so was almost immediately established in factories, though with water, rather than steam, supplying the power. As in England, spinning was first carried out in factories, while weaving was still left to hand-looms at home. In the woollen industry there was the same limitation to the use of power for the spinning processes, the other processes being done by hand, and the silk and linen industries did not use power at all until the 1840s. In Germany the textile industry was not the brightest aspect of the economic scene. Apart from the cotton industry in Saxony and around Elberfeld in the Prussian Rhinelands, the German textile industry was technically behind that in England and France.

Coal was the basic fuel for industry, and the coal-mining industry went on gaining in importance throughout the period. For every decade from 1830 to 1880 world output of coal increased by at least 60 per cent.

Britain remained by far the largest producer. In 1830 she was producing some 25 million tons a year, or four-fifths of the total world production. By 1850 she was producing some 50 million tons. She was fortunate in that five of her rich coalfields were on the coast, making export easier. But by 1880 other countries had started to catch up with her. She produced now less than a half of the total world production, but this still meant that in 1871 Britain was mining four times as much as Germany, and nine times as much as Belgium or France, and in 1880 still almost twice as much as Germany and France combined. In 1830 the German coalfields of the Ruhr, the Saar and Aachen were already being mined. Although French coal production increased, from the middle of the century it fell well behind that of Germany, and Belgium continued to produce slightly more coal than France. Germany became less dependent on imported British coal, especially in the Rhine valley. Early in the period it became possible to mine far deeper for coal, and new deeper mines were opened in the British Isles, North France, Belgium and the Ruhr, though the first pit was not opened in the Ruhr until 1841. The machine was used in coal-mining for transporting coal to the surface, pumping out water and in air, but not for the actual hewing which remained a primeval labour. In spite of the vast increase in coal output, it could not quite keep pace with the demands of other industries. There was a shortage of coal in the highly productive years 1871 to 1873, and the price of coal rose more quickly than other prices.

In other industries—paper, chemical, canning, cement and so on—important technical advances were made in the period. With the discovery of aniline dyes in 1866 the chemist became an important figure in industry. Other inventions of immense significance for the future were made, but did not have time before 1880 to be developed economically. In the 1860s Werner von Siemens, the brilliant German inventor, conceived the idea of the dynamo. In the shape of the electric telegraph, electricity had already been applied to communications. Now it would one day be available for power and lighting. In 1876 the internal combustion engine was invented.

To keep pace with Europe's ever increasing industrial output and her ever diversifying technical achievement, economic institutions were developed and perfected. The concept of the firm became more complex. The joint stock company continued to take over the role formerly played by the individual or the family. In France already in the eighteenth century the concept of the *société en commandite* had been formed: that is, a company in which an individual investor could remain a sleeping partner and would never be held liable for more than his personal investment, whereas the active partners were liable without limit. The concept had been given legal recognition by the Code Napoleon. It had the obvious advantage of encouraging outsiders to invest freely in an enterprise, while the active partners would in theory have a full sense of responsibility for policy. A later development, the *société anonyme*, in which all shareholders enjoyed limited liability, did not become common in France until the last years of the Second Empire, although in Belgium two hundred such companies already existed in 1857.

In Britain joint stock companies with limited liability had existed since the seventeenth century, but they could be founded only by Royal Charter or private Act of Parliament; two eminent examples were the East India Company and the Bank of England. In 1837 a Registrar of Companies was appointed, and after 1844 new joint stock companies could be founded by application to the Registrar. It was by then realized that the foundation of limited liability companies should not only be made more generally possible, but should be positively encouraged. Without limited liability a rich landowner, by investing a few pounds in a company, could endanger his whole fortune in the event of the company going bankrupt. British Acts of Parliament in 1855 and 1862 at last legalized the limited liability company, and made investment a far less dangerous step. It was now far easier for manufacturers to find capital. The 1862 Act went farther than other governments had gone, by obliging companies—in return for limited liability—to inform the government of the names of its directors and shareholders, and to publish annually an audited balance sheet. Similar laws were passed in France in 1867 and Germany in 1870.

While the financing of industry in Great Britain was largely the work of private enterprise, on the continent more responsibility for providing or collecting capital was accepted by the state. Napoleon III appreciated the need for credit if French industry was to be developed. The *Crédit Foncier* and the *Crédit Mobilier* were both founded in 1852—the same year as the Empire itself, and with the emperor's blessing. Both helped to finance the ambitious rebuilding of French towns carried out under the Empire. The *Crédit Mobilier* suffered from the excessive expenses of Haussmann's rebuilding of Paris[1]—expenses which were not immediately productive—and from the loss of the Mexican loans.[2] Founded by the Péreire brothers of Bordeaux with the express purpose

[1] See below, pp. 376–7.   [2] See below, p. 317.

of emancipating Napoleon and French finance from the Rothschilds, the *Crédit Mobilier* loaned large sums to the government. The brothers Péreire accepted the socialist doctrines of state expenditure once recommended by Saint-Simon. But they also loaned money abroad, especially for railway building, and to private companies. In Germany the credit system was primitive before unification. The royal governments of the German states provided capital, as did the Prussian government for the coal mines owned by the crown in Silesia. Individual capitalists and families continued to found companies on their own initiative, as did the Krupps at Essen. But in the 1850s banks were founded for the provision of capital in Austria and Darmstadt on the lines of the *Crédit Foncier* and *Crédit Mobilier* in France.

One last characteristic of the industrial revolution must be stressed: the growth of cities. Ancient cities, like London, Paris or Lyons, which acquired new industries, grew at a great rate, and wherever there was industry there was a degree of urbanization. But there was a still more striking growth in the north and midlands of England, where towns which had barely existed before the industrial revolution multiplied their populations throughout the nineteenth century. Manchester, Liverpool, Birmingham, Sheffield and Leeds became great, thriving, populous cities in a few decades. Not even the most loyal native of these cities would pretend that they added much to the beauty of Europe, but there can be no doubt that they added great wealth and power to Britain. In Germany, too, large cities grew very quickly. At the start of the century only two German cities had more than 60,000 inhabitants— Berlin with some 200,000 and Hamburg with just over 100,000. By 1871 eight German cities had populations of more than 100,000. They, too, brought wealth and power, if not joy and beauty. In later chapters the human suffering[1] and ugliness[2] attendant upon the industrial revolution will be considered, but here the more positive aspect must be stressed. Industry in itself, considered independently of the politico-social system in which it was introduced, could raise living standards, just as it had contributed to a rising population. In the long run, industrialization brought life, and it brought life more abundantly.

[1] See chapter VI. [2] See chapter XIV.

V

Agriculture, Trade and Commerce

While the most important economic development of the half century was without doubt the movement of industrialization, a very large majority of the people of Europe continued to devote their lives to agriculture. Even in England and Wales more than half the population still lived in the countryside in 1830, though by 1870 this was no longer true, since by then 55 per cent of the population was urban. If a large area of western and central Europe—France, Germany, Austria, Switzerland, the Netherlands and Sweden—is taken together, it can be said that only 30 per cent of its population lived in the towns in 1870, but even 30 per cent represented a great drift from the countryside since 1830 and contrasted sharply with the position in Russia and the Balkans,

BIBLIOGRAPHY. The basic economic histories mentioned for the previous chapter are, of course, relevant here. Agriculture has understandably had rather less attention than industry for this period. Two recent works by J. Blum deserve mention: *Noble Landowners and Agriculture in Austria, 1815–1848* (Baltimore, 1948), and *Lord and Peasant in Russia from the Ninth to the Nineteenth Century* (Princeton, 1961), and an older work is still valuable for Russian agriculture: G. T. Robinson, *Rural Russia under the Old Regime* (London, 1932). For the Balkans there is a collection of vivid contemporary accounts, with a scholarly and informative commentary by members of the staff of the School of Slavonic and East European Studies—*Contrasts in Emerging Societies. Readings in the Social and Economic History of South-Eastern Europe in the Nineteenth Century*, edited by Doreen Warriner (London, 1965). A recent study of British agriculture which has sections also on social conditions and the poor law is Christabel S. Orwin and Edith H. Whetham, *History of British Agriculture 1846–1914* (London, 1964). For the history of free trade there is a wealth of literature, much of it associated with the lives and policies of the men involved. Lucy Brown, *The Board of Trade and the Free Trade Movement, 1830–1842* (Oxford, 1958) deals with the policies and the opinions of the personnel of the Board of Trade, British governments and parliaments in the early part of the period, and for the movement of opinion in the country there is N. McCord, *The Anti-Corn Law League 1838–1846* (London, 1958). For commercial treaties and customs unions in the period the primary sources must still be consulted since no comprehensive secondary study where towns were still small and few and there had been no reason for a desertion of the land.

The general pattern of agricultural development before 1830 had been a movement away from communal or feudal organization towards commercialization and a cash economy. Crops and animals were now bought and sold, when in the past they had been bartered or consumed by their producers. Agricultural standards had been going up since the eighteenth century: new crops had been discovered, livestock were bred and reared more efficiently and new farming techniques were explored. Improvements were usually the work of individual farmers, who were becoming the rule in the west, though in Russia communal methods persisted even in the nineteenth century. In France, west Germany, north Italy, the Netherlands and Denmark the peasant farmers tended to own their land, while in areas on the whole more backward—Spain, east Germany, south Italy and Hungary—large landowners leased their fields to tenant farmers. England, in this respect like the poorer countries, was also farmed mainly by tenant farmers.

In the period more immediately preceding 1830 agriculture had experienced a difficult transition from the Napoleonic wars to the totally different conditions of peace. But by 1830 prices had started to rise again, after the disastrous fall in 1815. The accelerating increase of population provided agriculture with large new markets and stimulated higher production, though the increase did not have the same effects in

has been made, but several chapters of W. O. Henderson, *The Genesis of the Common Market* (London, 1962) are relevant, while *The Zollverein* (Cambridge, 1938) by the same author is still the only short, clear account of the Prussian customs union from 1818 to 1871. Karl Brinkmann, *Die preussische Handelspolitik vor dem Zollverein und die Wiederaufbau vor hundert Jahren* (Berlin, 1922) is an important study of Prussian economic policy, and A. H. Price, *The Evolution of the Zollverein, 1815–1833* (Ann Arbor, 1949) gives a detailed account of the formation of the Zollverein. A classic of German nationalist literature, Heinrich von Treitschke, *Deutsche Geschichte im neunzehnten Jahrhundert* (Leipzig, 5 vols., 1879–95) is still a major source for material on the Zollverein, though it is, of course, heavily slanted in favour of Prussia. For the Cobden Treaty there is A. L. Dunham, *The Anglo-French Treaty of Commerce of 1860* (Ann Arbor, 1930). On business cycles at the beginning of the period there is R. C. O. Matthews, *A Study in Trade Cycle History: Economic Fluctuations in Great Britain, 1833–1842* (Cambridge, 1954), and for another theme briefly mentioned at the end of this chapter, L. H. Jenks, *The Migration of British Capital to 1875* (New York, 1927) remains the authority. The importance of the U.S.A. for the British economy from the beginning of the period is illustrated by J. Potter, *Atlantic Economy, 1815–1860: the U.S.A. and the Industrial Revolution in Britain* in L. S. Pressnell, Ed., *Studies in the Industrial Revolution* (London, 1960).

all countries. In eastern and southern Europe growth in production often failed to keep pace with the rise in population, with the result that the peasant remained as poor as ever, and in some areas—in the kingdom of the Two Sicilies, for example—he became ever more impoverished. But in western Europe better and more intensive farming, and above all the growth of large, hungry towns, made life a little easier for the peasant. The picture, however, was influenced by the current laws of inheritance. In France the Code Napoleon allowed for equal inheritance by all children, so that here, and in countries with similar laws, farms and estates would often be fragmented during a period of rising population. In England, where the eldest son inherited the whole estate, which was anyhow farmed by his tenants, no such fragmentation occurred. In the farther east of Europe—in the great empty plains of Russia, Rumania and Hungary—new lands were cultivated, but in the west there was less living space and greater pressure for reformed methods. Unfortunately vast areas of peasant holdings all over Europe were not amenable to improvement: the farms were too small for experiments, and no capital was available. Peasants do not make successful capitalists: they are reluctant to borrow, and in the nineteenth century were mostly too poor to be able to save. Over most of Europe the agrarian system had ceased to be feudal, and yet had not become, in any full sense, either capitalist or socialist. It was left to the burgomaster of Weyerbusch, near Bonn, Friedrich Raiffeisen (1818–88), to realize that the peasant's main difficulty was his inability to get credit in a manner suited to his pride. Raiffeisen observed the economic distress in the German countryside during the depression of 1846–47, and decided to do something about it. In 1862 he founded the first system of cooperative peasants' banks (the *Darlehnskassenverein*), to give the farmer an element of social security when times were bad.

The economy of Great Britain depended less on agriculture than did the economies of other countries, but it was in Britain that some of the bigger changes had been experienced. The farming aristocrats and gentry of the eighteenth century had introduced improved methods in an almost dilettante spirit, but with immense consequences; and until the mid-nineteenth century Britain remained in the lead in agricultural, as in industrial, improvement. In the 1840s in Britain new methods of fertilizing were rendering unnecessary the old custom of leaving land fallow for long and frequent periods. About the same time the process of land enclosure, which had started centuries earlier, was almost completed. The few patches of common land remaining in 1830 had nearly all disappeared by 1880. The English countryside had taken on the appearance that the unspoilt areas have today: small, self-contained farms, with neat, if sometimes oddly shaped, fields and woods.

Throughout the period the English land-owning class retained a large share of political and economic power. The landed nobility, the Russells and the Stanleys, alternated in government with the new men, the Peels and the Gladstones. In 1870 over half of England and Wales was owned by 2,250 people; though English agriculture was administered by a quarter of a million tenant farmers, and worked by a million landless labourers. British agriculture enjoyed considerable prosperity until the mid-1870s, both before and after the repeal of the Corn Laws in 1846.[1] Then, abruptly, in 1873 things changed for the worse. The depression was caused by an accumulation of adverse factors: from 1874 to 1882 freak weather conditions ruined all but two crops; after the Civil War and the opening of the Middle West by the spread of the railways, wheat production in North America provided massive competition, which was further increased by growing exports from Australia after 1860; the sharp increase in grain exports from Russia and Rumania did not help the British farmer. By 1880 the great age of British agriculture was over.

More dependent upon agriculture was the Irish economy. The predominance of the potato and the lack of other crops meant that the potato blight of 1845–47 caused the horrors of a famine which has dug itself into the Irish national consciousness as deeply as the 1914 war has into the English consciousness.[2] The homogeneous nature of Irish agriculture was thus one basic weakness in the economy. Another weakness was the absenteeism of the landlords, who were mostly English aristocrats with careers in London, or with other estates in England. In such cases management of the estate was left to a tenant or a bailiff. As the population rose steeply before the famine, the landlords charged higher rents while the tenants were left with even smaller holdings. The Irish peasant earned enough to cover his rent with the small produce, animal or vegetable, of his own plot, and ate the inevitable potato. The problem of land shortage was solved—if that is the word—by the famine, but other hardships for the Irish farmer remained. Like peasants in all poor areas he lacked capital with which to make improvements; the law gave him no security of tenure should he fall behind, however temporarily, with his rent; and if he succeeded in enlarging his miser-

[1] See below, p. 96 and pp. 184–5.
[2] See below, pp. 191–2.

able hovel or constructing out-buildings, he had no legal rights to such improvements. Gladstone's Irish Land Acts did something to remedy these grievances,[1] but by then the social and political ills of Ireland had become too bitter to be cured by paternalism.

The French peasant was far more prosperous than the Irish and more independent than the English farm labourer. In the French Revolution the great estates of the crown, the Church and the aristocracy had been broken up, and while much of the land was bought by the rich bourgeoisie, much of it also filtered down to the peasants themselves. The building of the railways after 1850 brought about a big change in French agriculture. Farms which had in the past been remote and isolated could suddenly send their produce to more distant towns. With a slowly growing market for bread it made sense to devote more land to wheat, the production of which increased by about a half in France in the period. For every five acres growing wheat in 1870, two acres were growing wines, but wine production had bad fluctuations. In the 1850s it fell by two-thirds as a result of the oidium pest. After a quick recovery, a second, more disastrous, pest appeared, in the form of phylloxera. In the last five years of the period the wine crop fell off by some 70 per cent, spreading considerable distress over many areas of France.

The movement of enclosures was not so final and complete in France as it was in England. Even in the days of the Second Empire common land accounted for as much as 10 per cent of France, as it had in 1815. Much of the common land in France was covered with woods, but much of it also was pasture, and at the disposal of all the village. The small size of the peasants' holdings made investment in machinery unprofitable, so that by 1880 French agriculture was still largely unmechanized and, by English or American standards, archaic in its methods.

The reduction of English tariffs in the 1840s and the improvement in the shipping services across the Channel opened large markets to French agriculture. Towards the end of the period French dairy produce, especially cheese, and some fruit and vegetable delicacies—strawberries, asparagus, mushrooms—were exported to England, though production of luxuries of this kind was to increase enormously in the 1890s. Wheat remained the chief crop, its production steadily increasing, and the potato became an important feature of the peasants' economy after 1850. But slowness in applying scientific methods prevented France from producing as much wheat per acre as other western countries, and by 1860 she was importing wheat. As in England bad

[1] See below, p. 192.

harvests in the late 1870s increased the depression created primarily by American competition.

German agriculture passed through years of acute crisis in the early part of the period. The serfs had been emancipated in Napoleonic days under French influence, and in Prussia the edict of 1807 had abolished serfdom in principle, but there had been no expropriation of land and by 1848 the German peasants were impoverished by high rents, and ready for revolution. The potato famine hit the German peasants only less terribly than the Irish, and food riots ensued. To prevent social revolution the ruling classes in Germany made major concessions. The peasant was made effectively free and independent, and given a holding of his own in return for compensation payments which were not ruinous to him. But for many the reforms came too late. Poverty on the land caused many Germans, like the Irish of that generation, to emigrate to America. East of the Elbe the class of the land-owning peasant did not emerge at all. Rather the old pattern of large estates owned by the Junkers and worked by landless labourers persisted. Towards the end of the period industrialization caused the inevitable drift from the land and the German labourers on the Junkers' estates were partly replaced by immigrants from Russian Poland or Russia proper. The Junkers administered their own estates. In Germany as a whole there was virtually no tenant farming of the English variety, and when the Empire was set up in 1871 three-quarters of the agricultural land was owned by the peasants themselves. The process of enclosure quickened in Germany in the period, but the common land was often simply partitioned by the smaller peasants rather than being enclosed by large landowners. For the German economy as a whole agriculture was already less important by the end of the period. Between 1865 and 1875 Germany changed from being a food-exporting country to being a food-importing one.

In the Habsburg territories Vienna was the financial centre and chief market of a great agricultural region. The different parts of the Empire tended to specialize in their agricultural products, Austria herself breeding livestock, Hungary producing grain and Bohemia sugar. Under the Bach system[1] after 1849 a generous redistribution of the land took place. Over three million freed peasants were given land, which had been lopped from some 100,000 large estates. In Bohemia and Austria proper the imperial government paid one-third of the compensation, the local *Landtag* found another third, leaving only a third to be paid by the

[1] See below, p. 271.

peasant himself. In Hungary no compensation was demanded from the peasant at all. The contrast here with the practice in Russia after 1861 is striking.

The Balkan countries at the beginning of the period had large tracts of good fertile land which had not been cultivated. It was calculated in 1839 that one-quarter of the cultivable land of Hungary had been left untouched. The Great Hungarian Plain, which stretches for over three hundred miles in one direction and over one hundred in the other, was used mainly for pasture, especially for horses. The lack of timber or stone for road-building, and the fact that the rivers and streams were mostly subterranean, discouraged arable farming. The mountainous areas of Serbia, Bulgaria, Bosnia, Montenegro and what was to become Rumania were understandably mainly pastoral, but even the plains of the Danubian principalities were uncultivated: at the start of the period only about a sixth of the land of Moldavia and Wallachia was cultivated. The Balkans, whether forming part of the Ottoman Empire or the Habsburg Monarchy, were equally underdeveloped, partly because of the tax system, which prevented the accumulation of credit, and so of economic growth, partly because of the ignorance and conservatism of the population. But as the period proceeded more land was cultivated. Maize, in particular, was grown on the dry plains, and potatoes in the moister hills.

In the Danubian principalities there were larger landowners than elsewhere, but Prince Alexander Cuza,[1] first ruler of the United Principalities of Moldavia and Wallachia, whose stormy reign lasted from 1859 to 1866, tried to do something for the peasants. In 1864 he abolished serfdom and feudal dues and gave the peasants a greater share of the land.

Of the great climatic belts of the land mass of Russia only one provided rich agriculture, and even that was not dependable. In the far north was the totally uncultivated tundra. South of the tundra was an infertile belt of forest, allowing very little cultivation. Even the belt of very fertile, black earth, on which the most populated regions were centred, was subject to grave weather variations: if there was enough rain the land could be highly productive; if—as too often—there was too little rain and too much wind, there could be great distress, and sometimes famine. The basic unit of Russian agriculture was the village commune or *mir*, with its primitive assembly or 'meeting' of villagers, and executive officer or Elder. Through the *mir*, rights in the land

[1] See below, p. 283.

among the peasants were held in common, everyone's cattle grazed on the common land, and regulation of the occasions for ploughing, mowing and reaping were drawn up in the village meeting. The legal rights of the *mir* and its exact jurisdiction were never clearly defined. Since most of the members of the *mir* were serfs it was clear that their lords or squires could overrule their decisions. In the same way the concept of the ultimate ownership of land was less certain in Russia than in the west. The squire believed that he 'owned' the land, but so did the peasant, and to decide who was right is merely to define terms. The familiar claim of the serfs—'We are yours, but the land is ours'—gives some idea of the current concept before 1861.

The existence of the *mir* perpetuated old practices of farming in small strips, sometimes only three or four paces wide, and leaving fields fallow in rotation. Sometimes as much as a fifth of all the land was wasted as marginal land and boundaries. But the poverty and lack of capital experienced by Russian agriculture was quite as responsible as the communal or manorial methods for the slow arrival of improvements. It was in Russia, however, that the greatest single change in organization of agriculture took place, when, in 1861, Alexander II emancipated the serfs.[1] The peasants became proprietors of half the cultivated land in Russia, though not as individuals, but in their collective capacity as the *mir*.

In spite of the legal revolution of emancipation, social conditions did not change for the better in Russia.[2] But in western Europe increased consumption and new habits of the middle class influenced agriculture. Thus the custom of eating butter on bread was adopted by the upper classes in England and other parts of northern Europe. The Danes in particular spread the habit, which proved a boon to Danish dairy farming. Agriculture in Denmark was organized on a modern pattern. Farmers with an average of seventy acres each were proprietors of most of the land in Denmark by 1880. Holland, in contrast, remained a country of small holdings of less than twelve acres—a country with a concentrated population both of men and of beasts.

The agriculture of the Mediterranean countries continued to produce wine, fruit and olive oil, in addition to wheat, as it had done for centuries. Italy produced more silk than any other European country, and more wine than any other country but France. Italy was self-supporting in wheat, and could export olive oil. Agriculture was more prosperous in the north than in the centre, and far more prosperous

[1] See below, pp. 109, 277–8.   [2] See below, p. 109.

than in the south. There were few small peasant holdings. In the south the land was divided into great estates, or *latifundia*, owned by a few landowners, many of whom were noblemen. In the north the peasant was more independent, though not always a landowner himself. He had been freed from serfdom in the mid-eighteenth century, and his relations with his landlord were often regulated by the institution of the *mezzadria* (share-cropping): the produce of the peasant's labour was shared on an even basis with the landlord, who provided—as well as the land—the heavier implements and buildings, and paid the taxes. The *mezzadria* was practised commonly in Tuscany and Umbria, but was not uncommon throughout the northern half of the peninsula. The economy of Spanish agriculture was not unlike that of Naples, which had, indeed, been derived from Spain in the seventeenth century: estates were large, landowners mighty, the labourers free but under-paid and wretched.

By its nature, the development of agriculture is not given to sudden changes or striking revolutions. But trade and commerce—the processes linking the industries and agricultures of different countries and regions with each other—are more subject to changes in theory and policy. In the half century under consideration the principle of free trade, evolved by French and English philosophers in the eighteenth century, was experimented with on a large scale by European governments, and then abandoned. In the words of Walter Hallstein, himself a central figure in an attempt in the mid-twentieth century to lay the foundations of a united Europe on the soil of the commercial philosophies of the eighteenth and nineteenth centuries, '. . . free trade has so far remained a rather distant ideal. The nearest approach to this ideal was made in the twenty years following the Cobden Treaty of 1860; but by 1880 the goal had already begun to recede once more . . .'[1] High tariffs, intended to protect the national economy from foreign competition, had at the best a fluctuating effect before 1840. Protection rendered social distress during periods of business recession still more acute. When the trade cycle brought hunger, tariffs increased that hunger. The great expansion in world trade which followed the relaxing of protection after 1840 was no coincidence. From 1800 to 1840 world trade did not so much as double itself; from 1840 to 1870—a shorter period —it multiplied itself by four. In this great expansion of trade, Britain played the central role: the exports of her new and growing industries,

[1] Walter Hallstein, *United Europe* (Harvard University Press, Cambridge, Mass., 1962).

the imports of raw materials for the factories and food for the workers, and the export of capital which provided credit in sterling abroad for the purchase of English manufactured goods, were three interrelated and self-perpetuating movements.

Opposition to the movement of free trade in Britain came mainly from the farmers and landowners who believed that their income would be threatened by competition from cheap foreign food. In France opposition came from the industrialists who feared the competition of cheaper manufactured goods from England and Belgium. In government circles opposition sometimes came from finance ministers who believed that the revenue received from tariffs could not be replaced, though this fear was often due to a lack of imagination. Sir Robert Peel in England introduced the income tax as an alternative and more reliable form of revenue in 1842. The British Board of Trade was a very early convert to free trade. As president of the Board of Trade in the 1820s, William Huskisson, a minister on the left wing of a Tory government, had already lowered some import duties. Huskisson respected the free trade philosophies of Adam Smith and David Ricardo, but as a member of a government representing the landed class he could move only with caution. When the Whigs came into office in 1830 they brought with them a few younger ministers with very liberal ideas on trade. Most doctrinaire of all was Poulett Thomson, who was only thirty-one in 1830. As vice-president of the Board of Trade from 1830 to 1834 he was already the moving figure in the department, and from 1834 to 1839 he was president of the Board. He left a strong mark on the attitude of the department as a whole, and was thus an important pioneer of free trade in Europe. The son of a business man, Thomson was in many ways typical of the age ushered in by the Great Reform Act of 1832. Arrogant and dogmatic, he preached Ricardian principles, but neither the Whig governments of the 1830s nor the majority of the House of Commons showed the same enthusiasm for free trade. Small reductions of customs duties and tariffs were made, but they were not presented as a great change of commercial policy, nor did they have any significant effect on the economy.

Only with the Conservative ministry of Sir Robert Peel from 1841 to 1846 did the great switch to a *laissez-faire* policy begin on a broader scale. By 1841 the movement for free trade in the country had centred on an attack on the Corn Laws. In their most unpopular form the Corn Laws dated from 1815 when they had imposed a high tariff on imported corn to protect home-grown corn in freak economic conditions. A group of parliamentary radicals founded an Anti-Corn Law Association in London in 1836 to demand total repeal of the tariff, and in 1838 a similar and more effective body was formed in Manchester. The next year it was renamed the Anti-Corn Law League. For the first years of the Whig period after the Reform Act of 1832 the government's financial policies had seemed successful, but a change for the worse was now taking place. There was a bad deficit in 1838. The price of bread rose steeply. The number of paupers grew. Lancashire was experiencing a grim depression. In these circumstances the Anti-Corn Law movement fell into the able hands of Richard Cobden.

The son of an unsuccessful Sussex farmer, Richard Cobden was born in 1804. He left school at the age of fifteen, and worked first as a clerk and then as a commercial traveller. Having saved enough money to secure his independence, he went into business on his own in Manchester and proved highly successful. Travelling in America and the Mediterranean in 1835 and 1836, he developed a taste for political economy and public affairs. His background coloured his ideas, and his ideas were to have a marked influence on the course of European history. He was to become a hero in the eyes of John Morley, Herbert Spencer and a whole generation of liberal thinkers, yet to the twentieth century his intellectual limitations appear as striking as his accomplishments. A hard man, he was remarkable for astuteness rather than imagination, and his self-confidence often bordered on conceit. In the age of Darwin, he believed in the superstitions of phrenology. Yet his politico-economic ideas were clear-sighted and persuasive. His belief in free trade was linked to an abhorrence of aggressive foreign policy and military expenditure. He opposed Palmerston's policy of intervention and gunboat diplomacy, and believed that Britain should content herself with growing rich and influencing other countries by her wealth and her example. Other governments would soon realize that if they discarded aggressive policies and large armies along with economic protection they would quickly expand trade and acquire a new kind of power. 'States will all turn moralists in self-defence', Cobden wrote.[1] He believed that the example set by the U.S.A. of great economic energy and expansion coupled to political isolationism was the one which European states should emulate. 'Let governments have as little to do with one another as possible, and let people begin to have as much to do with one another as possible', he wrote.[2]

[1] John Morley, *The Life of Richard Cobden* (London, 1894), vol. I, p. 107.
[2] *ibid.*, p. 106.

In the Anti-Corn Law League Cobden's most influential support came from the Quaker John Bright (1811–89), the son of a textile manufacturer. Together the two men carried the movement to ultimate victory. The history of Peel's 1841–46 ministry and his final abolition of the Corn Laws is a central part of the history of England and must be told in that context.[1] But repeal in 1846 opened the era of free trade in England and in Europe, and might have done so more suddenly had not the Crimean War intervened. In spite of the abolition of all duties on imported corn, and the reduction or abolition of many other duties on foreign food, British food prices did not fall for at least twenty years after 1846. Nor did the other countries of Europe immediately abolish tariffs, but in the course of the 1850s and 1860s France, Germany, Italy, Belgium, Holland and Switzerland all liberalized trade. In Belgium Corn Laws similar to those in Britain were repealed in 1850. Freer trade was encouraged in Austria in the Bach era of the 1850s.[2] The Minister for Trade, Baron von Bruck, removed the trade barriers between the various parts of the Empire—Austria proper, Hungary and Lombardo-Venetia; and trade with Germany was officially encouraged. Prohibitions on imports were abolished and tariffs against German goods were lowered. In 1853 Buol negotiated a commercial treaty with Prussia to the advantage of both countries. But a much more significant movement in the history of the German economy had for long been developing: the Prussian Customs Union or *Zollverein*.

As early as 1818 Prussia had started on a course of commercial reform. Maasen's tariff law of that year abolished many internal duties and allowed most raw materials to enter the country free of charge, while imposing a heavy tax on foreign goods crossing Prussian territory. Karl Georg von Maasen, director general of taxes from 1818 to 1830 and finance minister from 1830 to 1834, the year of his death, thus did much to strengthen the Prussian economy. His law of 1818 encouraged some small neighbouring German states to enter a customs union with Prussia. In doing so they surrendered a portion of their sovereignty, since they not only adopted the Prussian tariff but were obliged to welcome Prussian customs officials on their soil to work the system. In the course of the 1820s the Prussian system expanded, notably by the signing of a customs union with Hesse-Darmstadt, which, as a comparatively large and important state, retained the right to appoint her own customs officials.

In 1830 three rival economic associations existed in Germany. In

[1] See below, pp. 184–5. [2] See below, p. 271.

97

addition to the union of Prussia, Hesse-Darmstadt and the diminutive states attached to them, a treaty had been signed between Bavaria and Württemberg in the south in 1828, and a Middle German Commercial Union had been formed the same year. Hanover, Brunswick and Saxony, the three chief members of the Middle German Commercial Union, had not joined in a full customs union as the other two groups had done. Their object was mainly one of defence against a Prussian stranglehold on trade in Germany: they wanted to keep open the roads from the ports on the North Sea to Frankfurt-am-Main and Leipzig. They therefore agreed not to enter any customs union until 1834—the date when Prussia's union with Hesse-Darmstadt would be due for renewal, and to keep up and expand a road system outside the Prussian customs union. To a German nationalist historian like von Treitschke their task was to seem merely a wrecking one. The immediate aims of the Commercial Union, and the more ambitious attempts to become a full customs union, were undermined by the action of Friedrich von Motz, Prussian finance minister from 1825 to 1830. Von Motz's share in laying the foundations of the *Zollverein* was as great as, if not greater than Von Maasen's. Motz encouraged the building of roads through Meiningen and Gotha, linking Prussia with Bavaria, Württemberg and Frankfurt-am-Main. In 1829 he persuaded the Dutch government to carry out the 1815 Treaty of Vienna as regards the freeing of trade on the lower stretches of the Rhine—an obligation they had hitherto failed to perform.

The Middle German Customs Union was thus already toppling in 1830. A vital member, Hesse-Cassel, experienced great economic distress and revolution in 1830, and the next year joined the Prussian union. By doing so she was breaking her treaty with the Middle Union, which soon collapsed. In 1834 the *Zollverein* came into formal existence when the Prussian Union was joined by Bavaria and Württemberg, who had previously failed in their attempt to draw Baden and the small Rhine states into their orbit. The greater Union now contained some twenty-three million people and covered a significant area of central Europe. Nor were the creators of the *Zollverein* blind to its possible political significance, even though their immediate concern was the prosperity of their own states. Before his death in 1830 Motz urged the link with the Bavaria-Württemberg Union in a memorandum to Frederick William III. Motz pointed out that neither the German Confederation nor Austria had done anything to further the economic union of Germany, and that Prussia's duty was now plain: by creating the *Zollverein* she could bring prosperity to Germany and at the same time isolate Austria politically and strategically. In the next ten years other German states joined the *Zollverein*, though not with Motz's vision of a greater Germany, so much as to escape from immediate economic difficulties. Nor was the Union so strong in these early days as it could have been. At the *Zollverein* Congress any member state could veto a measure: not until the Congress was replaced by a Federal Customs Council as part of the North German Confederation in 1866 did a clear majority vote become sufficient to pass a measure.

Before Bismarck's day the tangible but limited achievements of the *Zollverein* were twice threatened by more ambitious projects. In 1848 the Frankfurt Parliament[1] planned to create a Germany united economically and politically, but the plan, of course, died with the Parliament in 1849. The second rival plan emerged from Vienna in 1850. Von Bruck's liberalizing of trade in Austria has already been mentioned. His attempt to create a great economic bloc linking the Habsburg empire with the rest of Germany was looked upon favourably by agricultural interests in the Habsburg lands, but on the whole opposed by Austrian industry. Southern Germany wavered, but the Prussian authorities, as was to be expected, presented a determined opposition. Rudolf von Delbrück of the Prussian Ministry of Commerce swayed the decision against Austria by securing the membership of Hanover for the *Zollverein* at this critical moment. Prussian commercial policy towards the rest of the world was less protectionist than Austrian, so that liberals in Germany tended to sympathize with the *Zollverein*, but Delbrück's achievement in resisting the plans of Bruck was no small one in view of the political supremacy of Austria in Germany in the years 1849–51 and the temporary political eclipse of Prussia.[2]

In May 1851 Bruck resigned from the Habsburg government, and the states of south and central Germany subsequently renewed the *Zollverein* treaties with Prussia. Thereafter Prussian economic supremacy in Germany was never seriously in question. When Bismarck came into power in 1862 he fully realized the political significance of the *Zollverein*, but on the tariff question itself he accepted the advice of Delbrück, whom he described as 'the right man in the right place'. The creation of the North German Confederation in 1866[3] cemented the wider economic union, though Hamburg and Bremen, now members of Bismarck's Confederation, still remained outside the *Zollverein*. The

[1] See below, pp. 213–15.   [2] See below, pp. 215–16.
[3] See below, p. 220.

declaration of the German Empire in 1871 completed the work of economic, as of political, unification.

The birth and growth of the *Zollverein* in the 1830s and 1840s has sometimes been contrasted with a supposedly negative and unimaginative commercial policy on the part of the July Monarchy in France. In fact French governments were aware of the significance of the *Zollverein*, and tried to compete with Prussia in the creation of a customs union, but met with insuperable difficulties. As Louis-Philippe's chief minister in 1841, Guizot tried to organize a customs union with Belgium, an idea which had been widely discussed ever since the revolutions of 1830 in Paris and Brussels. Thiers had made tentative moves very shortly before falling from office in 1840. In the summer of 1841 four conferences were held in Paris under Guizot's chairmanship. Guizot believed that from the French point of view there would be strong political advantages for which certain economic concessions might be justified, while the Belgians were looking for easier markets for their industrial output, but were reluctant to give up the smallest element of political independence. The Belgians proposed the abolition of customs houses between Belgium and France, and the establishment of a unique and identical tariff on other frontiers; but they insisted that only Belgian officials should patrol the frontiers of Belgium: to have French officials on Belgian soil would be incompatible with the independence and neutrality of Belgium. The French replied that they could not leave an unprotected French frontier with Belgium unless they could post their own officials on the other Belgian frontiers: France could not abdicate the right of protecting with her own officials the interests of French industry. King Leopold entered the dispute by writing a personal letter to Louis-Philippe explaining that the rest of Europe would not allow French officials in Belgium. The British government would certainly have opposed a Franco-Belgian customs union. The Belgian king hinted at the possibility of returning to an economic union with Holland, but the French feared even more that Belgium might join the *Zollverein*.

The situation changed suddenly in June 1842, when the French decided to increase their tariff on imported textiles. The decision was aimed not at imports from Belgium, but at British textiles, the export of which to France had just increased sharply. The Belgians protested, and the two governments quickly came to an agreement by which the ambitious project for a customs union was abandoned but the more limited objective of a commercial treaty was reached. Belgian textiles were to be exempted from the French tariff and Belgium made concessions to French commerce in return. Guizot was attacked from both sides for his commercial treaty with Belgium—from one side for abandoning protection at all, and from the other for having failed to secure a full customs union. But the assembly sanctioned the treaty.

Among free trade theorists in England, the purists—like Cobden and Bright—favoured immediate and unilateral reduction or abolition of tariffs. On the continent *laissez-faire* enthusiasts looked for customs unions with other countries and comparatively low tariffs aimed by the union at the outside world. But many in Britain and elsewhere preferred a more moderate and, as they believed, more realistic policy—the signing of commercial treaties by which two countries guaranteed each other tariff concessions. Such agreements were usually negotiated by the diplomats rather than economic advisers or ministries of commerce. Thus the British Foreign Office negotiated commercial treaties with the Italian states before the unification of Italy—with Naples in 1845, Tuscany in 1847, Sardinia in 1851, and—somewhat informally—with the Papal States in 1853. The most important of these was that negotiated in 1851 by Palmerston and the Sardinian minister in London, Emanuele d'Azeglio. Under Cavour, who became prime minister in 1852, Sardinia maintained a comparatively liberal commercial policy, and passed on the tradition of a qualified free trade to the kingdom of Italy in 1861.

In a sense the central event in the history of free trade in Europe was the Commercial Treaty negotiated by Richard Cobden and Michel Chevalier, one of Napoleon III's counsellors of state, and signed on 23 January 1860. The two men who eventually signed the treaty had been very largely responsible for it, since each had influenced his government in favour of the agreement. Chevalier's background makes an interesting contrast with Cobden's. Born in 1806, Chevalier started his career as a mining engineer. After the July Revolution he was converted to the ideas of Saint-Simon, and in 1832 was imprisoned for a year for Saint-Simonian activities. But he secured the protection of Thiers and was reprieved after six months. Thiers sent him to the U.S.A. to study methods of communication, and Chevalier subsequently made his name by writings on North America. In 1836 he was sent to England to study the industrial depression, and he thereafter combined academic, bureaucratic and political careers, securing a seat in the assembly. He had wholly abandoned his early socialist ideas and in 1848 attacked Louis Blanc's social policies.[1] From the beginning of the Second Empire he was patronized by Napoleon III, and had been a member of the commission which organized the Paris Exhibition of 1855. He shared with Cobden an admiration for the U.S.A. and a fervent belief in free trade. In this he was unlike most Frenchmen, with whom protection was popular. Only the shipping firms of Bordeaux, Marseilles and Le Havre and the silk merchants of Lyons had agitated for free trade.

Economic developments were initially kind to Napoleon III, as the 1850s witnessed the considerable industrial boom, ended only by the coincidence of the commercial crisis which started in 1857 and the war of 1859. Napoleon decided to end the slump by lowering tariffs and importing British, Belgian and German manufactured goods, to encourage French industrialists to seek markets abroad themselves and to modernize their plants. The most immediate and tangible aims of the French in seeking a commercial treaty with England were to secure a reduction of British duties on silk and wine, two of France's biggest exports. For this, Chevalier advised, it would be worth opening the French market to British manufactured goods. In 1859 Cobden persuaded Palmerston, the prime minister, and Gladstone, the chancellor of the exchequer, to let him visit Paris to make tentative and semi-official approaches, while Chevalier persuaded Napoleon to let him negotiate with the Englishman. Napoleon, typically, kept the negotiations a close secret, not only from the public, but from his own ministers. Just as the French foreign minister sometimes knew as little about the moves in his emperor's foreign policy as anyone in Paris, so, in 1859, was Napoleon's minister of finance wholly in the dark about the most important move in French commercial policy since Waterloo.

The treaty limited French import duties on British goods to 30 per cent of their value for the next four years, and thereafter to 25 per cent. Subsequent supplementary conventions signed on 12 October and 16 November 1860 fixed French duties at rates as low as 10 per cent. The British government, for its part, scrapped the duties on silk altogether, and greatly reduced those on wines and spirits. By Gladstone's 1860 budget the changes were made universal for imports of silk and wines from all countries, but France in practice had few rivals. The French reductions of duties, however, were valid only for British exports, and so encouraged other countries to reach commercial agreements with France. The 1860 treaty seemed to hold out great promise

[1] See above, p. 61.

to the British textile industry, but events prevented the full and immediate exploitation of it. The American Civil War intervened. The North's blockade of Southern ports prevented the raw cotton from reaching Lancashire, and spread the misery of the cotton famine. The British cotton industry no longer needed new markets, and in the event —due to coincidences which Cobden could not have foreseen—France gained more from the treaty than Britain. The export of British manufactured goods to France went up over the period 1860 to 1865, but then remained stationary or fell, while the exports of French silks and wines to Britain rose steeply after 1860, during years when conditions for both industries happened to be favourable.

The Cobden Treaty, like other commercial treaties of the period, included a 'most favoured nation' clause, by which any good terms granted by either power subsequently to other nations would be automatically extended to the other partner. The Belgian government signed further commercial treaties with both France and Britain in the course of the 1860s, and in 1863 the Scheldt was declared open to free trade. Meanwhile Napoleon III had turned his attention to the *Zollverein*, after Britain perhaps already the most important economic unit in Europe. Just two days after the signing of the treaty with England, Napoleon III approached the Prussian government, but at first received little encouragement. His motive was primarily political: an attempt to prevent an Austro-Prussian alignment, though he was now a convinced advocate of free trade. Hard negotiations with Prussia continued for two years, and a treaty was finally signed on 29 March 1862, six months before Bismarck came into office. Tariffs were lowered by both countries. French imports from the *Zollverein* would now have to pay no more than those from Britain or Belgium. This meant in particular that the tariffs on imported iron and textiles from Germany would be appreciably lower than in the past. Duties on wine and silk imported by the *Zollverein* countries from France would in return also be much lighter.

Besides the industrialized countries of the west, other parts of Europe and, in particular, Russia and the Scandinavian countries, moved towards free trade in the 1860s. But in the last decade of the period the trend was sharply reversed. Confidence in free trade to a great extent depends upon confidence in international peace. The Franco-Prussian war in 1870 destroyed confidence in the possibility of securing permanent peace in Europe, and the emergence of the new nation states of Italy and Germany helped to discourage the feeling of cooperation and interdependence between nations—a feeling so necessary to free trade. The increasing cost of military and naval armaments also encouraged ministers of finance to secure revenue by every possible means, including the age-old one of a tariff on imports. But the most direct and compelling economic cause for a return to protection in the 1870s was the overwhelming agricultural competition from America, and the collapse of the boom in 1873. One by one the European states again returned to high tariffs. Thiers, as President of the young Third Republic in France, went back to protection in 1871, and Bismarck reimposed tariffs on both agricultural and industrial imports after 1878 in Germany. Only in Britain was no attempt made to return to a system of protection for agriculture. What Cobden had called a 'tax on bread' was never to return. Farming was no longer so vital a part of the British economy that it could command political support. From the depression of 1873 British agriculture never fully recovered.

Economic crises at ever decreasing intervals occurred throughout the period. In England there were bad business crises in 1836, 1847, 1857, 1866 and 1873, all of them shared to some extent by other European countries. Already in 1836 the American economy played its part in causing the depression. The sudden end of a boom in the U.S.A. meant that many British exporters there could not collect debts. Credit became difficult to obtain in Europe, and the depression of the period 1838–41 ensued. Business improved in 1842, and for five years there was comparative prosperity, accompanied by the railway mania. Over-speculation in the railways, followed by a financial panic and accompanied by bad harvests in 1845 and 1846 brought grave economic crisis in 1847 in western and central Europe generally, and contributed to the revolutions of 1848. The quick economic recovery after 1848 owed much to developments in America as far as Britain was concerned. Gold rushes and the building of American railways stimulated the British economy, only to lead again to an exaggerated boom and the inevitable crash in 1857. Yet again recovery was quick, but yet again events in the U.S.A. —this time the Civil War—contributed to a crash, though the depression of 1866 was less a European than an English phenomenon, and was mainly the direct result of the cotton famine. After the last recession of the period, that of 1873, recovery was less quick, because American agricultural competition was permanent, and after the construction of the railway systems had been completed, no comparable opportunity for large-scale investment took its place. Economic historians are by no means sure of the precise causes of the trade fluctuations in the period. A general loss of confidence among investors is to some extent a psychological phenomenon and so defies precise definition in statistical terms. But it is clear that conditions in America were already influencing British trade at the beginning of the period, and Britain remained throughout the period the chief trading power in Europe.

Britain also remained the world's banker and the main source of foreign capital throughout the period. Especially to North and South America was there a great migration of British capital. About 1850 France, too, began to export capital, but on a much smaller scale. Increasingly until 1914 French capital flowed to eastern Europe, mostly in the form of government loans. But, like Britain, France invested in South America and the U.S.A. to a greater extent than in her own colonies. In the 1860s and 1870s the Germans too began to invest in American railways, but the rapidly expanding industries of Germany soaked up most surplus capital at home. While Britain remained the most important centre of commercial and financial activity in Europe, it was in Germany that the most striking economic change took place between 1830 and 1880. In the 1830s and 1840s Germany was a primitive region in economic terms. The towns did not have modern shopping centres of the kind which already existed in Britain and France; Germans bought domestic products only at the weekly market, and foreign products, if at all, at an annual fair. Yet by 1880 the medieval pattern of commercial life in Germany had disappeared and the apparatus of a growing industrial power had sprung into existence.

VI

Social Conditions

So diverse were the changes in the social conditions of Europeans in the nineteenth century that few generalizations can be made, without their being hedged around by so many qualifying phrases that all significance is squeezed out of them. It can, however, be said that a large middle class in western and central Europe enjoyed a rise in their standard of living very much greater than anything experienced since the middle ages in a period of comparable length. Concerning the mass of the population no such easy conclusion can be reached. For the rural population in many parts of western and central Europe standards were probably slowly rising, but this was less evidently true of eastern Europe, and in the industrial towns of Britain, France, Germany and Belgium a

BIBLIOGRAPHY. The general works of economic history mentioned for chapter IV are again relevant here. Studies concerned specifically with social conditions are usually either out of date or politically prejudiced. The scholarly treatment of social conditions in nineteenth-century Naples provided by Domenico Demarco, *Il crollo del regno delle Due Sicilie. La Struttura sociale* (Naples, 1960) may be cited as a model of the treatment needed for other parts of the world in the period. *Contrasts in Emerging Societies*, edited by Doreen Warriner, and already cited for the previous chapter, gives several vivid impressions of the conditions of the peasants of the Balkans. So far as the industrial workers are concerned, much work has been done on England, but mainly for the earlier part of the period. Contemporary accounts, and the use made of them and of surviving statistics by historians, are discussed in chapter I (pp. 10–12) but three key articles must be mentioned here. An optimistic interpretation of conditions in urban England at the beginning of the period is given by T. S. Ashton, 'The Standard of Life of Workers in England', *Journal of Economic History Supplement* (1949). A pessimistic answer is contained in E. J. Hobsbawm, 'The British Standard of Living, 1790–1850', *Economic History Review* (1957), and a balanced summary of the various arguments is made by A. J. Taylor, 'Progress and Poverty in Britain, 1780–1850: a Reappraisal', *History* (February, 1960). Of conditions in the British factories and legislation to improve them, J. T. Ward, *The Factory System, 1830–1855* (London, 1962) gives a good, straight account, fully based on the sources. An introduction to conditions in Germany is provided new kind of hardship was experienced among the urban workers, especially in the first twenty years of the period. Because the workers in factories and mines were a comparatively novel phenomenon, more attention was paid to their conditions by public and private enquirers than was paid to those of the poorer rural classes, though the peasants still greatly outnumbered the industrial workers. The available evidence—literary or statistical—on the peasants merely shows how greatly their conditions varied from one region to another. In France the peasants almost certainly shared in a general rise of the standard of living from the 1840s. Food consumption per head of population grew, and the improvement in the quality of food increased even more strikingly. Bread was no longer made from a mixture of all kinds of coarse cereals and vegetables, but was more often white, and the consumers in the towns could choose from different kinds and prices. The actual amount of bread consumed per head of population tended to decline, but only because other foods—notably the potato—became available. Not only did the consumption of meat increase after the

by Jurgen Kuczynski, *A Short History of Labour Conditions in Germany 1800 to the Present Day* (London, 1945). The book has interesting statistical tables and makes good use of the contemporary pamphlet literature in Germany, but it has an exaggerated Marxist standpoint and reaches eccentric political conclusions. An enquiry into the history of the working class had already started at the turn of the nineteenth and twentieth centuries, and two works of this period may be mentioned: Guenther K. Anton, *Geschichte der preussischen Fabrikgesetzgebung bis zu ihrer Aufnahme durch die Reichsgewerbeordnung* (Leipzig, 1891; new edition, Berlin, 1953), and E. Levasseur, *Histoire des classes ouvrières et de l'industrie en France 1789-1870* (Paris, 2 vols., 1903-4). A rather more recent and scholarly study is: E. Dolléans, *Histoire du mouvement ouvrier, 1830-1871* (Paris, 2 vols., 1936-39), while yet more recently a vivid and comprehensive account of conditions in one French industrial centre during the Second Empire has been provided by Pierre Pierrard, *La vie ouvrière à Lille sous le Second Empire* (Paris, 1965). Public health and the early preoccupations of British governments concerning it are dealt with in W. M. Frazer, *A History of English Public Health 1834-1939* (London, 1950), and, more specifically, in R. A. Lewis, *Edwin Chadwick and the Public Health Movement 1832-1854* (London, 1952). On trade unionism in Great Britain a classic is Sidney and Beatrice Webb, *The History of Trade Unionism* (London, 1894). Many volumes on trade unions have been published since then, but for the nineteenth century the Webbs' volume remains the most important. For a dramatic chapter in the history of labour in France a scholarly and sympathetic study is D. C. McKay, *The National Workshops* (Cambridge, Mass., 1933). For the lighter theme of the life of the middle class, a French series deserves notice: R. Burnand, *La vie quotidienne en France en 1830* (Paris, 1943) and *La vie quotidienne en France de 1870 à 1900* (Paris, 1947), and M. Allen, *La vie quotidienne sous le Second Empire* (Paris, 1947).

middle of the century, but French butchers were supplied with meat of better quality. The consumption of both wine and sugar increased strikingly over the period. Frenchmen drank less than 50 litres of wine per head of population in 1840; in the mid-1870s—just before the onset of phylloxera—they were drinking nearly 90 litres per head each year. From 1840 to 1880 the consumption of sugar per person more than doubled.[1] The German peasant had a less varied diet than the French peasant: he was more dependent on the potato, and drank less wine and more cheap spirits, spirits which were often distilled by his own landlord or employer. The German countryside was generally poorer: population was expanding so quickly that industrialization and agricultural improvement could not provide sufficient employment. Especially in the decades before intensive industrialization started there was considerable distress in the rural areas. Over a million Germans emigrated to the U.S.A. between 1830 and 1880, a large number of them during the acute depression before 1848. Famine conditions existed temporarily when the potato harvest failed in 1845.

Suffering worse hardships than the German peasants, and probably, with the Irish, the most wretched class in western Europe, were the agricultural workers of southern Italy and Sicily. When Garibaldi and his Thousand, most of them from the educated classes of Italians, landed in Sicily in 1860, they were appalled and astonished to find young boys dressed in skins like savages. Under the Bourbons the peasants of the Neapolitan kingdom were not only impoverished, but were becoming more so. Nowhere was so dense a population living on more slender natural resources. In the Province of Terra d'Otranto in 1835 one in thirteen of the population lived by begging.[2] The political unification of Italy in 1861 did not benefit the poor peasants of the south. It merely added to the perennial hardships of acute poverty, the dangers of a prolonged warfare between Bourbonist bandits and the new authority. To find standards as low as those of southern Italy the social historian must turn to the hungry millions of Russia.

In the mid-nineteenth century, of Russia's population of sixty millions, more than three-quarters were peasants. In 1830 the peasants of Russia thus accounted for nearly a fifth of the total population of Europe. Most of them were serfs until 1861, and some twenty millions of them

[1] Charles Morazé, *La France bourgeoise XVIIIe–XXe siècles* (Paris, 1946), pp. 44–7
[2] Domenico Demarco, *Il crollo del regno delle Due Sicilie. La struttura sociale* (Naples, 1960).

were owned or employed by the state. The serfs cultivated part of the land for their own use, and paid for it with their own labour. Although the landlord's legal jurisdiction over his serfs was nowhere clearly defined, he had the customary right of flogging them, sending them off to the army or on forced labour in Siberia. Alexander II's emancipation decree of 1861 has been noticed in two other contexts.[1] Most of the emancipated peasants remained on the land where their material conditions deteriorated. Their debts rose, partly because of the crushing burden of their redemption payments, partly because of the land hunger caused by the increasing population. The peasant's debt had a paradoxical effect: he produced enough grain to feed himself, and was yet starving. The grain had to be sold for export to western Europe in order to keep the wretched peasant out of a debtor's prison. Over the period from about 1800 to 1880 the death rate in Russia was actually rising— from about 25 to 35 per thousand. In many respects the peasants of Russia were more like those of Asia than those of western Europe.

A contemporary impression of a village eighty miles from Moscow in the 1860s shows to the full the remoteness and primitiveness of the peasant's life. Each family occupied a small wooden hut, some sixteen feet across, with a straw roof. A clay construction served both as a stove for heating and as a bed for some of the family, but most of the family slept on straw on the floor. Often there was no chimney; the smoke filled the room, before escaping from a hole in the roof, as it did in Stone Age dwellings. Yet the Russian peasant thought of himself as civilized, and in certain respects he shared the social habits of western Europe. If he ate on clay or wooden dishes and used a simple splinter of wood for a fork, he was also the owner of china dishes which could be used on special occasions. Nor did he look like a savage. The women made the family's clothes and wore dresses of printed linen, the men wearing blue linen or hemp trousers and red shirts on holidays. In the cold weather the men's jackets, made of untanned sheepskin, must have given them a more primitive appearance, as must their sandals, which were made of the bark of birch trees. Once every ten years or so the peasants would get themselves a pair of leather boots to wear on holidays, and in the 1870s the village started to grow flax with which felt boots could be made. The glory of the Russian household at a later period was the samovar, but samovars were not used by peasants until the 1870s when tea was introduced as a luxury, for special occasions. The peasants lived mainly on rye bread, cabbage soup, turnips, peas and porridge. Like the

[1] See above, p. 92, and below, pp. 277–8.

poor all over Europe they ate meat rarely. They knew that fish, and such delicacies as biscuits, were eaten by the rich: it was unlikely that they would ever be able to afford them themselves. And this particular village was, in all probability, richer than many villages in remoter areas.[1]

The peasants in the Habsburg Monarchy were alternately oppressed by their landlords, and protected by the paternal government in Vienna. Since the days of Maria Theresa and Joseph II, government regulations had given the Austrian peasant a measure of economic security, in the sense that his tax liability was firmly fixed by law and his land could not be expropriated. In this his conditions contrasted sharply with those of the peasant of the Ottoman Empire, from whom sums of tribute might be suddenly demanded, or with the Irish peasant for whom the sudden deprivation of his land was an all too common experience. Throughout the Habsburg Monarchy the law guaranteed the peasant a share of the land he farmed, even before emancipation in 1848, and limited the amount of labour the landowner could exact from him. The law applied equally, of course, to the peasant of Hungary, though the Hungarian nobles always tried to exact an illegal amount of labour from their peasants, and the farther away from Vienna the estate was, the less protection the peasant was likely to get from the government.

The peasants in the remote parts of the empire—in Transylvania or Croatia—were inevitably more oppressed. The peasants of the Ottoman Empire suffered from the irregular and crushing taxation system, though in Bulgaria there were pockets of agricultural prosperity caused by the proximity of the great market of Constantinople. Specialized Bulgarian agricultural occupations were the cultivation of tobacco, of rice, and of roses for perfume. The peasants of Serbia were perhaps as well off as any other inhabitants of the Balkans. Though Serbia did not secure full legal independence until 1878, she was in most respects autonomous throughout the period, and already in 1830 the land was divided into small farms owned by the native Serbs. The average Serb family lived a primitive existence, but was rarely hungry and had living conditions which were almost certainly better than those of Russian or Irish peasants, and probably better than those of the English or German rural labourer. Thus in the mountainous regions the Serb peasant had a house with stone foundations, roofed with shingles. Typically the peasant anywhere in Serbia ate beans, onions and bread made from maize, and in

[1] Sir John Maynard, *Russia in Flux* (London, 1941), p. 30 *et seq.* Other case studies of Russian family life were made by one of the founders of sociology, Frédéric Le Play, and published in his *Les ouvriers européens* (Paris, 1879).

winter, sauerkraut and fat bacon, in summer, milk, cheese and eggs. He drank a weak brandy made from plums. On special occasions he drank wine, and ate roast lamb or pork.[1] Those parts of the Balkans which had been emancipated from the Ottoman Empire thus had an economy based on the very small farm owned by the peasant himself. Generally speaking this kind of economy offered a tolerable, if simple, standard of living, but one which did not have the factors necessary for economic growth. On the other hand rural Hungary in the mid-nineteenth century consisted mainly of large estates, on which landless peasants suffered from wretched conditions and were exploited by the landowner, but from which a faster economic growth could ultimately be expected, once capital and the other factors needed for growth became available.

The pattern of conditions in eastern Europe was thus by no means a simple one. Nor did it follow that in countries of rapid economic growth conditions for the rural community were improving. In Great Britain agricultural workers were experiencing grim conditions for the first twenty years of the period, a marked improvement from about 1850 to the 1870s, and then a return to depression again, though never again to the poverty of the first half of the century. Between 1815 and 1830 large numbers of English smallholders became day labourers and wage earners as a result of the divorce between craftwork and agricultural work. The movement from cottage industry to the factories deprived those workers who stayed on the land of a part of their livelihood. Thus at a time when British agriculture as a whole was protected by the Corn Laws and the big landowners were still securing a large income from the land, pauperism was increasing among the agricultural labourers. Wages fell and great sums were spent by the parish on poor relief. Women and children became employed increasingly on the land as in the towns. The new Poor Law of 1834 was not universally enforced, and did not appreciably improve conditions even outside the workhouse.[2] Poverty in the English countryside during the first twenty years of the period was responsible for the high level of crime. The existence of plentiful grouse and partridge, reared by the landowner for sport, was a considerable incentive to poaching. When the poacher and his family were sufficiently hungry, even the stiff sentences of imprisonment and transportation usually

---

[1] From contemporary observations of the Serbian writer, Vuk Karadžić, in *Contrasts in Emerging Societies*, pp. 297–9.

[2] See below, p. 130.

imposed did not act as a deterrent. Widespread poaching was only the most practical of several forms of unrest on the English countryside in the 1830s and 1840s. Incoherent rural disturbances often drew anxious comment in Parliament. At the time of the Reform Bill crisis, in 1830–32, there were outbreaks of arson, and these recurred in bad periods for the next fifteen years. In Wales there were fewer day labourers on the land and more small tenant farmers than in England, though in the early years of the period no fewer grievances. The Welsh farmers agitated against toll houses on the turnpike roads, which made it expensive for them to reach larger markets, and against the 1834 Poor Law. In 1843 there were outbreaks of violence against the toll houses. Bands of men blackened their faces, disguised themselves in women's clothes, and destroyed toll gates and the houses of toll-keepers.[1]

Agricultural workers in England as a percentage of the total population declined throughout the nineteenth century, but the actual numbers remained remarkably constant for the twenty years of prosperity— 965,514 in 1851 and 962,348 in 1871. Only after the depression in the early 1870s did they start to decline, falling to 870,798 in 1881 and continuing to fall thereafter. Wages in this case confirm other evidence concerning conditions. The farm worker's wage fell from 1830 to about 1850, then rose until 1872, and then declined again.[2] There can be little doubt that the workers on the land shared in the prosperity of their employers from 1850 to 1872. Pauperism at last diminished, and although the poacher and his complement, the armed gamekeeper, remained constant features of the countryside, the widespread crime of the depressed period 1815 to 1850 disappeared.

Far more numerous than the agricultural labourers of England and living in a very different type of community were those of Ireland. The living conditions of the Irish peasants were no better than those of the Russians. They, too, lived in tiny, one-roomed cabins. The Irishman's hut was made of mud, stood only four or five feet high, and was without windows, chimney or furniture. The only light and heat both came from a turf fire. Usually the pigs and fowls occupied the same huts as their owners. In many parts of Ireland bread and green vegetables were unknown, so that the potato formed the peasant's only diet. Skimmed milk and sometimes only water and pepper served as a drink. The Irishman's

---

[1] David Williams, *The Rebecca Riots* (University of Wales, 1955).
[2] For very precise figures relating to the various regions of England, see Lord Ernle, *English Farming Past and Present* (London, revised edition, 1961, Appendix IX).

problem before the famine was simply to secure enough land to live on. Over-population kept the price of land very high, and the rents very much higher than in England. In 1836 out of a population of over eight million, no fewer than 2,385,000 received public or private poor relief.[1] Throughout the 1830s the potato crop failed on several occasions in the west of Ireland, resulting in famine. A foretaste of the Great Famine of 1845–47 was experienced all over Ireland in 1839. The Great Famine itself is an important event in the history of the United Kingdom and must be considered in that context.[2] Although the population of Ireland was reduced to a half by the famine, conditions for the individual peasant who remained did not noticeably improve. The landowners converted much of their land to pasture, which brought them good returns, but did not support many labourers. Towards the end of the period rents fell as a result of Gladstone's legislation, but the struggle for the land remained the basic issue in Ireland, only partly obscured by a growing movement of nationalist revolt.

While in Ireland the standard of living remained consistently low, as it did in the Highlands of Scotland, in urban England it fluctuated dramatically, depending upon the trade cycle and its effect on the rate of unemployment. The novels of Mrs Gaskell illustrate more vividly than any statistics the sudden change which could be caused in the 1840s in the life of a worker in Manchester by even a short spell of unemployment. When times were good in the cotton industry the worker would at least earn a living wage. If the picture provided by *Mary Barton* is a true one—and there is no reason to suppose that it is not—a worker could afford to take a day off in the spring to walk with his family out in the fields, which were not yet beyond walking distance from Manchester. If they ran into a family of friends they could invite them home for tea, and could afford to make special purchases for the occasion—purchases not only of extra bread and tea, but of milk, eggs, and a bottle of rum 'to warm the tea'. The cottage in which they lived would be small, but not devoid of comforts. If anything, it would be overcrowded with cheap furniture. All this would change with appalling suddenness if the head of the family lost his job during a period of depression. The furniture and any available personal possession would be pawned to pay for food. First the adult members of the family would accept hunger, and then the children also would be forced to go without food. Opium, which was

[1] *Third Report of the Commissioners for Enquiry into the Conditions of the Poorer Classes in Ireland*, 1836, p. 5.
[2] See below, pp. 191–2.

cheap, would help the men forget their pathetic surroundings, and stop the screaming of the smaller children by giving them some hours of sound sleep. Malnutrition would very probably lead to one of the diseases which are the inevitable companions of famine. A decline in living standards on this scale was caused by outbursts of unemployment on several occasions in the first twenty years of the period, the two worst occasions being 1830–31 and 1842. In Bolton, compared with the 8,124 men employed in the mills in 1836, only 3,063 were employed in 1842, and figures for smaller occupation groups are even more striking: 120 bricklayers employed in 1836, only 16 in 1842; 150 carpenters in 1836, only 24 in 1842.[1] Since the population was rising quickly in these years, it is clear that a considerable majority of the inhabitants of Bolton—and almost certainly of Lancashire as a whole—was unemployed in 1842. And the textile factories still accounted for the largest industrial group in England. The agricultural labourers formed the largest single social group, the domestic servants the second largest, but the textile workers came third. The physical wellbeing of this considerable section of the people of England was very poor. Disease increased with the growth of the new industrial towns. Typhus and dysentery were expected in the hot months. Many were killed by the cholera epidemics of 1831–32 and 1848 all over western and central Europe, but town-dwellers suffered more heavily than country-dwellers. In Manchester the expectation of life at birth in the 1840s was only twenty-four years.[2] The habit prevalent among the workers of Lancashire of taking cheap opium is mentioned not only in the novels of Mrs Gaskell, but in a very different kind of literary source. Thomas De Quincey, in the preface of his 1821 edition of the *Confessions of an English Opium-Eater*, had observed that many more people took opium than was commonly realized, and that on a visit to Manchester he had been told by 'several cotton manufacturers' that their workmen were acquiring the habit of taking opium, which was a cheaper way of getting intoxicated than by drinking ale or spirits, and so very popular in a time of low wages. De Quincey did not believe that these proletarian opium-eaters would readily go back to beer even if the times were to improve.

Only after 1850 did conditions in industrial Britain change for the

---

[1] H. Ashworth, 'Statistics of the Present Depression of Trade in Britain', *Journal of the Statistical Society*, v (1842), p. 74, quoted by E. J. Hobsbawm, 'The British Standard of Living, 1790–1850', *Economic History Review* (1957).

[2] William Ashworth, *A Short History of the International Economy* (London, 1952), p. 107.

better. Surveys made at the end of the period suggest that wages and living standards generally among the workers rose from 1850 to 1875. But for the first twenty years of the period statistics give a confusing and incomplete picture which sometimes seems to clash with all the contemporary accounts and literary evidence.[1] The standard of living in terms of real wages was probably higher in 1850 than it had been in 1750, though this is a vexed question upon which a great deal of academic argument has been lavished. And if there was any improvement from 1800 to 1850, it was certainly much less than the improvement from 1750 to 1800.

The staple food of the workers in mid-nineteenth-century Britain was bread and potatoes. The somewhat unreliable evidence available suggests that bread consumption was actually declining, per head of population, until 1850, but the consumption of potatoes may have been increasing. For the consumption of meat the sources are more reliable, though by no means absolutely conclusive.[2] They indicate a change for the worse in the early years of the period. While meat consumption per head of population rose throughout the eighteenth century, from 1800 to 1840 it declined. As regards the consumption of milk, butter and eggs there are no complete statistics. The growth of London and the large towns in the industrial areas meant that perishable farm produce had to travel further to reach its market and prices in urban centres would consequently be higher, but the spread of the railways mitigated this factor, by making transport much easier and quicker. Grazing land was still comparatively near the centres of Manchester and Liverpool when the first railways were built, so that there was no significant time gap during which dairy produce would have been effectively unobtainable. It is reasonable to suppose, then, that milk remained available, but expensive. There is evidence in contemporary literature that the working class drank milk with their tea throughout the period. As regards green vegetables again there is no direct statistical evidence, but the argument regarding dairy produce again applies.

The most basic of all statistics—though not the least confusing—are those provided by the demographer.[3] Most demographers agree that the rise in population in the late eighteenth century can partly be explained by a decline in the death rate, which may well have fallen by 25 per cent

---

[1] For a fuller discussion of the relative values of different sources, see above, pp. 10–12.

[2] See above, p. 11.

[3] For a discussion of the significance of population figures, see above, pp. 11–12.

from 1780 to 1810. But from 1810 to 1840 there was an appreciable rise in the death rate in Britain, and a sharp rise in urban centres. Taken with the very low life expectancy in industrial areas already referred to for the 1840s, the rising mortality rate cannot be lightly laid aside or explained away. It constitutes the most damning piece of evidence against the industrial society of England in the early nineteenth century. After 1840 the death rate remained steady for a while, but in the second half of the period it was slowly declining. The improvement since 1850 has taken place because disease epidemics have become rarer and much less devastating, because standards of nourishment have slowly risen, because medical practice and hygiene have improved and infant mortality has fallen strikingly. All these factors, of course, are related and interdependent. Any attempt to generalize about the physical conditions of the workers before 1850 must, however, be misleading, unless strong emphasis is placed on the contrast between good times and bad times. In England during years like 1836, when there was much employment, the workers were perhaps more prosperous than they had ever been. But during years like 1842 they were as wretched as they had ever been, and memories of past prosperity only heightened the suffering.

On the continent conditions in the industrial areas before 1850 were in most respects as bad as they were in England, sometimes worse. They were very much worse in the years of the freak depression, 1846 and 1847. Conditions among the workers in France and Germany were probably grimmer in those years than they had been in England in 1842. What evidence there is suggests that the cost of living rose in Germany from 1820 to 1850, when industry had only just started to move from the home into the factory. But as in England there was a great deal of fluctuation, with the cost of living in 1846 and 1847 being very much higher than in any other year. Normally during a depression wages were low, but prices were also low. In 1846–47 in Germany prices were much higher than usual, wages much lower and unemployment more widespread. Wages seem to have remained about constant since 1830, but declined sharply in 1845. If these facts are taken together, there can hardly be surprise in discovering that working-class riots contributed to the revolutions of 1848. Wages varied enormously from one part of Germany to another, and from one industry to another. Certain general trends, however, can be recognized as following developments which had already taken place in England. Thus in the textile industry the initial move from cottage to factory, which had already taken place in England, brought a sharp rise in cash wages and an appreciable rise in real wages. The decline in wages experienced in England in the early part of the period did not occur in Germany until later. The iniquitous practice of the truck system, by which workers were paid in kind instead of in cash, was practised in England and Germany. Workers were often obliged to accept goods which they did not want, and which they then sold at a loss. Even when the British, Prussian and Saxon governments passed anti-truck laws, they were often disregarded by the employers.

The pamphleteers writing of conditions in Germany stress the prevalence of drunkenness, especially among female workers, to an even greater extent than do similar writers in England. Drunkenness among children was also common in Germany. It was partly due to the low price of spirits, though consumption of alcohol did not diminish when money was not available for food. Cheap spirits in Germany, like opium in England, gave short periods of comfort and forgetfulness during phases of unemployment. In times of fuller employment the German urban workers probably ate worse than their English counterparts. One report states that among the linen weavers of Silesia meat was eaten only at Easter, Whitsun and Christmas, as a great delicacy, and then about half a pound usually served for a family of five or six. The average German worker could not afford to include clothing in his normal budget. The same piece of clothing would have to serve, winter and summer, for several years at a stretch, until it fell from his back in rags. In this respect also the German workers fared less well than the workers of Lancashire or Yorkshire, where cotton clothes were very cheap. But the industrial workers of Europe as a whole were inadequately dressed in the winter, and in the centre of the continent, where there are greater extremes of temperature, they must have suffered considerably.

After 1860, if not earlier, conditions in Germany at last improved. Wages rose steeply, but, since the cost of living rose also, real wages rose only slightly, and still fluctuated, though not so drastically as they had done before 1850. In the 1860s widespread and intense poverty disappeared, though large pockets remained. In 1868 an article in an official Prussian review,[1] after concluding that conditions had improved since the 1840s, unintentionally painted a depressing picture of life in Silesia: workers in the county of Landeshut had barely sufficient income to buy food; clothes could be obtained only by begging; a typical family in the town of Greifenberg lived on potatoes, bread, coffee, herrings and a very little butter. Still in the mid-1860s, then, many German workers could

---

[1] L. Jacobi in *Zeitschrift des Koeniglich Preussischen Statistischen Bureaus*, 1868, cited by Kuczynski, *op. cit.*

not afford meat or sugar, though their diet was a little more varied than that of the poor in most parts of Europe twenty years earlier. Silesia, anyhow, did not compare favourably with other parts of Germany where conditions in the age of Bismarck were appreciably better than they had ever been.

In France the working class had contributed to the revolution of 1830. Most workers were probably disappointed when no republic emerged, and still more antagonized against the July Monarchy when it became clear that it had little sympathy for them. The revolution was followed immediately by a depression in which the workers in the silk industry in Lyons in particular suffered from unemployment. Industries producing luxury goods suffered in an exaggerated form from a period of slump when middle-class spending was halted. Wages in Lyons at the start of the period were wretchedly low. The dispute over wages and an attempt by the workers to establish negotiating machinery ended in the armed rising of 1831 at Lyons, a rising which had to be suppressed by the army.[1] Again in 1834 there were five days of fighting in Lyons, and two days in Paris, between the workers and Louis-Philippe's troops. Although there was no armed rising of workers again until 1848, the revolts in the early 1830s were symptomatic of the bad relations between employers and workers under the July Monarchy. Conditions in French industrial areas during the reign were comparable with those in England or Germany. The familiar features—overcrowding and lack of hygiene in the slums, a high disease rate, the employment of women and children and phases of unemployment—characterized the period when the first large factories were being opened. The cholera epidemic struck France in 1831 and 1832, killing 18,400 people in Paris in six months, and generally affecting the urban areas more terribly than the countryside.[2] In the most densely populated areas the funeral arrangements broke down. Bodies were left unburied on doorsteps, waiting to be collected. Tuberculosis, too, was more prevalent in the towns than in the country, and was becoming more common throughout the 1830s and 1840s. Habitual drunkenness was a characteristic of the industrial workers, who drank *eau de vie* rather than wine, which remained the drink of the French peasant. In France, as in Germany, conditions reached the lowest point just before the revolution of 1848, and thereafter improved. On the whole the workers were more content under the Second Empire than under the July Monarchy, and with good reason.

[1] See below, p. 169.
[2] E. Levasseur, *Histoire des classes ouvrières en France* (Paris, 1867), vol. II, p. 9.

Besides Britain, Germany and France, a considerable industrial proletariat appeared in Belgium in the first part of the period. In independent Belgium in 1839 there were already some 30,000 workers employed in the coal mines alone. The general conditions of the Belgian workers were in some respects worse than elsewhere, in other respects better. Wages were lower than in England, and were spent to a surprising extent on drink and gambling, but housing conditions were appreciably better. In Belgium there had been no drift to the towns as there was in England. Industrialization had started in Britain long before the railways were built; it had been necessary for the workers to move into the urban centres, where building speculators had quickly constructed workers' houses, as cheaply as possible and with total disregard for hygiene, comfort or appearance. In Belgium, on the other hand, the building of the railways was one of the first aspects of industrialization. Railway fares were comparatively cheap, and the workers found it possible to live in the country and commute to work. There was therefore less overcrowding in Belgium than in Britain, but nowhere in Europe did employers feel any responsibility or show any concern for the often appalling housing conditions of the industrial workers. Living space near the factories and mines of England was almost as valuable as land in Ireland. From 1800 to 1850 rents in urban England rose. Domestic heating, on the other hand, became a little easier as the price of coal fell, though during times of depression in the 1830s and 1840s there sometimes arose the ironical situation in which men who had spent their lives'hacking at the coal face could not afford to buy enough coal to keep their families warm in the winter. In housing, as in everything else, conditions varied strikingly with the rotation of the business cycle. A family with employment might inhabit a tolerably comfortable cottage in good times, but when hit by unemployment were often obliged to move into a basement room without drainage or daylight.

Like coal, other domestic essentials became cheaper and more plentiful. Per head of population more soap and many more candles were produced in the first half of the century than in earlier times, and the production of cotton clothes in proportion to the population increased ten times from 1785 to 1840. In good times in the 1840s the workers of Sheffield and of the Northumberland and Durham coalfields could afford comfortable furniture and carpets on the floor. The English worker has usually had a tendency to acquire movable property rather than to spend money on a good diet. There is evidence that English workers in the mid-nineteenth century would sometimes have over-furnished homes and under-nourished bodies. The French, on the other hand, would retain virtually no possessions as long as food was short. The picture given in Zola's *L'Assommoir* of a worker's home in Paris under the Second Empire suggests that there would be nothing in the way of furniture beyond one or two scrappy and dilapidated objects.

Countless contemporary accounts describe the slums in all the larger cities of the British Isles. Bad slums could be found equally in London, Manchester, Liverpool, Leeds, Bristol, Glasgow, Edinburgh or Dublin. In London congestions of slums were notorious not only in the East End—in Stepney and Whitechapel, which were to remain traditionally poor areas in the twentieth century—but also near the rich quarters of the West End in areas which were later improved: in Bayswater, St Giles and even in King Charles Street, in the heart of Whitehall. Large areas of Dublin were perhaps poorer and filthier than anything else which could be found in the British Isles. In Scottish cities the houses of the poor were more like those of Paris and Lyons than English cities in one respect: whereas in England slums tended to be low clusters or rows of cottages of two storeys, in Scotland, as in France or Italy, they were more often of four, five or even six storeys. The total effect of insanitary and overcrowded conditions might thus be accentuated, even if the architectural effect would be less sordid. An impression of the slums in the Old Town of Edinburgh is given by a particularly lurid account in *The Artizan* in 1843:

> In this part of the town there are neither sewers nor any private conveniences whatever belonging to the dwellings; and hence the excrementitious and other refuse of at least 50,000 persons is, during the night, thrown into the gutters, causing (in spite of the scavengers' daily labours) an amount of solid filth and foetid exhalation disgusting to both sight and smell, as well as exceedingly prejudicial to health.[1]

Glasgow, Liverpool and the East End of London were typical of large ports, where housing conditions were particularly bad. Another example was Bristol, the scene of considerable working-class violence in 1831. Nearly six thousand workers' families were visited in Bristol in the late 1830s, and 46·8 per cent of them were found to be living in one room, and sometimes sharing this room with another family.[2] One large in-

[1] *The Artizan*, Oct. 1843, p. 230, col. 2, quoted in F. Engels, *The Condition of the Working Class in England in 1844, op. cit.*
[2] *Journal of the Statistical Society of London*, vol. 2 (1839–40), pp. 368 75, quoted by Engels, *op. cit.*

dustrial city in England with a slightly better housing record was Birmingham. Slum areas certainly existed in Birmingham, but there was less overcrowding, and disease epidemics were less devastating than in Manchester, Liverpool, or even nearby Wolverhampton. The comparatively good conditions in Birmingham were further improved in the 1870s when Joseph Chamberlain, the future colonial secretary, was mayor. Besides municipalizing water and gas supplies, Chamberlain carried through a big programme of slum clearance—the first of its kind —and laid out broad areas of parks and open spaces. But Birmingham was an exception even for the 1870s. Generally speaking the legacy of unplanned building in urban Britain from the early part of the period was to survive well into the twentieth century, until Hitler's bombs and a new attitude to town planning combined to abolish the worst of the slums.

In Germany as in England the really grim living conditions were experienced by the unemployed. So long as a man had work, however poorly he was paid, he could preserve tolerable conditions. For this reason the 1840s and 1850s in Germany supply examples of the most appalling living conditions, because in those years periods of depression led to stretches of widespread unemployment. In the earlier years— especially in the two decades before 1830—there had sometimes been an actual shortage of labour, and unemployment had been rare. But by the 1840s and 1850s those workers who were wholly or partially unemployed were sinking into a state of destitution. An observer of the towns of Silesia in the 1840s noted that living conditions were worse than in Prussian prisons. There were reports of as many as thirteen children and seven adults sharing a single room, and one writer, G. S. Liedtke, mentions that in Berlin in the 1830s he found 'five to seven' people sharing a makeshift wooden bed covered with straw and rags. The pamphleteers in Germany give very similar accounts to those provided by the parliamentary commissions in England: rooms whose floors are made uneven by the deposit of dirt on them, whose ceilings are so low that a tall man must stoop continually, and whose walls are streaming with moisture.

The poor quarters of the big French cities during the July Monarchy had one characteristic which made them yet more wretched than the newer cities of England: they had a larger population of permanent paupers in addition to the temporary unemployed. In England pauperism was a characteristic of the countryside as much as the towns in the 1830s; in France it was concentrated in the industrial areas, and especially in the north-east. The most terrible slums in France were found at Lille, though Mulhouse, Rouen and Amiens all suffered from areas of gross overcrowding.

The mere discomfort of having to live in a very confined space would have been less disagreeable if the authorities had made some attempt to provide adequate drainage and sewage. But in this respect nineteenth-century Europe was still at a more primitive stage than ancient Rome had been. No authorities, central or local, had adequate powers to enforce public hygiene. In England local government departments were beginning to acquire them, and in Russia after the 1860s the *zemstvos* could look after the public health of their own area, but in France, even under the Third Republic, the mayor had no such powers.

The reform in England came initially as a result of the energies of that extraordinary group of men who had accepted the ideas of Jeremy Bentham.[1] Edwin Chadwick (1800–90), a forbidding, uncompromising and efficient Benthamite, published his report on the *Sanitary Conditions of the Labouring Classes* in 1842. The report inspired the government to appoint a royal commission in 1843 to examine the health of towns, and the commission itself reported in 1845. By showing that the insanitary conditions of towns encouraged the spread of epidemics, the 1845 report frightened parliament into passing the Benthamite Act of 1848, which established a General Board of Health of three men, one of whom was Chadwick himself. The state was thus accepting responsibility for the health of the community, and in this it was unique in Europe. The General Board could establish local boards of health, though in practice it found that local vested interests limited or prevented its operation. Chadwick's aggressive manner antagonized everyone with whom he had to deal, and the General Board of Health was dissolved in 1858.

The brave attempt to diminish public squalor by state intervention had been premature. In a more modest way the City of London was at the same time dealing with its own problems on a local level. In 1848 the London Corporation appointed a Medical Officer of Health—the discreet and cultured Dr John Simon—who moved more cautiously than Chadwick to make the poor quarters of London more sanitary. The functions of the General Board of Health were incorporated with those of the Poor Law Commission in 1871, and transferred to the newly created Local Government Board, which was to operate until after the 1914 war, when the Ministry of Health was created. The whole movement of public health in England, in spite of errors and setbacks, was

[1] See above, pp. 51–3.

many years in advance of anything existing elsewhere in Europe. But in the great conglomerations of British slums the need for reform had been much greater.

Conditions inside the factories and mines were, of course, no better than those in the homes or on the uncleaned and unpaved back streets. The machines in the textile factories were not designed for the comfort of the worker. Deformities of one kind or another often resulted from the long hours of standing in one position of work. Often they were deformities of a comparatively mild kind, like bandy legs or flat feet, but often, too, they were more serious. A Leeds doctor in 1833 told a parliamentary commission that he had seen some 300 patients in his hospital suffering from distortions of the spine caused by too many hours of continuous standing. The worker in the coal mines had still more arduous conditions to contend with. The sheer unnatural physical exertion required by his job, the familiar lung complaints of the miner and the constant preoccupation with the danger of explosions aged him prematurely. If— as was probable—he had started work in the mine as a boy of eight or nine, his life as a mature man would be shortened at both ends, since puberty was usually delayed among miners, often by several years. Dr Southwood Smith in the famous *Report on the Employment of Children in Mines* of 1842 said that work in the mines 'protracts the age of childhood, and anticipates the period of old age, decrepitude and death'.

The length of the working day varied from one end of industrial Europe to the other, but it was almost invariably too long, not only for the health of the worker, but for the economic efficiency of the industry. In France under the July Monarchy it was sometimes as short as eight hours, but often as long as fifteen. In the south—even in Lyons—comparatively short days, of from eight to ten hours, were not unknown, but in the industrial north working conditions in this respect were very bad. In Amiens the working day was fourteen or fifteen hours long, excluding time for meals. In fact the workers usually spent some seventeen hours at work, including two hours for meals. It is interesting that even in this dark age the industrial workers allowed themselves longer for meals in France than in Britain or Germany. In the first decades of the nineteenth century the working day tended to increase all over western Europe, and was halted eventually only by government action. In Germany it continued to increase until about 1850. In the 1830s a working day of thirteen hours was common for men and women in Germany. As in

England, reports are common in Germany of men in their thirties whose carriage and features were already those of old men as a result of their long hours of labour.

The employment of women and children in factories and mines in the early nineteenth century, like the working day, increased in the first few decades. It then attracted a great deal of publicity, the consciences of some of the ruling class were shocked, and governments took steps in the middle of the century to remedy the situation. In Germany in 1816 about five times as many men as women were employed in the factories, which at that time were still, of course, very small ones. In 1850 there were only about three-and-a-half times as many men as women. German coal mines, on the other hand, unlike British mines, never employed more than a few women. In the German factories of the 1840s, 10 per cent of the workers were less than fourteen years old, according to official Prussian statistics, and in domestic industries child labour was used even more. In the linen industry in Silesia children aged four were employed.[1] Children were employed far less, however, towards the end of the period; conditions in the factories and mines in Germany, as elsewhere, improved, and, above all, the working day became much shorter. Only in one respect was there a surprising deterioration in Germany: fatal accidents in coal mines increased steadily from 1850 to 1870. From an average per thousand of 1·99 a year in the period 1852–1856, there was a rise to 3·09 in the period 1867–70. In view of the shortening hours of work there seems as yet no satisfactory explanation of the trend.

It was unlikely that conditions as inhuman as those existing in the factories and mines in the early part of the period would be allowed to continue indefinitely in civilized countries. But the difficulty faced by a parliament attempting to legislate to improve conditions, especially in the *laissez-faire* tradition of early Victorian Britain, was immense. The idea of the state interfering with the contract of employment was regarded with abhorrence. But a Factory Act had been passed as early as 1802 in England, and the Act of 1833 inaugurated the age of the factory inspector. It prevented the employment of children under nine; children from nine to thirteen were to work for no longer than forty-eight hours a week, and children from thirteen to eighteen for no longer than sixty-nine hours a week. Further factory legislation depended on the tireless agitation of a few individuals who did not have the support of either

[1] Alexander Schneer, *Ueber die Not der Leinenarbeiter in Schlesien und die Mittel, ihr abzuhelfen* (Berlin, 1844), quoted in Kuczynski, p. 27.

political party. Richard Oastler in the 1830s started a movement demanding a limitation of ten hours a day on all labour. But deservedly the most famous of all the philanthropists was a Tory nobleman and devout evangelical, Lord Ashley, later the seventh earl of Shaftesbury (1810–1885). Ashley took up the ten-hour movement, believing that it would be easier to enforce a limitation for all workers, rather than for women and children alone. There was much doubt as to whether the 1833 Act was being enforced. In the 1840s two further Acts were passed to mitigate the worst evils. The Coal Mines Act of 1842 was inspired by the grim account and pictorial illustrations provided by the *Report on the Employment of Children* already mentioned. The Act abolished entirely the practice of employing women and boys under ten below ground in the mines, and arranged for the appointment of inspectors to see that the law was enforced. The Factory Act of 1844 further regulated hours of work for women and children, limiting the employment of women to twelve hours and of children under thirteen to six and a half hours. It thus still fell well short of the demands for a ten-hour bill which was bitterly opposed by the liberal leaders, Cobden and Bright.

Cobden was in principle averse to parliamentary intervention in questions of labour. He believed that in practice children should be kept out of factories altogether until they were thirteen, but that the decision of the parent on the question should not be usurped by the government. He professed to believe that parents would not permit their children to endanger their health by working long hours. Working parents should not be 'suspected of the guilt of infanticide'. His advice to the working class as a whole was that they should become independent by saving the fare to America—£20 in the 1830s. The advice was unrealistic and hypocritical. Even when a worker had saved so large a sum as £20, he would still be very far from transporting himself, his wife and children to America and ensuring that they did not starve, before he found work on arriving there. Nor did Cobden want to see a shortage of labour in Lancashire as a result of mass emigration to America.

In sharp contrast to the arguments of the Manchester School, Ashley persisted with the ten-hour movement, which promised more sleep and better health to men who cared far more for these things than they did for a mirage of independence. He introduced an amendment to the 1844 Bill. Detailing the full horrors of female and child labour in the factories, he declared: 'We, in the height of our refinement, impose on the wives and daughters of England a burthen from which, at least during pregnancy, they would be exempted even in slave-holding states, and among

the Indians of America.'[1] He ended with a poignant peroration addressed
to the manufacturers: '. . . we fear not the increase of your political
power, nor envy your stupendous riches. . . . We ask but a slight relaxation of toil, a time to live, and a time to die. . . .' But Ashley's amendment was defeated on a subsequent reading. Three years passed before
his ten-hour movement succeeded. In 1847 he secured the support of
some of the more enlightened Whigs—among them Macaulay—and
many of the Protectionists who had their own grudge against the
government, and a ten-hour bill passed by substantial majorities. No
doubt many members of parliament felt that their vote had been
a wise one when, the next year, fifteen European capitals faced
revolution.

Some indication of the long working day in Germany in the 1830s
and 1840s is given by the modest nature of the demands of political
writers. 'Vincens Veritas', writing in 1848, urged the government of
Saxony to impose a twelve-hour working day, though J. C. Luechow
was already demanding a ten-hour day from the Prussian government.
Yet not until after the creation of the Empire in 1871 was even a twelve-
hour day imposed by law. Steps were taken, however, to limit the
exploitation of children. By a Prussian decree of 1839 no child under the
age of nine could be employed in a factory or mine, and no child under
the age of sixteen could be employed at night, or on Sunday, or for more
than ten hours a day. But since no inspectors were appointed until 1853,
the decree was not necessarily effective. Even so the absolute monarchy
of Prussia had proved itself more benevolent than the parliamentary
régimes of Belgium and Louis-Philippe's France where no such laws
existed.

Bavaria and Baden introduced legislation similar to the Prussian in
1840, but contemporary evidence suggests that none of these laws was
well observed. Exploitation of children continued in the 1840s. In 1853
a further reform was introduced in Prussia. Children under twelve could
no longer be employed regularly in factories, while children under fourteen could not work for more than six hours a day. Factory inspectors
were at last appointed, but, as in England, they had to operate against
the hostility both of the employers and the workers, who usually preferred their children to work and so to increase the family income.
Bavaria followed the example of Prussia for the second time by improving her legislation with regard to child labour again in 1854, and
Saxony followed suit in 1861. Germany's record in factory legislation

[1] *Hansard*, 1844, vol. LXXIII, par. 1100.

certainly compared well with France where there were still no factory inspectors in 1880.

If the state moved very slowly in its attempts to help the workers in the nineteenth century, it is also true that the workers themselves were slow to organize for collective action, and when they did so they found an unreasoning fear and hostility in the opposition of the ruling class. Great doubts as to the legality of trade unions are characteristic all over Europe in the period. In England the repeal of the Combination Laws in 1824 had in fact made trade unions legal. The first important figure in the history of trade unions was the early socialist Robert Owen. Born in 1771, Owen had been a manufacturer himself in Manchester from 1790 to 1800. He had then founded the model factory community of New Lanark to prove that it was not necessary for the new industrial proletariat to live in filth and ugliness. His second model community in New Harmony in the U.S.A. failed, and in 1828 he returned to England to indulge in less isolated working-class activity. After the Reform Act he became involved in the attempt to create a great single trade union of all the workers, called the Grand National Consolidated Trade Union. The Grand National was founded in February 1834. Several other similar, though smaller, working-class associations had been formed in the previous two or three years. The Grand National had an ambitious constitution with a Grand Council to meet twice a year in London. But it lasted for only six months in its original form. The four largest trade unions refused to sink their separate identities in the Grand National, and those groups and individuals who had joined disputed with each other.

The movement lacked both practical leaders and convinced followers. But 1834 was a year of many strikes and lock-outs. One incident above all others has been remembered for its tragic outcome. In the village of Tolpuddle in Dorset a group of workers had founded the Friendly Society of Agricultural Labourers in October 1833, to protect their interests by peaceful negotiation. In spite of the evidently pacific nature of the movement six leaders were arrested, convicted of administering oaths forbidden by law, and condemned to transportation to the convict settlement in Australia. Throughout the country employers and government agents threatened dismissal or legal action against unionists, with the result that the workers increasingly abandoned trade unionism and turned to the direct political action promised by the Chartist movement.[1] The first period of trade union activity was over.

[1] See below, pp. 183-4.

The second period may be said to have started with the foundation of the Amalgamated Society of Engineers in 1851. This association of dozens of small local unions negotiated with the employers, when possible, in a friendly manner, and helped workers when they were sick or had been sacked. Modern in appearance, the Amalgamated Society of Engineers did not practise masonic-type theatricals as earlier unions had done. Instead it tried to reassure the employers and appease the public. But the growth of the unions before the 1870s was not striking. There were a mere 100,000 members in the 1840s, and still only about a million in 1873. Gladstone's trade union Act of 1871 and Disraeli's Act of 1875 allowed trade unions to exert collective pressure for better standards, the 1871 Act allowing them to strike and the 1875 Act allowing them to post pickets during a strike. A new age of trade unionism in Britain was beginning, an age in which trade unionists would be more respected and less feared.

In France the history of trade unionism took a quite different, and at times more turbulent, path. The French industrial labourer inherited an unfavourable legal situation from Revolutionary and Napoleonic days. In 1791 associations between employers or workers had alike been declared illegal, and Napoleon's Civil Code laid down that in any dispute as to the wage which had been promised for a job, it was the employer's word which would be accepted. Not until late in the Second Empire was this clause repealed. The Code Napoleon also repeated the regulations against associations, forbidding groups of more than twenty men or any form of organizing or picketing a strike. In spite of the laws, the silk workers of Lyons in 1831 tried through their associations to persuade their employers to promise a minimum wage. Some employers were prepared to negotiate, but when others refused to accept any fixed figure, violence resulted. The workers took over control of the city, and the rising had to be suppressed by the army.[1]

After the revolt harsher legislation against trade unions was introduced. The *Devoir Mutuel*, organized by the Lyons silk weavers and numbering some 3,000, had helped to organize the revolt. The *Devoir Mutuel* had always been an illegal movement, but in 1834 a law prohibited association even of twenty men if they were linked in bigger unions. Yet the authorities did not interfere with a printers' union formed in Paris in 1839 for wage negotiations. Other skilled craftsmen also succeeded in organizing themselves under the July Monarchy, or in preserving organizations from earlier times. The ancient association of

[1] See also below, p. 169.

the *compagnonnage*, which had existed since the fifteenth century, survived until the mid-nineteenth century. Members of the *compagnonnage* were skilled craftsmen, who were unmarried and had not become masters, and who had to tour the country looking for work. Their full title was *Compagnons du Tour de France*, and their association ran its own inns or *pensions*, found them work, provided for them when they were ill and even black-listed bad employers. Most members of the *compagnonnages* had in the past been builders, though they had always included many kinds of craftsmen. Under the July Monarchy coopers and shoe-makers were allowed to join, but after 1848 the *compagnonnages* became in practice mainly an association of builders.

Trade unionism in the modern sense remained outlawed in France until the Second Empire. Napoleon III's cousin, Prince Jérome Bonaparte, interested himself in the fate of the workers, and acted as a liaison between them and the emperor. In 1862 a French workers' delegation visited London, with the blessings of the government, to discuss trade unionism with English workers. In 1864 Napoleon III, on the advice of the duc de Morny, president of the assembly, half-brother of the emperor and always a liberal influence, pushed through a law permitting association, and abolished that clause in the Code Napoleon which had specifically forbidden strikes. With the Third Republic the attitude of the government hardened. After the defeat of the Commune,[1] strong proletarian action was regarded more severely, but trade unions, for negotiating terms rather than taking industrial action, multiplied. The republican journalist, Barberet, helped to create pacific trade unions, under government protection, and by 1875 about 130 existed in Paris. Barberet, however, disapproved of strike action. Trade unions gave French workers very little real power in the 1870s.

In Germany the trade union movement in its modern form developed no sooner than in France. The ancient guilds were slowly abolished throughout the period, but in 1868 unions of skilled workers—right-wing politically—were formed through the initiative of Max Hirsch, the economist and journalist. Socialist unions grew up in Germany at about the same time, after legislation in Bismarck's North German Confederation had made them legal. In Belgium, too, trade unions were permitted to function effectively by law only in the 1860s, and were even then slow to develop.

[1] See below, p. 178.

The state in Europe had always been less inclined to let the working classes organize themselves than it had been to dole out charity to them when they were in desperate need of it. The concept of poor relief from the government was no new one in the nineteenth century. In England the Tudor poor relief, enlightened and humanitarian in its conception, had deteriorated in many cases into a mere subsidy for wages, paid out of the parish rates. It created paupers and kept wages low. The Poor Law Amendment Act of 1834 took the function away from the single parish, and erected the 'union'—a group of parishes, with one elected board supervised by central government control. Each union was to build a workhouse where relief would be given but only in return for hard labour. Outdoor relief would no longer be available. In the event not every union built a workhouse, and outdoor relief continued to be administered. But where the 1834 Act functioned it was much hated, as is apparent both from the novels of Dickens and from the ample political literature of the times. Men were segregated from their wives, and a distinctly penal spirit prevailed. Work was intended to be sufficiently arduous to deter anyone from entering until he had exhausted all possibilities of finding work outside.

The sad phenomenon of the rural pauper was much rarer in France than in England, and consequently no system of poor relief developed. But the revolutionary Second Republic in 1848 provided an example of a dramatically premature attempt to handle unemployment by direct state action. The establishment of the National Workshops, as the *Ateliers Nationaux* have always been called in English, was intended to recognize the 'right to work' by giving employment to the thousands who lacked it. The attempt and its abrupt abandonment led to the revolution of the June Days and so was a basic factor in the central political history of France.[1] In more normal times the Church in France had traditionally done the work of alms-giving, performed in England since the Reformation—until 1834, at least—by the justices of the peace in the parishes. Apart from the ill-fated attempt of the National Workshops, the French state did nothing until 1871, of a constructive nature, to help the destitute. The law of 1871 encouraged the departments to arrange for lunatics, orphans, the sick and aged to be given assistance. For the purpose, *bureaux de bienfaisance* were established, partly from charity and partly by local governments from taxes paid to them.

In Prussia the local governments undertook poor relief. The mayor of each town presided over a special committee which levied poor rates,

[1] See below, pp. 172–3.

and lodged paupers free of charge with households who would accept them. The treatment of the least fortunate members of society was thus appreciably more humanitarian in the most authoritarian of German states than in the *laissez-faire* atmosphere of early Victorian England.

Hobbes's often-quoted comment on the human condition was clearly relevant to the great majority of Europeans in the mid-nineteenth century, as it had been of all previous ages. But where the nineteenth century differed from earlier times was in the size of its middle class and the sharp rise in their standard of living. A large new section of society whose wealth was based, directly or indirectly, on industrialization, enjoyed a rising affluence. They could afford considerable expenditure on food, clothes and leisure. The European aristocracy had eaten more than was good for its health for several centuries; in the nineteenth century many more people could enjoy an excessive diet. For the French urban middle class a dinner of ten to fifteen courses was normal. In England the Victorian middle class, puritanical in other respects, regarded gluttony as the least of the sins, as Mrs Beeton's *Book of Household Management*, published in 1859, clearly indicates.

Fashions in women's clothes also reflected a growing prosperity, sometimes with unhappy aesthetic results. The classical lines of the First Empire and Restoration periods gave way to the lushness of a latter-day romanticism. Skirts became ever fuller, culminating, in mid-century, in the crinoline. A theme of endless wit at the hands of cartoonists and columnists, the crinoline accentuated the physical helplessness of women, but compensated by giving them an imposing presence. Male fashions became more austere as the period proceeded, but there was, of course, a large increase in the number of men who had to be correctly dressed according to the rigid dictates of convention.

The wealth of the middle class also gave them leisure time to kill. Lighter reading material, and in particular the novel, became available. Many new indoor games were invented. Card games were popular all over Europe. Idle provincial ladies obtained more intellectual excitement from a game of whist than from any other occupation. There was no parallel as yet of the twentieth-century mania for outdoor sport, but in western Europe horse race meetings were well attended. The leisure of the middle class was made possible by one of the largest groups of the working class—the domestic servants—who thus lived permanently in the upper-class world. Throughout the period they were one of the most numerous sections of society, as the vast numbers of servants' quarters

131

in countless rows of houses all over western Europe indicate. Compared with the factory worker or the poor peasant, domestic servants were well housed and fed. If 'going into service' involved a loss of freedom, and perhaps of pride, it brought with it better material conditions than those of the working class as a whole.

Prostitutes formed another very considerable section of urban society, especially in the capital cities. In London, the Haymarket and Regent Street were thronged with prostitutes after dark in the 1860s. In the rest of western Europe licensed brothels were the custom, and registered prostitutes were given regular, free medical examinations in an attempt to limit the spread of venereal disease. In Lille in 1841 there were forty-two registered brothels, their clean paint and bright blinds contrasting with the decrepit slums which surrounded them. When in Prussia in 1845 the licensed houses were closed the experiment was soon considered unsuccessful and abandoned in 1851. Only in England did governments prefer to believe that Evangelical missions could ultimately end prostitution, and that medical precautions represented collusion with vice.

In this case, as in many others, the ruling class on the continent was perhaps less hypocritical than that in England, but the middle class of nineteenth-century Europe as a whole suffered from the narrowness of outlook with which Matthew Arnold charged them in *Culture and Anarchy*. But with the narrowness of outlook went a single-mindedness necessary to create nation states which were strong and prosperous as units of international society. As the next chapter will show, they had also a sufficiently shrewd sense of self-interest to support governments who avoided long or catastrophic wars. But they had one blind spot: they showed too little concern for the welfare of the working masses whose labour was building the new industrial society.

VII

Diplomacy and Wars

The instruments of diplomacy

Whether the realistic terms of the 1815 treaties were chiefly responsible for the long period of peace that followed the settlement of Vienna can be doubted. But the fact must be noted that Europe had enjoyed fifteen

BIBLIOGRAPHY. There are a vast number of monographs and articles on nineteenth-century diplomatic history. A good, recent, general survey is the *Histoire des relations internationales* edited by P. Renouvin. Vols. V and VI (Paris, 1954–55) deal with this period. On the other hand there is very little on the diplomatic machinery itself, so that the first section of this chapter has had to be based mainly on primary sources. Reports of parliamentary commissions contain much material on the British diplomatic service, *Reports Committees* (1861), vol. VI, being the most useful. The Appendix to this report gives detailed information on the diplomatic services of other countries.

For the individual crises and questions considered in this chapter, Sir Charles Webster, *The Foreign Policy of Palmerston* (2 vols., London, 1951), is important for the 1830s. For the Eastern Question during the Mehemet Ali crisis and before the Crimean War, there are H. W. V. Temperley, *England and the Near East* (London, 1936), and a collection of articles, G. B. Henderson, *Crimean War Diplomacy* (Glasgow, 1947). A brilliant survey of the diplomatic context of the Italian Question in 1859 is Franco Valsecchi, *Europa 1859* in *Atti del XXXVIII Congresso di Storia del Risorgimento Italiano* (Rome, 1960). A more detailed study of the 1859 crisis is H. Hearder, 'La politica di Lord Malmesbury verso l'Italia, nella primavera del 1859' in the *Rassegna Storica del Risorgimento*, Jan.–March 1956. A sound recent study of Bismarck's early period is W. E. Mosse, *The European Powers and the German Question, 1848–1871* (Cambridge, 1958), while no substitute has yet replaced L. D. Steefel, *The Schleswig-Holstein Question* (Cambridge, Mass., 1932). A very short article with the basic bibliography is Frank Spencer, 'Bismarck and the Franco-Prussian War' in *History*, October 1955. For the Eastern Question at the end of the period, two from a number of good books should be mentioned: B. H. Sumner, *Russia and the Balkans, 1870–1880* (Oxford, 1937), and W. N. Medlicott, *The Congress of Berlin and After* (London, 1938). A reference work published in the nineteenth century is still invaluable: E. Hertslet, *The Map of Europe by Treaty* (4 vols., London, 1875–91), of which vols. II and III are relevant here.

years of uninterrupted peace by 1830. There had been brief military expeditions sent by one or other of the powers into Italy, Spain or Greece, to suppress or support revolutions there; Russia had waged a short war on Turkey in 1828; but there had been no major war, and no war of any kind between two or more great powers, since Waterloo. From 1830 to 1854 peace between the great powers continued. The Crimean War, which ended this long record, still did not disturb the peace of western Europe. It was drastically limited in space to a small peninsula, and the belligerent powers kept in constant touch with each other, through neutral Austria, until peace was patched up early in 1856. In 1859 war at last broke out in western Europe, but again it was a war strictly limited in time and place—to only two months of fighting, in north Italy. Bismarck's wars in 1864, 1866 and 1870 again never involved more than two great powers at once, and were, again, localized. The war of 1866 lasted for only seven weeks, and even the Franco-Prussian war of 1870 lasted for less than a year. In the final decade of the period an uneasy peace was continuously preserved; the powers settled their differences over the Eastern Question by negotiation, if sometimes reluctantly.

Perhaps no century since the fall of the Roman Empire has been so peaceful as that between 1815 and 1914. The widespread wars of the seventeenth and eighteenth centuries had culminated in the massive campaigns of Napoleon and his enemies. Nothing like this took place in nineteenth-century Europe. For once, the more terrible wars were fought outside Europe: the American Civil War of 1861–65; the South American war of 1865–70 which destroyed more than half the total population of Paraguay and left her with some six women for every one man. Compared with the horror of these two wars in America, the wars of the 1860s in Europe seem restrained and almost gentlemanly affairs.

Ability to settle international issues without resort to warfare was not, of course, entirely due to the skills or virtues of European rulers and their diplomats. But it is nevertheless true that the men who held power during the period were often more interested in the art of diplomacy than in governing effectively at home. Metternich, Palmerston and Bismarck were all diplomats first, and domestic rulers second. Nor did the military authorities often exert undue influence on government policy as they have done on occasions since 1880. It was essentially a civilian age, except, perhaps, in Prussia, and even in Prussia Bismarck kept his generals firmly under control. In more ways than one it was the heyday of diplomacy. Rulers were still, more often than not, landed nobles or aristocrats with a basic understanding of each other's aims and policies. But their means of communicating were greatly speeded up by the railway and the telegraph. Governments were more constantly in touch with each other than they had been in the past, and were more reluctant to make a sudden move to upset the *status quo* without preliminary consultation or negotiation with friends or potential enemies. The machinery of diplomacy functioned with only occasional lapses. Rarely had it worked so well before. Never has it worked so well since.

The diplomatic services of the European countries had become to some extent standardized in practice before the nineteenth century, but only in 1815 was the standardization made permanent by a formal treaty. Annex XVII of the Treaty of Vienna regulated 'the Rank and Precedence of Diplomatic Agents', and in so doing created a fixed international hierarchy of the permanent professional diplomats who were to conduct international affairs throughout the century. The regulation established three classes of 'diplomatic characters': ambassadors, ministers and *chargés d'affaires*. Within each class the diplomats would rank 'according to the date of the official notification of their arrival'.[1] In other words, there was to be order in the diplomatic world. The professional rank and length of service of the individual diplomat gave him precedence in a foreign capital no matter how weak the country he represented. Article VI of the Annex read: 'Ties of consanguinity or family alliances between Courts confer no rank on their Diplomatic Agents. The same rule also applies to political alliances.'[2] Here, then, was an international ruling accepted by the signatories of the Treaty of Vienna, and so, in effect, by all European nations—a ruling which took no account of the family compacts of the past, or of the close alliances of the future. The regulations for diplomacy laid down in 1815 may have been a very small path cut through the very large jungle of international relations, but the path proved a useful one throughout the nineteenth century.

The formal recognition of a common machinery for international negotiations could not alone, of course, keep the peace. It merely provided serviceable means for the peaceful settlement of disputes when no power was determined on war. In 1815 Metternich and Castlereagh regarded the future with apprehension, and hoped only for a period free from wars and revolutions, and controlled by the cautious conduct of international affairs. Only Alexander I had sanguine schemes for international peace, and by 1830 he and all he had stood for were very dead.

[1] E. Hertslet, *The Map of Europe by Treaty* (London, 1875), vol. I, p. 62.
[2] *idem*, p. 63.

But the forty years before the Crimean War gave the more rigid diplomatic forms time to establish themselves, and it was something of a shock, in 1854, when the Eastern Question proved incapable of peaceful solution. Especially did the English ruling class of Whigs and liberals feel that there must be more civilized and more economic methods of settling disputes than by sending large armies to the other end of Europe, and leaving thousands of young men for months in danger of death from cholera and gunfire. At the Congress of Paris in 1856, the chief British plenipotentiary, Lord Clarendon, brought forward a proposal for nothing less than the abolition of war. 'The calamities of war are still too present to every mind', he said, 'not to make it desirable to seek out every expedient calculated to prevent their return.' The treaty ending the war with Russia had already been signed when Clarendon brought forward his exalted proposal. Article VIII of the treaty had recommended that when any power quarrelled with Turkey—as Russia had done in 1853— it should seek mediation from a friendly state before resorting to force. Clarendon now proposed that the specific recommendation with regard to the Ottoman Empire should be applied to international society generally: instead of going to war, powers should seek mediation. Although his proposal came too late to be drawn up as part of the treaty, the protocol containing it was signed by all the plenipotentiaries of the powers assembled at Paris, no doubt with varying degrees of scepticism. In the years immediately after 1856 British foreign secretaries continually advised states involved in disputes to respect the Protocol of Paris and to submit their differences to mediation. But the process of formal mediation was never successfully used to settle a single issue of first-rate importance. The attempt to extend the methods of the old diplomacy to create a final substitute for war was a total failure. But that the attempt was ever made is evidence of the confidence placed in diplomatic machinery.

The diplomatic services and foreign ministries of Europe were already far more professional in character in 1830 than they had been in the eighteenth century and by 1880 the process had been carried much further. The British service retained a more amateur character than had those of most other west European countries, but even the British service was considerably more professional than it had been at the time of the foundation of the Foreign Office in 1782, and appreciably more so than it had been in the days of Castlereagh. Under Palmerston and until 1861, during the period when Britain was at the zenith of her power and when the British fleet held unquestioned control of the oceans of the world, the British Foreign Office was housed in a few small buildings in Downing Street. An English diplomat, Sir Horace Rumbold, described the 'old Foreign Office', as it was subsequently called, as 'dingy and shabby to a degree . . . a thorough picture of disorder, penury and meanness'.[1] By 1861 it was wholly unsuitable for the work that had to be performed there. The old building was pulled down, and the new building which has since served as the Foreign Office was built, to the designs of Sir Gilbert Scott, in the style of a Venetian palace, with a handsome façade on St James's Park. The staff, too, was still small in Palmerston's time, but was growing. From a mere fourteen at the end of the eighteenth century, it had reached thirty-one by 1832, and fifty-two by 1861. Under Palmerston the staff were given no responsibility, all decisions of policy, however insignificant, coming from the secretary of state himself. Even his permanent under-secretary, Mr John Backhouse, was little more than a clerk. By 1880 the permanent staff had acquired far more prestige, partly because of the deliberate policy of Clarendon. Under him and other foreign secretaries, the permanent under-secretary, Edmund Hammond, assumed a significant role. Hammond was permanent under-secretary for nearly twenty years, from 1854 to 1873, and inevitably came to advise on questions of policy, in a manner which Palmerston would have considered unconstitutional. Hammond's career, which culminated in the peerage, is an indication of the growing importance of the permanent officials of the Foreign Office.[2]

The British diplomatic service as a whole, like the Foreign Office, retained an amateurish character until the middle of the nineteenth century, but from then on it was steadily becoming more professional. Ranks and salaries in the diplomatic service had been organized and standardized in the eighteenth century up to a point,[3] but the method of recruitment and administration of the service had never been laid down, and remained a matter of patronage and privilege until well past the mid-nineteenth century. In 1830 attachés at the embassies and legations were still in most cases young friends, or even relatives, of the ambassador or minister, usually unpaid, eating at their patron's table and

[1] Sir Horace Rumbold, *Recollections of a Diplomatist* (London, 1903), vol. 1, p. 109.
[2] Dr Mary A. Anderson's unpublished thesis, 'Edmund Hammond, Permanent Under Secretary of State for Foreign Affairs', for the degree of Ph.D. of the University of London, deals admirably with this important figure in the history of the British Foreign Office.
[3] D. B. Horn, *The British Diplomatic Service 1689–1789* (Oxford, 1961).

sleeping under his roof. Canning called them: 'A couple of dozen of young men scattered over Europe; owing no allegiance and taking diplomacy only as subsidiary to amusement.'[1]

Canning himself had done something to reform the diplomatic service, though his reforms were not in every case permanent in their effect. In 1855 of the sixty attachés in the service, thirty-one were still unpaid, but regulations in 1862 laid down that after four years every attaché was to assume the paid rank of third secretary. By the end of the period nearly all attachés in the service were intending to make a career there, and the old type of dilettante diplomat was disappearing. In earlier days ambassadors and ministers had, more often than not, been appointed from outside the service as reward for past political activity or because of a change of the political government. But already by 1830 the majority of high-ranking diplomats had risen from within the service, though purely political appointments remained an occasional feature, especially for the four big embassies. By the 1850s it was unusual for a new foreign secretary to appoint a batch of his own men to embassies and legations; he was content with those there already, since in most cases they were respected career diplomats with no overt political allegiances. On the bottom rung of the diplomatic ladder attachés were appointed throughout the period by the foreign secretary himself, although, in the early days, selected in the first place by the ambassador or minister.

In 1856 Clarendon introduced a system of qualifying examinations set by an independent body—the three civil service commissioners—for all candidates to the diplomatic service, though they would still be selected originally by the foreign secretary from names submitted to him by ambitious parents. The government and Foreign Office could not yet swallow a system of open competition. All the same, the foreign service in 1880 was more thoroughly organized than it had been in 1830, appreciably larger, and less dependent on the political group in power.

The other European countries had improved the organization of their diplomatic services in a similar manner and had, in some important respects, carried the process of professionalization a stage further than that reached by the British service. The French and Prussian diplomatic services, in particular, were run on modern lines, and were not specifically limited to the aristocracy. The Austrian government, on the other hand, excluded all but rich aristocrats, and preferred members of the nobility. The Russian system, as might be expected, was the most

[1] In a letter in 1826, quoted in H. W. V. Temperley, *The Foreign Policy of Canning* (London, 1925), p. 265.

archaic, and was strictly limited to nobles and certain favoured professional classes. Sons of army officers, of priests and of central government officials, including even chancery messengers, could apply for entry, as could all court officials, including 'young choristers discharged from the court choir after loss of voice'—a pleasing example of imperial paternalism. Specifically excluded by law from applying were all merchants, peasants and anyone who paid taxes: in other words all the unprivileged classes. Jews were also excluded unless they had undertaken a certain amount of military service or had secured certain university degrees.

By 1860 the diplomatic services of all the great powers had inaugurated qualifying examinations for entry into the diplomatic service. In Austria three state examinations had to be passed, but no examination was specially set for the foreign service alone. In France under the Second Empire candidates were exempted from all examinations if they had a degree in law, but otherwise had to take written and oral examinations in English and German, and in the diplomatic history of Europe from the Congress of Westphalia to the Congress of Vienna. The Prussian regulations for entry were the most rigid of all. They had been laid down as early as 1827, and amplified by a cabinet order of 1842. A candidate had to have completed three years at a university and taken the two first examinations required for a bureaucratic career. He had to send with his application an account of his earlier education, written in French. If he was accepted he would serve for a year unpaid, and would then have to return to Berlin for a special examination for admission to the permanent ranks of the service. The special examination consisted of five papers in history, law and political science and, finally, oral and written tests in French. It was possible at this late stage for the candidate to be failed outright, without the chance of taking the examination again, but for those who passed the reward was a third secretaryship of legation. That Bismarck's diplomats were at least academically well qualified cannot be doubted.

The Russian system of recruitment was more like the somewhat arbitrary method of the British. Not until 1859 was a qualifying examination introduced, and even then, as in Britain, the final appointment still remained very much at the mercy of the secretary of state. In the first two years only five candidates sat Russian examinations. The 1859 reform was the work of Gorchakov, and laid down that candidates should sit examinations in Latin, German, English and international law, and should make a précis of diplomatic papers and write a memorandum in

Russian and French. The Russian examination, then, was realistically adjusted to the functions the diplomat would have to perform. The recommended reading list included, surprisingly, John Stuart Mill's *Principles of Political Economy*.[1] In all European countries high-ranking diplomats—ambassadors or ministers—could be appointed from outside the diplomatic service. In the Russian service all ambassadors and ministers were always appointed by imperial ukase, only secretaries and attachés being appointed by the Ministry of Foreign Affairs. The lower strata of the service in Russia were under strict military discipline, the heads of mission having judicial powers to punish their subordinates for any shortcomings.

But attachés were not much better off elsewhere. Both in the Austrian and French, as in the British service, they were more often unpaid than paid, and in the Prussian service they were not paid for their first year. They had then to be the sons of a class of parent who could afford to give them a private allowance, except in so far as they could still depend upon the head of mission for food and lodging. In the Austrian service all subordinates—secretaries as well as attachés—were fed and housed by the ambassador, unless they were married. In the Russian service the same custom was practised in cases when the head of mission was provided with a house by the government. In the Prussian service the ambassador or minister had to house his subordinates or provide them with a cash substitute, but the liability was covered by his initial allowance from the government.

The governments of the great powers in the period generally were showing greater readiness to provide embassies or legations for their agents, to make allowances for lighting and heating and to bear the cost of correspondence and office equipment, than they had done in earlier days. If the diplomatic services of Europe retained certain characteristics of a system of privilege and patronage, they were acquiring other characteristics distinctly modern and professional in character. They were, too, growing in size, as were the foreign ministries. In 1861, when the British Foreign Office employed a staff of fifty-two, the Prussian Foreign Ministry employed sixty-six, not counting the porters and domestics, and the French Foreign Ministry was still larger.

The machinery of diplomacy was speeded up in the 1850s by the spread of the telegraph. By the outbreak of the Crimean War in 1854 the countries of western and central Europe were connected by telegraph.

[1] *Report of Select Committee on Diplomatic Service*, British Parliamentary Papers, Reports from Committees (1861), vol. VI, Appendix.

It was possible for the British Foreign Office to send telegrams to Vienna, but connection with Constantinople had to continue by a horse-drawn messenger, since neither railway nor the telegraph had as yet crossed the Balkans. The more intensive organization of armies in the 1860s was ultimately to have an effect on diplomacy, since the elaborated general staffs were to exert a new kind of influence on policy.[1] The international problems of the twentieth century were to prove too great to be solved by the old diplomacy, but in the nineteenth century the traditions and resources of diplomats stood up well to the strains of international society.

The failures of diplomacy

The body of European diplomats taken as a whole may be said to have failed when it has become necessary for nations to go to war with each other—when it has become necessary for governments to call upon their generals and their armies to attain the ends of policy, instead of relying on foreign ministries and ambassadors. Short aggressive wars may sometimes have brought benefit to the aggressors, though it can never be conclusively proved that equal or greater benefits could not have been achieved by peaceful means. In the present discussion, anyhow, it will be assumed that the maintenance of peace, rather than the preparation of war, is the normal function of diplomacy. The outbreak of war in 1859 and 1870 may have been regarded by Cavour and Bismarck respectively as marking a diplomatic success, but in the broader context of Europe they must be regarded as major failures of diplomacy.

Diplomacy can, of course, fail in another sense. It can preserve the peace, but in so doing retain injustices and prevent reform. It was in this secondary sense that diplomacy failed in the period 1815 to 1854. In 1830, and for the next eighteen years, Vienna retained the key position she had secured in 1815. The Austrian chancellor, Prince Clement von Metternich-Winneburg, who had out-played Napoleon in diplomacy and had presided over the Congress of Vienna, still considered himself the arbiter of Europe. His influence was, in fact, declining in the Habsburg monarchy itself, and so in the world at large, but the conservative system which he had established appeared strong until 1848. Since 1815 he had nourished the doctrine that the four or five great powers of Europe should exercise the right of intervention in small states threatened by revolution, particularly in western Europe, and particularly if

---

[1] The emergence of General Staffs and military organization generally are dealt with under individual countries. See below, pp. 205 and 251.

revolution threatened to spread across frontiers. Canning had repudiated the doctrine and had insisted instead that the great powers should not intervene in the affairs of sovereign states, either for or against revolution, but should allow each country to work out its own destiny. The debate was further complicated by an extension of Canning's doctrine of non-intervention to include intervention by a second power against the illegal intervention of the first power—intervention to preserve the doctrine of non-intervention. Canning had thus intervened in Portugal in the 1820s to protect the constitutional government against Spanish or French intervention.

After the July Revolution in Paris in 1830, France, too, proclaimed that she would protect the doctrine of non-intervention—in this case more particularly in Italy. But when, in 1831, revolutionary governments established themselves in the Papal city of Bologna and the duchies of Parma and Modena, Austria ignored the doctrine of non-intervention and suppressed the risings. A French expedition to Ancona may have dissuaded the Austrians from occupying Rome, but it did not save the revolutions, nor was it intended to do so. The revolution in Poland in 1830 was also suppressed by foreign—in this case, Russian—troops, and protests from Britain and France proved unavailing. European diplomacy in the 1830s did not permit alterations in the despotic régimes of small states. The establishment of Belgian independence was an exception. More typical were the repressions of revolutions in Italy and Poland.

The grievances of the peoples of Europe came to a head in 1848 with revolutions in fifteen capitals. The influence of diplomacy suffered a temporary eclipse. The diplomats, and the statesmen who, like Metternich and Palmerston, were primarily diplomats, could do nothing to prevent the revolutions, just as they had done nothing to render them unnecessary. Metternich was driven from power by the revolution, and Palmerston's attempts at diplomatic intervention were on the whole ineffective. In western Europe only Piedmont intervened on the side of the revolution, her king, Charles Albert, taking advantage of the revolution in Milan to attack an embarrassed Austria. But in 1848 and again in 1849 Austria defeated Piedmont. The Second French Republic, established by the revolution of February 1848, remained preoccupied with her own affairs and did not raise a finger to help revolutionaries elsewhere. On the contrary, in 1849, she intervened against the revolution, by destroying the Roman Republic. The only other great power to intervene against revolution outside her own frontiers was

Russia, who assisted Austria in suppressing the Hungarian rising in 1849.

The restoration of conservative régimes nearly everywhere in Europe in 1849 suggested that the existing system of international relations tended to protect the *status quo*. Diplomacy could only preserve peace; it could not assist reform or political improvement. Such was its negative failing. Positive failings—failures to prevent war between the powers— number only four throughout the period: in 1854, 1859, 1866 and 1870. Each deserves to be considered in some detail.

In 1854 the map of Europe was very much as it had been in 1815. There had appeared two small new states—Belgium in the west, and Greece in the east. Austria had annexed the free city of Cracow in 1846, thus show- ing the hypocrisy of Metternich's protestations of respect for treaties, and for the 1815 treaties in particular. But, broadly speaking, it can be said that the Concert of Europe had preserved the *status quo*. Now, in mid-century, the apparent crumbling of the Ottoman Empire presented the powers with a problem which could be solved only by a constructive approach. Since the eighteenth century Europe had feared the break-up of Turkey and the great rivalries and disputes which this immense power vacuum would bring with it. In the event the Empire was to survive for many more years, in spite of the hopeless incompetence of her administration. In a crisis Turkey usually managed to find western allies, and in the last resort could rely to a surprising extent on the tenacity of her own soldiers. But in 1850 the end seemed finally in sight. Neither the reforms of the Sultan Mahmoud II, nor the persuasion and bullying of the British ambassador, Stratford Canning, could arrest the decline. The preservation of the Ottoman Empire continued to be the immediate policy of all the great powers, but at least one ruler, Czar Nicholas I, began to speculate on the steps which should be taken if and when the immediate policy had to be abandoned.

As early as 1844 the czar, on a visit to England, had discussed with the foreign secretary, Lord Aberdeen, what steps might be taken to partition Turkey peacefully when the need or opportunity arose. As on several other important occasions during his tenure of the Foreign Office, Aberdeen gave a false impression of complete agreement, but left no memorandum, and believed that he had in no way committed himself. Nine years later, in the early weeks of 1853, the czar returned to his project for a partition of the Ottoman Empire, in conversations with the British minister in St Petersburg, Sir Hamilton Seymour.

Russia was to occupy the Danubian principalities, and Britain was to get Egypt. Constantinople, since Catherine the Great's day regarded as a goal of Russian policy, was to become a free city. Although he did not mention it to Seymour, Nicholas also considered sending a Russian garrison to the Bosphorus, permitting Austria to garrison the Dardanelles, and giving Crete to France. By a coincidence Aberdeen was prime minister in 1853. His government was no firmer in dissuading Nicholas from his grandiose plans than it had been in 1844. But at least on the later occasion they pointed out that the Ottoman Empire was still far from ultimate collapse.

Meanwhile the czar had become involved in the dispute between Greek Orthodox and Catholic monks in the Holy Places of Palestine, with the Greek Orthodox Church looking to Russia for help, and Napoleon III extending his patronage over the Catholics. The dispute had raged throughout 1852. When the squabble of monks threatened to become a Franco-Russian war of prestige the Turks became alarmed, and tried desperately to placate both parties. Nicholas I decided that the Porte must be frightened into pursuing a pro-Russian line. In January 1853 he mobilized two army corps, and contemplated waging an immediate preventive war against Turkey, before the powers could come to her assistance. He had consulted with Britain over a possible partition of Turkey, but his mobilization now was a unilateral act, which could have brought war at once, and anyhow brought it appreciably nearer.

Russia and France did not go to war over the Holy Places, but so much friction had been caused that any additional issue would be considerably more difficult to solve. The Russians themselves soon introduced an additional issue. The Treaty of Kutchuk Kainardji had in 1774 given the Russian government certain ill-defined rights of guardianship over the Christian communities in the Ottoman Empire. In February 1853 the Russian minister of marine, Prince Menshikov, was sent to Constantinople to secure a formal recognition of these rights from the sultan. While the professional diplomats had to this point kept the tone of the Russo-Turkish dispute within comparatively safe bounds, Menshikov adopted a more belligerent approach, which antagonized the Turkish ministers. On 21 May he left Constantinople without a guarantee of Russian protectorate rights, and diplomatic relations between the two countries were broken off. Again the czar had acted without consultation with the other powers, and his next step was even more rash. He ordered his armies to move into the Rumanian principalities—an invasion of

Turkish territory which alone might have been expected to lead to war. But the British and French governments still hoped for peace, and advised the sultan not to resist the Russian invasion while it was limited to the principalities. The fleets of the western Powers, however, were moved to Besika Bay within close reach of the Straits. The basic concern of the British government was to preserve the security of the Ottoman Empire, thereby ensuring the overland route to India, and at the same time preventing Russia from becoming a Mediterranean power. Napoleon III had less immediate interest in the crisis, but a strong policy in the east and a sure alliance with Britain would give the young Second Empire the international prestige it badly needed if it was to survive. Even at this late stage in the crisis the professional diplomats almost averted war. Count Buol, the Austrian chancellor, called a conference of ambassadors in Vienna in July, and negotiations continued for some weeks. Not until October did the Turks, whose territory, after all, had been invaded by a foreign power, lose patience and declare war. Nor did the western powers immediately come to the aid of Turkey. They waited until February 1854, then presented an ultimatum to Russia demanding evacuation of the principalities, and when no answer from St Petersburg arrived, declared war at the end of March.

Whether the Crimean War was necessary or futile has often been debated. Two points should be made: the war was fought for very genuine reasons and involved very real interests, but this is not to say that war was the only means of securing those interests. For Nicholas I the war, once started, was a crusade, in which he was fighting for the welfare of the faithful, while France and Britain were allied to the infidel. He had not wanted to destroy the Ottoman Empire, only to share it out when it finally collapsed. But his two or three sudden, ill prepared, unilateral moves had landed him in a war in which Russian influence in central Europe was to be permanently diminished, while Russian strength in eastern Europe was to be curbed for twenty years.

The Franco-Austrian War of 1859 differed from the Crimean War in one important respect: none of the governments which fought in 1854 claimed to be fighting for the modern ideology of nationalism. Napoleon III refrained from any attempt to stir up a Polish rising against Russia. But in the war of 1859 both France and Piedmont openly claimed to be fighting for the 'principle of nationality'. Since 1815 Lombardy and Venetia had been Austrian provinces, and Austrian troops were in occupation of the legally independent duchies of Parma, Modena and

Tuscany, and of the Papal Legations. Napoleon and Cavour both believed that the foreigner should be driven out of north-east and central Italy, if not by diplomatic pressure, then by war. The Austrian government replied by denying the existence of an 'Italian Question'. In fact the Treaty of Vienna gave Austria full legal claims to Lombardy and Venetia, but even on the grounds of legitimacy the presence of Austrian troops in the central duchies and Papal States was unjustified. Count Camillo Benso di Cavour, prime minister of Piedmont since 1852 and perhaps the most successful diplomat of the nineteenth century, concentrated on the weakest link in Austria's case. He pointed out that Austria could not remain in Italy without abnormally large military forces. She was not established in Italy; she was encamped there.[1] Napoleon III accepted the argument. He hoped that a war for the Italian cause would rally liberal support for the Empire at home. But his policy in 1859 seems strangely quixotic in comparison with that of all his contemporaries.

While all the four contestants in the Crimea in 1854 went to war with extreme reluctance, two of the contestants in 1859—France and Piedmont—went into a war which they had been carefully planning for nearly a year. Napoleon III, no less than Cavour, was fully prepared for an armed assault on the Austrian position in Italy. The only difference was that Napoleon continued to hope, until the last moment, that an international congress might possibly provide Italy with the fruits of victory, without the expense, complications and dangers of war. Cavour was under no such illusion. Nor did Austria make any great efforts to avert war. Her stubborn refusal to negotiate in the end played into Cavour's hands. Of the three powers which remained neutral neither Prussia nor Russia was unduly distressed to see a Franco-Austrian clash in Italy. When the Russian chancellor, Prince Gorchakov, tried to mediate, he did so only from a desire to bring Russia from the position of a defeated nation back into the European game of diplomacy. Only the British government put the full resources of diplomacy at the disposal of peace. The British foreign secretary, Lord Malmesbury, feared a second Napoleonic era of conquest and an extension of the war to the Balkans. Even if such horrors did not materialize, Britain would lose markets in north Italy while the fighting lasted.

As early as July 1858 Napoleon III invited Cavour to meet him privately at Plombières, where it was agreed that France would join

[1] *Carteggio Cavour-Nigra*, vol. II, pp. 26–38. Cavour's Memorandum for the English government.

Piedmont as a full ally in a war to drive Austria out of Lombardy and Venetia, in return for the cession of Savoy and Nice to France, and provided Cavour could find a plausible *casus belli*. Historians have usually overlooked the fact that the initiative for the pact of Plombières was Napoleon's, but it is true that Cavour seized eagerly the opportunity offered to him. The pact was turned into a formal alliance on 18 January 1859. In the early weeks of 1859 Cavour stepped up diplomatic agitation against Austria's position in the Duchies. In March the Austrian and Piedmontese armies were mobilized. Malmesbury tried desperately to use British influence with the three governments to arrange mediation, and on 21 March 1859 Gorchakov proposed a congress for the discussion of the whole Italian question. Malmesbury supported the proposal with enthusiasm. The place, date, participants and even plenipotentiaries for the congress were discussed. For some days it seemed that sincere negotiations would take place. But in the last resort Austria was not prepared to discuss any territorial changes in Italy. On 2 April Malmesbury proposed the 'disarmament' of Austria and Sardinia, though he probably meant by 'disarmament' what in the twentieth century would be called 'demobilization'. Paradoxically Austria had mobilized her large army too soon for her own security. To keep it mobilized indefinitely was too expensive a proposition: Austria could not afford to wait while negotiations took their leisurely path. But to start the process of demobilization would leave Austrian Italy extremely vulnerable so long as the Sardinian army remained mobilized. For the first, but not the last, time the technical difficulties and dangers of mobilizing large armies contributed to the likelihood of war. Count Buol drew up an ultimatum demanding Piedmontese demobilization in three days. The ultimatum was delivered on 23 April, and formally rejected by Cavour on the 26th. Napoleon came to the aid of Piedmont as he had promised, and the first war in western Europe between two great powers since Waterloo ensued.

In the war of 1859, as in the Crimean War, both sides were fighting for important issues. The Franco-Piedmontese victory in 1859 was an imperfect one, because it left Venetia still in Austrian hands. Nevertheless it started a chain of events leading to the independence and unification of Italy within two years. Historians have tacitly assumed that the war of 1859, including as it did the two terrible massacres of Magenta and Solferino, was justified by the end it achieved. Certainly Austria seemed stubbornly resistant to purely diplomatic pressure in 1859, but in the long run the pressure of the powers brought to bear in open congress and through peaceful channels, may well have had its effect.

Instead, Cavour had secured an aggressive alliance, and had reached an end admirable in itself, but by immoral means.

The third of the four wars between European great powers in this period, the war of 1866, was also a civil war in Germany, and must be considered again in the context of domestic German history. In the general diplomatic history of Europe it marked a disastrous phase. From 1815 until the 1850s it had been generally assumed that war between the powers should be averted at almost any cost. In 1854 three of the powers had resorted to military force, but hopes of reaching a compromise settlement by diplomatic negotiation were never abandoned. The peace of 1856 included terms which were hard for Russia to accept, but it was far from being a dictated peace. After 1856 Napoleon III determined to revise the 1815 settlement, if necessary by war, but he would still have preferred a peaceful revision in congress.

The advent of Bismarck on the European scene in 1862 meant that a revisionist policy would be pursued much more relentlessly. He was determined to substitute Prussian domination in Germany for the Austrian domination that had been established in 1815 and restored in 1849–51 after the failure of the revolutionary movement of 1848. Bismarck was convinced that so basic a change in central Europe could be carried out only after the military defeat of Austria. Like Cavour before him, he did not imagine that Austria could be talked into renouncing her authority. On the other hand, as an aristocrat and landowner, Otto von Bismarck, a count after 1866 and a prince after 1871, did not want to disrupt the social order in Europe. He did not even want to destroy Austria. He believed his ends could be achieved only through blood and iron, but he did not intend more blood to flow than he considered strictly necessary. He knew that his opportunities and ability were great, but he knew, too, that even they had their limitations. If his wars were more consciously planned than most, they were also short and localized.

To involve Austria in war in 1866 Bismarck used two complex issues —the questions of Schleswig-Holstein and of the political organization of Germany. Obviously, neither was artificially created by Bismarck. On the contrary, both were age-old problems which had been accentuated by the events of 1848. But neither problem was necessarily beyond peaceful solution. A temporary solution had been found to the Schleswig-Holstein question in 1852 when the compromise settlement contained in the Treaty of London was reached through British mediation. Since then the temporary settlement had been disrupted by the Danish king,

Frederick VII, and Bismarck had seized the opportunity of allying Prussia with Austria in a short and victorious war against Denmark in 1864. The Danes had capitulated, and surrendered the duchies of Schleswig and Holstein to Prussia and Austria. In August 1865 the Convention of Gastein, signed by the two great German powers, permitted Austria to administer Holstein, and Prussia, Schleswig; but the two powers retained joint rights of sovereignty over both duchies. Between August 1865 and June 1866, when the Austro-Prussian War started, several arbitrary steps were taken on both sides. The accumulated effect of these steps was to make a diplomatic settlement impossible, and war certain.

Bismarck's plans for the war were made deliberately and systematically. In October 1865 he visited Napoleon III at Biarritz and secured a promise that France would remain neutral in a war against Austria. In April 1866 he secured an offensive alliance with Italy, not yet a great power, but an independent and united nation since 1861. The Italian alliance would present Austria with a second front. Italy agreed to enter the war if Prussia had engineered a dispute within three months. The terms of the Italian alliance suggest that Bismarck was preparing an immediate war. There is much evidence that he then proceeded, coldly and deliberately, to pick a quarrel with Austria. On 9 April—precisely the day after the conclusion of the treaty with Italy—he moved a major project of reform of the German Confederation in the Diet at Frankfurt: a constituent assembly was to be elected by universal suffrage. Such a project was wholly unacceptable to Austria, but it placed Bismarck in a strong position. Having confused the German constitutional question beyond recognition, he could await developments. Both Italy and Austria proceeded to mobilize their forces before the end of April. Prussia waited until May. As in 1859 the long period and great expense required by Austria for mobilization placed her in a false position.

The first and immediate cause of the war was not the constitution of Germany, but the Schleswig-Holstein question. In June the Austrian government instructed the Assembly of Holstein to discuss the future of the duchy. Bismarck declared the instructions to be a violation of the Gastein Convention and of Prussia's rights in Holstein. Prussian troops were ordered to invade Holstein. Not only was this an act of aggression against Austria, but it wholly ignored the feelings of the other great powers. On 14 June the Diet at Frankfurt voted Prussia an aggressor in Holstein, and on the 17th Austria declared war, ostensibly to fulfil the wishes of the German Diet. Italy declared war three days later. Once again Austria had taken several unilateral steps, but this time she was provoked even more outrageously than in 1859. On the other hand, this time her blunder was more catastrophic. The Prussian victory of Sadowa on 3 July was decisive, and the whole war lasted for only seven weeks. The Peace of Prague finally excluded Austria from both Germany and Italy.

The fourth and last of the wars between European powers in the period —the Franco-Prussian War of 1870—was the most far-reaching in its results. It not only completed the unification of Germany, but made her the strongest nation in the world in military terms, though Britain, of course, retained mastery of the oceans. Like the last war of Louis XIV, the war of 1870 had its immediate cause in the question of the Spanish succession. The revolution of 1868, which had forced Isabella into exile in Paris, retained the institution of monarchy but provided no obvious candidate for the throne. The Spanish Cortes finally offered it to Prince Leopold of Hohenzollern-Sigmaringen, who, like several princes before him, refused it. Bismarck, however, saw that something could be made of the situation and in May 1870, when the Cortes renewed their offer, Leopold accepted. News of his acceptance was published in France on 3 July 1870. The secrecy of the scheme up to then made it seem all the more sinister and distasteful to the French, who could hardly relish the prospect of a Prussian prince enthroned on their southern frontier. Napoleon III's foreign minister was a clerical and bitterly anti-Prussian nobleman, the Duke of Gramont. On 6 July Gramont made a fighting speech in the Assembly, saying that he hoped the Hohenzollern succession would still be refused, but 'should it turn out otherwise . . . we know how to do our duty without wavering or weakness'. The French government were right in assuming that Bismarck was behind the Hohenzollern candidature, but they had no evidence to prove it, and their assumption of Prussian guilt was in itself offensive.

The press played a violent part in building up war hysteria both in Paris and Berlin, much as it had in London in 1854, with one difference —the most abusive and angry of the Prussian papers were inspired personally by Bismarck. The use of the press to whip up an irrational popular campaign was an ugly precedent to be frequently followed in the twentieth century.

Bismarck believed that for Leopold to withdraw acceptance of the crown now would constitute a serious diplomatic defeat for Prussia, but against Bismarck's advice the Prussian king, William I, decided to bow to French wishes. For the second time the Hohenzollern family turned down the Spanish throne. The French government foolishly refused to rest content with so considerable a triumph. Gramont decided to ask William I to write personally to Napoleon, apologizing for the whole affair and expressing friendship for France. After consultation with Napoleon at St Cloud, Gramont made even this request stronger by seeking a guarantee from the Prussian king that he would never again give permission to Leopold to consider acceptance. The only possible justification for such a step was the argument that the Hohenzollern family had already changed its mind twice, and a guarantee was needed that they would not do so once more. But Prussia was not a small state that could be expected to lie down under such an insult. William I received the French ambassador, Benedetti, at Ems, in a somewhat casual manner, and explained that he could not possibly give a guarantee of the kind the French wanted. The first account of the interview arrived in Berlin from Ems by telegram, and was already firm in tone. Bismarck shortened the telegram, making it still more curt, and published it. To the world it seemed that the Prussian king had dismissed the French ambassador in the most peremptory and final manner.

France declared war on Prussia on 19 July, apparently for a question of honour and prestige. From a misplaced and ill-calculated sense of pride Napoleon III's ministers had involved him in a war in which his empire would fall in less than two months, and in which France would face rapid defeat and the loss of the rich lands of Alsace-Lorraine. The crisis which had brought on the war had revealed stronger militarist sentiment in both France and Prussia than there had been anywhere in Europe since 1815. The habit of conscription and the creation of larger armies had inevitably made French and Prussian generals more important people than they had been in the past. Both Prussia and France had increased and reorganized their armies between 1866 and 1870. The French army was equipped with the *Chassepot*—a new breach-loading rifle which had been briefly proved in action, and the untried *mitrailleuse* —a first primitive version of the machine gun. The big reform in the French system of recruitment was only partly complete in 1870, a factor which was almost certainly an incentive to Bismarck to fight the war then rather than a year or two later. On the other hand, the Prussian army was growing by some 100,000 each year, so that the argument of the arms race is by no means conclusive in any assessment of war guilt.

Historians have usually assumed that the Hohenzollern candidature was used by Bismarck purely as an excuse for picking a quarrel with

France, just as he had used the Schleswig-Holstein question for picking a quarrel with Austria. But Bismarck might well have been content with a Hohenzollern king for Spain, and a postponement of the war for several years, so that, when war came, France would have a hostile régime facing her on the Pyrenees. For that matter, the Schleswig-Holstein question was much more than a complication invented by Bismarck: it had been an issue of vital importance for Germany long before Bismarck came to power. The Hohenzollern candidature, too, was much more than an opportunity suddenly presented to Bismarck in 1870. He had decided to press for it before the end of 1866; he had sent confidential agents to Spain in the spring of 1869; he had spent a considerable sum of money in building up a party in Spain favourable to the idea. Bismarck was clearly enthusiastic for the Hohenzollern candidature for its own sake. This being the case, negotiation over the Spanish succession question would still have been possible if Napoleon and his ministers had been less stubborn or more imaginative. Bismarck could even argue that Leopold of Hohenzollern was less distantly related to Napoleon than to William I: Leopold's mother was a Beauharnais. But the argument was of doubtful validity. As an infantry officer in the Prussian army, Leopold had never been very conscious of his French blood.

Both the French and Prussians appeared sincerely to believe that the other nation was preparing a war of aggression. In a circular to his diplomatic agents on 14 July, Gramont wrote: 'While Prussia, pursuing a dynastic interest, has devoted all her energies to plans for European preponderance, France has had no object but to repulse an attempt calculated gravely to compromise her territorial security.'[1]

On the other side, the Prussians quite genuinely saw things differently. Friedrich von Holstein, of the Prussian foreign service, wrote in his memoirs: 'Bismarck handled the Hohenzollern candidature rather as one waves a lighted match over a gas tap to see if it is turned on. . . . From July onwards Bismarck wanted war, but Napoleon had wanted it before then.'[2]

In so far as both sides in 1870 had feared each other, the dispute had been open to solution by a general exchange of guarantees all round. But for guarantees to be effective they had to be recognized by the

---

[1] *Les origines diplomatiques de la guerre de 1870–1871* (French Foreign Ministry, 1910–32), vol. 28, p. 358.
[2] *The Holstein Papers*, edited by Norman Rich and M. H. Fisher (Cambridge, 1955), vol. I, p. 40.

Concert of Europe, and in 1870 the Concert of Europe was dormant. The temporary withdrawal of Russia and Britain from European affairs left France and Prussia facing each other in a naked struggle for prestige and predominance in Europe.

The successes of diplomacy

The causes of wars have formed the central theme of diplomatic history. Certain very important wars have inspired an immense amount of historical research and speculation. To the causes of the war of 1914, and in this period, of the war of 1870, countless historians in Europe and America have devoted their labours, and large collections of documents have been edited.[1] A somewhat distorted impression of diplomatic history has emerged. The occasions when negotiations failed and war ensued have been analysed out of all proportion to their intrinsic interest. The occasions when negotiations have succeeded, and potentially great and terrible wars have been averted, have received only a few monographs. Yet if the record of diplomacy has any lessons to teach they are more likely to be contained in the frequent crises which were successfully controlled, than in the rarer disastrous moments when the negotiators threw in their hands and war ensued. The study of the potential causes of wars which were, in the event, avoided, in the nineteenth century, is particularly rewarding. Europe came very near to two great, general wars over the Eastern Question in 1840 and 1878. It would be a salutary intellectual exercise for historians to trace the origins of these two wars *manquées*. They would find it no more difficult than it has been to distinguish the causes of wars begun, historically, as a consequence of clashes over the Eastern Question in 1854 and 1914. Economic historians would have no difficulty in tracing the 'underlying' economic motives for war in 1840 and 1878. Diplomatic historians could edit great volumes of documents, showing the point at which war became 'inevitable'. Instead, the historian is left with the less dramatic task of reconstructing crises which failed at the last moment to reach the climax of war.

The concept of the 'Concert of Europe' had originated in the grand alliance of the powers against Napoleon I, and had persisted after 1815, to include France also. It tended to mean in practice simply 'the majority of the powers', and any state or states in dispute with the majority was said to be ignoring the 'wishes of the Concert of Europe'. But that the phrase should survive at all showed that statesmen preserved an ideal of

[1] For details of documents on the 1870 war, see above, p. 5.

European agreement and unity of aim, even if the practice would often fall short of the ideal. Even after the so-called 'congress system' had collapsed, and the congresses of which Metternich was so fond had ceased to meet, the term 'Concert of Europe' was still bandied about by the diplomats. In 1880 it was still in use, and Gladstone in the eighties tried to give the idea new life.

The first test of the validity of the concept in this period came immediately in 1830 with the Belgian crisis. The domestic reasons for the revolution within the United Netherlands are considered in chapter X. When the revolution proved successful and the Belgians established *de facto* independence the question became an international one. The king of the United Netherlands, William I, appealed to the powers under the terms of the Vienna Settlement. Nicholas I was prepared to respond to the appeal with the despatch of troops to re-establish the Dutch king's position in Brussels, and the Prussian king, Frederick William III, was also sympathetic. Metternich was much less eager for intervention, and both Nicholas and Frederick William preferred to wait in the hope of securing a general agreement of the powers. The revolution in Brussels had broken out at the end of August. Louis Philippe had therefore been king of the French for less than two months, and was not prepared to assist the powers against the Belgians, who seemed to be favouring some kind of link with France. Two events in November finally made a joint European intervention for William impossible. The revolution broke out in Warsaw, and for some months was to keep the czar's armies fully occupied, and to retain the attention of both the czar and Frederick William. And in England the Tory government of Wellington fell from power, with the result that Palmerston arrived at the Foreign Office.

The western powers were now free to settle the matter in a more liberal sense, and a conference called in London in November agreed to recognize Belgian independence. The crisis appeared to have been brought under control, but the whole thing blew up again when the discussion of frontiers started. The initial settlement by the powers excluded Limburg and Luxemburg from Belgium. In reply, the Belgians, early in February 1831, offered the crown to the duc de Nemours, the second son of Louis-Philippe. Palmerston threatened war if the crown were accepted, and Louis Philippe discreetly declined the offer. The Dutch king had never accepted any part of the settlement. In August 1831 he felt strong enough to defy the powers and to try again to suppress Belgian independence by force. But by then Louis Philippe's conciliatory attitude had persuaded Palmerston to trust him, and a French army was allowed to enter Belgium to enforce the decision of the London Conference. In November a protocol readjusted the frontiers, now dividing Limburg and Luxemburg, and forming the east part of Luxemburg into a Grand Duchy united with Holland only in the person of its grand duke, who was to be William I.

The Belgian question thus provides a classic example of settlement by negotiation. It is true that Belgium was to some extent immunized against Russian, and perhaps Prussian, intervention by the Polish rising. But even if circumstances were favourable, the Concert of Europe must be credited with drawing up a compromise arrangement, and enforcing it. For once, international intervention was used not simply to maintain the *status quo*, but to change the map of 1815. The point was now established that the Treaty of Vienna could be changed peacefully if the major signatories were in agreement.

The greatest danger to the peace of Europe in the 1830s was provided by the Eastern Question. The revolution in Greece in 1821 had initially succeeded. But in 1825 the sultan had procured the assistance of one of the most remarkable men of the age—the pasha of Egypt, Mehemet Ali. Egypt was still legally a part of the Ottoman Empire, but Mehemet Ali had not only made himself independent of Turkish authority, but had improved the Egyptian economy and reformed the army to the point where Egypt was as powerful a state as Turkey herself. He had been asked in 1825 to reconquer Greece for the sultan, and an army under his son, Ibrahim Pasha, had occupied the Morea, only to be driven out by the powers, who, after years of negotiating, had finally decided to help the Greeks. On 3 February 1830 the London Protocol recognized a completely independent Greece.

Mehemet Ali had been promised the Morea by the sultan. The powers had cheated him of this reward, and the British had sunk his fleet in the battle of Navarino in 1827. He now determined to break with the sultan and conquer a kingdom for himself in Syria, where he would find timber to build a still larger fleet. In December 1832, Ibrahim Pasha defeated a Turkish army at Konieh, and Mehemet Ali's Syrian kingdom became a reality. Constantinople herself seemed threatened. Palmerston, still preoccupied with the Belgian question, did nothing to help the Turks, who turned to Russia in their despair. In February 1833 Nicholas I despatched a fleet to the Bosphorus, and Russian troops were landed on the Asiatic shore to protect Constantinople from Egyptian attack. The prospect of a Russian army fighting to defend Constantinople was almost as displeasing to Palmerston as the more familiar one of a Russian army conquering Constantinople to enable the czar to say a mass in Saint Sophia. Mehemet Ali was begged by the British to be content with his gains, and a Turco-Egyptian agreement saved the situation for the moment. None of the other powers was prepared to see a Russian army remain indefinitely on the Asiatic side of the Straits, but before the Russians withdrew they signed the important Treaty of Unkiar-Skelessi with the Porte on 8 July 1833. The treaty ensured that the Straits would be closed to Russia's enemies in time of war.

Russia was at the peak of her power and influence in 1833. Palmerston accepted the situation surprisingly placidly. A lesser statesman might have been frightened into war. But the reasons for British antipathy towards Mehemet Ali need to be further considered. He had, after all, done nothing to endanger British interests. He had carried through an agrarian and social revolution in Egypt, and introduced the kind of administrative reforms that Britain was always recommending to Turkey. A reforming power in the Middle East might have been thought to serve Britain's interests more effectively than did the effete Ottoman Empire. But from his early days Mehemet Ali had accepted French patronage, and Palmerston could see Egypt only as an outpost of French influence. In this role, Mehemet Ali seemed to be upsetting the balance of naval power in the Mediterranean. By 1837 he had built his new navy, which included eleven ships of the line, four of which had more than a hundred guns. Palmerston had no objection to eastern potentates who irrigated land and gave it to the peasants, but he preferred them not to build large fleets.

In April 1839 Sultan Mahmoud II foolishly renewed hostilities with Mehemet Ali in Syria. In June the sultan's forces were again completely defeated by the Egyptians. One disaster followed another. The entire Turkish fleet sailed off to Alexandria, and put itself at the disposal of Mehemet Ali. Finally Mahmoud II died, of that disease known to historians, though not to medical science, as 'a broken heart', and left a child as his heir. If the powers were to preserve the Ottoman Empire they would have to act quickly.

By the opening of 1840 nothing had been done, and in February of that year, Thiers came into office in Paris. A tough little man from the *midi*, leader of the French left in the assembly, Thiers had no intention of helping the other powers to solve the Porte's problems. In April he announced that France could not allow force to be used against Mehemet Ali. Palmerston ignored France, and carried Austria, Prussia and even Russia with him. After a conference in London, the four powers signed a treaty in July, pledging themselves to force a settlement on Mehemet Ali: he was to become hereditary pasha of Egypt—where he had before been in theory only an appointed governor, and pasha of southern Syria for life; but he was to give up his other conquests in the Middle East, Crete and Arabia, which he had conquered long before. Unless he accepted the settlement within ten days, southern Syria was to be withdrawn, and after another ten days the offer would be withdrawn altogether. In material terms the decision of the powers was not ungenerous to Mehemet Ali, but its imposition would be a blow to his pride. He rejected it, and was supported by an outburst of public opinion in Paris. In September a British fleet shelled Beirut, and landed troops. The Egyptians were obliged to abandon Syria.

Here, then, were all the makings of a general war, which would be fought not only in the east and on the Mediterranean, but also on the Rhine. A war fever swept France and Germany. Frederick William IV, who had just succeeded to the Prussian throne, posed as the leader of Germany against possible French aggression.

Peace was saved at the last moment by Louis Philippe, who persuaded Thiers to resign in October, and appointed a government bent on conciliation. The European Concert imposed its terms on Mehemet Ali, who was left simply as hereditary ruler of Egypt. Next summer, July 1841, a Straits Convention was signed by all the powers, including France: the Straits were to be permanently closed to foreign ships in peacetime. The Eastern Question had been stabilized for another decade.

As the period of short wars, the 1850s and 1860s cannot provide illustrations of the kind of successes achieved by the Concert of Europe in the 1830s and 1840s. In the four wars whose causes have already been considered, beneficial diplomatic achievements took the form of the localizing or shortening of the conflicts. Austria deserved—but did not receive—the gratitude of the peoples of Europe, for her great work in keeping the Crimean War within narrow geographical and temporal bounds. Count Buol persuaded the Russians to evacuate the principalities, and replaced them there with an Austrian army. While remaining neutral, Austria had thus sealed off the Balkans from the war. Her primary aim may have been simply to protect her trade route down the Danube. Had she been able to secure an alliance with Prussia, she may even have entered the war against Russia. Whatever Buol's motives, his action had the effect of preventing the spread of bloodshed. That the war was not fought to a military culmination was due also to Buol, whose ultimatum to Russia in December 1855 forced her to come to terms with the West.

Unfortunately the next ultimatum issued by Buol started the Italian war of 1859, a war in which Austria, far from being a neutral mediator, appeared to be the aggressor. In 1859 credit for localizing the conflict must go to Britain and Prussia. Malmesbury promised that Britain would remain neutral, but declared that the promise would be no longer binding if the war spread beyond Italy. He warned the Diet of the German Confederation very strongly against joining the war as allies of Austria. The Prussian foreign minister, Von Schleinitz, took the surprising line of telling the British government confidentially that he wished to align his policy with theirs. Malmesbury repeated that Britain would maintain a strict neutrality, and advised Prussia to do the same, though he made it clear that Britain would be neither surprised nor offended if Prussia chose to mobilize her army on the Rhine. The eventual mobilization of Prussian forces was probably the major factor in Napoleon's abrupt decision to end the war in the Peace of Villafranca. Once again the war had been stopped before it became a general one, and a war on the Rhine had been avoided.

That Bismarck's two wars of 1866 and 1870 remained limited to two or three major belligerents was due partly—though by no means entirely —to his own skill in isolating his enemies. Napoleon III was given the vague and unjustified impression that France would secure actual territorial gains from an Austrian defeat. On the other hand, Austria, as well as Bismarck, negotiated for French neutrality. France and Austria had been at war with each other only seven years earlier; Napoleon still hoped to conquer Venetia for Italy: there were distinct reasons why France should become an active ally of Prussia. The Austrians removed the danger by promising to cede Venetia to Italy even in the event of a Prussian defeat, and to consult Napoleon over any subsequent rearrangement of Germany. Napoleon must have imagined himself in a strong position, as a result of his negotiations with Prussia and Austria, when war broke out. The participation of Italy confused the issue in French eyes. It encouraged French liberals to sympathize with Prussia, even though they were doubtful about Bismarck's aims. Two days after Sadowa Napoleon held a cabinet meeting and decided not to intervene, nor even to mobilize his army on the Rhine.

Britain and Russia helped to hold the ring both in 1866 and 1870. British governments, and, still more, Queen Victoria, were not sorry to see a strong Prussia emerging. They believed that Prussia was more likely than Austria to solve the German question in a liberal sense. Russia had not fully recovered from defeat in the Crimea, and had an identity of interests with Prussia in Poland. These two factors were probably more weighty in preserving Russian neutrality than was any past scheming on Bismarck's part. That Austria remained neutral in 1870 may have been because Bismarck had given her lenient terms in 1866, yet it could equally be argued that, if the Prussian generals had been allowed to inflict a heavy defeat as they wished on Austria, she would have been physically unable to intervene in 1870. The attitude of the Emperor Francis Joseph was also significant. His brother, Maximilian, died in 1867 before a firing squad, as a result of Napoleon's bungling Mexican expedition; his ministers could hardly have asked him to help defend the Second Empire so soon after the tragedy. But Bismarck anyhow reinforced his position by reaching an agreement with the Russians. The czar was to mobilize his army on the Austrian frontier in the event of a Franco-Prussian war. Even so, the drawback to Austrian intervention might have been ignored, if it had been possible for Austria to sign a Triple Alliance with Italy as well as France. Such an alliance would have ensured Austria against a repetition of the 1866 war on two fronts. But the Italian government could not enter into such an alliance so long as the Austrians held the South Tyrol, and—much more important—so long as Napoleon's troops were in occupation of Rome. The possibility of a general war between two power blocks was thus avoided in 1870.

Britain in 1870 was pursuing a policy of isolation. The prime minister, Gladstone, was too good an economist to become involved in a continental war. If his foreign secretary, Granville, was less peace-loving, Edmund Hammond at the Foreign Office was strongly opposed to European involvement, and did not hesitate to urge a pacific policy. Britain, alone among the powers, had nothing to gain from intervention. Russia, Austria and Italy could all have gained points of advantage from a victorious war, but all three governments were wise enough to realize that the points of advantage were far outweighed by the expenses and dangers involved in spreading the fighting.

In the post-1871 world a great united Germany replaced France as the predominant power. Having secured as much as, and perhaps more than, he could have hoped, Bismarck was now eager to preserve the *status quo*. If anything, he was now on the defensive. He had succeeded too quickly and too completely, and dreaded a general reaction. He seems genuinely to have feared a conspiracy of Catholic forces against him, and, during the 'War in Sight' crisis in 1875, a French war of revenge. In the spring of 1875 he seemed even to be preparing for a preventive war against France, though he later denied having any such plans. Whatever his motives were, he abruptly forbade any further exports of horses to France, and so started a war scare. A German newspaper discussed the situation under the heading 'Is War in Sight?', and so gave the crisis the name by which it has since been known. If Bismarck in fact contemplated war with France, he was dissuaded by Gorchakov, who warned him that Russia could not witness the permanent destruction of France as a great power. Even the British government warned Bismarck against a second war with France. Only the Austrians showed sympathy for Germany by keeping silent.

In 1871 the anti-Prussian, Austrian Chancellor, Beust, had been replaced by the Hungarian, Count Andrássy, who did not inherit the old tradition of Austro-Prussian bitterness in Germany. In 1873 a loose *entente* of the three conservative powers, Germany, Austria and Russia, was formed, and called, somewhat prematurely, the *Dreikaiserbund*, or Three Emperors' League, though it was in no sense a binding close alliance. Its main weakness lay in the conflict of Austrian and Russian aims in the Balkans. The Austrian government, deprived of influence in Germany and Italy since 1866, was turning its attention eastwards. It seemed to the Austrian military authorities that the thin Dalmatian coastline, which was already Austrian, would be more easily defended if the far more considerable Turkish province of Bosnia and the smaller one of Herzegovina could be secured. Only a general could have so perverse an idea, but Andrássy, as a good Hungarian, was also painfully aware of the danger of Serbian autonomy to an empire containing a large minority of south Slavs.

Once again Turkish administration seemed to be crumbling, as the Ottoman government rushed into bankruptcy. Russian policy was divided. The chancellor, Gorchakov, now old and vain, wanted as always to maintain a peaceful policy, but felt strong personal spite and envy towards Bismarck. The ambassador in London, Count Peter Shuvalov, soon to be plenipotentiary at the Congress of Berlin, wanted full cooperation with the other powers, not least with Germany. The ambassador in Constantinople, Count Ignatyev, on the other hand, was urging the czar to take a strong line. Ignatyev reflected the hopes of the Moscow Panslav circles, who wanted to destroy Turkey-in-Europe and replace her by a strong Slav state in the Balkans. For the first half of 1875 the diplomats of Europe waited, some eagerly, some apprehensively, for what now seemed imminent—the final collapse of the Ottoman authority. In July the first crack appeared. The population of Bosnia rose in revolt against the Turk. The great Eastern crisis of 1875 to 1878 had started.

The consuls of the powers tried unsuccessfully to mediate in Bosnia, and in December Andrássy sent a note to the other Powers, recommending reforms in the Ottoman Empire. Nothing had come of the Andrássy Note, when Muslim riots in Salonika led to the murder of the French and German consuls there. In May 1876 Bismarck, Gorchakov and Andrássy met in Berlin, and drew up a memorandum proposing Turkish reforms and an armistice in Bosnia, and ending with the suggestion that 'effective measures' be taken if the reforms did not materialize. The Berlin Memorandum was presented to Britain, France and Italy as a finished document, to take or leave as they saw fit. Disraeli, who had recently come into office in London, refused to cooperate, and let it be known that he was deeply offended that he had not been consulted at an earlier stage. Britain had for half a century claimed an interest second to none in the Eastern Question, and Disraeli certainly did not envisage her policy as one of 'splendid isolation'. Before the other powers could move further without him, war broke out in the Balkans. In June Serbia and Montenegro attacked Turkey in support of their fellow Slavs in Bosnia and Herzegovina. The Serbs were defeated, but not before a rising had started in Bulgaria, where undisciplined Ottoman troops reacted by massacring about twelve thousand Christians. So frightful a reversion to barbarism in a European province made it difficult at that moment for any of the great powers to support Turkish rule in the Balkans any longer. In England Gladstone came from temporary retirement to publish a strong indictment of the Turk, in his pamphlet, the *Bulgarian Horrors*.

In April 1877 the czar, having fallen under the influence of the Panslav agitation in Russia and taking advantage of Disraeli's embarrassment over the Bulgarian atrocities, declared war on Turkey. By the Budapest Convention of some weeks earlier Austria had been squared: Andrássy had promised Gorchakov that Austria would remain neutral, on the understanding that she could occupy Bosnia-Herzegovina once Turkey was defeated. But with this one modification the Russian action was a unilateral one, and infringed the terms of the 1856 Treaty of Paris by which any intervention in Turkey was the responsibility of the Concert as a whole. The Russians expected to defeat the Turks very quickly. Instead they were held up by the brilliant Turkish defence of Plevna, which lasted into the winter of 1877–78. Once Plevna had fallen, the Russian advance continued towards Constantinople. But the siege of Plevna had given the British public some more weeks in which to forget the full horror of the Bulgarian massacres and to return to its previous conviction that the Turk was 'a gentleman'. Disraeli felt strong enough to order the British fleet to Constantinople—a second unilateral step, which also ignored international treaties on the Straits. Lord Derby, the foreign secretary, resigned in protest. The Russians made peace with Turkey without entering Constantinople.

The Treaty of San Stefano, signed in March 1878, was the work of Ignatyev, and did not bring the kind of settlement the other powers were likely to accept. For some weeks peace between the powers had been in danger; if anything the Treaty of San Stefano increased the danger. It marked the high-water mark of the Panslav movement, with the creation of a great Slav state of Bulgaria, including not only what was to become modern Bulgaria, but also Salonika to the south and Macedonia to the west. It enlarged Serbia and Montenegro and gave Russia important gains from Asiatic Turkey. At last Russia was enforcing one of her own projects for the partition of the Ottoman Empire in Europe. In doing so she was breaking not only the whole spirit of the 1856 settlement, but also specific and much more recent agreements with Austria.

In 1875 and 1876 Britain had refused to cooperate with the *Dreikaiserbund*, and so had prevented an intervention of the Concert of Europe in Turkey. Now that Russia had tried to force her own solution of the Eastern Question, Disraeli's government fell back on the more sensible policy of reconciling their interests with those of the other powers, and particularly of Austria. Britain and Austria united their demands for a European congress, and Bismarck, who had played a genuinely neutral role throughout, offered Berlin as a meeting place and himself as president of the congress. The other powers, including Russia, accepted. This time the Eastern Question was to lead to a European congress instead of a general war.

The Congress of Berlin assembled a distinguished company: Bismarck; Andrássy; for Britain, Disraeli and the new foreign secretary, Lord Salisbury, later to be prime minister three times for a sum total of over thirteen years; and for Russia, Gorchakov and Shuvalov. In a sense Russia was being called to the bar of the Concert of Europe. Her position was a difficult one, all the more so as her plenipotentiaries did not agree together. The chief plenipotentiary was inevitably the chancellor, but

Gorchakov was old and ill, and the real negotiator was Shuvalov. All the best features of the nineteenth-century diplomat were personified in Shuvalov. He realized that it was in the interests of his own country, then as always, to preserve the peace. He knew that the surest method of doing so was fully to understand the motives and aims of the other powers and to reconcile his own policy with those aims. A highly intelligent man and a skilled negotiator, he managed to save something for Russia from the wreck which the rash policies and foolish acts of men like Ignatyev had brought upon her. He earned the respect of all the other plenipotentiaries who were at pains to save his reputation with Alexander II from any excessive humiliations. Fortunately for Europe, Salisbury was also a diplomat of some calibre, while Andrássy at least knew when to limit his ambitions.

Inevitably the Congress reduced the great Bulgaria of San Stefano to less than half her former size, but Shuvalov preserved Sofia for the Bulgars, in spite of English opposition. The southern part of Ignatyev's Bulgaria was to be formed into an autonomous principality, called 'Eastern Roumelia', still under Turkish sovereignty but also under the protectorate of the Concert. Macedonia was to remain Turkish. Austria was to occupy Bosnia and Herzegovina, and Britain Cyprus, but all three were to remain under Turkish sovereignty. Little remained, then, of the Treaty of San Stefano, but equally, little remained of Turkey-in-Europe. Russia's wild experiment in Panslavism, which, it had been feared, would have extended her influence throughout the Balkans, was reduced to a pale shadow of its former self. On the other hand, something like a partition of the European Ottoman Empire was confirmed. Crises and difficulties lay ahead, when the terms of the Treaty of Berlin came to be enforced, but the dreaded Eastern Question had been handled successfully by negotiation.

In October 1879 Bismarck signed a treaty of alliance with Austria. Each of the two powers was pledged to help the other in the event of an attack by Russia, and to remain benevolently neutral in the event of an attack by a power other than Russia—in effect, by France or Britain. The Dual Austro-German Alliance was a first step in Bismarck's system of close alliances. In 1881 the Three Emperors' Alliance linked Russia with Austria and Germany in a formal treaty, not merely, as in 1873, in a vague agreement. In 1882 the Triple Alliance linked Italy in the same way with the two Germanic powers. Bismarck's aim in welding his close alliances was without doubt purely defensive. His 'Reinsurance Treaty' with Russia in 1887 appeared on the surface to be a final safeguarding of a system of security; but the alliance with Russia was not to last. Already before Bismarck's resignation in 1890 Russia was drifting into another orbit. In 1894 a close Franco-Russian treaty of alliance was signed. Two blocks now faced each other, and peace was maintained only by a balance of power, or, in the terms of the mid-twentieth century, a system of deterrents. The Concert of Europe was at last dead.

The term 'balance of power' has been applied indiscriminately to the whole period of diplomatic history from 1815 to 1914. But of the period 1815 to 1870, and to some extent even to 1879, the term 'general' or 'just' 'equilibrium' is more appropriate, and was at the beginning of the period more often used. Only very rarely were there two clearly defined power groups. Never were there close alliances between two powers except on the rare occasions when they were actually allied in war. It is not stretching the term too far to say that the Concert of Europe prevented, and was a substitute for, a crude balance of power. After 1894 the system of close alliances built up since 1879 tended to keep the peace through the imposition of terror rather than the application of argument. From 1894 to 1914 the great powers were careful not to touch the *status quo* in Europe for fear of bringing the whole close alliance system—with its binding clauses and its vast armies—into operation. A deterrent of this magnitude is likely to work successfully for many years. The balance of power established in 1894 kept the peace for two decades. But when it broke down it involved most of the civilized world in a war of appalling dimensions. Great military deterrents can never be trusted to keep the peace indefinitely, though they may be necessary as a temporary expedient while a safer system of collective security, with some central international authority, is slowly and painfully constructed. The European Concert in the decades after 1815 was an international authority, if an uncertain and ill-defined one. It kept the peace during a period of economic, social and political growth, and when it broke down in the second half of the nineteenth century, it did so slowly and without leading immediately to a world war. The Bismarckian system of alliances which replaced the old concept of the Concert marked a step backwards into an atmosphere of international violence, anarchy and fear.

VIII

The Western Powers:
France and Great Britain

Throughout the 1820s Great Britain, especially when George Canning
was at the Foreign Office, had alone among the great powers shown
some sympathy for the few constitutional movements which had
developed in western Europe. Bourbon France had for the most part
been aligned with the autocratic powers in resisting change of any sort.
But with the revolution of 1830 in Paris, England was suddenly provided
with an ally in her defence of constitutionalism. Ever since the two
nations had come into existence in the middle ages they had regarded
each other as natural enemies. In the eighteenth century there had been
long and costly wars between them. Britain had been the most constant
enemy of Napoleon I. Yet after 1815 the two countries were never to go
to war with each other again, and from the 1830s onwards there was

BIBLIOGRAPHY. A history of France since the death of Louis XIV, placed in a
deep perspective of the social and cultural scene, is Alfred Cobban's *History of
Modern France* (London, 2 vols., 1961). Vol. 2 covers the period 1799–1945.
J. P. T. Bury, *France 1814–1940* (London, 1949) is also a good, clear account. A
classic French work is the *Histoire de France contemporaine*, edited by E. Lavisse
in 8 vols. (Paris, 1920–22). Vols. 5 to 8 are relevant for the period, and C.
Seignobos's volumes, 6 to 8, are especially lucid. For a straightforward account
of the July Monarchy there is the second half of M. R. D. Leys, *Between Two
Empires* (London, 1955), and for a rather more popularly written life of Louis
Philippe there is·T. E. B. Howarth, *Citizen-King* (London, 1961). Douglas
Johnson's *Guizot* (London, 1963) is well based on the primary sources, manuscript as well as printed. D. McKay's *The National Workshops* (Harvard, 1933)
not only gives a sympathetic account of that institution, but has good general
chapters on the revolution of 1848 in France. For the Second Empire the fullest
account is still P. de La Gorce, *Histoire du second empire* (Paris, 7 vols., 1894–
1905). There are two good recent studies of Napoleon III in English: J. M.
Thompson, *Louis Napoleon and the Second Empire* (Oxford, 1954), and T. A. B.
Corley, *Democratic Despot* (London, 1961). The latter work is based only on the
printed sources, but on so thorough a knowledge of them that it ranks as a work

usually some kind of *entente* or understanding between them, an understanding only occasionally shaken by passing quarrels and operating in
a liberal sense in European politics. Liberal and nationalist refugees
from Italy, Poland or Hungary could now find a home either in Paris or
London. With the slow and uncertain emergence of an Anglo-French
entente, Europe acquired a new power factor of immense significance.
Yet internally the two nations developed along contrasting lines.

of reliable scholarship. For the Third Republic there is D. W. Brogan's attractive, if somewhat unorganized, *Development of Modern France* (London, 1940).
The two relevant volumes in the *Oxford History of England*, edited by G. N.
Clark, are E. L. Woodward, *The Age of Reform, 1815–1870* (Oxford, 1938) and
R. C. K. Ensor, *England, 1870–1914* (Oxford, 1936). They have both worn well,
and continue to serve as valuable reference works. A splendid history of England
covering the period to 1867 is Asa Briggs, *The Age of Improvement* (London,
1959), in the series, *History of England*, edited by W. N. Medlicott. The vividly
written E. Halévy, *A History of the English People in the Nineteenth Century*
(English translation by E. I. Watkin, 6 vols., 1927, revised edition 1950) is now
a classic. On the Chartists there has been no straight account to replace M.
Hovell, *The Chartist Movement* (London, revised edition 1925), but *Chartist
Studies*, edited by Asa Briggs (London, 1959), is an interesting collection of
studies of local Chartist history. Two works on the Anti-Corn Law movement
mentioned for chapter v (p. 85) are relevant here, as are the vast number of bio-
graphies of the Victorians which cannot possibly be listed. A lively account of
Spanish history for the period is included in A. R. Oliveira, *Politics, Economics
and Men of Modern Spain* (English translation by Jeëner Hall, London, 1946).
Three works on the political institutions of France must be mentioned: M.
Deslandres, *Histoire constitutionelle de la France, 1789–1870* (Paris, 2 vols., 1932),
which is still valuable for reference; P. Campbell, *French Electoral Systems and
Elections, 1789–1957* (London, 1958); and T. Zeldin, *The Political System of
Napoleon III* (London, 1958), which shows how the official party of the Empire
was built up and gives a sympathetic view of Napoleon III's institutions. On the
English parliamentary and electoral system there have been several scholarly
books since the war. Two can be mentioned here: N. Gash, *Politics in the Age of
Peel, 1830–1850* (London, 1953), an interpretation which has so close a feeling
for its period, that it seems at times to regret the subsequent emergence of
democracy, and H. J. Hanham, *Elections and Party Management: Politics in the
Time of Disraeli and Gladstone* (London, 1959). Several works written for students
of political science are yet historical in their approach. One of the better, if less
pretentious, of these is John P. Mackintosh, *The British Cabinet* (London, 1962),
about half of which deals with the period before 1880. On the armies and navies
two chapters in the *New Cambridge Modern History*, vol. x, edited by J. P. T.
Bury (Cambridge, 1960), are very enlightening: 'Armed Forces and the Art of
War: Navies', by Michael Lewis, and 'Armed Forces and the Art of War:
Armies', by B. H. Liddell Hart. For the French army the opening sections of
Michael Howard's *The Franco-Prussian War* (London, 1961) are admirable.

Political developments: France

The lack of stability in French political life throughout the nineteenth century was the direct result of the many strong currents of thought—liberal, socialist and imperialist—which had been awakened by the French Revolution. Traditions had been absorbed differently by the many and contrasting regions of France. While a republican and left-wing tradition prevailed and developed in Paris, a monarchical and clerical tradition died hard elsewhere. The Vendeé, and to a less extent other provincial areas, remained devoutly Catholic. Thus when Napoleon III was losing the sympathy of radical Paris in the second half of his reign, he was acquiring support from the remote fringes of the country, where clerical sentiment was abandoning hope of a Bourbon restoration and adopting the Empire as its favoured régime. But the spirit of the *ancien régime* had not readily accepted defeat. Although the Bourbon dynasty left the French throne for ever in 1830, its supporters continued a rearguard action for many years. But in 1830 Charles X, the last of the Bourbons, was removed with surprising ease. The appointment of Prince Jules de Polignac as chief minister was a grave error which united the opposition, constitutional and unconstitutional, against the régime. Polignac's experience had been only diplomatic and his knowledge of the domestic politics of France was inadequate. His faith in prayer and revelation alarmed the hard-headed business men and journalists of Paris. The assembly which met in March 1830 at once made it clear to their sovereign that they had no confidence in his new ministers. Whether the king had the right to appoint an executive government without reference to the majority in the legislature was now seen, not for the last time, to be the issue which underlay the whole constitutional struggle in France. Charles's immediate answer to the problem was to dissolve the assembly. The new assembly, elected in July 1830, provided the opposition with an even stronger majority. On 26 July Charles put into force Article XIV of the charter which empowered him to issue emergency decrees, apparently without sanction from the assembly. The next day he issued four ordinances which gagged the press, dissolved the assembly, reduced an already small electorate to about one quarter of its former size, and announced that new elections would be held under these changed regulations. A consideration of the text of the ordinances suggests that Charles had decided to destroy the constitution, yet, if so, his policy was very rash, for he had kept few royal troops at hand to deal with any resistance.

The press was the worst victim of the ordinances, and resistance to the king was led by the press. Liberal journalists declared that Charles had forfeited the allegiance of his subjects by trying to impose an illegal system upon them. Disturbances, and the erection of barricades in Paris, lasted for three days, but Charles submitted without resorting to heavy fighting, and fled to England and exile. In Paris the men with the most constructive and energetic policy were Adolphe Thiers (1797–1877), a young journalist and historian, and Jacques Laffitte (1767–1844), one of the leading bankers in Europe. They and their following of moderates decided to retain the monarchy but to replace the Bourbons by the younger branch of the family, the house of Orléans. The present duc d'Orléans was Louis-Philippe (1773–1850), whose father had played an influential role in the great revolution, had renounced his titles and taken the name of Louis *Egalité*. Louis-Philippe himself had fought at the great revolutionary victory of Jemappes, was believed to favour a liberal régime for France and would accept that symbol of the revolution, the Tricolor flag. It seemed possible that Louis-Philippe could reconcile the monarchy and the traditions of the revolution. On 9 August the assembly recognized him to be 'King of the French, by the grace of God and the will of the nation'. The republicans afterwards claimed that they had made the revolution of 1830 but had been cheated of the fruits of it by the rich middle class. But there was no consistent or loyal backing for a republic in 1830. The republican newspapers, the *Tribune* and the *Révolution*, had only a few hundred subscribers; the larger newspapers—Thiers's *National* and the *Constitutionnel* with its 22,000 subscribers—supported the establishment of the Orleanist monarchy, though they were later to be alienated from it.

The reign of Louis-Philippe, called, after the month in which it started, the 'July Monarchy', was one of peace externally, but of bitterness and endless friction internally. Louis-Philippe took pains to foster the concept of a citizen king. In spite of his royal blood, his life had not been sealed off from the rest of the world as that of Charles X had been. He could easily identify his interests and appearance with those of the middle class. Already fifty-seven in 1830, he deliberately cultivated a humble exterior. He sent his children to the state schools and made himself, in the Palais Royal, more accessible than any king had been before. He walked the streets of Paris unattended, and dressed like any other successful citizen. He avoided a close relationship with the clericals. He was popular with the richer classes, so long as he could guarantee them peace and prosperity, but he never created an attractive image of himself for wider consumption. Both to the left and to the right of his régime there were bitter enemies. Between 1835 and 1846 there were six attempts on his life. His power rested on a narrow basis. The charter of 1814 had been modified, but not radically. A high tax qualification still deprived a great majority of Frenchmen of the vote.

The July Revolution in Paris had been a comparatively peaceful one, but Louis-Philippe had to face violent insurrections in the provinces almost immediately after he had come to power. In November 1831 the silk workers of Lyons, having failed to secure a fixing of a minimum wage by negotiation, resorted to force, and eventually gained control of the city. The attitude to be taken by the new French government, which had so recently acquired power by revolution, was of immense concern and significance to the whole of Europe. The action of Louis-Philippe and his ministers showed that they were eager to identify themselves completely with the interests of the manufacturers. Not only was the rising suppressed by royal troops—as it inevitably had to be—but the government also hastened to deny the legality of any collective bargaining by employees. Of even greater military significance was a Bourbonist rising in the Vendée which took longer to suppress than the socialist rising in Lyons.

For these first years of the July Monarchy the press censorship had been lifted. In 1835 a law was passed which discouraged the more violently subversive articles, and from then onwards opposition to the régime followed more constitutional paths. From 1835 to 1848 the political struggle was centred on parliamentary activity rather than on popular insurrections. A situation not unlike the English two-party rivalry developed with Thiers leading the liberals and Guizot the conservatives. François Guizot (1787–1874), a cultured Protestant, believed that the richer classes should have power and responsibility commensurate with their stake in the welfare of the country. He was prepared to adjust his policy to suit the wishes of the new rich in France. When his proposed customs union with Belgium, Switzerland and Piedmont, intended to counterbalance the German *Zollverein*, was opposed by the industrialists, he obediently abandoned it. Guizot was Louis-Philippe's chief minister from 1840 to 1848, and throughout these years his policy was closely identifiable with that of the king, who repeatedly interfered in the game of political management.

The reasons for the fall of the July Monarchy can conveniently be classified under the four headings of economic, diplomatic, social and constitutional. By the opening of 1848 an ugly economic situation had developed. Both in 1846 and 1847 the corn harvest had failed. The rising price of bread led to depression in other industries, especially the textile industry. Over-speculation in railway development in France as in England, created a financial crisis. Unemployment had contributed to the revolution of 1830; in 1848 it was still more acute. The economic conditions for revolution were thus present, but Louis-Philippe's government would probably have retained at least the confidence of the middle class but for a rash diplomatic move which seemed to bring France suddenly, surprisingly and uncomfortably near a war with England. In the early days of his reign, Louis-Philippe had established an *entente* with England during the crisis accompanying the Belgian movement for independence. Since then he had pursued a conciliatory and even humble foreign policy which had antagonized the liberal and Bonapartist parties, but had almost certainly reassured the richer classes as a whole. The surprise was all the greater, when, in 1847, Louis-Philippe and Guizot resolved the tangled Spanish marriages question in such a way that an Orleanist prince would in all probability become king of Spain—an eventuality against which the British government had for some time been trying to insure. The resulting crisis with England, over a purely dynastic issue, suggested that Louis-Philippe was prepared to go to absurd lengths in order to marry his sons to the older royal families.

In social terms France had seemed on the verge of revolution since 1830. The socialist ideas of the Saint-Simonians, Fourier, Proudhon and Blanc have been considered in an earlier chapter; the grim conditions in the large industries which were growing up will be considered in their European context in a later chapter. It is sufficient to point out here that the only men who pleaded the cause of the factory workers in France were violent revolutionaries like Louis-Auguste Blanqui, or the extreme socialist writers. There was no equivalent in France of a respectable Tory philanthropist like Lord Shaftesbury. Attempts made by the government of the July Monarchy to improve conditions in the factories had been pathetically inadequate. Yet all these factors—economic, diplomatic and social—would not have brought matters to a head without the constitutional issue which demonstrated the struggle between authority and the majority of the people in glaringly simple terms.

The electorate had remained a mere 200,000 out of a total population of about 35 million by 1848. Nothing would convince Guizot that it could safely be enlarged. As opinion turned against him in the assembly he was obliged to resort to ever more corrupt measures to retain his majority. Louis-Philippe not only encouraged Guizot's political management, but seemed to regard his own survival as being dependent upon that of his minister. That symbol of a citizen revolution on which the power of a bourgeois monarch should naturally have rested, the National Guard, had been in existence since 1830, but its members had not been granted the vote. In 1847 a petition demanding at least this measure of reform was rejected. Bourbon legitimists, republicans among whom the socialists were prominent, and Bonapartists united in opposition against a government which was refusing to notice the vast social changes France was experiencing. Public banquets were held as demonstrations in favour of parliamentary reform. On 22 February 1848 rioting broke out, and for the next few days there was widespread disorder in Paris. Inevitably at a certain stage the nerves of the troops broke down; shots were fired; the barricades went up. In 1830 Charles X had been unable to rally troops for his immediate support. To his credit, Louis-Philippe refused even to consider a full-scale armed action against the crowd. Instead he abdicated in favour of his ten-year-old grandson, and on 25 February hastened to England.

The revolution was directed not only against the king and his minister, but also against the assembly which gave legal recognition to the monarchy. A majority in the assembly would probably have accepted a boy-king with the old queen as regent, but a revolutionary crowd invaded the House, and the Republic was declared simultaneously there and in the Hotel de Ville. In the assembly the initiative was seized by a republican of the classical liberal tradition, Alphonse de Lamartine (1790–1869). Lyric poet and author of the very successful *History of the Girondins*, Lamartine had made his reputation under the July Monarchy as a colourful orator rather than as a political leader of intellectual weight. He persuaded the assembly to appoint a provisional government consisting of himself and six other moderate republican leaders. Meanwhile, in the offices of the socialist *Réforme*, a second list of ministers was drawn up, this one including Louis Blanc. The rival provisional governments had the good sense to draw up a compromise, by which Blanc and a worker in the gas industry, Albert Martin, always known affectionately by his first name, were to share power with the right-wing republicans.

The February Revolution which created the Second Republic in France was the first of a wave of revolutions which swept the capitals of Europe throughout the spring of 1848. But nowhere else did revolutionary governments contain either a socialist philosopher or a workman. Once again, as in 1789, the French were making political experiments undreamt of in other countries. The Provisional Government in Paris at once declared for universal suffrage, and abolished the regulation which had restricted the National Guard to the middle class. These measures had the full support of all members of the government. Another measure, not at all to the taste of the right-wing ministers, was conceded to Louis Blanc—the creation of National Workshops. It has been the habit, especially among English historians, to pour scorn upon Blanc's experiment. But the revolutionary government was faced with a very real problem: what was to be done with the thousands of unemployed, who had perhaps made the revolution possible, but who might equally prevent any sound administration in future? A more ruthless government than this group of journalists, lawyers and writers might have drafted the men into the army and embarked on a 'war of liberation' like that of 1792. It is arguable that the establishment of a state workshop was a preferable solution. The failure of the National Workshops was partly due to the lack of sympathy from Blanc's colleagues for his scheme. Even the official charged with the administration of the workshops was sceptical. But more basic factors contributed to the failure. In the chaotic conditions of 1848 the workshops could not be run economically. Work could not be found for all, and the unlucky had to be provided with a dole. More unemployed flocked in from the provinces. Some useful work was accomplished: several Parisian streets were macadamized. But this first socialist experiment stirred up fears and hostility all over France. It divided the ministers themselves.

In the elections for an assembly held under the new republican constitution no fewer than 84 per cent of the electorate—the adult male population of France—voted. Of the 876 delegates elected a majority were very moderate republicans, only about a hundred were radicals, while there were a considerable number of Orleanists and some Legitimists. It was hardly surprising that such an assembly should exclude Blanc and Albert when appointing its new government, but the announcement that the two ministers had been dropped was the signal for a socialist rising on 15 May. Among the leaders of the rising were Albert himself and Blanqui, who had throughout the revolutionary period been regarded as the key figure on the extreme left. Historians have usually dismissed Blanqui as a freak, yet he had led the first revolutionary socialist party to be composed mainly of workers—the *Société des Saisons*—which had risen in 1839. Since then he had spent eight years in prison or a prison hospital. In 1848 he led the 'Central Republican Party', which had a very considerable working-class following. After the May rising he was imprisoned, and his removal from the scene gave the new government the courage it needed to close the National Workshops towards the end of June. A more formidable rising, though now a leaderless one, followed the closing of the workshops. The workers, faced with renewed unemployment or enrolment in the army, refused to disperse. The assembly declared a state of emergency, and placed the supreme executive power in the hands of General Cavaignac, a republican leader who had been on the other side of the barricades in 1830 and February 1848. After three days of bitter fighting, remembered grimly as the 'June Days', Cavaignac re-established the authority of the government, but not without the killing and deporting of thousands of Frenchmen. The June Days left a terrible mark on the Second Republic and on the subsequent history of France.

In the autumn of 1848 the supposedly definitive constitution of the Second Republic was drawn up. It placed the executive in the hands of a president, who was to be elected, not by the assembly, but by universal male suffrage. The election was held in the last month of this eventful year. Among the candidates were Lamartine who, as minister for foreign affairs, had successfully kept the Republic out of foreign adventures, Cavaignac, whose methods during the June Days were thought to have been needlessly cruel, and a prince who was personally far less familiar, but whose name called up an emotional response even from the most ignorant of Frenchmen—Louis-Napoleon Bonaparte.

Prince Louis-Napoleon (1808–73) was by 1848 the legitimate heir of Napoleon. His father, Louis Bonaparte, king of Holland, had been brother, and his mother, Hortense de Beauharnais, step-daughter of the great emperor. Napoleon's son and brothers and Louis-Napoleon's own two elder brothers were all dead. The series of deaths seemed to confirm the conviction which Louis-Napoleon had long held: that he was fated to become ruler of France. All his life he had been an exile under the law of 1816 banning the House of Bonaparte from France, a law confirmed by Louis-Philippe's first assembly. His two attempts at seizing power, at Strasbourg in 1836, and at Boulogne in 1840, had been pathetic failures, giving the July Monarchy no cause for alarm. But they had been made before the cult of the First Empire, which was a characteristic of the 1840s, had made itself felt. The so-called 'Napoleonic Legend' was partly the creation of a literary movement and partly a re-birth of popular Napoleonic sentiment, tolerated, and even occasionally encouraged, by Louis-Philippe. Thiers's *History of the Empire* had unintentionally contributed to the legend, and Louis-Napoleon's own *Napoleonic Ideas* had found a public. His *Extinction of Pauperism* had associated Bonapartism with an awareness of the need for social reform. In 1840 the king had arranged for the bones of Napoleon I to be brought back from St Helena and buried in Paris in the monstrous tomb at the Invalides.

In 1848 Louis-Napoleon could thus rely on the support of a great Bonapartist tradition, which he skilfully adjusted to the concerns of the day. His personal appearance was something of a liability, but this could be overcome. By no means an attractive figure, he was shy and awkward in public, but exercised a certain quiet charm in conversation. His electoral campaign for the presidency was well planned. He could not openly recommend a restoration of the Empire, but declared his approval of a republic based on universal suffrage. The accumulated effect of the Napoleonic Legend, the confusion and bloodshed of the Second Republic and the need for stability produced an impressive result. Louis-Napoleon was elected President by an enormous majority. Only a few outlying parts of France preferred Cavaignac. The rest of the country placed their confidence in a name and a tradition. By the terms of the constitution, Louis-Napoleon could remain President for only three years. To overcome this obstacle to what he interpreted as the will of destiny, the President took the law into his own hands. On the night of 1 December 1851, he carried through, with lightning efficiency, the most ruthless act of his political career—the *coup d'état* which gave him absolute power in France. The assembly was occupied by troops and the leaders of the political parties were arrested. A plebiscite was held, and another overwhelming majority for Louis-Napoleon enabled him to consider the *coup d'état* confirmed by the nation. A year later, on 2 December 1852, he assumed the title of 'Emperor Napoleon III'.

The Second Empire, like the July Monarchy, was to last for eighteen years. It retained the façade of a constitution, but abolished the substance. An assembly was elected, but prevented from exercising any power. Napoleon chose his own ministers, and nominated senators to an upper house. He used the election of 1852 to build up a government party throughout the country. Official candidates were nominated, usually from the rich or locally influential classes. Not a single republican deputy was elected until 1857. Opposition to the régime was carried on, not in the assembly, but in the salons, or by exiles in England,

Belgium and Switzerland. Support for the régime rested on the army, business men and the priests, who kept the peasants to the government party line in rural elections. Napoleon succeeded where Louis-Philippe had failed: in winning the clericals away from their Bourbon allegiances. Under the authoritarian régime there was an absurd atmosphere of official suspicion. A newspaper was warned by a prefect for publishing the statement: 'The Emperor made a speech which, according to the Havas agency, provoked cries of "Vive l'Empéreur" several times.' The prefect thought he could detect a note of scepticism in the report. Events for the first half of the reign were thus in the field of social and economic development and foreign affairs, rather than of internal politics. While France slept politically, the railways were built, industry expanded, Paris was rebuilt on a magnificent plan. And the prestige of France as a great power was restored.

Before the Empire had been in existence for two years it was involved in a major war with Russia—the first time France had been at war with another power since Waterloo. Napoleon's object in entering the Crimean War lay in his desire to consolidate Catholic support at home and an English alliance abroad. In 1852 and 1853 the Catholic and Greek Orthodox Churches had disputed certain ritualistic and property rights in the Holy Lands. The French and Russian governments had supported their ecclesiastics, and the clash had become one of national prestige. A quite separate dispute between Russia on the one hand and Turkey and Britain on the other enabled Napoleon to weld together a close Anglo-French alliance, and in 1854 the two western powers went to war in defence of the Ottoman Empire against Russian aggression. For France and Britain the Crimean War was a static, badly planned affair, and the victory after nearly two years of stalemate was a dismal one. The contrast with the dynamic campaigns of Napoleon I could hardly have been more striking. But for an authoritarian government any kind of victory is better than none at all. The Peace Congress of 1856 was held not at London, or Vienna, but at Paris. French prestige was restored after forty years of eclipse.

Napoleon had not sought the help of Polish revolutionaries in defeating Russia. The need to keep at least the friendly neutrality of Austria had made it essential that Poland, Italy and the Balkans should rest undisturbed by revolution. But no sooner had the congress assembled in Paris than it became clear that Napoleon was prepared to take up the cause of nationality even in the teeth of Austrian opposition. As a young exile in Rome in 1831 he had supported the Italian revolution against the pope. It was even rumoured that he had taken the Carbonari oath. During the years after 1856 he gave diplomatic support to Rumanian nationalists, and in Italy drew up an understanding with Piedmont which led to war against Austria in 1859. Napoleon's Italian policy and his secret agreements with Cavour can better be dealt with in the context of Italian history. Their significance for France lay in their influence upon the internal security of the Second Empire. Throughout his reign Napoleon was trying to reconcile two conflicting traditions—the tradition of the Catholic monarchy of Louis XIV and the tradition of the Revolution. In Italy this led to an impossible paradox. At one moment Napoleon was launching great armies to enable Piedmont to unite Italy under her authority. At the next moment he was giving the pope active military support against the emerging Italian kingdom. The effect on both liberals and Catholics in France was to astonish, to irritate and finally to antagonize them. The war of 1859 was not popular in France, yet it went far towards the creation of Italy, and placed Napoleon at the peak of his power in Europe.

The second half of the reign of Napoleon III witnessed striking constitutional reforms at home, but a steady decline of French influence abroad. The political relaxation started in 1859 with the granting of an amnesty, which encouraged many exiles to return, though some, like Victor Hugo, refused to trust the 'man of December'. From 1861 the assembly was allowed to vote each item of the budget. The press censorship was relaxed. A few moderate opposition newspapers—both Orleanist and republican—appeared. But the reforms did not make Napoleon's government more popular; rather did it encourage stronger opposition. In 1863 thirty-five opposition delegates were elected, including all the representatives of Paris and several prominent figures—Thiers, Jules Favre and Jules Ferry. Two or three years later Napoleon began to suffer from bladder trouble, and by 1869 he was seriously ill. In the general elections of 1869 the government candidates obtained only 42 per cent of the total votes cast. Napoleon decided to push through the creation of his 'Liberal Empire'—to alter the underlying principle of his régime. In September 1869 the ministers were made responsible to the assembly, and in January 1870 a former opponent of the Empire, Emile Ollivier, became prime minister, but did not carry the bulk of the republicans with him. For the last few months of its life the Second Empire had become a parliamentary system, and Napoleon III a constitutional monarch with much the same responsibility as Queen Victoria enjoyed in England.

The increasing loss of favour of the Empire with the French electorate was due very largely to Napoleon's disastrous foreign policy in the last decade of his reign. First and most spectacular of the tragedies had been the Mexican expedition of 1861, which was to have led, according to Napoleon's dreams, to a liberal Catholic empire preventing the further spread of Anglo-American barbarism in the New World. His choice as Mexican emperor was the liberal-minded Maximilian, brother of Francis Joseph of Austria. By 1867 the Mexican experiment had led to complete disaster. The French forces were withdrawn, leaving Maximilian to be shot by the Mexican revolutionaries. Meanwhile Napoleon's policy in Europe had been ineffective and weakened by his Mexican commitments. He had failed to secure any advantage from the Austro-Prussian War of 1866, and the presence of his troops in Rome prevented the creation of an alliance with Italy and Austria afterwards. In 1870, with the emperor already a dying man, France was dangerously isolated.

To become involved in a war with Bismarck's Prussia in 1870 was the Second Empire's last and greatest mistake. It cannot be considered a personal error of Napoleon since he had handed policy over to his ministers. Rather was it the fault of the incompetent foreign minister, the duc de Gramont, and of the prime minister, Ollivier, who was too weak in the assembly to risk a humiliation at the hands of Bismarck. The war started on the first day of August 1870, and on 3 September the news reached Paris that a great French army had been forced to surrender at Sedan and the emperor was a prisoner. At once the republicans in Paris proposed that a government commission should be formed, but on the following day the ministers produced a document, signed by the empress, appointing a regency council of five deputies.

As on so many previous occasions the Paris crowd swept into the assembly chamber, and the republicans succeeded in establishing their 'Government of National Defence', of which General Trochu, governor of Paris under the Empire, was president. The government also contained Jules Favre and the young deputy for Marseilles, Léon Gambetta (1838–82). The Republic was proclaimed not only at Paris but at Lyons, Bordeaux and Marseilles—a contrast with the republican movement of 1848 which had been a purely Parisian one. A revolution had been accomplished without bloodshed. The Government of National Defence survived until the end of the war, but it was cut into two before the end of September by Prussian military victories and the siege of Paris. The chief ministers remained in the besieged capital, but three delegates had already left to govern the provinces, first from Tours and then from Bordeaux. On 6 October Gambetta made his spectacular escape from Paris by balloon, to fortify the provincial government and to bring its actions into line with the wishes of Paris. From the day of his arrival in Tours he became the real government of the provinces. Even after the surrender of France's greatest army under Marshal Bazaine, Gambetta refused to accept defeat. The government in Paris also refused to admit the hopelessness of the situation, but the Prussians were not their only cause for alarm. Socialists in the National Guard and a growing party organized by Blanqui were demanding the election of a commune by universal suffrage. The government closed the political clubs. They had already sent Thiers to the German headquarters to negotiate an armistice.

Paris surrendered on 28 January 1871, and a new assembly was elected on 8 February. In Paris many socialists were returned. The departments under German occupation and the south-east chose republicans, but the rest of France preferred opponents of Gambetta, either Orleanist or Bourbonist. The assembly met at Bordeaux, refused to proclaim the Republic, but elected Thiers, now, at seventy-three, at the peak of his popularity, 'head of the executive power'. His first function was to make peace with Bismarck—a peace which lost France Alsace-Lorraine and its one-and-a-half million people. But in Paris the National Guard had not disarmed, the eastern suburbs were strongly socialist, and the assembly's peace was bitterly resented. A 'Republican federation of the National Guard' with a central committee of sixty was established on 15 March, and three days later the socialist insurrection began. The mayors of Paris, among them the young Georges Clemenceau, tried to secure a compromise agreement from the assembly, but without success. Alongside the central committee of the National Guard a commune was elected, nearly a third of its delegates being members of the First International,[1] and another third followers of Blanqui. The republican calendar and red flag were adopted.

The commune rising led to the most terrible civil war in the nineteenth-century history of France. About 20,000 lives were lost. Thiers's government shot several thousand rebels after they had been taken prisoner. Thousands more were deported or imprisoned. Military trials continued to deal with cases until 1876. The socialist movement in France was broken for many years to come.

The assembly which had been elected in February 1871 had full

[1] See above, p. 64.

sovereign powers in the absence of any alternative, and retained them until January 1876. During these five years it took upon itself the role of a constituent assembly, and provided France with the constitution of the Third Republic. The monarchists together—Orleanists and Bourbonists—were the largest group in the assembly, but neither party alone could command a majority over the republicans. A few extra Bonapartists were elected in July 1871. In August Thiers was elected president, but he still regarded himself as responsible only to the assembly. As regards the administration of the country this cautious parliamentary government had a good record: the budget was balanced, the indemnity was quickly paid to the new German Empire and the German occupation ended in 1873. But in political terms the régime was a repressive one: newspapers were closely controlled and not allowed to be sold in public, and in 1874 a censorship of the theatre was imposed. The Church recovered much of its lost authority. Sacré-Cœur was built as a symbol of the defeat of the revolution.

Thiers steered a middle course between Gambetta's left-wing following in the assembly and the demands for a restoration of the monarchy. But by May 1873 his position had become impossible, and the little old man who had played so central a role since 1830 resigned his office. He was replaced by a government of monarchists who ruled France from 1873 to 1876 under republican forms. Marshal MacMahon was elected president on the assumption that he would prepare the way for a return of the monarchy. The difficulty with establishing a monarchy is that a king has to be chosen. It was easy and natural for barbarian tribes in the Dark Ages to select kings to lead them in battle. It was not too difficult, even in the nineteenth century, to find monarchs for small new Balkan states. But with France in the 1870s it was another matter. The Houses of Bourbon, Orleans and Bonaparte could all advance claims, though the only two which could be taken seriously were those of the Count of Chambord, grandson of Charles X, and the Count of Paris, grandson of Louis-Philippe. The Count of Paris eventually agreed to accept the claims of Chambord to be 'Henry V', in return for the recognition of himself as heir to the throne. But the monarchist cause collapsed when Chambord refused to accept the Tricolor. On 30 January 1875 the assembly declared by a majority of one vote that France was to remain a republic. The danger of a return to the atmosphere of the Restoration period was averted.

The new assembly, elected by universal suffrage under the constitution of 1875, provided a large republican majority. The president,

MacMahon, at first accepted the situation and appointed a ministry which could command support in the House, but a bitter dispute over clerical control of education and the lost temporal power of the pope ensued. In May 1877 MacMahon replaced the left-wing ministry by a conservative one, adjourned the assembly, and finally had it dissolved by the senate. In the subsequent election the president played an active role: he presented a list of official candidates as the Second Empire had done; he prevented the publication of many republican papers. Even so, the elections gave the left-wing groups a majority of about one hundred. MacMahon at last accepted the inevitable, and thereafter did not attempt to impose a ministry on the assembly against its wishes. The precedent had been established that the government was to be responsible to the assembly and not to the president. It was of immense significance for the future of France.

Gambetta and Thiers had combined forces against the president during the crisis of 1877. The death of Thiers, the same year, left Gambetta, surprisingly, as his heir in the leadership of the left-centre. In 1879 MacMahon resigned the presidency, and Jules Grévy was elected in his place. A lawyer of *petit-bourgeois* origins and an anti-clerical, Grévy was a typical father-figure of the Third Republic.

The extraordinary political convulsions which France had experienced in the century which preceded the establishment of the Third Republic had done little to hinder her steady economic growth. Her prestige as a great power had been re-established by 1856, and up to that date at least her industries had developed more quickly than those of any power other than Britain. But from 1856 to 1870 France was, comparatively speaking, a declining power in Europe. In both economic and military terms Prussia was fast catching up. Blunders in foreign policy contributed to French isolation, and the disaster of 1870 left her with two great powers, Germany and Italy, on her frontiers. But the national genius was not yet exhausted. By 1880 the European prestige of France was already returning. If the subsequent decades were to be marred by public scandal and corruption they were also to restore France to a big place in the world.

Political developments: Britain

In contrast with the sudden changes in the government system of France, Great Britain experienced a more gradual evolution. A conservative spirit directed the policies of British political parties mainly because of a habit of mind acquired in the long wars with revolutionary and Napoleonic France. Complete victory in 1815 had given Britain security from external attack, a security which she enjoyed throughout the nineteenth century. She did not have to rely on a large army for home defence, and could exert influence in Europe through her immense wealth. While France was experiencing revolution and counter-revolution in the period 1830 to 1880, British political institutions were slowly developed and adjusted. The outward forms of the English constitution and the myth of its perfection were both preserved, while the real centre of power was appreciably shifted. The first great shift of power was the result of the Reform Act of 1832, which gave the vote to the middle class and made the ruling aristocracy increasingly dependent on the good will of the newly enriched manufacturers. In geographical terms the Act in the long run shifted the centre of power from the agricultural south to the recently industrialized north.

The Duke of Wellington (1769–1852) had become prime minister in January 1828. His central role in the defeat of Napoleon had given him a unique reputation and position in Europe in the years after Waterloo. But his political attitude was already becoming an anachronism. He had no concept of cabinet solidarity, a constitutional feature which had been emerging since 1815. He regarded himself as responsible to the crown rather than to cabinet or parliament. By 1830 he had quarrelled with both the left and right wings of the Tory party and could no longer keep the government together. William IV was obliged to turn to the Whigs who had not been in office since the war. Lord Grey (1764–1845) was asked to form a government. Charles Grey, the second earl, had agitated for parliamentary reform before the end of the eighteenth century, but in recent years he had been neither an active nor inspiring leader of the Whigs. A landed nobleman, he was determined to preserve the rights of property, but he had the good sense to see that the time had arrived when a Whig government could profitably put itself at the head of a reform movement. On 1 March 1831 Lord John Russell introduced a Bill granting a large measure of parliamentary reform: taking away members from the smallest boroughs, giving representation to the large new towns in the north, and radically reducing the property qualifications for the vote. The Tories at once declared the Bill a revolution which would destroy 'the natural influence of rank and property': it was an act of robbery since the seats in the small boroughs were pieces of financial property. The Whigs themselves were driven by no desire for democracy, but were convinced that only a generous measure of reform could prevent revolution.

The Reform Bill crisis lasted for fifteen months. Two Bills were defeated and before the third was passed Grey was obliged to dissolve the House, fight a general election and engage in a fierce struggle with the House of Lords. Furious reform agitation spread from Birmingham, where Thomas Attwood's 'Political Union of the Lower and Middle Classes of the People' had been founded in 1829, to London and the south. There were mass disturbances in the winter of 1830–31, reaching a climax in a considerable mob rising in Bristol. The eventual passing of the Bill in June 1832 was greeted with rejoicing throughout the country. By extending the franchise and redistributing seats, the 1832 Act increased the electorate by almost exactly a half. Both reformers and opponents had expected a more striking change in the size of the electorate but in so far as it introduced a new class to political influence the Great Reform Act deserves to be considered a revolution no less—and perhaps more—than do the events of 1830 in Paris.

After victory the Whig cabinet would gladly have rested from its labours, but it was driven to further reforms by two very different radical groups—the pious Evangelicals and the materialist Benthamites. The Evangelicals persuaded Grey's government to pass two significant measures in 1833: acts abolishing slavery in the British Empire and regulating the employment of children in the factories. The Benthamite measure, the Poor Law Amendment Act of 1834, scrapped the system of outdoor relief which had been in operation since the Napoleonic wars, and arranged for the building of the workhouses which were to become so familiar a feature of the Victorian scene. Designed on strictly rational, if inhuman, lines, the Poor Law Act proved cruel in operation. In the workhouses men were separated from their wives and life was made as grim and arduous as possible. The Act was bitterly unpopular and contributed to the rise of the Chartist movement of working-class protest.

The Reform Act had altered the aristocratic nature of neither the Tory nor the Whig parties. They shared a common distaste for the radical group in the House of Commons, and a common fear of working-class movements. New leaders emerging in 1834 moved the Tories perceptibly to the left and the Whigs to the right. Sir Robert Peel (1788–1850), a hard-working and serious man, took over the leadership of the Tory party. As the son of a manufacturer, he inevitably brought a new outlook into what had tended to be an exclusively landowning party. In an address to his constituents at Tamworth, Peel declared in 1834 that the Reform Act, which he had passionately opposed, must now be accepted as permanent. The new Whig leader, William Lamb, second

Lord Melbourne (1779–1848), was a self-indulgent and good-humoured nobleman, who resisted further reforms and declared that Benthamites were 'all fools'. He succeeded Grey as prime minister in July 1834, but had given way to a Tory government under Peel before the end of the year. The Whigs had fallen from office after their eventful four years partly from incompetence in administration. They were unfortunate in possessing no competent financier—no Huskisson, Peel or Gladstone. The Whigs were bankrupt in financial ideas as the Tories were in political ideas. Peel fell from office again in April 1835, and was replaced by Melbourne's second cabinet, who were still in office when William IV died in 1837.

The new monarch, Queen Victoria (1819–1901), was a naive but self-willed girl who had just passed her eighteenth birthday. Under her the monarchy was to abandon its direct influence on government policy, but it was to acquire an aura of moral respect which it had never known before. The new respectability owed much to the personal character of the queen, but perhaps still more to that of the young German prince, whom she married in 1840—Albert of Saxe-Coburg-Gotha (1819–61).

If at one end of the social scale Lord Melbourne and the young queen lived in a peaceful and elegant world, at the other end of the scale the late 1830s were a period of social clamour and protest. The Chartist movement grew out of hatred of the Poor Law and was encouraged by the early trade union movement. It formed part of that wide working-class movement which was an important undercurrent to political developments at Westminster, and which was not directly affected by the passing of the Reform Bill. That the Chartist movement failed to secure its demands was partly due to its spasmodic nature. It did not keep up a sustained effort for more than a few months at a time. It slackened when working-class conditions momentarily improved—in years of good harvests, or during the short periods of full employment. It disappeared completely when the 'hungry forties' had given way to the more prosperous fifties. The People's Charter which formed the basis of the movement was published in May 1838. It demanded six points, all of them of a political nature: annual parliaments, universal male suffrage, equal electoral districts, the removal of property qualifications for M.P.s, a secret ballot and payment for M.P.s. All the points were regarded as extravagant by the ruling classes in 1838, yet five of them were, in the fullness of time, to be accepted. The charter was the work of William Lovett (1800–77) and Francis Place (1771–1854). Lovett, himself an artisan, had decided that political reform would have to precede the improvement of working-class conditions. Place, already quite an old man in 1838, had been one of the earliest moderate working-class leaders. The three Chartist petitions to parliament, drawn up in 1838, 1842 and 1848, marked a steady decline from the responsible and moderate working-class leadership of men like Lovett and Place in 1838 to the less responsible, yet vacillating, middle-class leadership of the Irish journalist, Feargus O'Connor, in 1848. No English parliament, anyhow, was ready to open its doors to the elected representatives of the working classes. In Westminster the term 'democracy' was still one of abuse.

Apart from a few of the leaders, the Chartists came from the working class. A cause which appealed to middle and working classes alike was the demand for repeal of the Corn Laws. In their most unpopular form the Corn Laws dated from 1815 when they had been introduced to protect home-grown corn in freak economic circumstances. Many people during the Reform Bill crisis had thought of parliamentary reform only as a means to an end, and the end was repeal of the laws which levied so high a tariff on imported corn that the price of bread remained unnaturally high. It was the great achievement of Cobden and Bright that they attracted the attention of the working classes away from Chartism to the movement against the Corn Laws, so that, in the period 1838 to 1846 when an ugly class war might easily have developed, a large number of the poorest workers were uniting their efforts with those of the manufacturers in a common struggle against the landowning classes.

When Peel formed his second ministry in 1841 there was great speculation on what tariff policy he would adopt. His government's administration was sound and energetic: tariffs were generally lowered and income tax was introduced, but in 1845 a substantial duty on corn remained and the price of bread was still high. Peel argued that the landed gentry was the class which had most consistently protected the traditional institutions of the country and their strength must not be destroyed. He added the less general argument—an argument which was to be used by the Tories in support of tariffs for many decades— that British agriculture had to be protected so that Britain could be self-supporting in time of war. But as the years passed and the debate, both in parliament and the country, became more heated, Peel's own convictions were shaken. Two of his most talented colleagues—Sir James Graham, the home secretary, and the young Gladstone at the Board of Trade—began to think in terms of total repeal. The potato blight in Ireland in 1845 and 1846 rendered the question an urgent one. Knowing

REPEAL OF THE CORN LAWS

that he would have the support of the Whig opposition, if not of all his own followers, Peel introduced a Bill removing all but a nominal duty on corn in June 1846. The Bill passed, but the Conservative party was split and Peel's period of power ended. Lord Aberdeen, Graham and Gladstone were convinced that Peel's decision had been right and honest, but the bulk of the Conservative party, and especially the farming interests, were appalled at his action, and turned elsewhere for leadership. They found it in two men whose alliance was to last for the next twenty years—Stanley and Disraeli.

Edward Stanley (1799–1869), who became 14th earl of Derby in 1851, had been secretary for war and colonies since 1845. A good orator, he took his political career lightly, and was always more interested in his racing stable. He owed his three periods of premiership to his personal popularity as a man rather than to any special political talents. For political talent he depended on his lieutenant, Benjamin Disraeli (1804–81). The son of a Spanish Jew, Disraeli had been elected to parliament in 1837. He had already been recognized as a skilful politician, if a flamboyant one, but it had not yet occurred to the Conservative party that this extraordinary young man would ever have to be trusted as a leader. In 1846 Disraeli attacked Peel in cruel and bitter terms, and the landed classes found, to their surprise, that he was their most eloquent spokesman.

The split in the Conservative party kept it from office for twenty years except for two short intervals when Stanley, by then Lord Derby, led conservative cabinets, but with a minority in the House. The period from 1846 to 1866 can thus be considered as a Whig era, an era of unequalled prosperity, when the men responsible for the rapidly expanding industries entrusted government to the old Whig aristocracy, who had given the middle class the vote in 1832, and were prepared for a policy of free trade. The grave social unrest of the 1830s and early 1840s was forgotten, and the Great Exhibition of 1851 seemed to herald a period of social harmony. There appeared no reason why the prosperity of the 1850s should not last for ever. It was an age of enormous economic developments, with accelerating industrialization using the network of railways which had already started to spread over the country in the 1840s. Production, wages and profits were all rising. The idea of free trade was now broadly accepted, and the term 'liberal' was becoming one of praise. Only in 1866 was there the first short slump, and only with the financial crash of 1873 did the period of prosperity reach a serious halt. Not until the 1870s did English agriculture fall into its long depression.

The central figure in domestic administration throughout the period was William Ewart Gladstone (1809–98), chancellor of the exchequer for most of the 1850s. The son of a rich Liverpool merchant, Gladstone had a brilliant academic career at Eton and Oxford. In his youth he had considered becoming an Anglican parson, and all his life he regarded his career as a religious mission. The most talented of the Peelites, he went with Peel himself into the political wilderness in 1846. Peel died in 1850, but Gladstone took office under another Peelite, Lord Aberdeen, in December 1852, in a coalition with the Whigs. Gladstone never again accepted office in a Tory ministry. In his 1853 budget he abolished most duties on imported foods and reduced by a half the duties on manufactured goods. Confident of the increase of national prosperity and determined to economize radically in government expenditure, he looked forward to the total abolition of the income tax.

He was awakened from his dream of a continual reduction of taxes and tariffs by the Crimean War. The eastern crisis which lasted through-out 1853 ended in 1854 by convincing the Aberdeen cabinet that the advance of Russian claims and influence in European Turkey could be stopped only by force of arms. In a buoyant and enthusiastic spirit the nation entered upon her first major war since Waterloo, allied to the young French Empire and the very senile Empire of the sultans. Tennyson reflected the spirit in the last lines of *Maud*:

> We have proved we have hearts in a cause, we are noble still,
> And myself have awaked, as it seems, to the better mind;
> It is better to fight for the good than to rail at the ill;
> I have felt with my native land, I am one with my kind . . .

But the public's enthusiasm could not survive the endless frustrations and disappointments reported from the Crimea. The sufferings of the troops in the winter of 1854–55 have become legendary, mainly as a part of the background to the early days of the career of that remarkable woman, Florence Nightingale. The gross stupidity of the army leaders was responsible for the virtual breakdown of all supply services. *The Times* raised a storm in the country. The Commons passed a motion of censure of the government in January 1855, and the pacifist Aberdeen, whose heart had never been in the war, resigned. Palmerston was swept into office on a wave of popularity.

Henry John Temple (1784–1865), third Viscount Palmerston, was a big man in every sense. As an Irish peer, he had sat in the House of Commons since 1807, but had always towered above group or party allegiances. As foreign secretary in the 1830s and again from 1846 to 1851 he had pursued a blustering policy which had not involved Britain in a major war, though it had scarcely increased her popularity in Europe. Under his leadership the country survived the Crimean War, and with France forced Russia to come to terms. At the time of the Congress of Paris in 1856 Palmerston enjoyed great popularity, but his greatest personal triumph came in the following year. He became involved, for the second time, in a small scale war with Imperial China. The war was condemned in the House of Commons and Palmerston was defeated on a vote of censure. Instead of resigning, he dissolved the House and fought an election solely on the merits of the Chinese Question and on British prestige. The candidates who supported Palmerston's line were everywhere given a large vote, and some of his most astute critics lost their seats. Palmerston had learned to interpret Mid-Victorian optimism in its more belligerent moods.

The minority government of Derby and Disraeli which was in office for fifteen months in 1858 and 1859 tried unsuccessfully to pass a parliamentary reform Bill. The Bill would have been moderate in its general effect, but radical in its treatment of county constituencies. Gladstone voted for it, finding himself in agreement with Disraeli on an important issue for the last time. Until the death of Palmerston in 1865, the Whigs made no great attempt to pass a further measure of parliamentary reform. Lord John Russell, unlike his chief, remained an enthusiast for reform, and in October 1865, when he formed his second cabinet, it seemed that his chance had come. Early in 1865 the Reform League had been founded on similar lines to the Anti-Corn Law League which had achieved such success twenty years before. The aim of the Reform League was rather to stimulate interest in parliamentary reform among the working classes than to give expression to any existing unrest. The lull in working-class agitation had continued throughout the 1850s and early 1860s, but with 1866 and 1867 a change came. Both were years of bad harvests; American corn was arriving; the Austro-Prussian War deprived British industry of markets; unemployment spread. To some extent Palmerston had been justified in his belief that the working class was not yet eager for the vote. But immediately after his death, with the return of bad times, working-class unrest reappeared.

Lord John Russell had become Earl Russell in 1861, and the Whig party had been assuming the name of 'Liberal Party'. They had a large majority in the House, but a majority sharply divided on the subject of parliamentary reform. John Bright and his followers on the left wing wanted a generous measure. Robert Lowe on the other wing eloquently and passionately opposed a large increase of the electorate. In March 1866 the Russell ministry introduced a Bill, mainly inspired by Gladstone, reducing the £10 household franchise in the boroughs to £7, and the £50 franchise in the counties to £14. But demand for reform in the country was still somewhat muted. The Bill passed two readings but was killed in the Lords. Russell resigned and Derby formed his third and last government with Disraeli chancellor of the exchequer and leader in the lower house.

Like his two previous governments, Derby's ministry had a minority Tory following in the Commons—a fact which makes its achievement in passing the second Reform Bill all the greater. The Liberal Bill had started reform agitation throughout the country, culminating in riots in Hyde Park for three days running in July 1866. In the course of the winter of 1866–67 Derby and Disraeli reached a radical decision. They decided to base their Bill on household franchise: all householders in the boroughs, no matter how low their rates, should get the vote. In 1859 Disraeli had spoken against the dangers of what he had contemptuously called a 'household democracy', but in 1867 he believed that it could be justified provided that it was based on rating and not rental. Ratepayers, he believed, would be responsible citizens with the interests of national prosperity at heart. Not all the Cabinet was convinced by this argument. Three members, including Lord Cranborne, the future earl of Salisbury, resigned. But Disraeli was successful at the Carlton Club where the party as a whole were prepared for his 'great experiment and leap in the dark'. The Bill became still more radical in its passage through the House. Disraeli meekly accepted amendments enfranchising compound householders and lodgers in certain circumstances, amendments which added half a million people to the electorate. In a sense the second Reform Bill was the work of a parliament rather than a government. Disraeli's conduct throughout was that of a brilliant opportunist. When the question of the lodgers' vote came up, he wrote to Derby's son, Lord Stanley, who was foreign secretary: 'I wish in the interval of settling the affairs of Europe, you would get up an anti-lodger speech, or a speech on the subject either way.' Disraeli would surely have rejoiced in Oscar Wilde's dictum that life is too important a thing to be taken seriously.

The 1867 Act roughly doubled the electorate. It gave the vote to the richer working classes, many of whom had not even agitated for it before 1866. Yet Robert Lowe's fears that it would open an era of revolution proved unjustified. Parliamentary life went on much as before, and no new radical party seized power as a result of the working-class franchise. Nor did the enlarged electorate show any gratitude to Disraeli. The general election of 1868 gave the liberals a majority of 112, and suggested that the voters shared Gladstone's conviction that Disraeli's Bill had been an insincere tactical move. Gladstone had convinced himself that right and progress were a monopoly of the Liberal party. In one of his more splendid flights of oratory in the House he declared: 'You cannot fight against the future. Time is on our side. The great social forces which move onward in their might and majesty and which the tumult of your debates does not for a moment impede or disturb are against you. They are marshalled on our side.'

Regarded with justice as the greatest living financier, Gladstone was now to earn his high reputation as a disinterested moral authority by his handling of the Irish question. The legislation of his 1868–74 ministry included an act disestablishing the Irish Protestant Church, and a first Irish Land Act, to which Gladstone had devoted three months' research in his usual meticulous way. Though there was much that Gladstone still did not know about Ireland, he knew so much more than Disraeli and his followers that they did not even dare to oppose the Bill, which was, anyhow, a moderate one. Of greater importance than the first Irish Land Act was W. E. Forster's Education Act, which arranged for the elementary education of children under thirteen and so made illiteracy a rarity in England. The Trade Union Act of 1871 seemed also enlightened in that it recognized the unions' right to exist, but it was rendered ineffective by a Criminal Law Amendment Act which virtually reminded the unions that picketing was illegal. A more typically Gladstonian piece of legislation was the Ballot Act of 1872, which made secret voting by ballot compulsory at parliamentary elections. The ballot had been demanded by the Chartists in the 1830s when wholesale bribery had made it more important than it was in the 1870s.

The fine record of Gladstone's first ministry did not save him from defeat at the polls in 1874. The pendulum swung, as it had done in 1868, and the Tories secured a majority of eighty-three. Disraeli phrased his programme as 'the maintenance of our institutions, the preservation of our empire, and the improvement of the conditions of the people'. The last phrase was no less sincere than the first two. The 1874–80 ministry put through a full programme of social legislation, and gave the Tory party a strong claim to having a greater concern for the working man than had the Liberal party. Disraeli's electoral victory was partly due to revised party organization—the establishment of the Central Conservative Office and the Local Conservative Associations. One of the two great English political parties was beginning to take on its twentieth-century appearance. The two most important measures of social reform carried through by Disraeli's 1874 ministry were the 1875 Artisans' Dwellings Act, which began the attack on the slums, and the 1876 Trade Union Act which legalized picketing. Less enlightened was the government's policy on imperial issues which involved Britain in wars with Afghans and Zulus and earned Gladstone's severe moral condemnation in his Midlothian campaigns of 1879 and 1880. In the elections of 1880 the liberals secured a majority of 137, due partly to Joseph Chamberlain's renovation of the party machinery.

When Disraeli died in 1881 he left behind him a rejuvenated Conservative party, only temporarily out of favour with the electors. The two great English parties had dominated domestic history throughout the nineteenth century. In 1880, each led by a man of genius, they gave vitality to as effective a system of representative government as any Europe had experienced.

The political and cultural history of England has always centred on London to an even greater extent than is the case with most capital cities, and until the nineteenth century London was very much larger than any other English town. She had already in 1800 a population of nearly 900,000, at a time when only fourteen other towns had even 20,000. By 1850 the population of London had swollen to 2,362,236, but by then seven other cities—Birmingham, Bradford, Leeds, Liverpool, Manchester, Sheffield and Bristol—had populations of over 100,000.[1] The significance of the new towns of the north and midlands in the economic life of Britain has been suggested in an earlier chapter; their political significance was not proportionate, though it was certainly not negligible. The Manchester School of economic thinkers in a sense triumphed over the traditions of the agricultural south in 1846.

The smaller nations of Great Britain, the Scottish and the Welsh, shared the domestic history of England from 1830 to 1880, in the sense that they were completely integrated politically. Only in Scotland was there any new expression of national sentiment, and this was of an ecclesiastical nature. A Presbyterian revival in the years after 1830 led to demands that the established Church of Scotland should be given greater independence from Parliament at Westminster. When the

[1] R. M. Hartwell, *The Industrial Revolution in England* (Historical Association Pamphlet, 1965), pp. 19–20.

demands were resisted by both Whig and Tory governments a schism in the Scottish Church resulted. Four hundred and seventy-four ministers left the established Church in 1843 and formed the Free Church of Scotland, which in the succeeding months built churches and collected funds on a scale unequalled by any other religious community in the British Isles in the nineteenth century.

If Scotland and Wales were comparatively happy countries without histories in the mid-nineteenth century, the opposite is true of Ireland. From 1830 to 1880 Ireland had plenty of history—a history crossing the grim watershed of the Great Famine of 1845-47. The main preoccupation of the politically conscious classes in Ireland before the famine was with the Act which had united the Irish and English parliaments in 1800. Repeal of the Act was demanded partly on nationalist grounds, partly for good practical reasons: if Ireland was ever to overcome her poverty, she would have to build up her few small industries, and this could be done only if they were protected from English competition. An English parliament would never grant tariff protection for Ireland, nor, before Gladstone, would it willingly interfere with the free contracts between landlords and tenants. Three-quarters of Ireland was owned by English landlords, usually absentees, leaving their tenants to provide farm buildings. The tenants had no legal rights to their improvements, yet if their rents were in arrears they were frequently evicted in the most cruel manner.

The leader of Irish nationalism before the famine was Daniel O'Connell (1775-1847). An impressive and noble figure, O'Connell hoped to secure repeal of the Union without resorting to armed force. Catholic emancipation had already been achieved in 1829, but only after violence. When possible, O'Connell tried to work with the Whigs, to the disgust of more extreme Irish nationalists who hoped for no more from Lord John Russell than O'Connell did from Peel.

The basic faults in the Irish economy—underemployment, too little land under cultivation and, above all, dependence on potatoes—became tragically apparent in 1846. The potato blight started in the autumn of 1845 and brought on one of the most terrible famines in the modern history of Europe. The population of Ireland, like that of the rest of Europe, had grown rapidly in the first decades of the century. From an estimated figure of 5 million in 1780 it had passed 8 million by the time of the 1841 census. And this was in spite of continual emigration. In 1841 Ireland had the fantastic birth rate of thirty per 1,000. Yet by 1868 the population had fallen to 5 million again. In a few years wholesale emigration, disease brought on by malnutrition, and downright starvation had removed a third of an entire people. Immediately after the famine Peel wrote of 'whole counties such as Meath and Tipperary' being 'depopulated and changed into prairies like those of America'. One final figure must suffice to emphasize the scale of the disaster: in July 1847, those receiving food from the relief authorities in soup kitchens and workhouses numbered 3,020,712.

The governments of both Peel and Russell had been inhibited from taking adequate measures by their dislike of government intervention in economic affairs and their respect for private property. Even after the famine the legislation of the British government showed more concern for the landlord than the peasant. In Ireland herself the famine had the immediate effect of discrediting the extreme nationalists: the problem was felt to be a social rather than a political one. But English apathy contributed to a revival of violent nationalism in the 1860s, when the Fenians formed their society around a hard core of emigrants returned from America. Not until Gladstone's advent to power in 1868 did an English statesman devote his whole attention to Ireland.

The established Protestant Church was one of the richest institutions in Ireland, and yet, over the greatest part of the country, it had only a tiny congregation. Macaulay had long before said: 'I am not speaking with rhetorical exaggeration . . . when I say that, of all the institutions of the civilized world, the Established Church of Ireland seems to me the most absurd.' Gladstone successfully passed through parliament a law disestablishing the Irish Church, and devoting half of its endowments to the relief of poverty and the development of education in Ireland. His first Irish Land Act was perhaps less beneficial, but at least a start had been made in curing the agrarian ills of Ireland. Disraeli did not continue the attempt during his 1874–80 ministry. In 1880 most of the people of Ireland were as wretched as they had ever been, but they had at least found a sympathizer in the greatest living liberal statesman, and a more effective leader than they had known in the past in Charles Stewart Parnell.

If the relations of the British government with Ireland were a cause for shame, their relations with the rest of the world were more often a cause for pride. The relations between Europe and the other continents are considered in a later chapter, but something must be said here of the nature of British foreign policy in Europe. Because her navy was so much larger, and her army so much smaller, than those of any other power, Britain could always exert greater influence on coastal districts. She had decisive influence in the Mediterranean, but virtually none in central Germany. The need to keep open the route to India necessitated a strong position in the Mediterranean. So long as France was the only rival in that sea, the situation was comparatively safe, but if a Russian fleet ever appeared there, the security of the Empire would be threatened. Constantinople and the Straits thus became, in Temperley's words, 'the first strategic position in the world', and to defend them it appeared necessary to support the effete empire of the Ottomans. The logic of this argument had not been fully accepted by Canning, but in the course of the 1830s, with Palmerston at the Foreign Office, it became a basis of British policy.

Defence of the *status quo* in the east appeared to Palmerston necessary even if it involved war. In the west peace was necessary for Britain, even if it demanded adjustments in the 1815 settlement. Western and central Europe still provided the chief markets for British exports. Even short wars in which Britain was neutral—like that of 1866—affected her adversely. Trade slumped, unemployment increased and working-class agitation flared up. To defend peace in the west Palmerston realized that reforms were needed in the absolutist countries. The terms in which he recommended reforms to the monarchs of Austria, Spain and the Italian states were resented and seldom heeded. Occasionally—as in the securing of Belgian independence—Palmerston succeeded in adjusting the 1815 settlement while avoiding war.

Palmerston dominated British foreign policy, whether as foreign secretary, prime minister or in opposition, from 1830 to 1865. The ten years which followed his death were years of isolation, with Britain sometimes ingloriously excluded from European affairs, sometimes ineffectively but voluntarily standing aside. In the Eastern Crisis of 1875–1878 Disraeli reasserted Britain's position in European diplomacy, but in doing so made foreign policy once more an issue in party politics. Something like a bi-partisan policy can be traced from the Crimean War to 1875, but with the arrival of Disraeli and Gladstone as alternating prime ministers, foreign affairs were to be as hotly debated as domestic ones. In spite of the heat of the debate the issue was not one of life or death for the nation. From 1830 to 1880 her security was never really threatened. Her wealth and her navy gave her prestige and influence, even when statesmanship and armies were lacking.

Anglo-French relations

At the opening of this chapter it was suggested that Anglo-French relations were of immense significance for the history of Europe in the nineteenth century. The developments of 1815 to 1830 had shown how politically stagnant the continent could become when France aligned herself with the eastern powers. Britain alone could do little to foster the Benthamite concept of 'improvement' on the continent. But with the revolution of 1830 in Paris the Conservative bloc in Europe was broken at the moment when the Whigs replaced the authoritarian Wellington in London. So far as constitutional ideas were concerned, both Palmerston and his successor at the Foreign Office in 1841, Lord Aberdeen, felt a basic identity of aims with the July Monarchy. But the sympathy in their political philosophy was often rendered of no account by clashes of vital interests. One such clash came in the eastern Mediterranean in the crisis of 1839–41. Louis-Philippe's government gave technical and diplomatic support to Mehemet Ali, the governor of Egypt, in his rebellion against the sultan, and when Palmerston gave active naval support to the sultan, the Anglo-French *entente* was temporarily broken. It was saved only by the resignation of the belligerent Thiers. Aberdeen's relations with Guizot in the early 1840s were happier, but even then there were irritants like Spain and a crisis in Tahiti. The question of who should marry Queen Isabella of Spain created Anglo-French friction, which increased as the poor girl reached maturity. When Palmerston again replaced Aberdeen at the Foreign Office in 1846 things quickly came to a head. The resulting break in the *entente* seemed to give Palmerston a free hand in Europe. His policy in the vital months before the revolutions of 1848 seemed excessively radical and dangerous to Guizot, though it was limited to advising European princes to grant constitutions. When the revolutions broke out, Palmerston was careful not to intervene.

From the moment when he secured absolute power in France, Louis Napoleon looked to England for moral support. Palmerston's prompt, if unofficial, approval of the *coup d'état* of 1851 added to the many grievances which Queen Victoria felt against him, and he was obliged to resign. Both in opposition and when he inevitably returned to office Palmerston remained a loyal friend of Napoleon. The Crimean War welded the two nations into a military alliance, and in the years after the Peace of Paris British and French troops were still fighting side by side in China. In spite of Napoleon's flirtations with Russia, and in spite of several sharp crises, like those following the Orsini attempt on his life and the French annexation of Savoy and Nice, the two governments continued to consider themselves as allies. Public opinion in the two countries was not so sure. Napoleon once likened the *entente* to two pyramids whose heads were leaning closely together, but whose bases were constantly slipping apart. He warned that if the process went too far both pyramids would crash to the ground. The English middle class was partly appeased by the free trade treaty which Cobden drew up with the French government in 1860. Napoleon had proved braver than Louis-Philippe and Guizot in dealing with the strong protectionist instincts of the French industrialists. But from 1860 to 1870 the two nations again drifted apart. Britain dissociated herself from the unbalanced schemes which marked the decline of Napoleon's foreign policy. She was strictly neutral in the war of 1870. Even so, after the surrender at Sedan and six months' imprisonment in Germany, Napoleon sought refuge in England. He died in 1873 at Chiselhurst in Kent.

The Third Republic played a modest role in Europe for its first ten years. There was no strong reason either for hostility or friendship with England. In 1880 relations between the two countries were less intimate, but also far less dangerous, than they had been earlier in the century. It seemed unlikely that they would ever go to war against each other again, but even if they were closely allied they could no longer guarantee a liberal or a peaceful future for Europe. Everything now depended on Germany.

Spain

A country which had played a central role in Anglo-French relations was Spain, and it will be convenient to deal briefly here with Spanish internal political developments.

In one respect Spain had a greater resemblance to Russia than to England or France: she was almost completely lacking in any group which could be called 'a middle class'. The Spanish nobility had avoided contact with trade or business, and since the expulsion of the Jews in the fifteenth century there had been nothing resembling a commercial class. Political issues were disputed by the landowners, the clergy and professional men, with the result that political ideas were —again, as in Russia—of an extreme nature. By 1830 many of the nobility were impoverished, and the class as a whole was effete. The peasantry, on the other hand, ignorant and illiterate though it was, showed remarkable fighting spirit in the frequent civil wars, as it had

done against Napoleon. Here, then, were all the constituents for acute
political instability: a strong Church and proud landowning class,
army officers and intellectuals with ideas of undiluted democracy, and
a clash between the doctrines of Loyola and Rousseau. The struggle
over political ideologies was further exacerbated by the weakness of the
crown. Even the principle of succession was a subject for dispute. Since
the Bourbons had come to Spain in 1701, the Salic Laws, by which only
a man could be sovereign, had been observed. In 1830 Ferdinand VII,
having married four times without securing a son, issued a Pragmatic
Sanction, by which his newly born daughter, Isabella, was to be recognized as his heir. His brother Don Carlos, Ferdinand's heir according
to the Salic Laws, denied the legality of the Pragmatic Sanction. To all
Spain's other misfortunes was added that of a disputed succession.

When Ferdinand died in 1833 the struggle for power began. Isabella,
a child of three, was proclaimed queen, and her mother, Maria Cristina,
regent. The civil servants of the old king stood by the regent, while
Carlos was supported by the monastic orders, most of the clergy, the
towns of Castille and the Basques. Carlos wished to preserve an absolute
monarchy in Spain, forcing Maria Cristina to fall back on the liberals
for support. England and France sympathized with the regent, the autocratic powers with Carlos. The unhappy reign of Isabella II lasted until
1868, when it was ended by violent revolution. The fates were not kind
to the young queen. As she reached the age of maturity the whole of
Europe occupied itself with the task of finding her a husband. In 1846,
at the age of sixteen, she was married to her first cousin, who was impotent. Compensation was provided by a series of lovers and indulgence
in ostentatious religious piety. Meanwhile the political forces unleashed
in 1820, and intensified by the revolutions of 1848, fought for her kingdom. In 1834 the regent had issued a royal charter granting a limited
constitution, very like that granted by Louis XVIII's charter. The more
conservative of the constitutionalists, the *moderados*, had stood by the
1834 charter, but the advanced liberals, the *progressistas*, had demanded
nothing less than the democratic constitution of 1812. With the split in
the constitutionalist party, the temporary agreement between France
and England on Spanish affairs was also broken. France now supported
the *moderados* and England the *progressistas*. While the charter of 1834
had not made the executive responsible to the assembly, it had nevertheless brought about a significant change in the nature of Spanish government: it had replaced court favourites by political ministers. In 1836
the *progressistas* secured control of Spain, and the next year introduced

a constitution based on that of 1812 but with great improvements of a practical kind.

The 1837 constitution marked a high watermark of nineteenth-century liberalism in Spain. But the civil war was by no means won. Espartero, the liberal leader, was overthrown in 1843 and the *moderados*, supported by France, seized power. Their conservative constitution of 1845 survived throughout Isabella's reign. The queen herself favoured the re-establishment of absolutism, and her minister, Narvaez, formerly a leader of the *moderados*, became increasingly authoritarian. Attempts to overthrow the constitution of 1845 failed until a wider revolutionary movement in 1868 drove the queen herself into exile.

With the throne vacant, Spain once more became a matter of great concern to the European powers. A constituent assembly drew up a constitution not unlike that of 1837, and offered the crown to Leopold of Hohenzollern, thereby starting the crisis which led to the Franco-Prussian War. The crown was eventually accepted by an Italian prince, Amedeo, son of Victor Emmanuel II. At last Spain had an enlightened and moderate monarch, but the bitter political feuds continued. In 1873 Amedeo abdicated in disgust, and for some months anarchy ensued, with the republicans momentarily in power in Madrid and a more sinister absolutist movement developing in the Basque provinces. The monarchy was restored at the end of 1874 in the person of Alfonso XII, son of Isabella, and the reign of Alfonso lasted until 1886. Endemic civil war and endless Anglo-French intervention had made Spain the scene of one of the saddest stories of nineteenth-century Europe. The proximity of the developing civilizations of Britain and France only threw the sufferings and poverty of Spain into sharper relief.

Political institutions

That both France and Britain were becoming more efficient states in the period 1830 to 1880 is undeniable. That France was throughout the period suffering from grave political instability and that constitutional development in England lagged behind social change is also evident. France retained the logical administrative pattern given her by Napoleon I, though attempts to democratize the French civil service failed. In both countries the number of bureaucrats increased appreciably, and in Britain the civil service was being converted from a system of privilege into a regular profession recruited by openly competitive methods.

Some form of electoral system for a central assembly persisted in both countries; only in France was the central assembly for a short while under the Second Empire unimportant and impotent. The various constitutions—good, bad or indifferent—under which Frenchmen lived, were alike in giving France a more uniform and homogeneous political life than that provided in England by an unwritten constitution and the two complex Reform Acts of 1832 and 1867. In France, particularly under the July Monarchy, corrupt methods were used by the government itself to undermine an already very limited constitution. In England corruption was endemic on a lower level—in the constituencies, and was recognized by the innocuous definition of 'electoral management'. The 1832 Act removed the most glaring abuses, but it left a still complex electoral pattern. Fifty-six sparsely inhabited—or even uninhabited—boroughs were disfranchised, 111 members, who had represented no one, thus losing their parliamentary seats. Thirty-two other boroughs were deprived of one of their two members. Seven large English towns, the largest being Manchester and Birmingham, and four London districts were given two members each and so represented in parliament for the first time. The vote was given to all householders in the borough constituencies who paid £10 or more a year in rates. In the country constituencies the Act was less simple; the vote was given to £10 copyholders and £50 leaseholders, in addition to the £2 freeholders who had always possessed it. A somewhat mixed assortment of householders, only broadly identifiable as 'the upper and middle classes', thus constituted the British electorate from 1832 to 1867.

Nor did the 1832 Act dispose of all members of parliament who owed their seats quite simply to financial influence. If it abolished all the 'rotten boroughs', over forty 'pocket boroughs' remained—boroughs, that is, where the patron can be definitely named, and where no political contest was necessary or possible at election time. In short, the sizes of constituencies no longer contrasted so extravagantly, but there were still wide divergencies. The south of England still had many more members per head of population than the north had. Not surprisingly, then, the House of Commons of the period 1832 to 1867 was still a very aristocratic body. The titled members—baronets and sons of the nobility—were almost as numerous as before, although there were appreciably fewer landowners as a whole, and a sprinkling of middle-class members voiced radical opinions which had found no expression in the House before 1832.

Since the vote depended on a property qualification, people who were getting richer would become automatically enfranchised. The size of the British electorate increased enormously from 1832 to 1867 in spite of the absence of any further Reform Bill, partly because of the increasing wealth of a considerable class, partly because of the great growth of population. But in practice a large number of these potential new voters did not use their privilege. The 1832 Act had instituted a registration of electors. A great many people did not trouble to register or preferred not to pay the registration fee of one shilling. The legislation passed by the reformed parliament was better informed and more effectively drafted than it had been in the past. One of the results of Bentham's influence on the British governmental system was the practice of appointing royal or parliamentary commissions to collect the relevant facts before Bills were prepared for debate. The many commissions which sat in the early and mid-Victorian period provided parliament with exhaustive data and increased the efficiency of its legislation.

The constitution of 1830 in France gave power to an oligarchy not so unlike that which ruled England between the two Reform Acts. From 1830 to 1848 France, like England, was a constitutional monarchy in which a property qualification was needed for the vote. In theory William IV and Victoria reigned by inherited right while Louis-Philippe was king 'by the grace of God and the will of the nation'. In practice Louis-Philippe retained a hold on executive policy to an extent not attempted by a British monarch since George III. The Orleanist king had neither the authority of popular suffrage nor the right of legal inheritance—a point which would have worried the English less perhaps than it did the French, who have always prided themselves on their logic. The lack of a logical justification for Louis-Philippe's crown partly explains his determination to retain a practical hold on political power.

The July Revolution—like the 1832 Reform Act—did not bring a complete change in the social order, but gave power to a wider group of men. The upper legislative house lost half of its old members, who refused to take an oath to Louis-Philippe. It lost its hereditary rights, and throughout the reign had little political influence. The lower house became the only real arena for political disputes. It was elected by men over the age of twenty-five with the necessary property qualification. The delegates themselves had to be over thirty, and came mostly from the middle class, with a sprinkling of large landowners. The lower house was thus less aristocratic than the English House of Commons, but its electoral basis was far narrower. Only about 170,000 Frenchmen could vote: one out of two hundred, compared with one out of thirty in the U.K. after 1832.

The grave limitation of the French electorate contributed to the political extremism of the revolution of 1848 and to the democratic nature of the institutions of the Second Republic. In the course of 1848 and 1849 no fewer than three elections were held by direct universal manhood suffrage: two elections for the assembly and one for the president. For the first time in history western Europe experienced the working of a full democracy. The results showed that the masses in France were more conservative than the middle classes who had made the revolution. In the election for a constituent assembly in April, of the 900 delegates elected only twenty-six came from the working class; three were bishops, fifteen priests and one was a monk. There were as many Orleanist delegates as radical-socialists; and in the second election for an assembly, in May 1849, the monarchists were still more numerous and the socialists still fewer. The results showed that radical Paris was opposed by the conservative provinces. In February 1848 Paris had gained the upper hand, but with the elections the provinces asserted their authority. Louis-Napoleon tried to hold the balance between them, initially with some success.

The most important constitutional innovation to be adopted by the president, who was soon to make himself Emperor Napoleon III, was the plebiscite, an idea inherited from Napoleon I. After the 1851 *coup d'état*, $7\frac{1}{2}$ million Frenchmen recorded their approval of Napoleon's action, while only 700,000 voted against him. A plebiscite was used again to confirm the constitution of 1852 which inaugurated the Second Empire. The constitution allowed for a two-chamber legislature, both chambers devoid of real power. The lower house was a very small one— of only 260 members, and for that reason could be easily packed with government supporters. Its sessions were not published by the press; its president was nominated by the emperor; it could vote only on proposals from the emperor or his council of state. Napoleon presided at all meetings of ministers at the Tuileries; in no sense did his ministers form a united, responsible cabinet such as had already emerged in England. They were appointed personally by the emperor, and remained responsible only to him. They were few in number: Walewski, the illegitimate son of the great Napoleon, Persigny, Morny and three or four others, most of them fellow-adventurers of Louis-Napoleon in the past. In the early years of his reign Napoleon spoke with contempt of parliaments. He probably sincerely believed that an Empire, buttressed by an occasional plebiscite, was a better guarantor of popular sovereignty than an assembly in which political parties competed for power.

But his constitutional reforms in the years 1860 to 1870 brought the assembly back into the forefront of political life, and gave Frenchmen once again a measure of choice as to who should govern them. Since the assembly had, throughout the life of the Empire, always been elected by universal manhood suffrage, the introduction of the principle of ministerial responsibility to the assembly provided a genuine parliamentary democracy for the last few disastrous weeks of the reign.

Great Britain, meanwhile, had avoided a headlong rush to democracy, but had, on the other hand, prevented one man or one party from holding power for too long or with too little restraint. When, in January 1867, Napoleon was issuing a decree which allowed political meetings to be once more held in public, England was passing through the constitutional crisis from which the second Reform Act was to emerge. The electorate of England and Wales had already passed the million mark before the 1867 Act, which brought it up, very nearly, to two million. In the period 1867 to 1880 working-class voters were in a clear majority in the towns of Great Britain. But the 1867 increase in the electorate was by no means uniform. It was much greater in the borough constituencies than in the country constituencies, until Gladstone's Act of 1884 did something to redress the balance. Within the country constituencies the agricultural areas were better represented than the small towns and industrial villages—than, for example, the mining valleys of south Wales. On the other hand, in the borough constituencies it was the urban and industrial influence which became stronger. The biggest increase in the vote went to the large cities, while the small countrified boroughs often increased their electorate by only a half. In the south of England many of the small boroughs which had enjoyed a favoured position since 1832 were in 1867 deprived of one of their two members.

People called into political existence by the 1867 Act included large numbers of small shopkeepers and traders, besides industrial workers in the larger boroughs, and in the smaller boroughs an appreciable number of agricultural labourers. But the agricultural workers in particular were still very open to the influence of their employers or landlords. The introduction of the secret ballot in 1872 might have been expected to deal a final blow at electoral management, but the available evidence suggests that its effect was strictly limited. No subsequent parliamentary reform in the nineteenth century had the political significance of the 1867 Act. It increased the working-class vote enormously in certain regions, especially in Scotland and the north of England. A striking example is Warrington, which in 1866 had an electorate of 768 of whom 149 were fairly described as 'working-class'. In 1872 the electorate had grown to 4,848, the new voters being almost entirely working-class. This kind of change clearly amounted to a complete social revolution, but its effect on the nature of parliament was to some extent annulled by other factors. In spite of the redistribution of fifty-three seats, the 1867 Act still left a grossly unfair variation in the sizes of constituencies. Portarlington, with 3,000 people and only 140 electors, sent a member to parliament, while Liverpool, with 500,000 people and 6,000 electors, still, with Birkenhead, sent only four members to parliament. Portarlington, not surprisingly, had a patron, the earl of Portarlington, who had his son returned to the Commons from 1868 to 1880, just as he had done from 1857 to 1865.[1] To say that England was either a democracy or a plutocracy after 1867 would be equally false. She was a mixture of both.

The effect of a working-class majority in so many of the constituencies of England and Scotland was far less than had been expected. In 1880 there was still no working-class group in parliament. But the increased numbers going to the polls had brought about a change of another kind. It had become necessary for the electoral mechanism of the two national parties to be improved and tightened. In 1874–75 the Conservatives had renovated their party organization, and in 1879–80 the Liberals followed their example, and took the process still further. The less attractive accompaniments of the British democracy were making their appearance.

While England was living under the régime of the second Reform Act, France was experiencing the agonies of the war with Prussia and the rising of the Commune. The constitution which emerged from the struggles of the years 1871 to 1875 was that of a parliamentary régime based on universal male suffrage. The Third French Republic differed from its predecessors in being founded on no written constitution, but on four laws; it was essentially an empirical foundation, not expected to last. In the event it proved more durable than any constitution since 1789. The political role of the president of the Republic was a nearer approach to that of the English monarch than Louis-Philippe's had been in practice or Napoleon III's had been in law. The president could perform no political function except through his ministry, and was soon regarded as a purely ceremonial figure. The ministers were the real governing body. They were formed into a cabinet on the English model, and stated by law to be collectively responsible under their own 'presi-

[1] H. J. Hanham, *Elections and Party Management: Politics in the time of Disraeli and Gladstone* (London, 1959).

dent of the council'. The 1875 constitution in France was thus profiting from experience in England, where cabinet solidarity and the prime ministership had slowly emerged as a practical method of government. The ministers of the Third Republic were dependent upon a vote of censure in the lower house only. The lower house, elected every four years by universal suffrage, was thus, like the House of Commons in England, indirectly the sovereign body. The president of the Republic nominated the ministers, but parliamentary precedent, as in England, quickly obliged him to appoint them from the majority party in the lower house. The president himself was not elected directly by the people, as Louis-Napoleon had been under the Second Republic, but by the two legislative houses, for a period of seven years.

The Third Republic was similar to the English constitution in many ways, but in some respects it was more democratic. The head of the state and the upper house were both elected. The lower house was elected by all adult Frenchmen regardless of their financial status, and the delegates, once elected, were paid a salary. At last France had a working constitution, with real guarantees of personal freedom and equality before the law—the principles promised by the great revolution nearly a century before. In 1880 the two great powers of western Europe were ruled by parliamentary régimes based on the recorded consent of a wide electorate.

If the constitution of a country decides the ultimate questions of power and individual freedom, the administrative system has a direct bearing on the welfare of the population. Purely political developments will perhaps always attract more attention from the historian than administrative developments, but no study of European society is complete without a consideration of the bureaucracies of the various nations. Throughout the period the French civil service was a more highly developed one than the British, a fact due almost entirely to the work of one man—Napoleon I. Just as in the field of law France retained the main points of the Code Napoleon after 1815, so did she leave virtually intact the administrative institutions of the Empire: the *conseil d'état* and the system of prefects. The *conseil d'état* remained the central bureaucratic body, a group of legal and technical authorities who helped the various political governments with problems of administration and so formed a link between the ministries and the central government. The prefects were nominated by the government in Paris to control local government in the provinces through the sub-prefects and mayors. Under the July Monarchy, Second Republic and Second

Empire they continued to have a strongly centralizing effect. Only in 1871 were the departments of France given a degree of autonomy for the first time since their creation. Under the Third Republic the powers of the prefects were at last limited to some extent by the establishment of locally elected bodies.

In France the civil servant enjoyed a higher prestige than the politician. Aristocrats were always content for their sons to take up bureaucratic appointments. But if the French civil service was efficient and respected, it was also authoritarian and worked on a system of patronage. Already under the July Monarchy attempts had been made by liberals in the assembly to introduce an element of competition into the system of recruitment for the civil service, but the government had evaded the issue. The position had been complicated by the large number of civil servants among the deputies themselves—the most corrupting element in the parliamentary life of the July Monarchy. Out of 459 deputies in 1845, 190 were government servants. The Second Republic was preparing to place the civil service on a more democratic basis, but had no time to accomplish anything. Napoleon's liberal Empire in its very last months was considering the question, and the Third Republic throughout the first ten years of its existence debated reforms in the administrative system, but in 1880 the situation was much as it had been in 1830. The attitudes of officials were still conditioned by excessive centralization: they were too obsessed with the well-being of the state and too little with the interests of the individual citizen. The central civil service was already in the 1830s larger and more professional in France than in England, and both services increased the numbers of their officials considerably over the period. Rough figures suggest that the central civil service in France employed 130,000 officials in 1839, and 220,000 in 1871. The increase was taken up mainly by the Ministry of Education and the Post Office. The Ministry of Finance actually declined in size over the same period.

In Great Britain there had been no sweeping innovations in administration as there had been in France under the Revolutionary governments and the First Empire. In 1830 British administrative practice of the eighteenth century was still in force. The system was based on the justices of the peace—amateur, honorary administrators, performing their duties as part of the obligation of land and property owners towards the community. Only after the Reform Act of 1832 did a few Benthamite measures start the creation of permanent administrative machinery. Most important of these was the Municipal Corporations

Act of 1835, which arranged for the election of local municipal governments by all householders. The central event in the history of the British civil service in the nineteenth century was the report of the Northcote–Trevelyan committee in 1853. It recommended that government clerks and officials should be selected by open competition in examinations set by an independent body. John Stuart Mill and Macaulay both praised the imaginative sweep of the report, but there was great opposition from all those who wanted to preserve the ancient system of patronage. Three civil service commissioners were appointed to conduct qualifying examinations in 1855, but not until 1870 was really open competition introduced for appointments in the civil service.

If government in France and Britain was beginning to perform new and more complex administrative functions, its primordial task of defending the community from external attack remained. The principle of universal conscription introduced by the French Revolution had been of immense significance for the future of Europe. At the restoration it had been replaced by the old system of a standing army, but the July Monarchy had brought back conscription which in one form or another survived thereafter. Napoleon III introduced a special fund into which conscripts could pay to obtain exemption and which could be used to finance the recruitment of regular professional soldiers. Conscripts who preferred to serve were placed on the reserve after five years, but the system did not create a potentially vast army like that being created in Prussia, where far more men were being trained and placed on the reserve. In 1870 Prussia, with a smaller population, had an appreciably larger army than France. More important, Prussia in 1870 had an integrated and highly efficient general staff.[1] Only after the war did France acquire a general staff in the modern sense, and even under the Third Republic the minister of war performed some of the functions which in Germany were more effectively carried out by the general staff. A minister of war usually has a double function: he must represent the wishes of the political government to the army, and the needs— material and strategic—of the army to the government. In France the minister of war felt a strong loyalty to the army rather than to the government, and tended to forget his responsibilities to the electorate. In Prussia already in 1866 the general staff formulated and coordinated strategy and then pressed it on the king; in France even after 1870 there was no body which exercised quite such clear-cut powers.

The British army was singularly archaic at the start of the period

[1] See below, p. 251.

compared with that of France. The eighteenth-century balance between a militia in the hands of the local gentry and regiments of royal troops was still preserved. The regular troops were still contracted by individual officers for their own regiments in 1854. Only in 1871 was control of the militia taken from the hands of the local gentry and given to the War Office. For the greater part of the period control of the army was in a state of utter confusion. The relationship between the commander-in-chief, the secretary *for* war and colonies and the secretary *at* war depended upon the arbitrary behaviour of the three men concerned. The commander-in-chief remained far too independent of parliament and the cabinet, especially when the post was held by the queen's cousin, the Duke of Cambridge, as it was from 1856 to 1895. That Britain survived the career of the Duke of Cambridge was due entirely to her navy, which was, of course, far the more important of the two services.

The Admiralty, as the ministry responsible for running the navy, originated in the period. Before 1832 the Admiralty was responsible for naval policy, but not for the actual administration of the navy, which was the responsibility of the Navy Board. In 1832 Sir James Graham took a big step in rationalizing the system by amalgamating the two bodies and placing the whole ministry—called collectively the 'Admiralty'—under a minister responsible to parliament, the First Lord. Graham's reform tended to make the political chief too powerful, in the sense that he interfered with matters which the admirals themselves felt to be purely internal ones. In 1872 George Goschen reorganized and modernized the Admiralty in such a way that the permanent naval officers had full control over their own affairs, while the First Lord retained the supreme authority necessary in a parliamentary state.

Many English institutions had survived from a remote past, and many French institutions looked back to the glories of the Revolution and the Napoleonic era. But the real nature of society was changing rapidly in both countries. As population increased, industrialism quickened and education was extended, the public became more politically conscious. If the period is taken as a whole, it can be seen that both France and Britain had been moving towards democratic institutions between 1830 and 1880. The mechanism of government had been to some extent rationalized, in a manner of which Bentham would have approved. Many of the characteristics, good and bad, of democracy, which de Tocqueville had anticipated, were by 1880 making their appearance.

IX

The New Nations:
Germany and Italy

The two biggest political events in the history of Europe from 1830 to 1880 were the extension of the sovereignty of the House of Savoy over the whole Italian peninsula from 1859 to 1870, and the acceptance by William I, king of Prussia, of the offer from the German princes of the title of Emperor of Germany in 1871. The more important of the two events was clearly the unification of Germany, which emerged as the most populous country in Europe after Russia, and without exception the strongest military power. Yet so far as constitutional forms went

BIBLIOGRAPHY. As an introduction to the histories of the two countries for the period there are two small volumes in a series published by the Cambridge University Press: E. J. Passant, *A Short History of Germany, 1815–1945*, with additional sections by W. O. Henderson, C. J. Child and D. C. Watt (Cambridge, 1959); and H. Hearder and D. P. Waley, eds., *A Short History of Italy* (Cambridge, 1963), more than half of which deals with the post-1815 period.

For German political developments an excellent recent account is Golo Mann, *Deutsche Geschichte des 19. und 20. Jahrhunderts* (Frankfurt, 1959). Another broad narrative of German history since the eighteenth century, dealing well with the intellectual background, is Koppel S. Pinson, *Modern Germany* (New York, 1954). A German classic covering the whole period is Heinrich von Sybel, *Die Begründung des Deutschen Reiches durch Wilhelm I* (7 vols., Munich and Leipzig, 1889; English translation by M. L. Perrin, New York, 1890). Of the many works on the revolutions of 1848 Sir Lewis Namier's penetrating essay, *The Revolution of the Intellectuals* (London, 1944), deals more with Germany than elsewhere, but certainly does not err on the side of over-generosity to the Germans. For Bismarck the standard biography is Erich Eyck, *Bismarck, Leben und Werk* (3 vols., Zürich, 1941–44), of which a shortened English version is *Bismarck and the German Empire* (London, 1950). A. J. P. Taylor, *Bismarck: the Man and the Statesman* (London, 1955) makes an interesting psychological study of Bismarck, as does a yet more recent and a wholly convincing and authoritative short life: W. N. Medlicott, *Bismarck and Modern Germany* (London, 1965). A good recent study of the unification of Germany is Otto Pflanze, *Bismarck and the*

the Italian achievement was the more complete. Germany remained a federation of ancient states. The new Italy was an integrated nation state: all the former kingdoms and duchies other than that of Sardinia-Piedmont were dissolved, and no transitional phase of federalism was considered necessary. In practice the distinction did not matter very much. In terms of political power two new nations had appeared in the world, each with a strong sense of national identity, a single foreign policy and a single sovereign monarch.

Development of Germany: the Period of Unification, 1815–1871 (Princeton, 1963), and an admirable history of the war of 1870 by a leading military historian is Michael Howard, *The Franco-Prussian War* (London, 1961).

An important recent study of developments in Italy over the period is made by the sections written by Alberto M. Ghisalberti and Giuseppe Talamo in vols. III and IV of *Storia d'Italia*, edited by Nino Valeri (5 vols., Turin, 1959–60). An older work still worth consulting is C. Spellanzon, *Storia del Risorgimento e dell'unità d'Italia, 1748–1918* (7 vols., Milan, 1934)—a magnificent edition with over a thousand illustrations. For the first years of the period there is the very readable book by E. E. Y. Hales, *Mazzini and the Secret Societies* (London, 1956). Two sympathetic biographies of Mazzini are G. O. Griffith, *Mazzini, Prophet of Modern Europe* (London, 1932) and A. Codignola, *Mazzini* (Turin, 1946). For the central role played by Pius IX a liberal, Catholic interpretation is E. E. Y. Hales, *Pio Nono* (London, 1954) and events from 1846 to 1848 are well covered by G. F.-H. and J. Berkeley, *Italy in the Making* (3 vols., Cambridge, 1932–40). On Cavour a sympathetic and scholarly study is Adolfo Omodeo, *L'opera politica del Conte di Cavour* (Florence, 1945), while a different impression of Cavour comes from a significant study of the culminating moment of the *Risorgimento*, by the English historian, Denis Mack Smith, *Cavour and Garibaldi in 1860* (Cambridge, 1954). Until recently the National Society had been neglected, but there is now an excellent study—Raymond Grew, *A Sterner Plan for Italian Unity—The Italian National Society in the Risorgimento* (Princeton, 1963). The opening chapters of Denis Mack Smith, *Italy. A Modern History* (Ann Arbor, 1959) cover the last ten years of the period.

As usual, there are fewer reliable studies of institutions than of historical developments, but many historians and lawyers studied the constitutional form and working of the German Empire during its short life. One of the more massive of these studies was Paul Laband, *Das Staatsrecht des Deutschen Reiches* (2 vols., Freiburg, 1888), and a good discussion is Burt Estes Howard, *The German Empire* (London, 1906). On the unification of Italian institutions an important series, *L'organizzazione dello stato*, under the general direction of Alberto M. Ghisalberti and Alberto Caracciolo, is now almost complete. Of the eleven volumes, two of the more relevant for this chapter are *Il Parlamento nella formazione del regno d'Italia*, edited by Alberto Caracciolo (Milan, 1960), and *Le forze armate*, edited by Piero Pieri (Milan, 1962). The volumes contain selections of documents central to the theme, with introductory discussions by the editors.

Political developments: Germany

The policy of Metternich still dominated Germany in 1830, a policy, that is, which believed that prompt and effective repression of any liberal or nationalist aspiration was necessary for the safety of society. So far as the July Revolution of 1830 in Paris was concerned, Metternich was more alarmed for its effect in Germany and in Italy than in France herself, where the new régime soon showed that it would suppress radical revolution. In some of the larger German states there were immediately demonstrations and riots—in Würtemberg, Bavaria, Baden, Hesse and Nassau. Agitation was centred on demands for the constitutions required by Article 13 of the Federal Act of 1815, or, where constitutions already existed, on the appointment of a liberal ministry and the broadening of the constitution. Revolutionary sentiment in Germany was kept alive by the universities, as it had been since 1815. Outbreaks of open revolution forced the princes of Brunswick, Saxony and Hesse-Cassel to abdicate, and their successors introduced constitutions. In Hanover, as in England, William IV succeeded to the throne in 1830, and after the British Reform Bill had been passed, Hanover, too, was provided with a constitution, though a very narrow one. For four years the constitution survived in Hanover. Then, in 1837, William IV died, and Victoria succeeded in England, but in Hanover, since a woman could not be sovereign under the German Salic Law, the throne passed to Ernest Augustus, Duke of Cumberland and a son of George III. Cumberland had been living in England, where he was thoroughly disliked. Almost his first step was to abolish the 1833 constitution in Hanover, and to dismiss seven professors from the University of Göttingen. Of the seven professors two were the brothers Grimm, and a third was the historian, Friedrich Dahlmann (1785-1860), who had drafted the 1833 constitution.

None of the political movements in the German states during the 1830s need necessarily have been connected with a desire to unite Germany, but in fact most individual liberals were also nationalists. Those, however, who were more preoccupied with the immediate unification of Germany than with political reform in the individual states were, for the moment at least, less realistic in their approach and less effective in their actions. In May 1832 some 25,000 nationalists met at Hambach to honour the idea of Germany, to drink and to talk wildly of the need for violent action. The Hambach Festival was not only nationalist and democratic but republican in flavour. Not

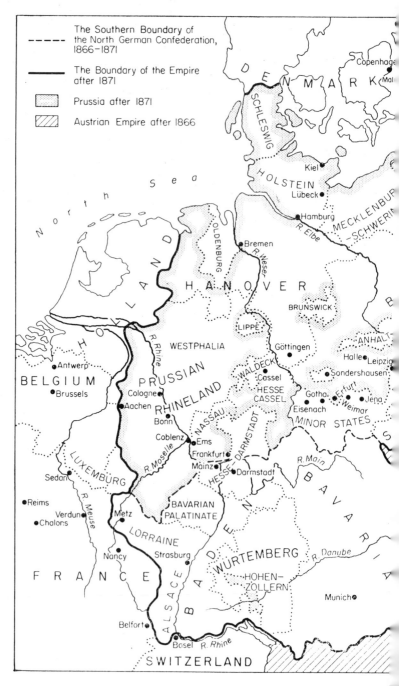

The Southern Boundary of
the North German Confederation,
1866-1871

The Boundary of the Empire
after 1871

Prussia after 1871

Austrian Empire after 1866

Copenhage

Mal

D E N M A R K

SCHLESWIG

North   Sea

H O L S T E I N

Kiel

Lübeck

MECKLENBUR
-SCHWERI

Hamburg

R. Elbe

OLDENBURG

Bremen

R. Weser

H   O   L   L   A   N   D

H A N O V E R

BRUNSWICK

B

LIPPE

ANHAL

Göttingen

Halle Leipzig

WESTPHALIA

Antwerp

BELGIUM

Brussels

PRUSSIAN

Cologne

Aachen

WALDECK

Cassel

HESSE
CASSEL

Sondershausen

Gotha Erfurt

Eisenach Weimar

Jena

MINOR STATES

S

RHINELAND

R. Rhine

Bonn

NASSAU

Coblenz

Ems

HESSE-DARMSTADT

LUXEMBURG

R. Moselle

Frankfurt

Mainz

R. Main

Sedan

Darmstadt

B A V A R I A

A

HESSE-DARMSTADT

Reims

Verdun

Chalons

R. Meuse

Metz

BAVARIAN
PALATINATE

B A D E N

LORRAINE

Nancy

Strasburg

WURTEMBERG

R. Danube

FRANCE

ALSACE

HOHEN-
ZOLLERN

Munich

B A D E N

Belfort

Basel   R. Rhine

SWITZERLAND

3. THE UNIFICATI

WEDEN

Memel

Baltic Sea

Königsberg

Danzig

EAST
PRUSSIA

WEST
PRUSSIA

POMERANIA

Stettin

BRANDENBURG

POSEN

Berlin

R. Vistula

Warsaw

RUSSIAN
POLAND

SILESIA

Dresden

Breslau

SAXONY

Teplitz

Sadowa

Carlsbad

BOHEMIA

Königgrätz

Prague

MORAVIA

Troppau

GALICIA

Olmütz

Nikolsburg

AUSTRIA

HUNGARY

Pressburg

Vienna

R. Danube

Salzburg

Buda

Pesth

Holstein

GERMANY

surprisingly, Metternich was alarmed. He persuaded the Frankfurt Diet to tighten its control over the internal affairs of the German states, so that the universities and the press could be more closely controlled. Paradoxically he was trying to strangle German nationalism by giving more authority to the Confederation—the only all-German institution. The nationalists increasingly regarded the Diet as their enemy. In April 1833 an armed rising tried to take possession of Frankfurt itself, but was put down. Metternich summoned a conference of German ministers in Vienna in March 1834, and again convinced them of the need for repressive action; but from the most significant movement in Germany in the 1830s—the extension of the Prussian customs union[1]—Austria was excluded.

Politically Prussia played a negative role in Germany under Frederick William III, who reigned until 1840. The king was personally respected, and the administration of Prussia was more efficient than that of other German states, with the result that the lack of a constitution was less apparent. The landed aristocracy, the Junkers, were the ruling class, but there was sharp hostility between town and country, especially between the newly acquired towns of the Rhinelands which had once been occupied by Napoleon, and the rural areas in the east. Stein's municipal ordinance of 1808 had given the towns the right to elect their governments, but the representative principle had not been extended to the administration of the countryside. The result was that the usual alignment between the town and liberalism on one hand, and the countryside and conservatism on the other, was even more marked in Prussia than elsewhere. Metternich's influence over Frederick William III's government was exerted through the Austrian Chancellor's friend, Johann Ancillon (1766–1837), after 1832 foreign minister in Berlin. Ancillon had been tutor to the Crown Prince, who became King Frederick William IV in 1840. An unstable romantic, the new king was alternately to make liberal gestures and to abuse the liberals in full-blooded terms. He began by relaxing the censorship—only to impose it again when he felt that the press was going too far, and by reinstating the racist historian and poet, Ernst Arndt, in his chair in the University of Bonn from which he had been ejected as long ago as 1819. Dahlmann and the brothers Grimm, exiles from Hanover, were also found university posts in Prussia.

Frederick William IV appeared as a potential leader of nationalist Germany for another reason. During the Mehemet Ali crisis in 1840[2]

[1] See above, pp. 97-100.   [2] See above, pp. 156-7.

Thiers's government in Paris adopted a belligerent line against the other powers, and especially against Prussia. The result was a wave of Francophobia in Germany. Schneckenburger's song, 'Die Wacht am Rhein', expressed the spirit of the moment, and it was fully realized, perhaps for the first time, that the watch on the Rhine was kept not by Austria, but by Prussia. Louis-Philippe's decision to drop Thiers was greeted with rejoicing in Germany, where it was felt that Frederick William IV had stood firm in the name of the whole of Germany, although the French surrender almost certainly owed more to Palmerston's policy than to the attitude of Prussia. But between 1840 and the year of revolutions Frederick William did not increase his prestige as a national leader. Rather, he disappointed the Prussians by his half-hearted movements towards constitutionalism. But he still had the best claim to a German crown if the *Grossdeutsch* party, who wanted to include Austria in the new Germany, were defeated, and the *Kleindeutsch* party, who wanted to exclude Austria, were successful. When news of the February Revolution of 1848 in Paris arrived, many strands seemed to be brought together in a great German national upheaval: the aims of the liberals to secure constitutions in the separate states of Germany, the hope of the middle class to dislodge the Junkers from positions of power in Prussia, the need of the unemployed for food, and finally the dream of the nationalists of a united German state.

In March 1848 Germany seemed to be experiencing the dawn of a new era, an era of freedom and fraternity. Everywhere there were demonstrations in favour of liberal reform, and everywhere the rulers seemed to be taken up in the general enthusiasm. Constitutions were introduced, liberal ministries appointed, broad reforms and civil liberties granted. In Berlin there were initially clashes between the crowd and the troops, but after three days Frederick William abolished the censorship and on the fourth day he ordered the troops to withdraw and allowed the crowd to arm itself. On the sixth day he declared that he was ready to lead a united Germany and that Prussia should be 'merged in Germany'. In Frankfurt the Diet had responded to the spirit of the time by accepting the nationalist flag of black, gold and red stripes as the flag of the German Confederation. A group of liberals in Heidelberg meanwhile took the initiative for the election of a German national parliament. They invited the states to send representatives to a *Vorparlament*, or preparatory assembly, at Frankfurt. The *Vorparlament* met on 31 March—the last day of this month of exhilaration—and arranged for the election of a National Assembly by universal suffrage.

The Frankfurt Assembly itself met on 18 May. From the professional classes—about two hundred of them lawyers and about one hundred professors—the delegates were all idealists, and yet they did not quite sustain the excitement of March. They were revolutionaries neither in a social nor a political sense. They had no more sympathy for socialist ideas than had the great majority of ministers established in Paris by the February Revolution. Nor did more than a few of them want a republic. But in the spring of 1848 hopes for a liberal, united Germany still stood high. An enlightened Habsburg archduke, John, the uncle of the Emperor Ferdinand, was given the title of Imperial Regent, until an emperor of Germany should be created. As yet, however, the authority of the Frankfurt parliament had no basis of power, and it was the function of the Schleswig-Holstein question to demonstrate this failure.

Holstein was traditionally considered a part of Germany: it had been within the boundaries of the Holy Roman Empire, and was a member of the German Confederation. Schleswig, on the other hand, was not a member of the Confederation, but both Holstein and South Schleswig were German-speaking. However, the king of Denmark was also Duke of Schleswig and Holstein. In January 1848, a new king, Frederick VII, succeeded to the titles. Determined to integrate Schleswig with Denmark, he moved troops into the duchies, whereupon a pro-German, nationalist revolution ensued, accompanied by insistent demands all over Germany for intervention by the new federal government. The Frankfurt parliament had to depend on Prussian arms, and prevailed upon a reluctant Frederick William to intervene in the name of united Germany. In August the Prussians accepted the Armistice of Malmö, which was a compromise and in no sense a permanent one, and was regarded as wholly unsatisfactory by German nationalists. After a further spell of fighting negotiations dragged on until 1852, but the importance of the Schleswig-Holstein question for 1848 was that the military impotence of the Frankfurt parliament had been revealed. So long as it depended upon the armies of Prussia and Austria it had no real authority in Germany. It could survive only so long as the revolution was triumphant in Berlin and Vienna.

It was in the Austrian territories that the revolutionary movement received its first shock.[1] The re-establishment of the old authorities in Vienna suggested to Frederick William IV that he had been pusillanimous in going so far with the revolution in Berlin. In his heart he

[1] See below, pp. 268–70.

had retained a blind faith in the divine right of monarchs and a contempt for the liberals. In May of 1848 he had allowed the election of a national assembly in Berlin by universal male suffrage, and he had appointed a liberal ministry. But in October, after the reaction in Vienna, he replaced the liberal ministry by an ultra-conservative one, including as minister of the interior, the man who was to emerge as the leader of reaction in Prussia, Otto von Manteuffel (1805–82). Before the end of the year the Prussian revolutionary assembly had been dissolved, and an authoritarian constitution had been enforced by the crown.

Frederick William IV's most important decision was yet to be made. The Frankfurt parliament had finally settled on a democratic, federal empire as the form for the new Germany, and had voted to exclude all the Habsburg territories. On 28 March 1849 the parliament elected the Prussian king as hereditary emperor, but Frederick William rejected the offer. His emotional reaction to the choice which for a few weeks lay before him was a mixed one. At one moment he spoke of refusing to pick up a crown 'from the gutter', of the need for a unanimous offer from the princes, of monarchy depending upon divine right and not on elected assemblies; but at the next moment he admitted that Frederick the Great would have accepted, but that he himself was 'not a great ruler'. The individual German governments felt that the moment had come to withdraw from the Frankfurt experiment, and started to recall their delegates, but the people of Germany did not passively accept the Prussian king's betrayal of liberal nationalism. After his refusal of the imperial crown many risings in favour of the Frankfurt constitution broke out in Germany, but were suppressed by the Prussian army. Frederick William's brother, later to be King William I, as commander of the army played the dominant role in the repressive movement. Those delegates of the Frankfurt assembly who bravely remained in session removed to Stuttgart, and finally had to be driven away by the army.

The Prussian king still hoped to create a German union based on monarchical legitimacy, and the goodwill, though exclusion, of Austria. In March 1850 a parliament of the German states met at Erfurt, but— not surprisingly—the Austrian government was hostile. In the face of Austrian opposition and the hesitation of several of the more important states the Erfurt Union was soon abandoned, and in May 1850 the Austrians restored the 1815 Diet of the Confederation. For a moment it seemed that Prussia might resist the reassertion of Austrian leadership by force of arms, but Manteuffel, who had been made foreign minister in November 1850, and became prime minister next month, feared a war against Austria, with whom Russia might well be allied. At a Prusso-Austrian meeting in Olmütz in November Manteuffel virtually accepted Austrian leadership in Germany. So far as German nationalism was concerned the revolution of 1848 had achieved no tangible result.

The 1850s were a decade of prosperity and political quiescence in Europe, apart from the Crimean War and the Italian Question, in both of which Prussia played a virtually neutral role. Manteuffel ignored the constitution as much as he could, enforcing decisions of his government in an arbitrary manner by using the police. But in 1858 two events seemed to promise a better future. Frederick William IV was at last recognized as being permanently insane, and his brother William became prince regent. In the general elections for the Prussian parliament, or *Landtag*, the moderate Liberals gained a great victory, with 210 seats, as opposed to only 59 Conservative seats and 58 Catholic Centre seats. The liberals thus had a clear and strong majority in spite of the conservative nature of the electoral system. William had dropped Manteuffel but was dismayed at the results of the elections. In 1861 the mad king died and the prince regent became William I. In spite of the role he had played in 1849, his accession was greeted by the liberals as the beginning of a new era. In fact he was an unimaginative army officer, who, as the second son, had been given only a military training and not expected to succeed to the throne. His real interest was the army, and if he came to hate the liberals it was mainly because they opposed him in his attempts to strengthen and reform the army.

When, during the Franco-Austrian War of 1859, the Prussian government had mobilized its army on the Rhine, the mobilization had been sluggish and incompetent. William, as prince regent, had decided that radical military reforms, and above all an increase of the army, were needed. In 1860 the *Landtag* was presented with a Bill for army reform. The Bill antagonized the liberals by its proposal to integrate the *Landwehr*, a semi-civilian, middle-class, reserve force, with the regular army, and so to deprive the liberals of armed allies. The Bill further proposed to increase recruitment per year by more than one half, and generally involved considerable additional expenditure. The liberal majority procrastinated. They passed the budget for increased expenditure for the year, but refused to accept the military reform in principle. To fight the battle of the middle class against the Junkers and the army a new political party was founded in 1861. The 'Progressive Party', as they called themselves, were frankly eager to unite Germany in a liberal sense, but had only modest objectives in their quarrel with the Prussian crown. In the dispute over army reform they had already lost the first round by accepting the government's programme for a year and so enabling the reorganization which involved destruction of the separate identity of the *Landwehr*. But the formation of the Progressive Party strengthened parliamentary opposition, and in 1862 the majority rejected the Army Bill.

William I was supported in his determination to secure the army reforms by the illiberal minister of war, von Roon, who encouraged him to proceed regardless of the vote in parliament. It was arrogant advice. In the successive elections during the years of the crisis enormous liberal majorities were returned to the Prussian parliament. A very wide popular movement, by now including peasants as well as the urban middle and lower classes, supported the Progressive Party. All the material for revolution seemed present, but the leaders of the Progressive Party would not even encourage passive resistance. The government had no difficulty in collecting taxes which had not been sanctioned by parliament, and so were in fact illegal. But William's position was a dangerous one. After contemplating abdication, he decided instead to seek a chief minister who would be ruthless enough to continue government in blatant disregard of the great majority of parliament. In September 1862, following the advice of von Roon, he sent for his ambassador in Paris, Count Otto von Bismarck.

Born in 1815, Bismarck had inherited his powerful intellect and imagination from his mother, a determined woman of middle-class origins. Bismarck's father was a dull-witted Junker, who gave him nobility, social position and wealth, but nothing else. Enrolled in the University of Göttingen, Bismarck led a wild life, over-spending, over-drinking and fighting numerous duels, but eventually graduated and entered the Prussian civil service for a half-hearted and undisciplined career of four years. In 1848 he bitterly and scathingly opposed all aspects of the liberal-nationalist movement, and in the spirit of reaction which prevailed in 1851 he was sent as Prussian delegate to the Diet of the restored Confederation. At Frankfurt he acquired a taste for diplomacy and a conviction that Austria would have to be regarded as the enemy until Prussian supremacy in Germany had been secured. He was at Frankfurt for seven years, until, in 1858, he was sent as Prussian ambassador to St Petersburg. During his three years in Russia he became familiar with the weak but well-meaning czar, Alexander II, and a man who was to be Bismarck's rival for many years—the chancellor, Gorchakov. In April 1862 Bismarck was given the Paris embassy, but after only five months was recalled to Berlin to lead the government. He brought with him a professed aversion for abstract principles, and especially for those of the French Revolution. Up to a point he was an Hegelian: he believed that God's truth was being revealed in history, and that it was not for a statesman to erect fixed principles, nor to pursue abstract ideals. All that he could do was to interpret God's will as it became apparent through the movements of the times. Bismarck's sense of moral responsibility was a mystical and an essentially anti-humanist one. He told the English ambassador: 'I attach little value to human life because I believe in another world.' He was at least free from hypocrisy; in one of the clearest statements of his belief in *real Politik*, he wrote: 'The only sound business of great states is egoism, not romanticism. It is unworthy of a great state to fight for anything that does not form part of its own interests.'[1] This kind of statement has contributed to the picture of the 'Iron Chancellor', a picture in which the stability and balance of his personality have been exaggerated. In fact Bismarck was a volatile and highly-strung man, very different from the traditional image of the Junker which he at times liked to assume.

In his first interview with the king in 1862, Bismarck secured a free hand in the formulation of policy, after declaring that his only aim was to preserve the authority of the monarchy. In rather the same way he approached the *Landtag* by apparently offering to work with them. Rather dramatically he produced a small olive branch, but then went on to assure them that force was necessary in Germany. His famous claim that 'speeches and majority resolutions' would not decide 'the great questions of the time', but that decisions should be reached only 'through iron and blood', was thus included in a speech which was intended to offer conciliation to the progressives. It may well be that on this occasion Bismarck was carried away by his own eloquence, though the fact remains that he did not intend to concede a single point. He continued to collect taxes without parliamentary sanction, and censored the press in the teeth of adverse votes in parliament.

His interest in domestic affairs, however, was always secondary to his interest in foreign policy. In 1863 the first important issue of foreign affairs presented itself to him in the shape of the Polish Revolt against Russia.[2] While Britain, France and even Austria protested at the Russian repression of the revolt, Bismarck came to a quick understand-

[1] E. Eyck, *op. cit.*, p. 29.   [2] See below, pp. 278–9.

ing with Alexander II's government. He sent Count von Alvensleben to St Petersburg to assure the czar of Prussian sympathy in the crisis, and he mobilized half the Prussian army on the Polish frontier. By the Alvensleben Convention the Prussian and Russian governments promised each other mutual assistance, if necessary, to suppress a Polish revolt, and, more specifically, to allow each other's troops to cross the frontier in pursuit of Polish political refugees. Bismarck later claimed that his policy during the 1863 Polish crisis was planned with a view to securing a Russian alignment for the wars which he would have to wage for the unification of Germany. Probably his motives were concerned with more immediate issues. Although the Poles in Prussia were not rebellious in 1863, Bismarck was preoccupied with this large foreign minority. He always saw the Poles—whether subjects of Prussia or Russia —as enemies of the Prussian state. In 1861 he had written of them in a letter to his sister: 'I have every sympathy with their situation, but if we want to exist we cannot do anything but exterminate them. The wolf, too, is not responsible for being what God has made him, but we kill him, nevertheless, if we can.'

While Europe was still concerned with what had happened in Poland, the Schleswig-Holstein question was reopened by the death of the Danish king, Frederick VII, in November 1863. The new king, Christian IX, signed a reformed Danish constitution which seemed to prepare the way for the full annexation of Schleswig. Christian IX's succession in Denmark was through a female line. In Germany it was held that the duchies came under the Salic Law, that Christian therefore had no legal claim to them and that the legal successor was the Duke of Augustenberg. Through the tangled confusion of succession disputes and the claims of the duchies to autonomy Bismarck was now to cut a straight track. His approach was brutally simple. He decided neither to accept the Danish solution nor to support the German nationalists in their candidacy of the Duke of Augustenberg, but to annex both duchies to Prussia. In an extraordinary interview with William I, Bismarck reminded the king that all his predecessors on the Prussian throne had added fresh territories to the kingdom: William I should make Schleswig-Holstein his contribution. The king was at first appalled at the suggestion, and believed that Bismarck was drunk. But in the course of the next two or three years Bismarck not only convinced the king, but utilized Austria in an alliance against Denmark. The diplomatic history of the Schleswig-Holstein question from 1864 to 1866 and of the outbreak of the Austro-Prussian War of 1866 has been considered in another context.[1] In summary it can be said that the two rival great powers in Germany went to war as the result of bitter disagreement over Schleswig-Holstein, and fierce dispute in the Frankfurt Diet over rival proposals for a constitution for Germany, a constitution to reform or to replace the Confederation. The Seven Weeks War was itself perhaps the central event in the nineteenth-century history of Germany. It finally settled the long dispute for supremacy in favour of Prussia over Austria.

The quick Prussian victory in 1866, culminating in the Austrian defeat at the battle of Königgratz or Sadowa, owed a great deal to Helmuth von Moltke (1800–91), chief of the Prussian general staff. With von Roon, Moltke had turned the Prussian army into a modern fighting machine. He made good use of railways, the telegraph and the needle-gun. He had personally invested in a railway company as early as 1844. In some respects he was more forward-looking than Bismarck. Moltke foresaw to an astonishing degree the nature of twentieth-century war-fare: he prophesied that universal suffrage and mass conscription would lead to total war in the sense that they would demand extravagant and over-simplified propaganda, depicting the enemy as totally evil, and such propaganda in its turn would mean that war had to be fought to the unconditional surrender of one side or the other. But Bismarck's war of 1866 was the exact opposite of the democratic wars of the future. His objectives were essentially limited. The preliminary peace of Nikolsburg in July, confirmed by the definitive Treaty of Prague on 23 August, took territory neither from Austria nor from the south German states who had been Austria's allies—Baden, Württemberg and Bavaria. The treaty, however, annexed to Prussia the considerable state of Hanover, Hesse-Cassel, Nassau, Frankfurt and, of course, both Schleswig and Holstein, thereby adding over three million people to the population of Prussia. Much more important was the exclusion of Austria from the new Germany by the creation of the North German Confederation, dominated by Prussia. William I was to be president and commander-in-chief of the North German Confederation, Bismarck its chancellor, and a lower house or *Reichstag* was to be elected by universal suffrage.

The war of 1866 totally altered the political situation in Prussia herself. The very day that Sadowa was fought, elections were held and the conservatives increased their members in the *Landtag* from 38 to 142. The progressives and groups aligned to them were reduced from

[1] See above, pp. 148–50.

253 to 148. The progressives were thus only just the largest party in the *Landtag*, and many of them now sympathized with Bismarck. After the victory of 1866 a new party was formed, the National Liberals, but to support Bismarck, who seemed to be uniting Germany and who had introduced universal suffrage for the North German Confederation. In fresh elections in 1867 the National Liberals secured 101 seats, leaving a rump of only 48 liberal members who still opposed Bismarck. Already before the 1867 elections, but after the victory of Sadowa, the *Landtag* had passed a law retrospectively declaring Bismarck's measures since 1862 to have been legal, in spite of adverse parliamentary votes. The cynical doctrine that might is right was securing an increasing number of adherents in Germany.

The unification of all the German states north of the river Main into a Confederation far more closely integrated than the 1815 Confederation had ever been, marked the first and most important step in the political unification of Germany. To include the states of south Germany, which were predominantly Catholic, in the union, would involve overcoming their strong temperamental aversion to Prussian leadership. Bismarck believed that this could be done only if the whole of Germany was threatened with a common enemy, and the most obvious potential enemy was France. From 1862 to 1867 Bismarck's relations with Napoleon III had been reasonably friendly, but the growth of Prussian strength made the French apprehensive, and after 1867 increasingly hostile. The question of the Hohenzollern candidature for the Spanish crown and the diplomatic origins of the Franco-Prussian War of 1870 have already been discussed.[1] The crisis developed very quickly—more quickly than that of 1866—and culminated in the longest and last war fought in western Europe in the century between 1815 and 1914.

If the military genius of Moltke had been a significant factor in the war of 1866, it proved still more triumphant in 1870. With the armies of the allied south German states at his disposal, as well as the Prussian army—now a very large one—he was the centre of a formidable military force. In less than three weeks well over a million men were mobilized in Germany and almost half of them had been transported to the front by the railways. The Prussian mobilization had not worked too smoothly in 1866, but by 1870 Moltke had perfected the modern methods of handling great numbers of men, and transporting them by rail. Realizing that the new defensive weapons—machine guns and artillery—

[1] See above, pp. 150–1.

made offensives against defended strong-points too costly, Moltke evolved the principle that strong-points should, if possible, be by-passed. Thus it was that the largest French army, under Marshal Bazaine, was shut up in the fortress of Metz in August 1870, within the first few weeks of the war, and left there while the Prussians advanced on Paris. The second great blow suffered by France was the defeat of the army under Napoleon's own command at Sedan on 1 September. The French Second Empire fell two or three days later after a republican revolution in Paris,[1] and four months later the German Second Empire was founded. On 18 January 1871 William I, king of Prussia, was proclaimed German Emperor in the Hall of Mirrors at Versailles. Bismarck read the proclamation to the assembled princes and dignitaries of Germany, a proclamation which made it clear that the title was a revival of the Holy Roman Emperorship renounced by Francis II in 1806. The interim of sixty-five years when there had been no German *Kaiser* was over.

In his memoirs Bismarck created the impression that the unification of Germany was almost exclusively the result of his personal diplomacy, and the impression has often been accepted with too little reflection. Though much certainly depended on Bismarck's policy, he had the advantage of powerful factors which would have existed whoever had been chief minister in Berlin. The *Zollverein* had already made most of Germany a single economic unit. The industrialization of Germany was gathering momentum by 1862. The population was increasing more quickly than in France or in most parts of Europe. The railways had been built. An efficient and reliable civil service and a well educated and qualified diplomatic service were at the disposal of the Prussian government. Above all a large and modern army was being created by Roon and Moltke. Even the diplomatic setting for the unification of Germany did not owe everything to Bismarck. Already in 1815 Prussia had acquired the Rhinelands with their strategic significance for the defence of Germany. After the defeat in the Crimean War Russia was no longer the great power she had been, and it was correspondingly easy for Bismarck to secure her goodwill as a major step in the isolation of Austria in 1866 and of France in 1870. After the death of Palmerston in 1865 Britain counted for rather less in Europe than she had done before: if she played an active diplomatic role in the Luxembourg crisis of 1867, under Gladstone's ministry in 1870 she was eager to keep out of continental affairs. Bismarck's diplomacy contributed towards

[1] See above, p. 177.

the neutrality of Russia and Britain in 1870, but it was not the main cause. It must still be said, however, that from 1862 to 1870 Bismarck made the best use of the forces at his command. He rarely, if ever, erred in his judgments of what was politically possible, and in diplomacy, as in war, it is the leader who makes the fewest blunders who is eventually victorious.

From the war of 1870 and its concluding Peace of Frankfurt, signed on 10 May 1871, the new Germany secured the provinces of Alsace and Lorraine, including the cities of Strasbourg and Metz, but excluding Belfort and an eastern strip of Alsace. France was also to pay an indemnity of five billion francs—about equal to two hundred million pounds—and a German army of occupation was to remain in north France until the indemnity was paid. In the event France paid the indemnity by 1873, with little effort.

Bismarck was to remain the dominating figure in Germany and Europe for twenty years after 1870. For the world they were years of peace, but Bismarck himself knew little peace of mind. His fertile imagination was continually foreseeing conspiracies against Germany and himself, and drawing up elaborate policies to avert the dangers. His first fear after 1871 was of a Catholic threat to the new Protestant imperial government. The *Kulturkampf*, or 'struggle for culture' between the Catholic Church and the Prussian state, started as a quarrel within the Church between those who supported the pope's dogma of Infallibility, proclaimed in 1870, and those German Catholics—the 'Old Catholics', as they were called—who refused to accept the new doctrine.[1] The 'Old Catholics' consisted mainly of a few liberal scholars; the bishops and priesthood of Germany naturally supported the pope's line. In March 1871 a new political party, the Centre Party, emerged in Germany to defend the Church against the encroachments of an all-powerful state. The Centre Party was to survive longer than the German Empire itself, and immediately acquired considerable sympathy, securing about seventy seats in the first elections for the *Reichstag* in 1871. Bismarck saw the movement as a danger to the very existence of the Empire, and decided to place the strength of the state behind the 'Old Catholics' in their struggle with the Church. The government patronized 'Old Catholic' teachers in the state schools, the Catholic department of the Prussian Ministry of Religion (*Kultus-Ministerium*) was abolished in July 1871, and the Jesuits were dissolved in Germany in June 1872.

[1] For the religious aspect of the dispute see below, pp. 351–2.

The culmination of Bismarck's assault on the pope came in May 1873, when the Falk Laws were passed. Dr Adalbert Falk was the Prussian minister of religion, and his laws brought the Catholic Church more closely under state control, in particular imposing government supervision over Catholic education, including education of the priests themselves. The struggle remained a bitter one for several years. Pius IX had become increasingly belligerent in his old age, and had no intention of passively accepting the persecution of the German Church by Bismarck. Early in 1875 the pope sent an encyclical to the German bishops instructing them to disobey Prussian laws which undermined the authority of the Church. Bismarck forbade publication of the encyclical. The medieval struggle between empire and papacy was being renewed, though the Empire was now dressed in the modern garb of the secular nation state. Many bishops and priests went into exile, and in 1874 a young Catholic attempted to assassinate Bismarck. The National Liberals supported Bismarck in the *Reichstag*, but the chancellor's hopes that a great new protestant group would form to defend the Empire against Catholic machinations was disappointed. His fear that the *Kulturkampf* was part of an international conspiracy against Germany, a conspiracy in which the pope, the French, the Belgians and the Poles were all involved, was also eventually shown to be groundless. When Pius IX died in 1878, Bismarck decided to seize the opportunity of the arrival of a new pope to put an end to a struggle which had grown too bitter. The new pope, Leo XIII, proved conciliatory, and direct negotiations were opened. In the course of the 1880s the Falk Laws were to be largely repealed, and the Catholic Centre Party found that on other issues after 1878 Bismarck's policy was in line with their own conservative sentiments.

They, like the chancellor, were opposed to socialist doctrine. The founder of active socialism in Germany was Ferdinand Lassalle (1825–1864), who organized the Universal German Workingmen's Association in Prussia in May 1863. Lassalle was opposed to revolution and regarded the achievement of political democracy, and especially universal suffrage, as the first aim for the workers. An understanding existed between Bismarck and Lassalle, who both hated the urban, middle-class liberals. But in 1864 Lassalle was killed in a duel, and thereafter German socialists were dominated by the Marxists. In 1869 the Social Democratic Workingmen's Party was founded by friends of Marx. After the rising of the Commune in Paris Bismarck developed a dread of socialism. In 1878–79 his policy changed in four senses: he reached a close alliance with Austria;[1] he used the mediation of the pope to make friends with the Catholic Centre Party; he broke with the liberals; and he started persecution of the socialists. A law was passed in October 1878 forbidding socialist publications and public meetings, and the police were instructed to enforce the law as actively as possible.

Bismarck's break with the large National Liberal party in the *Reichstag* was caused by the sudden change of his commercial policy. By the law of 12 July 1879 tariffs were imposed on imported agricultural and manufactured goods. For his alliance with the National Liberals since 1867 it had been necessary for Bismarck to pursue a policy of free trade. His change of policy was carried through with typical suddenness and brutality. In the *Reichstag* he blatantly spoke as a rich landowner claiming that he knew more about the needs of the country than the landless bourgeoisie who made up the Liberal party. In particular he attacked a previous ally, one of the leaders of the liberals, Eduard Lasker (1829–84), whom he jeered at as one of the men without landed property, 'the gentlemen whom our sun does not warm and our rain does not moisten'. The alliance with the liberals which had achieved so much had always been an unnatural one. In a sense Bismarck's new policy after 1878 marked a political home-coming. He had utilized the drive for freedom of the German middle class to create an authoritarian and militarist régime.

Political developments: Italy

The situation facing the forces of liberalism and nationalism in Italy in 1830 was apparently more hopeless than that facing the same forces in Germany. The German Confederation, however inadequate as a form of national expression, did at least provide a common meeting place for the delegates of the princes; in Italy there was no such confederation, but all the states were totally independent of each other. In Germany a few states had constitutions; in Italy there was not a single elected assembly in the whole peninsula. In one sense, however, the Italian nationalists were to have a more clear-cut case to fight for than the Germans had. A foreign power, Austria, occupied two of the richest and most Italian of Italian regions—Lombardy and Venetia. Austria made a more convincing common enemy for all Italians than France made for all Germans. But the revolutions which broke out in Italy in 1831 were mainly concerned with the securing of a change of government in the individual states, and were anyhow limited to central

[1] For Bismarck's diplomacy after 1870, see above, pp. 160–4.

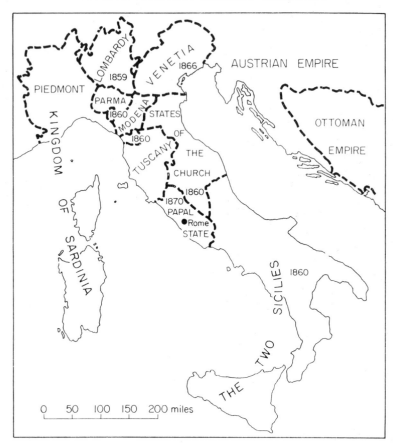

4. THE UNIFICATION OF ITALY

Italy. In February there were risings against the rulers of the small
duchies of Parma and Modena, and in Bologna and the nearby towns
of the Papal Legations, as the outlying northern part of the Papal States
was called, there was a movement to abolish the temporal power of the
pope. In the duchies some of the revolutionary leaders had vaguely
nationalistic aims, but the movement did not spread to Lombardo-
Venetia. One of the leaders in Bologna wrote that the revolution must be,
'in the end, national, not municipal', but no one in the Papal States
was more explicit. The more tangible aim in the legations was to get
rid of the pope's corrupt judicial system.

On the death of the pro-Austrian pope, Pius VIII, in 1831, an anti-

Austrian cardinal was elected, and became Gregory XVI. In spite of a determination not to be dominated by Metternich, Gregory was as conservative in his domestic policy as his immediate predecessors had been. He had no intention of surrendering any of the temporal power, or of reducing the clerical control of the administration. His reign as pope was one of the most static and least imaginative in the history of the papacy. A revolutionary assembly was elected in Bologna, but both this and the government established there—which called itself the Provisional Government of the Italian United Provinces—were dispersed by Austrian intervention, as were those in Parma and Modena. The liberals of Bologna, mostly from the professions, were not men of action, though many of them belonged to the Carbonari. The older secret societies, of which the Carbonari was the chief, were largely discredited by the failure of 1831. One young member of the Carbonari, Giuseppe Mazzini (1805–72), who was captured and imprisoned briefly in 1831, spent his days of forced solitude in planning a new secret society which would be less theatrical than the Carbonari, younger in its members, and more clearly dedicated to the concept of a free and united Italy. For the first time Italian nationalism received an articulate aim: freedom from Austria and the priests, and unity as a democratic republic.[1]

Released from prison, but exiled, Mazzini went to Marseilles, where he founded his new underground society, calling it *La Giovine Italia*, or Young Italy. Its immediate aim was to build up all over Italy little groups of idealists who accepted Mazzini's nationalist doctrines and would be ready for the revolution when it came or for any sacrifice demanded of them. Throughout the 1830s and 1840s the followers of Young Italy grew in number. As the nationalist educator of Italian middle-class youth Mazzini had a role of immense significance. But specific attempts at revolution failed. The authorities of Sardinia-Piedmont discovered a conspiracy in 1832. Charles Albert, who had become king the year before, was believed to have liberal sympathies, but did nothing to encourage such beliefs, suppressing the rising with some energy. Mazzini meanwhile moved to Switzerland and in 1834 tried to organize an invasion of Piedmont through Savoy by a small force of exiles. The attempt was again put down by the authorities with little effort.

In the 1840s a nationalist movement of a very different kind developed

[1] For a fuller consideration of Mazzini and his political ideas, see above, pp. 46–8.

in Italy. If European romanticism had produced the anti-clerical nationalism of Mazzini, it produced after 1840 a movement usually referred to as neo-guelfism—a movement which looked to the pope to lead a regeneration of Italy. In political terms the movement was somewhat impractical from the beginning, but in historical terms it was true that the popes of the middle ages had often protected Italy from foreign aggressors, and a cult of the middle ages was one of the aspects of the romantic revival of these years. The leading figure in the neo-guelf movement was the Piedmontese abbot, Vincenzo Gioberti. An exile until 1833, in 1834 Gioberti had attacked the Mazzinians after the failure of the Savoy expedition. Gioberti believed that an armed rising of the Mazzinian kind, even if it succeeded initially, would lead only to Austrian intervention. His own proposals were made in a work published in 1843, called *The Moral and Civil Primacy of the Italians*. As its title suggests, the book was a eulogy of Italian history and culture, which were contrasted with the prevailing lowly political state of Italy. The remedy Gioberti proposed was for the princes of Italy to retain their sovereignties, but to unite into a confederation under the presidency of the pope. There were weaknesses in Gioberti's scheme: in the first place, he accepted the survival of the princes and dukes only because he believed it would be too difficult to eject them, though, of course, he wanted them to introduce broad reforms in their own states; in the second place, the role given to the king of Sardinia was a vague one: Gioberti described him as 'the sword of Italy', but was not more explicit; in the third place, it seemed unlikely in 1843 that the pope would accept the presidency of Italy; and finally, Gioberti made no mention of Austria, who could not be excluded from his confederation without war.

Other moderate nationalists of the 1840s faced the problem of Austria more realistically. Both Cesare Balbo, in *Le speranze d'Italia*, published in 1844, and Massimo d'Azeglio, in *Degli ultimi casi di Romagna*, published in 1846, recognized that military or diplomatic action would be needed to drive the Austrians out of Italy. Balbo, like Gioberti, looked for a federal solution, while d'Azeglio stressed the need for continual non-violent agitation for the securing of domestic reforms. A Piedmontese nobleman and writer of sophistication, d'Azeglio believed that armies would one day be needed to obtain independence from Austria, but that meanwhile much could be done to modernize Italy by a campaign of verbal protest 'with our hands in our pockets'.

The works of Gioberti, Balbo and d'Azeglio were all great successes in Italy, but Gioberti's ideas in particular were remembered in 1846 when the liberal-minded bishop of Imola became Pope Pius IX. The new pope had read Gioberti, and felt warmly for the liberal-nationalist cause in Italy. His first move was to grant a political amnesty by which many future revolutionary leaders were released from the papal prisons. He then went ahead with other reforms and modernizations, planning railways, judicial and fiscal reforms, and granting freedom to the press, so that by the beginning of 1848 there were nearly a hundred newspapers in Rome, at a time where there was no unofficial newspaper in Vienna. In October 1847 freedom of the press was also granted in Piedmont, where Charles Albert was under considerable pressure to introduce the more rudimentary of liberal institutions. At last a thaw was setting in all over Italy, though as yet none of the monarchs had dared to grant a constitution.

Sicily had the distinction of being the scene of the very first revolution of 1848—even earlier than the February rising in Paris. On 12 January a revolutionary movement started, demanding Sicilian autonomy from the Neapolitan kingdom, and a month later King Ferdinand II, faced with a liberal movement in Naples as well, granted a constitution for the whole of his kingdom. This time no Austrian intervention had been possible, because Pius IX had refused to permit the Habsburgs to move troops across the Papal States. As everywhere in Europe, constitutions blossomed quickly in Italy in February and March of 1848. The Grand Duke Leopold II gave Tuscany a constitution on 17 February, and on 4 March Charles Albert found it impossible to halt on the path of reform, and introduced his famous *Statuto*. It has been the custom among English historians until recently to speak of Charles Albert's *Statuto* as a 'liberal constitution', though the only thing liberal about it was the mere fact that it had been granted at all. It gave the vote to only a small minority of adult males, and it left strong executive authority in the hands of the king. But it at least opened the door to a heated debate among the aristocrats and professional classes of Piedmont on the great issues of the day. The pope had already introduced a *consulta*—an advisory council containing laymen—and on 14 March 1848 he broadened this into a genuine, if very limited, constitution, by increasing the electoral and secular elements.

The Austrian provinces were now the only considerable part of Italy without some form of representative government. From the beginning of the year there had been great agitation in Milan. Young

Milanese had started a campaign of protest against Austrian rule in the form of a boycott of tobacco, which was a state monopoly. As a patriotic gesture everyone gave up smoking. Austrian soldiers who made a point of smoking cigars provocatively in the streets were attacked by groups of Italians, and disorder spread. The general in command of the Austrian army was Radetzky, eighty-one years old in 1848, but still an accomplished general and much loved by his troops. But the old man's dealings with Milan were foolishly severe, and the news of the fall of Metternich was enough to lead to open revolution on 18 March. For the famous *Cinque Giornate*—five days of street fighting—a civilian revolutionary army grappled with one of the most highly trained armies in Europe, until Radetzky withdrew his troops, not only from the city, but back upon the traditional defensive position of the Quadrilateral—the four fortresses of Mantua, Peschiera, Legnano and Verona which guarded the entry to Austria. A leader of the revolution in Milan was one of the deeper and more intelligent speculators on the nationalist question—Carlo Cattaneo (1801–69), who personally favoured a republican and federal solution for Italy, but who for the moment hoped that an armed rising of the whole country would make possible the summoning of a central constituent assembly, which could then decide democratically on Italy's future.

On the last of the Five Days of Milan a revolution succeeded in Venice also. The leader in Venice was Daniele Manin (1804–57), a lawyer of Jewish origin who had specialized in defending legal cases of a political complexion. Manin had been imprisoned in Venice by the Austrians, and the first action of the crowd in the March Revolution was to release him. The Austrian general in Venice, more civilized than Radetzky, withdrew his army at once from the city, after only two or three people had been killed. The Venetians proclaimed a restored Republic of St Mark with Manin as its president, and on the same day Piedmont declared war on Austria. The provisional government in Milan had appealed to the Piedmontese government for help, and Charles Albert, alarmed at what his own radical subjects might do, had been prevailed upon to go to war. He now found himself at the head of an armed national movement, for many elements of which he felt distaste and distrust. In April an army, partly of regular, partly of volunteer troops, left the Papal States for the war in the north, under the command of General Durando, a soldier of fortune who had already served in the armies of Piedmont, Belgium, Spain and Portugal.

The attitude of the pope to the war was clearly now of vital significance. Pius IX had become a great national leader in the eyes of most Italians. The cry 'Viva Pio Nono' had been forbidden in Austrian Italy. If the pope were to express his approval of the war and to turn Durando's army into an official force, the movement would become a crusade as well as a revolution. But Pius IX was essentially a man of peace who had never intended to lead a war against Catholic Austria. On 29 April he issued an encyclical declaring that Durando's army had been instructed merely to protect the Papal States, and that for the pope to 'undertake a war against the Germans' was 'wholly abhorrent from our counsels'. Coming at a moment of high excitement for Italy, when a Neapolitan army under the revolutionary general, Pepe, had arrived in the north to fight alongside the Piedmontese, Lombard, Venetian and papal forces, the pope's announcement was the first setback in the nationalist war. The second setback came in May when the Swiss mercenaries of Ferdinand II re-established his absolute authority in Naples, and the Neapolitan kingdom promptly withdrew from the war. The third setback was of a purely military nature, and far more serious. The Piedmontese had won a victory of secondary importance at Goito on 30 May, but in June Austrian reinforcements arrived and on 24 July Radetzky won a crushing victory at Custozza. The Piedmontese were obliged to evacuate Lombardy, and on 9 August an armistice was signed by which Charles Albert withdrew his claims to the Austrian provinces.

The repercussions of the pope's apparent betrayal of Italian nationalism had created a revolutionary situation in Rome. Radical and anticlerical sentiment, which in the past had been centred in Bologna and outlying parts of the Papal States, was now growing in strength in the capital itself. In an attempt to stem the tide Pius IX appointed as prime minister in September an enlightened and moderate man, Pellegrino Rossi, who had become a naturalized Frenchman and returned to Rome as a diplomat. In November Rossi was murdered, probably by an extremist of the left, and in the ensuing popular rising the pope escaped from Rome to seek refuge at Gaeta in the kingdom of Naples. A period of confusion followed, until, in February 1849, a constituent assembly proclaimed the Roman Republic, which was to survive for the first six months of 1849. The short-lived state had a remarkable record of liberal and social reform. It was a pure democracy, with an assembly directly elected by universal suffrage. Its executive consisted of three men, who took the title of Triumvir, and the chief of whom was Mazzini himself. By its taxation and pensions policy the Republic did something to help its more wretched subjects—the poor peasants and shepherds of the countryside, and the unemployed of the city. Mazzini remained dangerously accessible in a small office in the papal palace of the Quirinale. He refused to imprison political opponents or to censor opposition newspapers, in spite of the months of anarchy through which Rome had just passed, and the formidable external forces which were rallying to destroy the Republic.

Throughout the winter of 1848–49 the Italian Revolution survived only in Rome and Venice, where the Republic of St Mark still held out against Austria. But in March 1849 Charles Albert made another attempt. Again his motivation was rather the fear of revolution in Piedmont—and especially in Genoa, where Mazzinian sympathies were strong—than any love for the Milanese. This time, however, Radetzky had defeated the Piedmontese within two weeks. At the battle of Novara Charles Albert's army was again overwhelmingly defeated, and after several months of negotiations a definitive peace was signed, leaving Lombardy and Venice in Austrian hands, and imposing a large indemnity on Piedmont. Charles Albert abdicated in favour of his son, Victor Emmanuel II.

Once again the Republics were the sole survivors, but the Catholic powers of Europe were now conspiring to restore the pope. Not only were Austria and Spain preparing to send expeditions against the Roman Republic, but the French Second Republic, first under General Cavaignac and then under the president, Louis-Napoleon Bonaparte, were determined to give armed help to Pius IX. A French expedition landed at Civitavecchia in April, but to the surprise of Europe failed to occupy Rome. The defence of Rome familiarized the world with the name of Giuseppe Garibaldi, soon to be recognized as one of the great guerrilla leaders of history, if not the greatest.

Garibaldi had been born in Nice in 1807. As a sailor he had seen much of the world, and had led armies in South America. He had as a young man been attracted by the ideas of Saint-Simon, and then of Mazzini, but he was uneducated and had a political understanding which was limited, if astute. His remarkable powers as the leader of irregular armies came from his single-mindedness, his physical courage and the warmth of his personality. His resistance to Louis-Napoleon's forces in 1849 lasted until early July, when Garibaldi retreated with about 5,000 devoted followers across Italy to the Adriatic. Many of the 5,000 were killed or captured, but Garibaldi himself escaped. Meanwhile the Venetian Republic survived, in spite of acute food shortage, cholera and, in the last days, Austrian shelling, until 28 August. The revolutionary resistance of 1849 thus lasted longer in Venice than anywhere else in Europe.

On the face of it, it would seem that the republican achievement in 1848–49, though ultimately halted by the hostility of the great powers, had been more admirable than that of the Savoy monarchy. Republics in Rome and Venice—and a third in Florence—had resisted longer than other régimes, and Garibaldi had supplied the kind of epic story needed for the nationalist mythology. But in Piedmont something survived the disasters of 1849—Charles Albert's *Statuto*. The new king, Victor Emmanuel, refused to give Austria the satisfaction of withdrawing the constitution, with the result that the political debate over the future of Italy could continue only in Turin, among the Piedmontese upper classes and the exiles who had escaped there from other parts of Italy and whose role was to be a significant one in the next twelve years. In the period from the introduction of the *Statuto* in 1848 to the coming to power of Cavour in 1852 the three men whose writings had played so important a part in the moderate nationalist movement—Gioberti, Balbo and d'Azeglio—each occupied the post of prime minister in Turin. But none was particularly successful.

All political figures in Piedmont were quickly overshadowed by the witty debater and able administrator who was minister of commerce from 1850—Count Camillo Benso di Cavour (1810–61). The younger son of a noble family, Cavour had extricated himself from a miserable career in the army, made a great financial success of a farm provided for him by his father, and by 1850 was director of a bank and a railway company. Like Richard Cobden he was a man with great business ability who became interested in public affairs, with the difference that in Italy public affairs meant not only commercial and constitutional issues, but the struggle for national independence. Cavour had travelled in France and England, and met leading political figures. He had read the English classical economists and *laissez-faire* theorists and was a convinced advocate of free trade and parliamentary government. He had edited a newspaper, *Il Risorgimento*, after the lifting of the press censorship in 1847 and through its columns had pressed Charles Albert's government to make moderate reforms. As minister of commerce he was already the most active member of the government from 1850, and in 1852 replaced d'Azeglio as prime minister.

Cavour's achievements in his first years were all domestic ones: he gave Piedmont a healthy economy, established the authority of the state over the Church, and turned the 1848 Constitution into a more parliamentary one in some practical respects. In foreign policy he had no immediate aims. For some years he was to go on thinking of the unification of Italy as a highly dangerous project, having nothing to do with the practical aims of sensible statesmen. In a letter to Urbano Rattazzi, who was subsequently to be prime minister of Italy, written on 12 April 1856, after the Congress of Paris had finished its work, Cavour referred to Manin 'who wants the unity of Italy and other *corbellerie*'. *Corbellerie*, a coarse word, might best be rendered in this context as 'nonsense'. Not until, at least, 1859 did Cavour believe that the creation of a totally united Italy could be regarded as a political possibility. Yet he was more than a Piedmontese statesman pursuing a purely Piedmontese policy. He was continually identifying himself with an Italian cause and writing of the interests of Italy, or—a typical phrase of his—of 'our poor peninsula'. But if any improvements at all were to be introduced into the political situation of Italy, if Piedmontese independence itself were to be preserved in the face of Austrian pressure, Cavour believed that the friendship of Britain or France, and if possible both, had to be cultivated. Yet when Britain and France needed the help of any available troops in the war against Russia in the Crimea, Cavour did not hasten to intervene. Before he would agree to organize Piedmontese intervention, pressure had to be exerted from Paris and London, and Victor Emmanuel II, working in collusion with the French minister in Turin, had to threaten to appoint another ministry. The Piedmontese king's motives were a naïve desire to create a martial reputation for his army and for himself. Cavour's preoccupation was rather with the treaty of alliance signed on 2 December 1854 by France and Britain on the one hand, and Austria on the other, by which Austria promised diplomatic, but not yet military support against Russia. Cavour feared that a Franco-Austrian alliance would dangerously isolate Piedmont, and his decision to sign an alliance with Britain and France in January 1855 was thus an essentially defensive one. But the initiative had not come from him, and the policy was certainly not part of a deep-laid plan for the unification of Italy, although the small army of Piedmontese troops despatched to the Crimea in the spring of 1855 enabled Cavour to go as plenipotentiary to the Congress of Paris in 1856.

At Paris Cavour hoped to secure territorial gains for Piedmont— perhaps, at least, the duchies of Parma and Modena. He failed in this aim but obtained what was to prove more important—a closer contact with Napoleon III. After the Crimean War the French Emperor decided, for purely quixotic reasons, to do something for the 'principle of nationality', and above all for its application to the Italian Question. His meeting with Cavour at Plombières and the diplomatic preparations for the war of 1859 have already been discussed.[1] They constitute the first major diplomatic achievement by Cavour, and were responsible for the emancipation of Lombardy from the Austrians. The war was fought, by France and Piedmont on cne side, and Austria on the other, mainly in two large and bloody battles: Magenta on 4 June, and Solferino on 24 June. All armies suffered grim losses, but after Solferino the Austrian position was on balance the less tenable, and the Habsburg armies were withdrawn to the Quadrilateral. Napoleon III was now faced with the Austrian defensive line which had never been broken; he was personally nauseated by the bloodshed which he was witnessing himself as commander of the French armies; in France clerical opinion was hostile to the war which was likely to endanger the pope's temporal power; and the Prussians were mobilizing their army on the Rhine. Napoleon decided to end the war, though Venetia had not been liberated. On 11 July he met the young Austrian Emperor, Francis Joseph, at Villafranca. By the truce of Villafranca, confirmed by the subsequent Peace of Zurich on 10 November, Lombardy was surrendered to Napoleon, who ceded it to Piedmont, but Venice, of course, remained Austrian. Cavour was dismayed at the sudden termination of the war when only half the objective had been achieved, and resigned his office for the time being in protest.

In the course of the war of 1859, known in Italy as the Second War of Independence, revolutions had peacefully ejected the rulers of the duchies of Tuscany, Parma and Modena. The revolutions had been the work of the National Society, one of whose leaders was Manin, the Venetian hero of 1848. The National Society, a small group of moderates, had originally been republican, but in 1856 had come to an unofficial understanding with Cavour and were now working for an enlarged monarchy under Victor Emmanuel. Exactly what Cavour expected from them is open to question, but in 1859 they served him well. In the autumn, after Villafranca, representative assemblies in Tuscany, Parma and Modena voted for union with Piedmont. The key figure in Tuscany was the austere aristocrat, Baron Bettino Ricasoli, who had decided that annexation by Victor Emmanuel was the only moderate solution, and whose other title to fame rests in his work in restoring the Chianti vineyards. The governments of the great powers felt that the Italian situation was

[1] See above, pp. 146-7.

getting out of hand. Napoleon III was particularly concerned with the papal Romagna, where there had also been a revolution followed by demands of union with Piedmont.

When Cavour returned to office in January 1860 close relations with Napoleon were resumed. The French Emperor agreed to accept Piedmontese annexation not only of the three duchies of central Italy but also of the pope's province of Romagna, in return for Piedmont's cession to France of Savoy and Nice. Although Savoy and Nice were small areas of little economic significance, their loss was not likely to be popular in Piedmont. But all the changes of territory were confirmed by plebiscites in the areas concerned, and in March 1860 Savoy and Nice were ceded to France in a formal treaty, which would then need ratification by the Piedmontese assembly. Before ratification could be voted on a new parliament was to be elected on 5 May. It so happened that the date 5 May 1860 was to go down in Italian history for another reason, because on that day Garibaldi's expedition of the Thousand sailed from Genoa on the start of his amazing adventure.

Early in April there had been a rising against the king of Naples in Sicily, and although a month later the rising was known to have failed, Garibaldi decided to lead an expedition of irregulars, most of them Mazzinians, to Sicily. He had been in touch with the National Society, and had agreed to broaden the basis of his support by fighting in the name of 'Italy and Victor Emmanuel II' though the expedition did not, of course, have official Piedmontese support. The force, of little more than a thousand young men, many of them boys, transported in two small ships, seemed absurdly inadequate for its purpose. So many similar Mazzinian expeditions had failed in the past. A much larger force, led by Carlo Pisacane, socialist and one-time Mazzinian, had sailed to the coast of Naples in 1857 and had been easily defeated by Neapolitan forces. Cavour was strongly opposed to the expedition, which robbed him of the initiative in Italy. He believed that the alien and poverty-stricken southern half of Italy was not ready to be absorbed into the growing kingdom of the north. On 12 May Cavour wrote a revealing letter to Nigra, his confidential agent in Paris:

The ministry could not have lasted if it had tried to stop Garibaldi. With the elections on, and depending on the votes of every shade of moderate liberal to counter the opposition and get the French treaty through, I could not take strong measures to stop him . . . At the same time I omitted nothing to persuade Garibaldi to drop his mad scheme. What with La Farina's assurances and the failure of the Sicilian insurgents, I never thought he could possibly go.[1]

La Farina was Cavour's connection with the National Society. The advice that Garibaldi would find too many difficulties even to leave Genoa was credible enough at the beginning of May 1860, and the moderates found some comfort in the belief that a successful expedition was highly improbable. For Garibaldi even to make the attempt would be bad enough; for him to succeed would be a disaster. Massimo d'Azeglio wrote that he feared the immediate annexation of the south more than he feared a second battle of Novara. Yet by 11 May the Thousand had landed at Marsala, by 27 May they had taken Palermo, and in August they crossed the Straits of Messina to the Neapolitan mainland. By this time the force was greatly augmented by volunteers from all over Italy. On 7 September Garibaldi entered Naples in triumph, and in the last campaign on the Volturno he was in command of an army of some 57,000, and the ancient Bourbon kingdom of Naples had fallen to him.

Throughout the spring and summer of 1860 Garibaldi and the democrats had held the initiative in Italy. They now decided to march on Rome, a step which would almost certainly have brought French intervention. Cavour undermined this dangerous project by arranging for a Piedmontese invasion of the Papal States. With the claim that the revolutionary situation in the Papal States could not be handled responsibly by the pope's forces, Cavour marched an army into the pope's territory, where they defeated a papal army at Castelfidardo on 18 September. With Victor Emmanuel himself at its head the force then marched south to intercept Garibaldi. The meeting of the two armies—representing such different concepts of the new Italy—did not lead to a clash. Garibaldi quietly withdrew to his home on the small island of Caprera off the coast of Sardinia, handing over his conquests to the king of Piedmont, and his irregular army was subsequently disbanded. The whole of Italy except the area around Rome, and Venetia, was now in the physical control of Piedmont, but an administration and constitutional framework remained to be constructed. Plebiscites were held in Naples, Sicily and the papal provinces of the Marche and Umbria to confirm the presumed wish of the inhabitants to become subjects of Victor Emmanuel II, king of Italy. Since there was no practical alternative, and in the prevailing nationalist enthusiasm, the affirmative votes

[1] D. Mack Smith, 'Cavour's attitude to Garibaldi's expedition to Sicily', *The Cambridge Historical Journal*, 1949, p. 364.

were in a great majority. The 1848 Constitution of Piedmont was now extended to the whole of the new kingdom of Italy, and the first national parliament met in March 1861. Cavour became the first prime minister of Italy, but was not to hold the office for long. On 6 June 1861 Europe was shocked to hear of the death of Cavour at the early age of fifty-one.

Subsequent Italian historians in the nineteenth century, and, following them, English historians in the early twentieth century, were to overstate Cavour's achievement by suggesting that he had always planned to unite Italy and that he had utilized Garibaldi for his own purposes. Cavour's achievement was in fact so great that there is no need for such exaggeration. Concentrating on the independence rather than the unification of Italy, he had secured the French alliance which had led to the liberation of Lombardy in 1859, and he had prevented French intervention when the duchies and Romagna were linked with Piedmont. In the spring of 1860 he would have halted Garibaldi's plans had he dared, but in the autumn he wrested leadership from the democrats, and the kingdom of Italy which emerged was—for better or worse—very much the kind of régime he wished.

In his last days Cavour had been considering the Roman Question. The pope had, of course, been bitterly antagonized against Piedmont ever since secularization of the state had started in 1850, and more intensely when Cavour annexed a large proportion of the Papal States in 1859 and 1860. Pius IX had been deeply disappointed with the violent outcome of his initial moves to liberalize the Papal States, and subsequently tended to leave political affairs in the hands of his secretary of state, the astute but corrupt and conservative Cardinal Antonelli. Cavour's successor as prime minister of Italy, the Tuscan, Bettino Ricasoli, had a more hostile and puritanical attitude to the Catholic Church and was less likely to compromise. Rome was still occupied by French troops, and Italian democrats and Mazzinians demanded that they should be driven out. Garibaldi returned from Caprera and built up a volunteer army in Sicily for the conquest of Rome. Ricasoli fell from office in March 1862, and his successor, Urbano Rattazzi, had to deal with the dangerous situation which was developing in the south. He decided that Garibaldi must be stopped. In August 1862 Garibaldi and his force, who had crossed to the toe of the Italian mainland, were attacked and defeated by royal forces at Aspromonte. Garibaldi himself was wounded in the foot and imprisoned for a few weeks. The incident was an acute embarrassment to the new régime, and an indication that it considered the revolution over.

The apparent ease with which Piedmont had taken over the kingdom of the Two Sicilies was deceptive. Large forces of disbanded troops from the Neapolitan army, and brigands of all kinds, fought a guerrilla war against the kingdom of Italy for the first five years after 1861. They fought either from religious motives, or from a sense of loyalty to the House of Bourbon, or from simple resentment against the men from the north who had come to rule them. They represented one of the dead-ends of history—a movement whose justification would be attempted by no school of historians.

Besides Rome, Venice still remained outside the kingdom. Mazzini had not accepted the Italian monarchy of Victor Emmanuel and remained in exile, but his followers in Italy concentrated on agitation for the annexation of Venice, once Aspromonte had shown that the road to Rome was temporarily blocked. Not until 1866, however, was the government ready to take steps for the acquisition of Venice. Then, with the Prussian alliance, Italy fought her Third War of Independence against Austria. From the Italian point of view the fighting itself was disastrous. The Italian high command failed to move its armies into positions from which it could fight, with the result that an Austrian army defeated an Italian force about twice its size. The second battle of Custozza, fought in June 1866, was by no means a crushing defeat, but resulted in an Italian retreat. The naval war was if anything more disreputable for Italy. In the Adriatic an Austrian fleet defeated a more modern Italian fleet at the battle of Lissa. But in the tradition of the House of Savoy, Italy secured her objectives by diplomacy rather than by force of arms. Negotiations with Napoleon III, the alliance with Bismarck and the Prussian victory at Sadowa gained Venice for Italy.[1]

Meanwhile the French had withdrawn their garrison from Rome, following the terms of the September Convention of 1864, by which Italy agreed to protect Rome from attack and to move her capital from Turin to Florence. Napoleon III accepted the argument that the choice of Florence as capital was a renunciation of Rome, but it could equally have been argued that if the capital had been moved once it could as easily be moved a second time. Garibaldi regarded the September Convention as a betrayal of the Italian cause, and in 1867 raised another voluntary army. This time he crossed the frontier without interference from the Italian authorities, and initially defeated the papal forces. But the French government reacted quickly, sending back to Rome an army issued with the new breech-loading rifle which the Prussians had used

[1] For the diplomatic history of the 1866 war, see above, pp. 149–50.

so effectively against the Austrians the year before. In November 1867 Garibaldi was defeated by the French at the battle of Mentana. Italy had to wait another three years for Rome, and again she was to secure her objectives as a result of Bismarck's policy. In 1870 Napoleon III, needing all available men in France, withdrew his garrison from Rome even before he had suffered a major defeat. After Sedan an official Italian force fought its way into the city against stiff papal resistance. At last Italy had secured the only capital which seemed historically the logical one. By the Law of Guarantees the Italian government unilaterally settled the pope's affairs: he was to remain in secure possession of the Vatican, to have his own postal service and to draw a pension from the Italian state. Pius IX ignored the Law of Guarantees, did not touch his financial allowance and aggressively cultivated a new image as the 'prisoner of the Vatican'. In the event, the loss of temporal power was to give the papacy higher spiritual authority than it had enjoyed for several centuries.

From 1861 until 1876 Italy was ruled by the successors of Cavour, who were called simply the 'party of the Right'—*la Destra*. They kept the régime based on the interests of the middle class, but were on the whole honest administrators, free from corruption if lacking in imagination. After the epic struggles of the *Risorgimento* the era was bound to be one of anticlimax, and men like Giovanni Lanza, prime minister from 1869 to 1873, or Marco Minghetti, prime minister from 1873 to 1876, were not likely to fire the imagination of the young nation. *La Sinistra*—the party of the Left—came into office in 1876, with Agostino Depretis as head of the ministry. They were mostly one-time Mazzinians who had accepted the monarchy. Depretis himself was a cynic who secured and maintained the prime ministership by calculated and amoral political management. The parties of the Right and the Left did not have the same formal organization or consistency of principle as the two parties in England at this time. This meant that in Italy more shades of political opinion could emerge from the voting of the delegates in parliament than was possible in the already over-disciplined party procedure in England, but it also opened the door to more corruption in the Italian assembly. Depretis used every form of patronage and bribery that was available to him in retaining the support of a majority. This system, known as *trasformismo*, ignored old political loyalties and prevented the growth of a party system.

The unification of Italy in the middle years of the century had been, in Gladstone's words, 'among the greatest marvels of our time'. If the spirit of the *Risorgimento* was partly lost in the years after 1861, it is yet true that the achievements of the new kingdom in securing recognition as a great power, and in integrating the many and varying institutions of the Italian states, was a considerable one. A study of those institutions will show that the accomplishments of the men who ruled Italy after the death of Cavour were as significant as the events of 1859 and 1860 were spectacular.

Political institutions

A small middle class in both Germany and Italy had been influenced by the French Revolution and the institutions brought to their countries by Napoleon. In both countries, then, there was available a constitutional tradition springing from the ideas of 1789, but in Italy no constitutional element of any kind survived the 1815 settlement. In 1830 King Ferdinand II of Naples, who ascended to the throne that year, Francis II, Emperor of Austria and sovereign of Lombardo-Venetia, Pius VIII, prince of the Papal States, Charles Felix, king of Sardinia, and the dukes of Tuscany, Parma and Modena were all, without exception, autocrats. In Germany on the other hand the constitution of the Confederation recommended to the princes that they should introduce constitutions, and though the great powers, Austria and Prussia, remained absolutist, three of the states in the south—Bavaria, Baden, and Würtemberg—and two of the states in central Germany—Saxe-Weimar and Hesse-Darmstadt—had limited, but written constitutions.[1] But the more liberal régimes of the medium-sized German states were unfortunately to have little significance for the future of Germany.

Of primary importance, on the other hand, were the political institutions and traditions of Prussia. The scattered and geographically artificial nature of the Prussian state had made a centralized and authoritarian government a necessity, and since the early eighteenth century Prussia had developed a strong military tradition. The king was essentially a military commander and his absolutism seemed a necessary condition of the survival of the state. Neither Frederick William III, nor Frederick William IV, who became king in 1840, would have voluntarily done anything to modify their absolutism, but by 1840 there was a rising demand that the Prussian king should recognize the original aims of the Confederation to the extent of granting some form of constitution. The steps taken by Frederick William IV before the revolution of 1848 were

[1] See also above, pp. 31–2.

wholly inadequate. In 1841 he arranged for the provincial estates—local bodies which he had inherited from Frederick William III—to elect representatives who in 1842 met as a central body in Berlin for an advisory and purely temporary function. They were specifically told that they were not a popular assembly, and the experiment was not repeated for five years. In 1847 the king went a little farther. He summoned all the provincial estates to sit as a united *Landtag*, but again made it clear that he was not granting a constitution in the French sense. The *Landtag* sat in Berlin for a few weeks, but found that it was to be given neither real legislative powers nor control over government expenditure. In other words it was to be a parliament in none of the normal senses, nor was it even to sit regularly.

The March Revolution in Berlin in 1848 temporarily changed Frederick William IV's attitude, and the constituent assembly which met in May was at first allowed to draw up a comparatively radical constitution. But the work of the constituent assembly went through a double process of watering down. In the first place, in drafting the constitution in December 1848, the government restored the executive authority of the king; and in the second place the electoral system was changed in a conservative sense in May 1849. The constitution which emerged in 1849 was to remain in force in Prussia until 1918, and was therefore of great importance during the unifying of Germany and as an influence on the political climate throughout the life of the Empire. There was a *Herrenhaus*, or—to give it a literal translation—a House of Lords, and a lower assembly, or *Landtag*, elected by universal male suffrage, but indirectly through colleges of electors, and by a system which divided the electorate into three classes according to the amount they paid in taxes. The system ensured that the richer section of the population was far better represented than the poorer. One class of voters—electing one third of the members—accounted for 83 per cent of the electorate. The *Landtag* certainly had full legislative powers: it could introduce, debate and pass or reject laws. It had in theory the power to vote or withhold taxes, but it had no other control over the executive. The one feature which made Prussia—and subsequently Germany—an authoritarian rather than a democratic régime was the lack of ministerial responsibility to the assembly. The king—and subsequently the Emperor—appointed and dismissed his ministers, and they were responsible to him alone.

The *Landtag* which was in practice elected by the three-class system was less conservative than might have been expected. The largest group of delegates were the landowners, and there were many manufacturers, merchants and civil servants: government employees, as in the July Monarchy in France, were not excluded from sitting. Among the leaders of the more active liberal and nationalist groups there were some landowners, but university professors figured prominently. Politically minded academics were commoner both in Germany and France than in England. There was no secret ballot, so that it might have been expected that the Junkers would bring pressure to bear on their peasants or tenants to vote for conservative deputies, but the very large liberal majority returned from 1859 to 1866 suggests that such could not have been the case. There is something of a paradox in the apparently illiberal nature of the electoral system and the liberal majorities which it produced. What the Prussian constitution and electoral system did was to enable a powerful middle class to emerge and prevent the working class from having adequate representation. Lassalle's parliamentary socialist party remained small in the 1860s in spite of the spread of industrialization.

The revolution and reaction of 1848 and 1849 thus stamped Prussia with the constitutional character which was to last until the first world war. In contrast the constitution drafted in 1848–49 for united Germany by the Frankfurt parliament was never to be put into practice, but its potential importance was so great that it must be considered. It was the result of much debate and learned speculation. The Frankfurt parliament had contained several major groups of opinion, from a group of republicans on the left, including Vogt and Ruge, who wanted a federal, but highly centralized, democracy, through a left-centre, who wanted a monarchy with very little autonomy for the states, and a right-centre, which included Arndt, Dahlmann, Jacob Grimm and Gagern, who had been president of the parliament when it first met, and all of whom were constitutional monarchists, to a right wing, which included Radowitz, the Prussian minister, who wanted to preserve a great deal of autonomy for the states. The constitution they finally settled upon was a federal empire, with an hereditary 'Emperor of the Germans', and a two-chamber legislature. The upper chamber, or *Staatenhaus*, was to be formed partly by nomination, partly by election—50 per cent of the members would be appointed by the governments of the individual states, 50 per cent would be elected by the parliaments of the states. The lower chamber, or *Volkshaus*, was to be, as its name suggests, a wholly democratic body: it was to be elected by universal male suffrage, under a system of secret ballot. The ministers were to be responsible to parliament. Such a constitution, if it had ever functioned, might well have saved Germany, and the world, from later disasters.

More like the Prussian constitution of 1848–49, in that it was monarchical and restricted, the Piedmontese *Statuto* of 1848 was also to survive beyond national unification. It became, in fact, the constitution of the kingdom of Italy and the basis of Italian political life until the twentieth century. By Article 5 of the *Statuto* the king was declared the commander of the armed forces and to have the right to make all treaties, 'giving notice of them to the chambers when the interest and safety of the State permit'. The king could dissolve the assembly, but had to call another one within four months, and had to secure the sanction of parliament for all taxes. The upper house or *Senato* was to be nominated by the crown, but had to be chosen from specified kinds of dignitaries, who had to be over forty years of age: bishops or archbishops, government ministers, ambassadors, delegates of long standing in the lower house, judges, magistrates etc. The lower house or *camera elettiva* was to be elected by men over twenty-five, who could read and write, and who paid at least forty lire a year in taxes. This meant in practice that a minority of the adult male population had the vote, because, while the rate of literacy was high in Piedmont compared with the south, the tax qualification excluded the lower classes. A nationalist character was given to the electoral law which accompanied the *Statuto* by the extension of the vote to *Italiani*, even if they were not subjects of the king of Sardinia, provided they were resident in Piedmont. The large numbers of Lombard, Venetian, papal and Neapolitan political refugees in Piedmont could thus play a part in political life, and their cooperation was of great importance in the years to come.

In the first years of the working of Charles Albert's constitution, until Cavour's coming to power in 1852, the authority of the crown was too strong for the régime to be considered a parliamentary one. The several governments which came and went did so at the bidding of the king, rather than because of the wishes of the assembly. Victor Emmanuel II had an unsophisticated approach to politics, and it did not occur to him to play the role of constitutional monarch as interpreted by Victoria and Albert in England. But the arrival of Cavour brought a change, in that the post of prime minister acquired prestige in its own right, a prestige which the king preferred not to ignore. Cavour himself was sometimes happy to work through parliament, but his admiration of the English political system did not extend to the two-party system. His alliance or *connubio* in 1852 with Urbano Rattazzi, leader of the moderate left, which had been the closest thing to an official opposition, greatly strengthened his position in the Piedmontese assembly, but started the tradition of political manœuvering, without too much regard for principles or national parties—a tradition inherited by the kingdom of Italy. The question as to whether Cavour felt more responsible to the crown or to parliament is a vexed one, and perhaps the truth is that he felt sometimes one way, sometimes the other. Certainly he could wholly ignore neither the king nor the elected delegates. In this respect the régime in Piedmont was more genuinely constitutional than that in Prussia during the 1850s: in Prussia, in spite of the large and vocal parliamentary opposition, the ministers considered themselves the servants of the king, and the king was in full agreement with them on the point.

In both Germany and Italy in 1848 there developed strong democratic traditions which were subsequently ignored, and to an extent betrayed, by the ruling classes. While in Germany democratic sentiment produced the Frankfurt Constitution which was then destroyed by the Austrian and Prussian governments, in Italy there was the strong belief—held not only by the Mazzinians but by more cautious men, like Manin and Cattaneo—that a constituent assembly should be elected by universal suffrage, and should then democratically debate the form and process by which the Italian state should be created. In the event the Piedmontese government summoned no constituent assembly in 1860, but instead used the device, favoured equally by Cavour and Napoleon III, of the plebiscite. In the occupied—or liberated—territories of the king of Naples and the pope, the inhabitants were asked to approve or to disapprove annexation by Victor Emmanuel. One of the weaknesses which go with this kind of plebiscite is the grave doubt in the minds of the voters as to what would happen in the event of a majority of negative votes. The plebiscite was conducted by universal male suffrage, but once the majority of affirmative votes had been secured, the Piedmontese authorities imposed their own constitution—in effect, Charles Albert's Statuto of 1848—with negligible changes. Thousands of the illiterate Neapolitan peasants who voted in the plebiscite of 1860 were voting not only for the first time in their lives, but also for the last time. The literacy qualification for the vote excluded far more southerners after 1861 than it had done Piedmontese, because of the higher standard of elementary education in the north. In the new Italian kingdom the 443 members of the assembly were elected by only some 300,000 voters—in effect, by the rich and educated members of society. Cavour and the party of the right were not ashamed of the narrowly oligarchical character of the régime. They believed that the primary need of the new state was stability, and that a large bloc of illiterate peasant voters would not contribute to stability. Against this argument was the fact that the peasants were by no means a dormant or acquiescent section of the community. Throughout the whole *Risorgimento* period there had been numerous peasant risings—incoherent and undirected outbreaks of violence, whose only objects were the immediate ones of securing food or land, or burning down the town hall and so destroying the landowners' titles to their estates. Whereas in 1789 the French middle class had taken a few hesitant and half-hearted steps to identify their interests with those of the peasants by removing 'feudal' restrictions of land tenure or tax inequalities, the Italian middle class of the *Risorgimento* scrupulously avoided any identification of interests with those of the peasants. The Italian peasants were more heavily taxed after 1861 than before, and their discontent was to rise to serious proportions later in the century.

In contrast to the Prussian and Piedmontese constitutions the first German constitution created by Bismarck—that of the North German Confederation of 1866—was based on the principle of one man, one vote. Although it was the work of the monarchical governments, in the sense that it was drafted in Prussia under Bismarck's direction and accepted by the other German princes north of the River Main by formal treaty, the North German Confederation had some surprisingly democratic aspects. The ancient term *Reichstag* was used again for the lower legislative house, which was elected by universal manhood suffrage. The upper house, Federal Council or *Bundesrat* represented the states; it was composed not of deputies or plenipotentiaries with a will of their own, but of delegates of the states with specific instructions from their state governments on how to vote. The whole *Bundesrat* consisted only of forty-three vote-holding delegates, seventeen of whom were from Prussia. Since Prussia could count on the votes of some of her small neighbours she was able to hold control of the *Bundesrat*. The president of the North German Confederation was the king of Prussia, who had an official representative in the person of a chancellor, the first chancellor being Bismarck. After the war against France in 1870 each of the south German states independently agreed to join the North German Confederation, which was renamed the German Empire from 1 January 1871. The constitution of the German Empire was thus the same as that of the North German Confederation, and it is possible to consider the institutions of the Confederation and the Empire together, as they were, in effect, the same.

Both the *Reichstag* and the *Bundesrat* could initiate legislation, though in practice most laws originated from the *Bundesrat*. The *Reichstag* had, of course, the right of debating, and of accepting or rejecting laws originating from the *Bundesrat*, including the budget, and of ratifying treaties, though this was defined by Bismarck as meaning only treaties of peace, not treaties of alliance, which were usually kept secret. The *Reichstag* was elected not only by universal male suffrage, but also by secret ballot, and so was a fully democratic body, apart from the exclusion of women from the vote, but this exclusion was regular practice all over Europe throughout the nineteenth century. Bismarck defended universal suffrage after 1866, saying quite simply that 'the solid mass of population should predominate at the elections'. Like Napoleon III he saw the urban middle class as his ultimate enemy, and he sought to use the masses—especially the rural masses—as a counterweight. He foresaw that universal suffrage would not lead immediately to socialism, and he believed that it would if anything have a restraining effect on the radical minority in the middle class. In the long run he was mistaken: the social democrats were eventually to become a large party in the *Reichstag*; but one of Bismarck's most striking characteristics was his lack of concern for what might happen after his death. The contrast is clearly a sharp one between Bismarck's acceptance of universal suffrage and the reluctance of Cavour and his successors to allow more than a small minority of male Italians to share in the political life of the country.

If a wider range of public opinion could be expressed in the *Reichstag* of united Germany than in the assembly of united Italy, it is yet true that the kingdom of Italy was the more liberal of the two régimes. This was because in Italy the prime minister and his cabinet were more dependent upon the assembly than was the chancellor in Germany. In both countries the monarch had more authority than is the case in genuinely parliamentary régimes, but in Italy the ministers looked for support to parliament whereas in Germany Bismarck could afford to ignore the *Reichstag* more safely than he could disregard the Emperor. A great deal of Bismarck's time, skill and nervous energy went into the struggle to persuade his Emperor of the wisdom of the policy he was proposing. Bismarck always succeeded in carrying the Emperor with him, so long as William I lived, which was until 1888, so that for these years Bismarck was the real ruler of Germany, though the Emperor held the ultimate executive power had he ever desired to use it. The Emperor, or *Kaiser*, appointed and dismissed at pleasure not only the chancellor, but all imperial officials. He appointed the judges of the imperial court, or *Reichsgericht*, but could not dismiss them: the judiciary was thus independent. He was commander-in-chief of the German army, all members of which took an oath of personal allegiance to him. An attempt on the life of the *Kaiser*, even if unsuccessful, was punishable by death.

The role of the imperial chancellor was more eminent than that of a prime minister, since there was no cabinet to control him. He had a double function as head of the imperial administration and chairman of the *Bundesrat*. He had, then, to be a delegate of one of the states to the *Bundesrat*, and in practice this meant that he was always a Prussian delegate. The Emperor was by definition king of Prussia, and inevitably appointed one of his own Prussian delegates to the *Bundesrat* as chancellor. Had he, for example, as a gesture of generosity, appointed a Bavarian delegate as chancellor, the anomalous situation would have arisen that the king of Bavaria could have deprived the Emperor of his chancellor merely by replacing his delegate at the *Bundesrat*. The four successors to Bismarck as chancellor were consequently all Prussians.

The civil service of which the chancellor was the head was at first a decentralized one. When the Empire was established in 1871 it was decided that the administrative systems of the various states should be left intact, but that they should all be supervised at the top by the chancellor. A civil servant appointed by the chancellor would thus come under the regulations of his own state, which may vary considerably from those of other parts of the Empire. The system proved too complicated to work smoothly and in March 1873 a code of regulations for all imperial administrative officers, based mainly on the Prussian system, was introduced. The Prussian civil service had a good record. There had never been much corruption, and the Prussian officials who had worked the *Zollverein* had earned a reputation for efficiency. German civil servants were divided into two classes—'direct' officers appointed by the *Kaiser* or the chancellor, and 'indirect' officers, initially appointed by the sovereign of the separate state, but then coming under the authority of the *Kaiser*. As regards finance, the German Empire, like most federations, was not highly centralized, the imperial government depending on contributions from the states, or *Matrikularbeiträge*. But the imperial authority had income of its own apart from that coming from the states and from its property: it imposed taxes on railway tickets and cheques, both of which were too mobile to be handled by the separate states, and it had a large income from customs duties. It was partly with a view to increasing the specifically imperial revenue that Bismarck imposed the high protective tariffs in 1879.

If the administration of Bismarck's Germany was in many respects more centralized than that of most federations, it was very much less centralized than that of united Italy after 1861. The integration of Italian institutions after unification was an astonishing achievement. The laws, the administration, education and the armed forces were all united and standardized in the teeth of strong opposition from local prejudice, deep-seated traditions and vested interests. In most cases it was a question of imposing Piedmontese systems and practices. As far as the legal system was concerned, an exception to the usual drive for standardization was allowed in the case of Tuscany, where a tradition started under the influence of Beccaria in the eighteenth century had created more advanced legal codes than those of Piedmont and in some respects more civilized ones than even the Code Napoleon. The death sentence had long ago been abolished in Tuscany, and the new Italian authorities could hardly reimpose it. Tuscany, then, was allowed to keep her own penal code. Administrative unification, on the other hand, was carried out quite ruthlessly by a few capable and devoted ministers. Piedmont had adopted a French type of local administration, dividing the country into provinces under prefects, and communes under mayors, and this system after 1860 was imposed on the rest of Italy with little regard for regional sentiment. In the same way the great variety of financial systems were integrated into a single one by such capable ministers of finance as Marco Minghetti and Quintino Sella. There had been great diversity of financial practice even within the old states: the practice in Sicily had been different from that on the Neapolitan mainland, and the several administrative areas of the Papal States had differed from each other. The very principles underlying public taxation and expenditure had varied from one state to another. They now had to be reconciled, and the various public debts had to be united and dealt with on a national basis. The whole process of standardization of institutions took some years, but by 1870 it was virtually complete.

To the question whether the unifications of Italy and Germany were really conquests by Piedmont and Prussia of the rest there is no simple answer. So far as the adjustment of the administrative systems is concerned it is clear from what has already been said that both Piedmont and Prussia behaved very much like conquerors, and Piedmont, perhaps, rather more so than Prussia. But in political terms the Piedmontese were more careful to merge in Italy, than the Prussians were in Germany. Turin was the capital of Italy for only three or four years; the capital was then moved to Florence, and finally Rome. Berlin remained the capital of the German Empire, although, like Turin, it was remote from the centre of the country and did not have the cultural and artistic heritage of several other German cities. The first prime minister of Italy was inevitably the Piedmontese, Cavour, but the second was the Tuscan, Ricasoli, and of the nine men who were prime minister before 1880 only five were Piedmontese. Nearly all the German chancellors in the life of the Empire were Prussians. Victor Emmanuel II was blamed by many Italians for not changing his title to 'Victor Emmanuel I' of Italy: to retain the numeral II seemed to imply that Piedmont had merely annexed the other parts of Italy. When William I of Prussia became German *Kaiser* he had no such problem, but his son became Frederick III, although the eighteenth-century Prussian Kings, Frederick I and Frederick II, had not been rulers of Germany. But both the Piedmontese and the Prussians felt that their predominant positions in the new nation states were justified by the initiatives they had taken and the efforts they had made in the process of unification. The Piedmontese in particular had fought wars of independence in 1848, 1849 and 1859, and had sacrificed two of their own provinces— Savoy and Nice—to the cause of unification."

The Piedmontese army, though small compared with those of the great powers, had performed an important function in 1859 and was the nucleus of the army defending the nation after 1861. Those units of the Neapolitan army which were still in existence, and the smaller official forces of the central duchies were incorporated in a national army, but in 1860 Garibaldi had disbanded many of the Neapolitan troops who had surrendered to him, and many of these disbanded forces subsequently joined the brigands in the civil war against Italy. There was a certain irony in the fact that the Piedmontese government refused to incorporate even the officers from Garibaldi's own Army of the South, as it was called, into the national army, though commissions issued by the ex-king of Naples were recognized by Victor Emmanuel. After a great deal of bitterness an Italian army was created, but the unification of the navies of Piedmont and Naples proved more difficult, and the attempt to integrate them into a single force was not even made for some years.

In the process of Italian unification Cavour's diplomacy and Garibaldi's civilian volunteers had played more important roles than the Piedmontese regular army, but in the process of German unification the Prussian army had played a role second to none. In any consideration of Prussian or German institutions the army must be given a prominent place. The Prussian army had combined a primitive respect for caste with the most modern military technique. Thus it carried out striking reforms in organization in the 1860s, and yet was still controlled by the old nobility. Only noblemen held commissions in the famous guards regiments. For the cavalry regiments officers were nearly always taken from the nobility, and even among the officers of the infantry there was only a small minority of commoners. Above all, the generals at the top were Junkers with fixed prejudices against the middle class. Yet these men in the 1860s were the first to perfect the use of modern weapons, especially the breech-loading rifle, which made the infantryman much more effective; they were the first to use artillery fire in a concentrated, modern manner; they were the first to use the railway effectively for mobilizing vast numbers of troops: the French in 1859 and again in 1870 fell into considerable confusion in their use of the railways; and, above all, the Prussians were the first to evolve an efficient general staff.

In 1857 Moltke was appointed chief of the general staff. Though sharing the political and social prejudices of his class, Helmuth von Moltke (1800–91) was a man of wide culture and deep insight. With his delicate features, quiet manner and love of Mozart, he was anything but a typical Prussian officer. The general staffs of other powers, and of Prussia before Moltke, were essentially office workers for the commander-in-chief, who would himself accompany the army in the field. Moltke realized that war had now become too technical, and armies too large, to be handled in this manner. He turned the general staff into the brain of the army—a central headquarters where railway movements for mobilization could be planned and whence the operations of all the armies in the field could be coordinated and directed with the use of the telegraph. Sadowa was the first major battle in history in which one side could draw upon the intelligent speculations of a general staff and in which all movements of a vast army were coordinated in a modern manner. The overwhelming defeat of the Austrians was not due to the tactical skill of the Prussian commanders in the field nor to the courage of the Prussian troops. It was due solely to the plans of von Moltke and the use he made of the general staff.

The distinction between a federal state and a confederation of several states is perhaps most clearly illustrated by a study of the command of the armed forces. In the German Confederation from 1815 to 1866 there were numerous armies under separate commands, but with the creation of the North German Confederation the armies were united under the single command of the king of Prussia. Thus, although the term *Bund*, translated as 'Confederation', was used for both organizations, it is clear that the creation of the North German Confederation already constituted the unification of many states into a single, federal state, and the declaration of the German Empire in 1871 merely re-emphasized what had already happened, and extended the union to include the southern states. Under the Empire the armies of the German princes remained in existence, but no longer in separate, independent existence. The officers and men took a double oath of allegiance—to their own prince and to the Emperor. Common equipment and a common uniform were introduced for the whole German army. The expenses for the army were met by the imperial authorities; martial law and regulations for conscription and discipline were controlled by the central government. The navy was still more completely united. Only Prussia had a navy of any size before unification, so that in 1871 the navy could simply be considered an imperial force, under the command of the king and emperor.

This chapter has been concerned with the points of contrast in the movements for the unification of Germany and Italy, but the points of similarity are also striking. In both cases peoples with long, rich and turbulent histories had been deprived for some centuries of political unity, and had secured it in the single decade of the 1860s, as the result of revolution, war and diplomatic agility. In neither case was the constitutional form under which unity was achieved to last for very long. The German Empire survived for only fifty-three years and the kingdom of Italy for only eighty-six years. In the twentieth century the nationalist movements in both countries were to go sour and produce the sick and destructive phases of fascism. But the idea of political nationality in Germany and Italy was to survive two world wars and to constitute an important part of the image of Europe.

X

Experiments in Moderation: Belgium, Holland and Switzerland

Three small countries of western Europe, Belgium, Holland and Switzerland, followed patterns of historical development from 1830 to 1880 which have much in common. All three countries had shared the violent and colourful past of the rest of western Europe. All three countries experienced internal violence and bloodshed in the 1830s. The twentieth-century image of the three countries—smug, over-civilized and self-satisfied little democracies—is based only on the last century of their histories. Since 1848, it is true, all three countries have evolved an ordered political life in which disputes formerly leading to bloodshed have been settled by debate and votes in the assembly hall. Almost overnight these three ancient European communities discovered that even bitter religious and political issues could be settled within a system of constitutional rules and without resort to the older barbarisms. The

BIBLIOGRAPHY. The classic history of Belgium is H. Pirenne, *Histoire de Belgique* (Brussels, 1929), of which vols. VI and VII deal with this period. A recent study of the birth and evolution of the Belgian constitution is J. Gilissen, *Le régime représentatif en Belgique depuis 1790* (Brussels, 1958). Sir Charles Webster's *Foreign Policy of Palmerston* (London, 1951), vol. I, deals well with the diplomatic history of the movement for Belgian independence. For Holland there is in English, G. Edmundson, *History of Holland* (Cambridge, 1922), and the historical section of E. Van Raalte, *The Parliament of the Kingdom of the Netherlands* (The Hague, 1959). A standard history of nineteenth-century Switzerland is W. Oechsli, *Geschichte der Schweiz im 19. Jahrhundert* (Leipzig, 1903–13), of which an abbreviated version in English occurs in chapter VIII of the *Cambridge Modern History*, vol. XI (1909). The *New Cambridge Modern History*, vol. X, touches only briefly on the Low Countries and Switzerland. A recent history of Switzerland in English is E. Bonjour, H. S. Offler and G. R. Potter, *A Short History of Switzerland* (Oxford, 1952), and E. Bonjour is also the author of *Swiss Neutrality* (London, 1946, translated by M. Hottinger). A good constitutional history with the relevant documents is W. E. Rappard, *La constitution fédérale de la Suisse, 1848–1948* (Boudray, 1948).

questions at issue remained largely the same: what should be the relations between Church and State? Who should control education? How large a section of the community should be allowed to elect representatives in government and parliament? But these questions, basic and vital though they are in any society, were found to be capable of settlement within a universally accepted institution of debate—a parliament.

Political developments: Belgium

The union of Holland and Belgium under the Dutch king, William I, in 1815 had been one of the less successful parts of the Vienna settlement. The economic and strategic motives which had seemed to justify the union proved less potent than the religious and cultural sentiments which were offended by it. William I had shown a sympathy for Belgium's economic needs, but neither he nor his officials could understand the claims of Belgian Catholics nor the enthusiasm of Belgian liberals. That short-lived movement, the liberal catholicism associated with Lamennais in France, had encouraged a temporary union of liberals and Catholics in Belgium, and the 1830 revolution in Paris infected the citizens of Brussels with its spirit.

Popular demonstrations in Brussels in August and September 1830 were led by the usual revolutionary types—the lawyers and journalists. Rioting quickly developed into armed revolution. The Belgian leaders in the old parliament of the United Netherlands—men like de Gerlache and de Brouckere—were seeking only administrative separation, and this the king granted late in September when the revolution had already established *de facto* separation. But the bloodshed already caused by the king's attempt to reoccupy Brussels antagonized the Belgians to the point where only complete independence was acceptable. Crowds of miners and peasants had flocked into Brussels, while the middle-class leaders left. A more extreme group formed an 'administrative commission', which later assumed the title of 'Provisional Government'. On 4 October 1830 they proclaimed the independence of Belgium and announced that a national congress was to be elected.

The Belgian Question had already become a major issue in European diplomacy. The declaration of Belgian independence constituted an infringement of the 1815 settlement. British and French interests were vitally involved. Metternich could congratulate himself for having abandoned claims to Belgium in 1815, but this was small comfort in 1830 when a revolutionary fever seemed to be again spreading across

Europe. That the powers settled the Belgian Question without resort to war showed that the 'Concert of Europe' was not a wholly meaningless phrase. The Conference of London, attended by the five powers, was dominated by a new figure on the European scene—the English foreign secretary, Viscount Palmerston. The Conference sat throughout the Belgian crisis and passed through some dangerous phases. Palmerston was obliged to bully in turn the Belgian revolutionary congress, the French, the eastern powers and the Dutch. The settlement which emerged was very much to his liking. Although William I was not to accept defeat until April 1839, the powers signed a treaty recognizing Belgium as an independent state on 15 November 1831. The Belgian national assembly had already been persuaded to elect Leopold of Saxe-Coburg as king. He was uncle of the future queen, Victoria, and an intelligent and able man of forty-one. Belgian neutrality was guaranteed by the powers. An enthusiasm among many Belgians for a link with France had alarmed Palmerston, and he had persuaded the Belgian congress and the other powers to accept the idea of perpetual neutrality, to place Belgium once and for all beyond the ambitions of her closely related neighbour.

A new state, with a respectable constitutional monarchy, had appeared in western Europe. Its king, who reigned until 1865, quickly acquired throughout Europe a reputation for political astuteness. In the early years of his reign Leopold's personal prestige was a source of unity to his kingdom, but as Belgian political parties grew in influence the king's power declined and his attitude appeared increasingly conservative. The clerical-liberal coalition which had carried through the revolution ruled Belgium for the early part of Leopold's reign, but a split soon started to appear. The liberal newspaper, L'Indépendance, founded in 1861, took an anti-clerical standpoint.

With the common enemy defeated, Catholics and liberals became rivals for control of education, even while they could, for the time being, share the government of the country. The king of Holland had founded two state universities in Belgium—Ghent and Liège. The Catholics replied with the revival of Louvain and in 1834 a liberal university was founded in Brussels. That the Catholics and liberals continued to form coalition governments from 1831 to 1847 was mainly due to the deliberate policy of the king, who refused to summon a one-party government and so prevented the growth of ministerial responsibility to the assembly. Though essentially undemocratic, Leopold's policy gave the country a sense of unity in its early years. But it did not give political stability:

from 1831 to 1847 there were seven ministries; and his authoritarianism could not survive the liberal outburst of 1848.

With St Petersburg and London, Brussels was one of the very few European capitals to escape revolution in 1848. In the summer of 1847 the liberals won the election and Charles Rogier, a leader of 1830 and the most distinguished liberal statesman of the period, was made prime minister. For the first time the principle of ministerial responsibility was clearly recognized. After the February Revolution in Paris, Rogier acted quickly, mobilizing the army, expelling Marx, but at the same time wisely passing important electoral reforms. Satisfaction was felt at the increase of the electorate from 46,000 to 79,000. The deputy Delfosse expressed the general feeling in a declaration which was to become famous: 'To go around the world the ideas of the French Revolution need no longer pass through Belgium'.

From 1848 to 1880 Belgium enjoyed a two-party parliamentary system, very similar in most respects to the English system. The liberals were in office for the greater part of the time, but with the Catholics always forming a strong opposition. The main issue remained control of education. The peasants in the northern, Flemish part of Belgium tended to support the Catholics, while the industrial classes in the southern, Walloon region tended to be liberal and anti-clerical. The liberal governments pursued a classic economic policy, in the 1860s freeing overseas trade and signing commercial treaties with France and Britain. Belgium had become the most highly industrialized part of the continent. Her coal production in 1841 was greater than that of France or Germany, though by 1871 Germany had rushed ahead. But the tax qualification for the vote kept the industrial working class out of political life until after 1880. Not until 1885 was a workers' party founded, and no working-class members were to be returned to parliament until after the constitutional reform of 1893.

Political developments: Holland

Before accepting Belgian independence, William I had fought several stubborn military campaigns against the Belgians and a French army representing the Concert of Europe. A Dutch garrison in Antwerp had been besieged by British naval and French land forces. The wealth that William's sound economic policy from 1815 to 1830 had procured for Holland had been squandered in a decade of war. The Dutch people had at first sympathized with their king in his struggle against the Belgians, but as the war brought increasing hardship the Dutch grew disillusioned with its aims. Partly because of growing unpopularity, and partly to enable him to marry a Belgian Catholic, William abdicated in 1840. He had been an autocrat and had bungled the Belgian Question, but on economic and social issues his policy had always been sound. In the last years of his reign he had organized a commission to examine the evils of child labour. After his abdication the commission was dropped.

The period of Dutch history from 1840 to 1880 was dominated by the figure of Johan Rudolf Thorbecke, professor of law at Leiden, who built up the Liberal party and turned it into an engine of government. William I's successor, his son, William II, was a sensible monarch who did not wish to retain the near autocracy of his father. In 1848 he appointed a commission, which included Thorbecke, to draft a new constitution. The result was by no means a radical document, but it had the effect of saving the Dutch from violent revolution in 1848, just as the electoral reform had saved the Belgians. The opening of parliamentary life in Holland as in Belgium was marked by an alliance between liberals and Catholics. About a third of the population of Holland was devoutly Catholic, and encouraged to take an active part in politics by their priests. When Pius IX established a Catholic hierarchy in Holland in 1852, to fight, as he put it, 'the evils of the Calvinist heresy', a new Protestant party, calling itself the 'Anti-revolutionary Party', was formed. But the liberals and Catholics remained allied in defence of the constitution, which permitted the ideal later to be recommended by Cavour—'a free Church in a free State'. On constitutional grounds the Catholics were clearly justified in organizing their own Church, even though Holland was a predominantly Calvinist country, but the tone adopted by the pope and priests in exercising their rights was needlessly provocative. The tact exercised by Catholics in England, and especially by Cardinal Wiseman, at the time of the establishment of the hierarchy there, compares favourably with the indiscretions of Dutch Catholics. The new Calvinist party received hysterical support, and was carried to victory at the polls. For many years Dutch politics was preoccupied with the religious rivalry, and, as in Belgium, the question of control of education became the central theme.

The period after 1850 was one of prosperity and economic growth. The exploitation of Java had largely overcome the economic difficulties of the 1840s. The reign of William III, 1849 to 1890, was one of peace and stability. Until his death in 1872 Johan Thorbecke retained his position in the country solely as a parliamentary figure. He gave the

Dutch middle class a political consciousness, and presided over the maturing of their constitutional system.

Political developments: Switzerland

Even more striking in its sudden switch from an era of civil violence to one of peace and order was the history of the Swiss Confederation in the mid-nineteenth century. The 1815 settlement had recognized a loose confederation of twenty-two cantons. Switzerland at the Restoration harboured primitive institutions in some of the cantons: torture, religious intolerance, press censorship. But from 1828 to 1848, the period usually called the 'era of regeneration', a new spirit swept the country. In many cantons democratic reforms were introduced, including freedom of the press and even universal male suffrage. From 1830 to 1833 ten cantons introduced radical institutions. The democratic movement was stimulated by the professional classes—lawyers, doctors, parsons and writers; but it was running against the reactionary tide prevalent in other parts of central Europe, and it was by no means universally acceptable all over Switzerland. Opposed to the liberal or radical cantons were the Catholic cantons. The liberals wanted not only internal reforms in the individual cantons, but a more closely integrated federal state, a greater measure of centralization. The Catholics opposed centralization, because a strong federal government would deprive the Catholic cantons of their hold on education. As in the Low Countries bitter religious rivalry had survived from the sixteenth century, but now centred itself almost entirely on the issue of control of education.

The basic split in Swiss political life led to civil strife in 1831 in Basle, and in Neuchâtel, where the situation was complicated by the sovereignty held over the canton by the king of Prussia. At times throughout the 1830s the federal government tried to intervene to prevent religious war in the cantons, but not always effectively. In the mixed canton of Aargau a radical government in 1841 suppressed a Catholic rising and then dissolved the monasteries. In the important Catholic canton of Lucerne secondary education was placed in the hands of the Jesuits, and a radical rising of protest defeated. In both the federal government proved too weak to mediate successfully. Its impotence opened the way to civil war.

In 1845 a secret armed league was formed of the seven Catholic cantons, Lucerne, Uri, Schwyz, Unterwald, Zug, Freiburg and the Valais—the *Sonderbund*. In the following months the secret leaked out, and in July 1847 the Federal Diet passed a motion declaring the *Son-*

derbund a breach of the constitution. The war which ensued was no longer simply domestic strife within individual cantons, but a war between cantons, a struggle for power throughout Switzerland. Even so, it was not a war involving great destruction of life or property. The liberal forces under G. H. Dufour easily defeated the forces of the *Sonderbund* in July 1847, before Metternich and Guizot could intervene. The restrained nature of the fighting made it possible for the victorious side to grant a wise and conciliatory peace, a peace which took the ultimate form of the constitution of 1848. Under its new constitution Switzerland was to enjoy a much stronger federal government, and a legislature based on universal suffrage. Seldom in European history has so radical a constitution proved more successful. The history of Switzerland from 1848 to 1880 is one of almost undisturbed calm. The Neuchâtel Question, with its external complication, alone produced anything approaching a crisis, and even this was solved in 1857, when Frederick William IV renounced all concrete rights in the canton, retaining only the honorific title of 'Prince of Neuchâtel'. The stability of Swiss society in the second half of the century is unique in European history. From 1848 to 1918 the same party—the radical party—kept its majority in both legislative houses. The same executive officers were continually elected to power. The Swiss had complete confidence in their constitution and in their chosen rulers. Their neutrality was consistently recognized. They were apprehensive, but in practice untouched, by the adventures of Napoleon III and Bismarck. In the centre of a dramatically changing Europe the small democratic Republic remained a haven of security.

Political institutions

The Belgian constitution of 1831 is of central importance in the history of Europe. It became a model copied by other liberal monarchical constitution makers. In some of its features it reflected the spirit of 1789 and borrowed from the constitution of the July Monarchy in France: it recognized the sovereignty of the people and included a declaration of the rights of citizens; the monarch was obliged to swear an oath to the constitution. In other respects, as in the care with which the judiciary was kept independent of the state, it reflected the British constitution, but Belgium after 1831 was in some respects more democratic than Britain, even after the Reform Act of 1832. Both Belgian legislative houses were elected, not, it is true, by universal suffrage, but the tax qualification for the vote was a very low one by the standards of 1831. Article 63 of the constitution allowed for ministerial responsibility to parliament, but this was to some extent rendered ineffective until 1848 by the considerable powers given to the king as personal head of state: he could veto legislation and dissolve parliament. The existence of a second chamber was regarded by many as a serious limitation on democracy. The left wing of the revolutionary congress in 1830 had quoted Rousseau in support of a single chamber, but the majority opinion had been expressed by J. B. Nothomb, who defended the idea of an upper house on the grounds that there were two classes in existence, 'those who sell their labour and those who buy it'. The senate which was written into the constitution was certainly a conservative body: senators had to possess great wealth, and to be at least forty years old.

The Belgian constitution of 1831 was, then, very much a question of checks and balances, a mixture of monarchic, aristocratic and radical elements. But unlike the British or French constitutions of the time it allowed for its own revision. The Whigs in England made much of the claim that the 1832 Act was a definitive measure, a 'rock bottom' for the constitution. The Belgian constitution, on the contrary, anticipated a subsequent broadening of the electorate. The generous extension of the right of suffrage in 1848 enabled the constitution to survive unchanged until the social disruption of 1885 to 1890.

The 1815 constitution of the United Netherlands remained valid for Holland until 1848. It provided for an Estates General elected by the provincial estates and having no control over the ministers or the executive government. Such a system would not have seemed revolutionary in the seventeenth century, though it had appeared liberal in contrast with the prevailing spirit of 1815. The executive government was, quite simply, the king, whose personal power was actually increasing until 1840. Royal decrees were used to keep government going without reference to parliament. Parliament began to be a force in the land only in 1840, when it rejected the budget by fifty votes to one—the one vote being that of the unfortunate minister of finance, who, understandably, resigned. The growing self-confidence of parliament in 1840 contributed to the king's decision to abdicate. In 1848 the new king, William II, took the initiative in reform by appointing a Royal Commission to draft modifications in the constitution. The resulting document prepared the way for Holland to become a modern parliamentary state. The ministers were now to be responsible to parliament, though the king was still to be president of the council of state. There were to be two legislative chambers, of which the lower, or 'second' as it was called, was to be elected by direct suffrage. The vote was to be based on a tax qualification, which in practice created an electorate of all classes down to, and including, the small businessmen and shopkeepers. The upper, or 'first' chamber was to be elected by the provincial estates. As in Belgium, it consisted of only the very richest tax-payers: only one out of every three thousand would be eligible for election to the first chamber. Although the senators elected tended to be of the moneyed rather than the landed property-owners, they looked back with nostalgia to the days when the king and the old aristocracy had enjoyed exclusive power.

Since the old assembly, before 1848, had been elected indirectly, by the provincial estates, there had been no opportunity for the growth of political parties. The term 'liberal' had only the vaguest significance until 1848, and even from 1848 to 1880 no permanent organizations of political parties developed. After appointing the Royal Commission in 1848 to revise the constitution, William II entrusted Count Schimmelpenninck with the task of forming a united cabinet on the English model. Hitherto the ministers had been responsible to the king individually and not as a single cabinet. A permanent system of cabinet government had not yet been established. Schimmelpenninck could not keep his government together, but he had indicated the path along which a truly parliamentary government would have to go. Thorbecke's government from 1849 to 1853 was by no means a united cabinet, but it was never without a majority in parliament. In a minor crisis from 1866 to 1868 the doctrine of ministerial responsibility to parliament rather than to the crown was decided once and for all. There was, then, a striking resemblance between constitutional developments in Holland and Belgium, though the Dutch system was appreciably more conservative and the Dutch political scene less lively.

Like Holland, Switzerland acquired her modern constitution in 1848. The 'Federal Pact' of 1815 had re-established Switzerland as a very loosely knit confederation—little more, in fact, than an alliance of sovereign states, not unlike the German Confederation of 1815. The constitution which was erected after the war of the *Sonderbund* replaced the Federal Pact by a single federal state. Switzerland became the first modern type of federation in European history. Only in the U.S.A. could a parallel be found. At first sight it appears strange that a type of constitution which serves so effectively for so large a country as the U.S.A. could serve equally effectively for so small a country as Switzerland. But the cantons of Switzerland, like the broad states of the U.S.A., are to a degree separate worlds, but worlds separated by high mountains rather than by great distances. The constitution of 1848 gave Switzerland a legislature bearing a marked resemblance to the American one. There were two chambers, one, the Council of States (*Ständerat* or *Conseil des Etats*), elected by the cantons, the other, the National Council (*Nationalrat* or *Conseil national*), elected directly by the people. Each canton returned two members to the Council of States, while the National Council was elected by all males over the age of twenty— 22,000 votes returning one delegate. In contrast with the cautious, oligarchic systems in force in the Low Countries and Great Britain, here was a parliamentary system based on the principles of pure democracy. Only in the Swiss executive government was a more moderate system adopted. The Federal Council (*Bundesrat* or *Conseil fédéral*) consisted of seven men elected by the two chambers. It elected its own chairman annually, but the chairman did not have any more power than his six colleagues. There was to be no danger of any one man acquiring too much power in the federal government. Swiss statesmen have retained a modest anonymity in Europe from 1848 to the present.

Of all the experiments made in 1848 the Swiss was the most lasting and among the most original. Yet a still more original addition to the constitution was to come with the revision of 1874 which inaugurated the Referendum. It now became possible for 30,000 citizens or eight cantons to propose a legislative measure by direct petition. The measure was then submitted to a universal popular vote. If it secured a straight majority it became law without further reference to the legislative authorities. To collect 30,000 signatures was to prove a comparatively easy task if a measure justified consideration. The Swiss were to make great use of their referendum, although, typically, always in the most moderate spirit. The more original in appearance Swiss institutions became, the more placid and respectable became Swiss society. If domestic stability is the main aim of government, the Swiss experiment of 1848 must be considered one of the most triumphant in history.

The internal peace enjoyed by Belgium, Holland and Switzerland from 1848 to 1880 owed something to their freedom from involvement in foreign wars. All three countries were wise enough to remain neutral in foreign struggles. Belgium and Switzerland were covered by an international guarantee of perpetual neutrality. Belgium had been the battlefield of many armies in the past, and was to be in the future. But in the 1830s the movement that gave her independence gave her also immunity from war for over eighty years. Not that the Belgians were eager for the guarantee of neutrality. Rather was it imposed upon them by the wishes of the great powers, and especially by the supposed needs of British foreign policy. Palmerston wanted to keep France out of the Low Countries. The Belgians were anything but neutral in their attitude to European affairs. Neutrality as applied to Belgium was thus a novel idea imposed upon her from outside. The reverse was true of Switzerland. Neutrality had emerged as a basic principle of Swiss foreign policy in the seventeenth century. In 1815 the Congress of Vienna had formally recognized the 'perpetual neutrality' of Switzerland, partly as a bribe to persuade the Swiss to accept the whole territorial settlement. The powers continued to regard Swiss neutrality as a concession benevolently granted to the Swiss. Metternich seemed to think that it implied that the Concert of Europe had rights of surveillance over Switzerland. When the Swiss harboured liberal refugees from Germany, Italy and Poland and even allowed them to write in the press and to take up teaching posts in the schools and universities, Metternich protested. He was outraged by Mazzini's absurdly unsuccessful revolutionary expedition into Savoy in 1834, and talked of placing an armed ring around Switzerland until she had expelled her foreign refugees. The revolutionaries themselves were not always so grateful as they should have been for the refuge provided by Switzerland. They claimed that Switzerland, as a free country, should not be neutral, but should come out openly on the side of liberalism. Mazzini, as a refugee in Switzerland, even wrote that Switzerland should go to war against royalist Europe, and so start the general European Revolution which he was always expecting. In 1847 when Metternich wanted to intervene in defence of the *Sonderbund* Palmerston strongly opposed him. To the credit of the British government it always stood by the 1815 guarantee. But neutrals are seldom loved by the rest of the world, and the European powers could not yet foresee the great benefits to be rendered by a neutral Switzerland in the twentieth century.

In terms of institutions there were clearly great contrasts between the Low Countries and Switzerland. Both Belgium and Holland were monarchies; Switzerland was a republic. Belgium and Holland were single united states; Switzerland was a federation of autonomous cantons. In Belgium and Holland universal male suffrage was withheld until the twentieth century; in Switzerland it was granted in 1848 and retained. It would be too much to dismiss these differences as superficial, but the similarities of the basic political struggles in the three countries were perhaps more significant. In all three countries the ancient hatreds of Catholic and Calvinist for each other had survived into the nineteenth century, but had become confused by the emergence of a strong liberal, secular—largely agnostic—movement. Calvinism had become less coherent as a political influence than Catholicism. Sometimes, as in Holland, devout Protestants saw the liberals as their bitter enemies; sometimes, as in Switzerland, Protestants were aligned with radicals against Catholics; sometimes, as in Belgium at the beginning of the period, Catholics were aligned with liberals against a Protestant authority or in defence of constitutional rights. Whatever the party alignment, religious fever was still an important factor in political life, though operating now in a nineteenth-century context: the struggle between Church and state was now centred on the fight for the control of education.

Religion and education in the nineteenth century were usually the preoccupations of the middle class.[1] The electoral systems in Belgium and Holland gave political power to the middle class, and to some extent deliberately excluded working-class interests from parliamentary debates and measures. In Belgium in particular heavy industrialization had brought its own problems. It was a grave shortcoming of the Belgian system that vital social issues were discussed only by socialist revolutionaries, and ignored by the legally elected representatives of the nation. In Switzerland, where the industrial working class was much smaller, the more democratic system allowed the new problems to be aired in a constitutional manner. Before 1870 the governments of the more enlightened Swiss cantons attempted to limit hours of work in factories, to prevent exploitation of women and children and unhygienic conditions in industry. Their attempts had the effect merely of driving industry to the less enlightened cantons. One of the objects of the 1874 revision of the constitution was to allow the federal government to legislate for the protection of industrial labour at a national level. Subsequently much suffering was prevented by federal measures. In this, as in so much else, the apparently extremist institutions of Switzerland worked smoothly and safely for the welfare of the whole population.

It is the fate of all institutions to become ultimately archaic. If the Belgian and Dutch institutions of the period appeared inadequate sooner than did those of Switzerland, this is partly because they had been introduced earlier. It can hardly be denied that all three of these small countries gave their inhabitants greater freedom and security than was enjoyed in most parts of Europe.

[1] For a discussion of religion and education see chapter XIII.

XI

Central and Eastern Europe: Austro-Hungary; Russia and Poland; the Ottoman Empire and the Balkan States

Political developments

The three most easterly Empires in Europe, the Austrian, Russian and Turkish, were all declining in the nineteenth century. By 1923 they had all perished. Attempts at reform, carried out sometimes despairingly and never confidently, were nowhere successful for any length of time. The Habsburgs tried to preserve their heterogeneous monarchy by repeated constitutional experiments; the czar, Alexander II, hoped to modernize and humanize Russian institutions; even the sultans periodically tried to rejuvenate their diseased Empire; all three failed to make any radical improvements.

Yet, in a territorial sense, of the three Empires only the Ottoman was diminishing. Austria was obliged to surrender Lombardy in 1859

BIBLIOGRAPHY. An introduction to the history of the Habsburg Monarchy throughout the period is provided by the central sections of A. J. P. Taylor, *The Habsburg Monarchy 1809–1918* (London, 1947). There is good background material on the nationalities in the Empire, followed by a comparatively detailed history, in R. A. Kann, *The Multinational Empire: Nationalism and National Reform in the Habsburg Monarchy, 1848–1918* (New York, 2 vols., 1950). The classical biography of Metternich is H. von Srbik, *Metternich, der Staatsman und der Mensch* (Munich, 2 vols., 1925), and an interesting recent study with many quotations from Metternich's writings is G. de Berthier de Sauvigny, *Metternich et son temps* (Paris, 1959). Good works by Austrian historians dealing with the period are the essay by Hugo Hantsch, *Die Nationalitätenfrage im alten Österreich* (Vienna, 1954), and Georg Franz, *Liberalismus. Die Deutschliberale Bewegung in der Habsburgischen Monarchie* (Munich, 1955), a more detailed survey to 1867. For the period of the Dual Monarchy, the first half of A. J. May, *The Habsburg Monarchy, 1867–1914* (Harvard, 1951) is relevant, and a good short history of Hungary, of which three chapters cover the period, is C. A. Macartney, *Hungary* (London, 1934). A great number of histories of Russia in English have appeared and Venetia in 1866. Also in 1866 she was driven from the dominating position she had assumed in Germany since 1815. But in 1878 she was allowed to occupy the not inconsiderable Turkish region of Bosnia-Herzegovina, and her influence in the Balkans was increasing: she was becoming an eastern rather than a central European power. The Russian Empire was growing in size, as it expanded in central Asia. The Ottoman Empire, on the other hand, was retracting physically, as the resurgent Balkan nationalities, patronized by one or other of the great Christian powers, were pushing the Turks out of south-east Europe. The dynamic element in the nineteenth-century history of eastern Europe is provided by the emergence of the self-conscious nationalities. By 1880 the Poles

recently. One of the best is Lionel Kochan, *The Making of Modern Russia* (London, 1962). Sir Bernard Pares, *A History of Russia* (London, 1937) remains a classic introduction, while B. H. Sumner, *A Survey of Russian History* (London, 1948) has an unusual approach, in that it is not a narrative history, but rather an impression of modern Russia placed in a historical perspective. A lucid and more straightforward account is H. Seton-Watson, *The Decline of Imperial Russia* (London, 1952), of which the first third deals with the reign of Alexander II. In the absence of full-length scholarly lives of Alexander II or of his chancellor, Gorchakov, there is an excellent brief account—W. E. Mosse, *Alexander II and the Modernization of Russia* (London, 1959). A full account of the revolutionary undercurrent of the period is Franco Venturi, *Il Populismo Russo* (Milan, 1952), translated as *Roots of Revolution* (London, 1960), and a lively study of a central institution is Sidney Monas, *The Third Section. Police and Society in Russia under Nicholas I* (Harvard, 1961). Two works of fine scholarship on Poland by R. F. Leslie, *Polish Politics and the Revolution of November 1830* (London, 1956) and *Reform and Insurrection in Russian Poland, 1856–1865* (London, 1963), give an interpretation which is emancipated from the traditions established by the sympathizers with Polish nationalism, and set the story in a fuller politico-social context. For the Turkish and Balkan history of the period W. Miller, *The Otto-man Empire and its Successors, 1801–1927* (3rd edn., Cambridge, 1927) is still a useful introduction, but for the latter part of the period covered by Miller there is now an important piece of scholarship—Bernard Lewis, *The Emergence of Modern Turkey* (Oxford, 1961), of which the first half is relevant for this volume. A nineteenth-century work dealing with the Turkish reform movement, the *Tanzimat*, is still very good: E. Engelhardt, *La Turquie et le Tanzimat* (Paris, 2 vols., 1882–84), and the same theme has been studied recently in Roderic H. Davison, *Reform in the Ottoman Empire 1856–1876* (Princeton, 1963). On the Balkan countries after or during their emancipation from the Ottoman Empire there is much literature. Two works on Rumania, in particular, deserve mention: T. W. Riker, *The Making of Rumania* (Oxford, 1931) and a shorter work, W. G. East, *The Union of Moldavia and Wallachia, 1859* (Cambridge, 1929), which in fact covers the period from before the Crimean War to the union of the princi-palities in 1859. Other works on the diplomatic history of the Eastern Question are mentioned in the bibliography for chapter VII.

were still subjects of the czar; the subject nationalities in the Habsburg Empire had not secured independence, though the Hungarians had won autonomy and equality in the Dual Monarchy; Macedonians and some Bulgars were still under Turkish rule. But some nationalities had already secured complete independence. Greece had already been independent in 1830, Serbia and Rumania since 1878; Bulgaria was still nominally under Turkish sovereignty, but autonomous. Whether they had secured absolute independence, virtual independence, or were still, in fact as in law, under foreign rule, it was these nations who were to inherit power from the ancient empires. Their spasmodic risings, sometimes successful, sometimes tragically unsuccessful, provide the highlights in the political development of the region during the decades.

Austro-Hungary

From 1815 to 1848 the Habsburg Monarchy was politically in a state of almost complete stagnation. Ultimate power rested with the Emperor, who alone was sovereign, but neither Francis I (1792–1835) nor Ferdinand (1835–48) had the temperament or the executive ability to make the reforms demanded by growing sections of opinion. Their principal minister, Prince Clement von Metternich, realized, at least, what were the main administrative weaknesses of the monarchy, and frequently recommended specific reforms, but he, too, lacked the temperament for enforcing change. He prophesied doom with evident relish, but advised reform without conviction. If the black picture of Metternich painted by liberal historians in the last century was exaggerated, the reaction against it in this century has gone too far. Metternich would be surprised to learn that in the mid-twentieth century he could count on more than one apologist in the U.S.A. Recent historians have even been prepared to accept Metternich's characterization of himself as a *socialiste-conservateur*, determined to restrain the ambitions of the *bourgeoisie*. It is true that Metternich's bitterest enemies—German nationalists like Jahn, Arndt, Jordan or Richard Wagner—were aggressive, antisemitic and intolerant, but this is no reason for mistaking Metternich's own intolerance and lazy fatalism for enlightenment or statecraft.

It is, again, true that under Francis Metternich did not have full responsibility for internal affairs. Internally Francis was his own chief minister, and even the minister of police, Count Sedlnitzky, was probably more influential than Metternich. In 1826 a more distinguished rival had appeared with the appointment of Count Kolowrat, a Bohemian nobleman, as minister. Kolowrat became the Emperor's chief adviser on domestic issues, though Metternich remained the author of foreign policy. Kolowrat tried to persuade Francis to reform the chaotic finances of the monarchy, but found his advice ignored, as Metternich's had often been before him. Kolowrat, not for the last time, offered his resignation, but was persuaded to withdraw it. Metternich made much in later years of his continual proposals of reform and their continual rejection, but it is significant that he never saw fit to resign, nor even to threaten resignation. If Kolowrat was vain and open to flattery, Metternich was pusillanimous and cynical.

When Francis died in 1835 he left instructions to his heir, Ferdinand: 'Govern and change nothing.' Ferdinand suffered from rickets and epilepsy, and was simple-minded. He was incapable equally of governing or of changing anything himself, but would sign any document placed in front of him. If either Kolowrat or Metternich had been a determined reformer, something might have been made of the situation. As it was they were content to prevent each other from taking action. Francis had been one of ten brothers, of whom five survived him. The youngest, least intelligent and least liberal of the five, Louis, managed to assert himself as the strongest man in Austria after 1835. A dilettante of great charm, Louis played Metternich and Kolowrat off against each other, but was a poor substitute for an effective emperor. Austria in 1848, like France in 1789, was to face the greatest revolution in her history with a vacuum where there should have been a government.

A foretaste of the storm to come had been provided early in 1846 by a rising of Polish nobility in Galicia. Metternich's government had utilized a peasant rising against the Polish nobility to defeat the nationalists. Subsequently government troops restored order and the Habsburgs seized the opportunity of suppressing the Polish free town of Cracow. Thus one of the last acts for which Metternich was partly responsible was a violent infringement of the 1815 settlement which had guaranteed Cracow her independence, and which the chancellor had always declared sacred.

The more serious revolutions which swept the monarchy all started in March of 1848. Vienna, Prague, Budapest, Milan and Venice were all engulfed in a revolutionary wave. Although the Germans in the Empire were not more numerous than the Hungarians, and only about half as numerous as the Slavs, Vienna was by far the largest city. Consequently it was in Vienna that the economic crisis of 1848 was felt most sharply, and it was in Vienna that the first rising took place. On 12 March demonstrators demanded a constitution, and on the 13th there was a clash with the troops. The Habsburg court decided that a sacrifice must be offered to liberal feeling, and Metternich was very reluctantly persuaded to resign. Two days later the court published a manifesto lifting the press censorship and promising a constitution. The revolution seemed to be succeeding in Vienna without violence.

More serious enemies of the Habsburgs than the radicals of Vienna were the Hungarian nationalists, who had found an impressive leader in the young lawyer, Louis Kossuth. The old Hungarian Diet was the vehicle of the revolution in Budapest. The March Laws, passed by the Diet, gave Hungary responsible government and complete autonomy from Austria. The simple-minded Emperor, in the grip of the revolution in Vienna, accepted the March Laws. Kossuth had won a revolutionary victory by wholly legal methods. But the movements in Vienna and Budapest were mainly upper-class affairs, unlike demonstrations in Prague which were more representative of the people as a whole. The Czech nationalists secured their triumph on 8 April when the Habsburgs promised a constituent assembly for the historic kingdom of Bohemia. In Croatia, Moravia, Galicia, Dalmatia and Transylvania the early stirrings of submerged nationalist groups achieved successes. By mid-May the revolution was successful all over the Empire, and the Habsburg authority, although ostensibly still respected, was clearly crumbling.

Poor Ferdinand and his frightened relatives cut themselves off from the revolution on 17 May by escaping from Vienna to Innsbruck. A month later the revolution suffered its first reverse. The imperial forces in Prague were under the command of the strong militarist, Prince Windischgrätz, who had consistently avoided the use of force against the nationalists. On 12 June his wife was accidentally killed during a riot in Prague. Five days later, without waiting for orders from Vienna, Windischgrätz bombarded Prague and subsequently established himself as military dictator. It is not too much to say that the Habsburg monarchy was saved from ultimate collapse by an angry man's love of his dead wife.

In July the position in Italy[1] was rectified by General Radetzky's victory over the Piedmontese, who had gone to war with Austria in March, and in September the Habsburgs enlisted help from another quarter. The Croats had demanded autonomy from the kingdom of Hungary in March. Vienna had accepted their demand by allowing the Croats their own governor, the Baron Jellačić, but had suspended

[1] See above, pp. 229–31.

him from office in June, when he had denied the Hungarian Diet any authority in Croatia. By September the court had realized that the Hungarians were their most dangerous enemies. Jellačić was reinstated, and allowed to lead an army against the Hungarians. The imperial government henceforth used incipient south Slav nationalism as an ally against the dominant nationalism of the Magyars. It was now a question of open war between the Hungarian revolution under Kossuth and the imperial forces under the command of Windischgrätz and Jellačić. The Habsburgs put their house in order to face the crisis by appointing as minister another strong man, Prince Felix Schwarzenberg, and in December, by forcing the wretched Emperor to abdicate. Ferdinand was succeeded by the eighteen-year-old Francis Joseph, who was to reign for sixty-eight years and who was, at least, in full command of his wits.

The Hungarians had assembled an army with surprising speed, and for the first half of 1849 held their own against the imperial forces. Budapest could even claim that she was fighting for the legitimate rights of Ferdinand, king of Hungary, who had granted the March Laws and had been subsequently wrongfully deposed, though this argument could have little sincere appeal to Hungarian radicals. In April it was abandoned; Hungary was declared an independent republic under the presidency of Kossuth. For four months the Hungarian Republic survived. In June Schwarzenberg decided to take a drastic step. He asked formally for the assistance of Russian troops, and czar Nicholas I, glad of an opportunity to destroy a revolution which was so near Poland, quickly complied. In August the Hungarian forces surrendered to the Russians, and the prolonged threat to the Habsburgs vanished. Kossuth escaped to Constantinople and, finally, to England, but in Hungary the Austrian general, Haynau, a pathological sadist, organized wholesale executions.

Schwarzenberg's régime lasted until his death in 1852. So far as the questions of the constitution and the nationalities were concerned, it was bleakly repressive. The last remnant of the revolutionary authority in Austria itself, a constituent assembly meeting at Kremsier, had been dissolved in March 1849, and replaced by a constitution whose elaborate façade of liberalism failed to conceal the absolute nature of the power wielded by the Emperor, his ministers, bureaucracy and army. All parts of the Empire, including even Hungary, were to be integrated under Vienna as they had not been since Joseph II's day. Only in terms of social reform did the revolutionary ideas retain some influence. Emancipation of over three million peasants was put into effect, land being sold to them on generous terms.

Schwarzenberg himself was mainly preoccupied with German and European affairs. In Germany he reasserted Austrian supremacy and rejected the Prussian challenge.[1] On his death Count Buol was made foreign minister, and was to be responsible for Austrian neutrality during the Crimean War. In 1856 Austria found herself isolated. Buol tried to compensate for isolation by an aggressive and arrogant refusal to discuss the Italian Question with the Concert of Europe. As a result Austria was defeated by France and Piedmont in 1859, and obliged to surrender Lombardy.[2] The principal minister for domestic affairs during these years was Alexander von Bach, who had helped to implement Schwarzenberg's policy of rigid integration and germanization after the defeat of the revolution in 1849. This policy, and especially the repression in Hungary, came to be associated with Bach's name. The nationalities who had been loyal to the Habsburgs in 1848—the south Slavs and the Rumans—were, like the Hungarians, refused any form of national expression by the 'Bach system'. Only the danger of a fresh Hungarian rising during the war of 1859 induced Francis Joseph to drop Bach and his policy. In the course of the two years following the end of Bach's bureaucratic and authoritarian régime, two separate constitutional experiments were tried in an attempt to diminish the widespread unpopularity of the imperial government. The October Diploma in 1860 resurrected the provincial diets and arranged for them to send delegates to a central diet, which would, however, be at once an aristocratic and a weak body. Only the conservative nobility, who had hated the Bach system, were conciliated by this archaic measure. The middle classes and all liberal-thinking men were deeply disappointed. In Hungary the pacific and moderate liberal Francis Deák rejected the October Diploma, and became a national leader. Francis Joseph was quickly made aware of the total inadequacy of his concession. To try yet another solution he appointed as chief domestic minister Anton von Schmerling, who had undeservedly earned the reputation of being a liberal from 1848 to 1851. Schmerling's February Patent in 1861 claimed to be a modification of the 1860 October Diploma, but in fact constituted a quite separate experiment. It was appreciably less aristocratic, and created two central assemblies in which the middle class would have much say. But its electoral regulations were weighted heavily in favour of the German-speaking parts of the Empire, against both

[1] See above, pp. 215–16.   [2] See above, p. 235.

Hungarians and Slavs alike. Even so Déak was at first prepared to give the constitution a trial. Schmerling, however, was not prepared to negotiate changes demanded by the Hungarians. In the summer of 1861, with the German-speaking delegates behind him, Schmerling declared in the assembly that 'the constitution of Hungary was forfeit in law and abolished in fact' by the revolutionary behaviour of the Hungarian Diet. The authoritarian system of Bach was again enforced in Hungary. The Emperor had virtually admitted the failure of his constitutional experiments.

The crisis of 1866 which brought defeat at the hands of Bismarck's Prussia[1] was far graver than the crisis of 1859 had been. It called for more radical measures, and measures which this time had to succeed if the monarchy was to survive. The Habsburgs were helped in their difficult task by the realistic attitude of the Hungarian leaders. Déak had never abandoned the idea of negotiating with Vienna. Another Hungarian leader had emerged in the person of Count Julius Andrássy, who was still more eager to come to an understanding with the Habsburgs in order to prevent the emergence of the various Slav movements against the Magyars. Andrássy persuaded Francis Joseph permanently to abandon any federal solution. A dual Austro-Hungary would be able to accept Bismarck's offer of conciliation after the Seven Weeks' War and the Peace of Prague, which was felt to be not ungenerous to Austria, although it deprived her of the rich province of Venetia. The possibility of an Austro-Hungarian settlement at the expense of the Slavs was increased by Francis Joseph's appointment of the Saxon, Count Ferdinand Beust, as minister. In February 1867 Andrássy was permitted to form a separate Hungarian ministry. By June the Dual Monarchy was established. Hungary was given complete autonomy: home rule and a separate set of laws. Defence, foreign and financial policy were still to be united, and the two nations were to be linked by a customs union. On 8 June 1867 Francis Joseph was crowned king of Hungary in Budapest, but he himself regarded dualism as only a temporary expedient. It was modified in 1868 when Croatia was given a large degree of autonomy within Hungary, and in 1870 Francis Joseph was again playing with the idea of federalism. Again it was Andrássy—now an important influence in the monarchy—who persuaded him of the merits of dualism.

After 1867 the Austrian half of the monarchy was ruled by a cabinet more modern in appearance than that ruling the Hungarian half.

[1] See above, pp. 148–50 and 220–1.

Middle-class ministers, who considered themselves 'liberals', were available in Vienna, while in Budapest offices were still held by landed aristocrats. The Austrian prime minister, Prince Charles Auersperg, reintroduced trial by jury, which had disappeared under Bach's régime, and did much to secularize marriage and education. Opposition to Auersperg's ministry therefore came from the clericals as well as the Slavs, among whom the Czechs were his bitterest enemies. In 1870 Francis Joseph worked with a short-lived conservative ministry in his attempt to reimpose federalism. After the attempt had failed, another liberal ministry, under Prince Adolph Auersperg, a younger brother of Prince Charles, was formed in November 1871, and in 1873 liberalized the electoral system, though still leaving the franchise restricted to tax-payers. In that year, 1873, a financial crisis undermined the public's confidence in Auersperg's government with unhappy results for the future of liberalism in Austria.

The *Ausgleich* or 'compromise' with Hungary, as the establishment of the Dual Monarchy had been called, was renewed in 1877, and in a sense economically favourable to Hungary. The Emperor's foreign minister during these years was the Hungarian, Andrássy, under whose direction the foreign policy of Austria reasserted itself after the humiliation of 1867. Driven out of Italy and excluded from German affairs, Austro-Hungary was eventually to find her opening in the Balkans. Andrássy handled the eastern crisis of 1875 to 1878 with some skill. Reaching understandings with Britain and Germany he prevented an advance of Russian influence in the Balkans.[1] In 1878 Austria emerged from the Congress of Berlin with the right to leave her troops and administrators in the Turkish provinces of Bosnia and Herzegovina. Next year Andrássy negotiated a close treaty of alliance with Bismarck. The Dual Austro-German alliance of 1879 was to remain the most constant diplomatic feature in Europe until 1914 and the war which was to form the last chapter in the six hundred years of Habsburg rule.

Russia

While both Francis I and Francis Joseph appointed their own ministers and did not hesitate to dispense with them at will, they nevertheless delegated considerable power to those ministers who retained their good favour. In Russia there was far less delegation of power. As sovereigns, the Romanovs were absolute in every sense of the word. Heads of Church and state, they presented a semi-divine image to their far-flung

[1] See also above, pp. 161–3.

subjects. The history of government in Russia throughout the nineteenth century is the history of the five men who in turn occupied the imperial throne.

During the period under consideration only two czars reigned—the grim and powerful Nicholas I (1825–55), and the more enlightened, but less effective, Alexander II (1855–81). With Nicholas I czarist Russia reached the peak of her power. Under his predecessor and brother, Alexander I, Russia had defeated Napoleon, and had secured a position of authority in international politics. Under Nicholas himself Russian influence in central Europe, through his agents and his dominance over German princes, was immense. After his impressive intervention in Hungary in 1849 and until the outbreak of the Crimean War in 1854, Nicholas was almost certainly the most powerful man in Europe. It required an alliance of the two richest nations, Britain and France, to defeat him in the Crimea, and to push back Russian influence from central Europe and the Balkans. Before becoming czar in 1825, Nicholas had been absorbed and happy in his role as an army commander. A large, handsome man, he had little difficulty in dominating his subordinates. But, although ultrasensitive, he had a brutal manner, and was not loved, except by his simple and pretty wife, Alexandra, a German princess. Several of Nicholas's tutors had been German, and German was the language of his household. His happy domestic life was shattered by the death of Alexander I in 1825, and the doubt as to who should succeed. The Decembrist rising in St Petersburg in favour of the reluctant Constantine, who remained in Warsaw, almost prevented Nicholas from succeeding, and for a long day threatened his life. The strain of this 14 December, at the end of which Nicholas ordered the artillery to fire on the crowd, had a profound psychological effect on him. His character was still further hardened and acquired a note of strident cruelty. By the end of the day his wife, the Empress Alexandra, had developed a nervous facial twitch which was never to leave her.

Neither a well-educated nor a self-indulgent man, Nicholas drew his strength of character from a chilling sense of responsibility. He believed that his duty towards Russia was to prevent the spread of the ideas of 1789 to a country which was still less ready for them than France had been. The most striking feature of his reign was the repression of any freedom of expression. In 1826 Nicholas had re-established the secret police which Alexander I had abolished. Positive achievements by his government were very slight throughout his reign. A new code of laws which came into existence in 1832 was merely a collection of existing decrees and customs, with no attempt made to liberalize them. For all the severity of the czar's rule, the country was not well administered. Apart from a few currency reforms, the ministers of Nicholas I could find no answer to the increasing gap between the government's income and expenditure, beyond floating new loans. By 1853 the national debt had reached the equivalent of £144 million. From the moment of his accession Nicholas was faced with grave peasant discontent. Every year before the Crimean War there were twenty or more outbreaks of violence among the serfs. That the peasants were not totally unconscious politically, nor totally ignorant of the world outside, is evident from the sharp increase in risings in 1848, when there were no fewer than sixty-four.

Much more dangerous to the régime than disturbances among the wretched Russian peasants, was the threat from the Polish nationalist aristocracy and intelligentsia. The autonomous kingdom of Poland which Alexander I had created under his own sovereignty in 1815 had given little satisfaction to Polish nationalism. Where official Russian policy in Poland had been enlightened—as, for example, in education —it had been at the same time anti-clerical, and had so united the Polish Church with the nationalist movement. Before the death of Alexander I the Polish gentry had grown embittered, and secret societies had been formed. Nicholas postponed calling a diet until 1830. By then opinion in Poland was enflamed by the July Revolution in France. Revolution broke out on 7 (19) November 1830, and at first met with astonishing success. The Russian army withdrew from Warsaw, and Polish independence and union with Lithuania was declared. But in spite of its success the revolution was by no means a great popular movement. The aristocrats and gentry who led it were very little concerned with the welfare of their peasants. Nor was the czar's army likely to be held at bay for long. In May 1831 the Polish revolutionary forces were defeated at Ostrolenska and in September the Russians re-entered Warsaw. Terrible retribution for the Poles followed. While Nicholas had executed only five Russian rebels after the Decembrist rising in St Petersburg, executions of Polish revolutionaries now ran into hundreds. Nicholas declared the Polish constitution abolished, and left Poland with only a partial administrative autonomy. The Polish revolutionary leaders who escaped capture went into exile and for the rest of the century tragic colonies of Polish exiles remained in western Europe, and especially in Paris.

As it began in violence so the reign of Nicholas I was to end in violence—the more general violence of the Crimean War. The causes of the war are considered in another chapter.[1] For Nicholas it was a crusade in defence of the Balkan Christians, an assault on the revolutionary doctrines of Napoleonic France and, once the fighting in the Crimea had started, a defence of the sacred soil of Russia. Unfortunately the czar's religious zeal was not matched by the ability of his commanders nor the efficiency of his army. Defeated on the river Alma in September 1854, in the first important battle of the war, the Russians were spared the loss of Sebastopol only by the shortsightedness of the British and French commanders who failed to march immediately on the great port and naval station. The delay allowed the Russian general, Todleben, to fortify Sebastopol with great speed and effectiveness. His fortifications—the only creditable military achievement of the war—preserved Sebastopol from Anglo-French attack for an entire year. Sebastopol finally fell in September 1855. Nicholas I had died in St Petersburg six months earlier.

Russia emerged from the Congress of Paris in 1856 with her influence in the Balkans much dimmed. Her claims as the protector of the Christian subjects of the sultan had been firmly rejected; instead the Concert of Europe was now to preserve the Ottoman Empire as a wholly independent power. Part of Bessarabia north of the mouths of the Danube was ceded by Russia to the autonomous principality of Moldavia, and the czar could no longer keep a fleet on the Black Sea, which was declared demilitarized. Equally important was the loss of Russian influence in Germany. From 1856 to 1870 Russia was a second rate power. The new czar, Alexander II, son of Nicholas I, was a man of thirty-five in 1855. A grandson, on his mother's side, of Frederick William III, he was nephew both of the reigning Prussian monarch, Frederick William IV, and of Bismarck's king, William I. Like his father, Alexander had certain Prussian characteristics. He liked military parades, and was insensitive to intellectual, literary or artistic enjoyments. But there was in Alexander a strain of human compassion wholly lacking in Nicholas. Unfortunately it was not coupled to any energy or strength of character. Mildly fond of his pleasures and wellbeing, Alexander was already stout at the age of twenty. He had great respect for his father and certainly did not see himself as having to reverse his father's policy. Nevertheless his accession permitted a thaw in Russian political life. Two unpopular ministers were dismissed. The Catholic Church in Poland was given greater freedom. More important, the

[1] See above, pp. 143–5.

Russian universities were liberalized and expanded. The government gave scholars grants for travel abroad. Books censored by Nicholas could now be published. Such were the preliminary steps taken even before Alexander's coronation in September 1856. At the time of the coronation a manifesto was issued releasing political prisoners, cancelling unpaid taxes, suspending recruitment to the army for three years and further modifying restrictions on travel outside Russia. The manifesto constituted something of an amnesty granted by the czar to his burdened and beleaguered subjects.

In the 1840s the future Alexander II had been given by his father the task of presiding over committees considering the difficult question of the serfs. Nicholas had not been wholly unaware of their sad condition. In the past, bankrupt aristocrats had frequently auctioned their serfs in such a way that whole families were broken up. In 1841 Nicholas had forbidden this callous practice for the privately owned serfs, and his minister of state lands, General Kiselev, had considerably relieved the burden on the state peasants. But the numerous peasant risings already mentioned made it only too evident that the suffering of the bulk of the serfs had not been appreciably alleviated under Nicholas. Alexander's desire to emancipate the serfs was partly due to the influence of his strong-willed empress, Mary. Other influences in favour of emancipation were exerted by a minority of Alexander's ministers—most influential of whom were the Freemason, Lanskoy, minister of the interior, and Gorchakov, minister of foreign affairs—as well as by the merchants and radical writers. A majority of the ministers and all but a very few of the landed aristocrats were opposed to emancipation. In 1856 the czar tried to prepare the minds of his aristocratic subjects for the coming social revolution by declaring: 'The existing manner of owning serfs cannot remain unchanged. It is better to abolish serfdom from above than to await the time when it will begin to abolish itself from below.' For the next few years Alexander and the reforming ministers met considerable opposition from the nobility, but by 1861 resistances and procrastinations had been overcome and the Edict of Emancipation was published on 17 March (5 April western style).

The serfs were not only freed by the Edict, but were given land, so that more than half the cultivable land in Russia, after 1861, was held by the peasants. But the serfs had to pay stiff compensation to their former owners. Their economic conditions did not improve as the result of emancipation. If anything, they became worse, as the peasants wrestled with heavier taxation, frequent famines and a growing population without a corresponding increase of cultivated land. Emancipation inevitably involved Russia in a complete change of her social and legal system. The laws by which peasant life was administered and the apparatus of village government had to be adjusted and renovated. Alexander's legal reforms were happier in their consequences than emancipation itself. Drafted by an *ad hoc* commission, they were enforced by the czar in 1864. They introduced trial by jury, in courts open to the public, and through an entirely new judicial system they went far to abolish corruption and create a fresh spirit of impartial justice. The only drawback was the shortage of trained lawyers without whom the new system could spread over Russia only very slowly. In certain parts of the Empire, including Poland, trial by jury was never introduced. But the emancipated peoples of Russia were now equal before the law. In this respect Alexander's reforms brought the social revolution that France had experienced in 1789, and other countries of western Europe in a more piecemeal fashion in the years between. In another respect Alexander's reforms underlined the communal character of Russian rural life. From 1865 onwards the *zemstvos*, or village assemblies, were established. Elected by landowners, they were essentially aristocratic bodies, and could always be overruled by the local government officials. But they did useful educational and medical work in the villages. Their urban counterparts, elected town councils, came into being in 1870.

In Poland also Alexander was prepared for concessions. The Polish nobles were allowed to form a nationalist organization called euphemistically 'the Agricultural Society of Poland'. They were satisfied initially when Alexander in 1861 appointed committees to consider Polish grievances, and gave Poland more extensive local autonomies. As in the rest of the Empire, greater freedom of expression was allowed, though Alexander warned the Poles—in words which were to become notorious —'*point de rêveries!*' Neither the Catholic Church nor the more radical and poorer gentry were appeased by the concessions. The revolt of 1863 was the immediate result of the ill-advised attempt to press suspect Polish nationalists into the army. Alexander's government tried to stir up the Polish peasants against their landlords, and was successful at least in keeping the peasantry neutral and unsympathetic to the revolt.

The Polish Question was not purely a domestic one. Polish autonomy had been granted by the 1815 settlement. Both Britain and France claimed responsibility for Poland in that they were signatories of the Treaty of Vienna. The governments of Palmerston and Napoleon III protested that the Poles had a right to some degree of self-government. Napoleon threw away the close understanding he had built up with Russia since 1856, and to no effect. Only Bismarck, who had his own Polish minority to think of, approved of Alexander's crushing of the revolt by armed force. The failure of the 1863 rising ended the sad story of Congress Poland. The 'kingdom of Poland' ceased formally to exist, and became instead, in 1866, the 'Vistula Region' of the Russian Empire. The power of the Polish nobility was deliberately broken, but Alexander did not step back from his policy of emancipating the Polish serfs. On the contrary, seeing the peasants as allies against the Polish gentry, he gave them more land than the emancipated Russian serfs received. The peasant communes in Poland, too, were given wider powers. It may well be that the mass of the population in Poland gained in material wellbeing as a result of the failure of Polish nationalism, though this aspect of the question could not be appreciated by liberals in western Europe.

The thaw which Alexander had encouraged, and which had led to violent revolution in Poland, led in Russia to great intellectual turbulence, student riots, the founding of revolutionary societies and Alexander's own death by assassination. Several attempts were made on his life from 1866 onwards. After the failure of non-violent socialist movements a revival of terrorism characterized the 1870s. The organization 'People's Freedom' specialized in assassination. In March 1881 it reached the peak of its ambition by assassinating the czar himself. After attending a military display in St Petersburg, Alexander was returning to the Winter Palace when a bomb was thrown at his carriage. One of the soldiers escorting him, and a poor tradesman's boy who was watching, were killed. Alexander bravely but foolishly stepped out of his carriage to see who had thrown the bomb and who were the victims. A few minutes later a second member of 'People's Freedom', a Polish student, threw a second bomb, and the czar was killed. His reign which had started in high hope had ended in futile tragedy.

There is a unique dichotomy about the nineteenth-century history of Russia. Whereas in western Europe the intellectuals often played a role in the central domestic histories of their countries, in Russia the intelligentsia were deprived of all responsibility and could have no continuing influence on events. The régime had no place for them, and their attitude to the régime was consequently a purely destructive one. Their main preoccupation was not how the régime could be improved, but rather the exact nature of the Utopia which would be built when the régime was destroyed. A brief history of revolutionary groups must be told as a story almost wholly distinct from that of the governments of the czars.

The aristocratic intelligentsia had failed to seize power in the revolution of 1825, and no similar attempt at armed revolt was made during the period covered by this book. But speculation of a revolutionary nature continued. Initially the great debate was between the Westernizers and the Slavophils. The Decembrist rising had been planned by men who looked to France or Britain, or even the U.S.A., for an example. The westernizing case was put in an extreme form in 1836, when Peter Tchaadeyev, an aristocrat and ex-officer, published the 'Philosophic Letter' in a Moscow paper, *The Telescope*. The letter pointed out that Russia had remained isolated from the great movement of western civilization, and declared that her only hope was to turn to the west, and to western Christianity or Catholicism. Among the names of those who in these early days looked to the west were some which were to become famous: Herzen, Belinsky, Turgenev and Bakunin. These men condemned the régime of Nicholas I because it was not based on reason and did not permit individual freedom. They believed in the constitutions and free institutions which were achieved momentarily by the 1848 revolutions in the west. The Slavophils—Khomyakov, the brothers Aksakov and Kireyevsky—had condemned the reign of Nicholas I for the opposite reason: because it looked too much to the west, and especially to Prussian bureaucratic models. They believed that previous czars, and notably Peter the Great and Catherine the Great, had betrayed the original traditions of Russia by their westernizing policies. They did not look for individual liberty, but for a development from the *mir*, or village community, into a more truly cooperative commune. They pointed out that the west had not solved her social problems. They did not want parliaments on the western model, but rather a revival of the traditional consultative assemblies of the sixteenth and seventeenth centuries. They emphasized the importance of the Russian Orthodox Church as a defence against western materialism.

The debate was continued in private by the aristocratic intelligentsia, and had no effect on political life. The clear distinction between Westernizers and Slavophils was lost when several of the former visited western Europe and saw for themselves the evils associated with an industrial society under apparently liberal régimes. Alexander Herzen went to Paris enthusiastically in 1847, but was deeply disappointed in conditions under the July Monarchy. The failure of the 1848 revolutions brought further disillusionment. Herzen was completely converted to the movement against westernization, and became convinced that the peasant commune was a great blessing for Russia. The next logical step in the intellectual development of the disillusioned Westernizers was to study the socialist writings of the west. Vissarion Belinsky, who died in 1848 of tuberculosis at the age of thirty-eight, had read Proudhon, Fourier and Blanc, and was convinced that only a complete social revolution could cure Russia's ills. After the accession of Alexander II the intelligentsia were preoccupied by the need to emancipate the serfs. Both Herzen and socialists like N. G. Chernyshevski welcomed emancipation in 1861, but were saddened by its ineffectiveness to remove suffering. In the 1860s the Populist movement, which based its hopes on the village commune, developed as a characteristically Russian form of socialism. Chernyshevsky's novel, *What is to be done?*, was published in 1863. Blending the ideas of Owen and Fourier with those of John Stuart Mill, it painted a rather joyless and ascetic Utopia. Another leading exponent of Populism, Nicholas Konstantinovich Mikhailovsky, born in 1842 into the lesser nobility, became a professional journalist in the 1860s. His work, *What is Progress?*, provided a humanist answer to Herbert Spencer.

In the 1870s the Populists moved physically into the villages to preach socialist ideas to the peasants. Members of the intelligentsia— and especially university students—took posts in the villages or poor areas of the towns as doctors, teachers or even labourers. After the famine of 1874 in the Volga district several thousand of the intelligentsia moved into the region to share the life and distress of the peasant. Although the 'To the People' movement had made no visible impression on the peasantry, the government decided to suppress it. Perhaps a half of the intelligentsia involved in the movement of 1874 were arrested. A similar movement in 1875 met with a similar treatment from the government, and in 1877 mass trials of Populists were held in St Petersburg, though the sentences passed were comparatively lenient. Since the 'To the People' movement was treated as violent revolution the intelligentsia began to abandon their non-violent tactics.

The ruthless communist organization, 'Land and Liberty', with rigid discipline and a select terrorist membership of about two hundred, was founded in 1876. A young member of 'Land and Liberty' was George Plekhanov, who was later to bring Marxism to Russia. In 1879 the movement was split into two, the majority of the members of 'Land and Liberty' forming 'People's Freedom', while the minority, led by

Plekhanov, assumed the title 'Black Partition'. 'People's Freedom' concentrated purely on terrorism, believing that a mass rising of the people would never take place spontaneously, but that the path to revolution must be prepared by assassination, and especially by the assassination of the autocratic emperor himself. Plekhanov, on the other hand, believed that single acts of terrorism were futile, and that the ultimate goal of giving the land to the peasants must remain the main point in the revolutionary creed. Although it was 'People's Freedom' who won the immediate achievement of killing Alexander, it was Plekhanov who was to be the major influence on the future course of Russian socialism, and it was from Plekhanov that Lenin, the greatest professional revolutionary in history, was to receive his training.

The Ottoman Empire

If Russia was only half European, both Nicholas I and Alexander II were western in temperament and outlook. The other large Empire of eastern Europe—the Ottoman Empire—and its rulers, had absorbed nothing of the west. Mahmoud II, sultan of Turkey from 1808 to 1839, was an oriental despot maintaining his European Empire by terror and violence. His attempts at westernization were more superficial and less sincere than Peter the Great's had been. The story that his mother was French is no longer acceptable.[1] He spoke neither French nor any other western language. But his policy of ruthless centralization was initially successful. He failed to bring Egypt or Greece back under his authority, but succeeded nearer home, where—in Rumelia and Anatolia—rebellious governors and nobles were called to heel or eliminated.

By 1830 Mahmoud had lost Greece, but had at least established his personal authority at Constantinople. For the greater part of his reign the capital had been at the mercy of the Janissaries, the military caste which had played a central role in Turkish history since the fifteenth century. By the nineteenth century they were no longer effective as an army but kept a stranglehold on government. In 1826 Mahmoud established a new military corps, loyal to him personally. His action provoked the Janissaries into revolt, but the civilian crowd supported the sultan's troops and the Janissaries were defeated. Over six thousand of them were massacred, leaving Mahmoud at last the real ruler of the Ottoman Empire.

Greece had secured her independence from the Ottoman Empire by the long wars of the 1820s. After this epic struggle and the passionate

[1] Bernard Lewis, *The Emergence of Modern Turkey*, p. 76.

support given to the Greeks by the liberals, devout Christians and poets of western Europe, Greece's first decades of independence were inevitably an anti-climax. Later in the century Italian history was to follow a similar pattern of wild enthusiasm leading to disenchantment. The first king of independent Greece, Otto I, was an unhappy choice. A Bavarian prince of seventeen in 1832 when he was given the throne, Otto reigned for thirty years. At first reluctant to grant a constitution, he was at last obliged to do so by revolution in 1843–44. It was, however, too limited a constitution to satisfy the politically minded Greeks, and after a troubled reign Otto was deposed in 1862. The next year a happier choice was made. A Danish prince, also aged seventeen, became George I and almost immediately a democratic régime was introduced. A single assembly was to be elected by universal manhood suffrage— a system which seemed worthy of the political traditions of ancient Greece.

The Danubian principalities of Moldavia and Wallachia, which were one day to constitute the greater part of modern Rumania, were in 1830 known to Europe simply as 'the principalities'. They were under the suzerainty of the sultan, but since the days of Catherine the Great Russia had claimed special rights of intervention. After a brief war against Turkey to establish her claim, Russia remained in occupation of the principalities from 1829 to 1834. It was from these years that the modern Rumanian nationalist movement dates. After the Crimean War Napoleon III replaced the czar as the main champion of the Rumanians. Their immediate aim was to unite into a single principality under an elected *hospodar*. In the face of Austrian and Turkish opposition and English doubts, but with the diplomatic help of France and Russia, the principalities secured their single prince in 1859. Colonel Alexander Cuza, a Rumanian idealist, reigned from 1859 to 1866 and pursued a radical policy in favour of the peasants. In 1862 the principalities assumed the national name, Rumania. Strong vested interests opposed Cuza, and in 1866 he was kidnapped and forced to abdicate. A more conservative group gave the crown to Prince Charles of Hohenzollern-Sigmaringen, and secured the approval of the sultan. The Treaty of Berlin in 1878 recognized the full independence of Rumania, which had never ceased to be autonomous within the Ottoman Empire. At least one nationalist movement had succeeded without too much bloodshed.

As a result of insurrections under two rival families, the Karageorgevich and the Obrenovich, the Serbs had won their autonomy from the sultan as early as 1817. In 1830 Milosh Obrenovich was recognized as the hereditary prince of Serbia, but the years from 1830 to 1860 were marked by violent struggles for power between the two dynasties. Under Michael Obrenovich, from 1860 to 1868, the Serb nationalist movement seemed to be at its strongest and most successful. An able and well-educated man, Michael had a broader vision than his ignorant predecessors. He hoped to unite not just the Serbs, but all the Balkan races, in a common war of liberation from the Turks. He won the respect of the powers and in 1867 the last Turkish troops were obliged to evacuate Serbian territory. His assassination in 1868 by a supporter of the Karageorgevich was a tragedy for Serbia, but under his great-nephew, Milan, complete independence was granted by the powers in the Treaty of Berlin in 1878.

Serbia was to have an eventful history in the twentieth century, but the Victorians found the epic story of the small mountain kingdom of Montenegro more to their taste. Tennyson romanticized it:

> O smallest among peoples! rough rock-throne
> Of Freedom! warriors beating back the swarm
> Of Turkish Islam for five hundred years . . .

The Montenegrins were Serbs distinguished from their kinsmen of Serbia proper by their unique history: they alone of Balkan states had retained complete independence from the Turk—a fact formally recognized by the sultan in 1799. The record of independence was temporarily ended in the mid-nineteenth century when a Turkish army under the brilliant Omar Pasha, a Croatian convert of Islam, invaded Montenegro and enforced Turkish sovereignty. From 1861 to 1878 Montenegro was legally a part of the Ottoman Empire, but its independence was again recognized by the Treaty of Berlin.

Last of the Balkan states to emerge was Bulgaria. Few people in the west knew of the existence of the Bulgars at the time of the Crimean War, though the Bulgarian nationalist movement developed quickly afterwards. In the 1860s Bulgarian revolutionary leaders were in touch with Prince Michael of Serbia. The first successful expression of national identity was of an ecclesiastical nature. In 1870 the Bulgarian Exarchate, an independent branch of the Greek Orthodox Church, was recognized by the sultan, though declared schismatic by the Greek patriarch in Constantinople. The establishment of their own Church was partly owed to Russian support of the Bulgarians. It stimulated rather than satisfied the nationalist movement. With the rising of 1875 and the massacre of Bulgarians by Ottoman troops in 1876, Bulgarian history became an important feature of international history.[1] Two opposing solutions to the Bulgarian Question were attempted after the Eastern crisis of 1875–78. The Russian solution, forced upon Turkey by the Treaty of San Stefano in March 1878, created a larger Bulgarian state than had ever existed before, or would ever exist again. It was rejected by the other powers. The solution offered by the Concert of Europe, contained in the Treaty of Berlin in July 1878, replaced the large Bulgaria by a small, autonomous principality still under the sultan's suzerainty, and a larger district, called Eastern Rumelia, still under the political and military control of Turkey. The European solution was to be rejected by the Bulgarians themselves after a few years. A period of strife and disorder was to follow until Bulgaria eventually secured her independence in 1908.

While the Greeks, Rumanians, Serbs, Montenegrins and Bulgarians were establishing a right to an independent existence, the Turkish régime itself was caught in the compulsive grip of a legal system based on religious dogma. To break loose by introducing modern reform involved risking the accusation of heresy. Mahmoud II took the risk when absolutely necessary to hold the administration of the Empire together. His death in 1839 left the sultanate in the hands of a boy, Abdul Mejid. It also cleared the path for more enlightened attempts at reform than any tried by Mahmoud himself. The astute minister Reshid Pasha, who had already enjoyed a distinguished career under Mahmoud, believed in more radical westernization. He drew up a reform decree, the *Hatt-i-Sherif* of Gulhané (or Rescript of the Rose Chamber), which was issued by the sultan in November 1839. It proclaimed what had been established by the Declaration of the Rights of Man in western Europe: the equality of all before the law and the right of the individual to life, liberty and property. Concrete reforms of administration and taxation were also promised, but as usual government policy in practice bore little resemblance to the intentions declared in the sultan's decrees. By the time of the Crimean War few real improvements had been made.

In the Crimea Britain and France expended much blood and money to preserve the Ottoman Empire against Russian attack. After the war the western powers felt some of that responsibility for the wellbeing of the Christians of the Empire previously claimed by Russia. Turkey was proclaimed a member of the Concert of Europe and the sultan's government was urged by the powers to reform his régime and to guarantee the

[1] See above, pp. 161–3.

security of the Balkan Christians. To justify Turkey's new status the sultan issued an Imperial Rescript or *Hatt-i-Humayun* on 18 February 1856, to accompany the Treaty of Paris. It repeated the principle of equality of all subjects, regardless of their religion, a principle already contained in the *Hatt-i-Sherif* of 1839, and again promised renovation of the tax system. It was the work of two reformers, Ali Pasha and Fuad Pasha, who had been the protégés of Reshid Pasha, and were now his political rivals. Both men had been born in 1815 and were typical of the westernizing movement. Ali Pasha was the son of a shopkeeper in Istanbul, while Fuad Pasha's father had been a famous poet and statesman. Though their origins were so different, the two men rose to high office by the same means: a career in the diplomatic service, and, above all, fluency in French. The *Tanzimat*, or Reorganization, as the whole reform movement since Mahmoud II's day was called, was largely French in inspiration. It was gravely weakened by three nearly contemporary events: the deaths of Fuad Pasha in 1869 and of Ali Pasha in 1871, and the defeat and eclipse of France in 1870–71.

More grave crises for the Ottoman Empire followed a few years later. The government had been borrowing heavily from abroad, and Turkish finances had never been put on a sound footing. In 1874 the Empire was faced with financial collapse. The sultan's government declared itself bankrupt, and repudiated half the interest owing on its loans. The next year the largest nationalist insurrection for many years broke out in Bosnia and Herzegovina and spread to Bulgaria. Serbia and Montenegro went to war in support of their fellow-Slavs. The Eastern Question was again a dominant issue of international history.[1]

In the midst of the crisis which ended in the Russo-Turkish war of 1877–78 and the Congress of Berlin, Constantinople experienced a shortlived political revolution. In the spring of 1876 riots in the capital secured the appointment as chief minister of Midhat Pasha, who was pledged to secure a parliamentary constitution. In December Midhat proclaimed a constitution, freedom of speech and the press. At last a genuinely liberal régime seemed possible. But Midhat had not secured the confidence of the new sultan, Abdul Hamid II, who had accepted the constitution only because he could see no way of avoiding it. When conservative forces rallied against Midhat, the sultan felt strong enough to act. In February 1877 Midhat Pasha was dismissed and banished, and thereafter Abdul Hamid allowed the constitution to lapse. But the new sultan was no proud and arrogant autocrat. After the 1875–78

[1] See above, pp. 160–3.

crisis he felt wholly dependent upon the powers for the survival of his régime. Even the appearance of magnificence disappeared from the Ottoman court. Abdul Hamid, his ministers and officials put aside bright oriental clothes and dressed in a modest western style befitting their poverty. Financially the régime was never to recover its independence. The Empire was to sink in status until in the twentieth century it became, economically if not politically, a colony of the great powers.

Political institutions

To compare Austrian, Russian and Turkish political life during the period 1830–48, is, of course, to compare three autocracies. The limitations on the absolute authority of the emperor in each case were of his own making. Sometimes even the most autocratic of rulers must delegate power to a minister or department. Whether such delegation of power constitutes a limitation of absolutism is largely a question of definition. Francis I left the formulation of foreign policy to Metternich, but was more jealous of domestic policy, which he usually kept in his own hands. Like his grandson, Francis Joseph, Francis I enjoyed the day-to-day routine of the bureaucrat, but unlike Francis Joseph, he was hopelessly slow and incompetent at it. His autocracy, however, was a less primitive one than that of Nicholas I in Russia, just as the Austrian territories were more civilized than Russia in that they were blessed with far more law and order. Russia was ruled not by a system of law at all, but by imperial decrees. What permanent laws existed were chaotic. Some of them had survived from the old Muscovite kingdom, some had been added by Peter the Great and others had subsequently been copied blindly from western systems. The collection of existing laws made under Nicholas was no substitute for a rational system like the Code Napoleon. The complete secrecy in which both criminal and civil law were administered permitted unlimited corruption. The government's attempts to counter corruption by appointing ever new courts of appeal merely lengthened the time needed to secure justice, and increased the number of bribes that had to be paid.

Neither in the Austrian nor the Russian governments was there anything approaching a modern cabinet. In Russia there were no permanent ministries. Both Nicholas I and Alexander II depended on *ad hoc* committees to get big measures enacted. There was in Russia, however, a 'state council', which drew up a budget and could modify legislation presented to it by ministers. But the activities of the state council were closely observed by the czar, and the czar's own *ukases* or decrees were not submitted to the state council. The nearest thing to a prime minister was the chancellor, who was chairman of the state council. Prince Gorchakov, as chancellor under Alexander II, acquired more real power than any other Russian minister in the period. But the imperial *ukases* were issued from the Personal Chancellery of the emperor, which was the ultimate ruling body.

In the absolutist régimes of modern Europe an important role has always been played by the police, whether regular or political, uniformed or secret. In Metternich's day in Austria the minister of police controlled a very thorough system of censorship and spying. Literature from the rest of Europe and especially from southern Germany was carefully scrutinized before being allowed over the border. Schiller's plays were heavily censored when they were not completely banned. Even Grillparzer, the Austrian dramatist who remained in fact loyal to the Habsburgs, could not write what he wanted. After 1830 and the revolution in Paris, the police régime in Austria grew more rigid and stupid. No Austrian student was now allowed to visit any foreign university. The most characteristic institution in Nicholas I's Russia was the secret police, which constituted the Third Department of the Imperial Chancellery. Virtually an extra-legal body supplementing the work of the uniformed gendarmerie, the Third Department had judicial powers to punish its victims. Besides preventing revolutionary conspiracy the Third Department fulfilled another, somewhat paradoxical, function: in a country without a parliament or an independent press it gave the government knowledge of the state of public opinion. Contemporary monarchs—Charles X and Louis-Philippe in France, or George IV in England—may have been offended at the disrespectful tone of the press but at least they were less in the dark concerning the sentiments of their subjects than was Nicholas I.

In Turkey the sultan did not have the services even of a political police force, but depended for the maintenance of his rule upon the army. The archaic nature of the institutions of the Ottoman Empire left the individual citizen with greater freedom than in either the Habsburg or the Russian Empires. The nationalist intellectuals of Serbia, the principalities, and later, Bulgaria, did not have to fear a highly organized police force. The army, after the destruction of the Janissaries, was kept loyal to the sultan, but given specific police duties. Mahmoud II created a new executive officer, the Serasker, who was commander-in-chief of the army, but also in charge of security and the maintenance of law and order in Constantinople. Under a strong and efficient man like Husrev Pasha, Serasker from 1827 to 1836, the new office could be one of great power, though always, of course, entirely dependent upon the sultan.

The existence of the ancient, aristocratic provincial estates in the Habsburg lands was a limitation on the autocracy of the imperial government in only the most abstract sense. They met rarely and when they did had no real power. But the Hungarian Diet was eventually to play a historic role not unlike that of the Estates General in France in 1789, and its composition is therefore of some interest. It had an upper house consisting of the greater nobility and bishops, and a lower house of the gentry representing both the urban and rural districts of Hungary. The Croatian Diet was also represented in the Hungarian lower house. As a result of the March Laws, passed by a newly elected liberal lower house in 1847, Hungary secured a constitution of the modern type with a popularly elected parliament and a responsible government. As a result of the 1848 revolution in Vienna, a constituent assembly met there also in July and deliberated until March, 1849. Its work, the Kremsier constitution, combined democracy and federalism, and may well have contained the answer which was to elude the Empire for the rest of its life. But the Kremsier constitution is only of historic interest, since Schwarzenberg never allowed it to function, but replaced it by his own sham constitution and highly centralized régime. Even so, the revolutions of 1848 serve to distinguish the Austrian Empire from the Russian. After 1848 Vienna was continually aware of the need to experiment with constitutional forms. Never again would the wholly negative approach of Metternich be possible. Since St Petersburg had no revolution in 1848 the czars continued to shelve the constitutional question for the rest of the century.

Schwarzenberg's constitution followed the Kremsier constitution in its one conservative feature: the regional divisions of the Empire were to follow historic rather than ethnic lines. Only in Galicia was a somewhat synthetic division into two régimes made by the creation of 'Ruthenia'. In Vienna there were to be two central assemblies while the local *Landtags* in the regions were given very little authority. The ancient and historic *Staatsrath*, or royal council of advisers who had virtually ruled Austria in Ferdinand's time, was now transformed into a *Reichsrath* of twenty-one members, all nominated by the Emperor. Thus did Schwarzenberg hope to integrate the Empire, to make the peoples forget the events of 1848. Francis Joseph was in complete sympathy with his minister and, in spite of lip service to 'the constitution of the kingdom of Hungary', he intended to end Hungarian separation completely and rule as emperor of a single empire no less than the czar did. Croatia-Slavonia and Transylvania were no longer to be part of Hungary but to be individual crownlands having an equal status to Hungary herself. Lombardy and Venetia were to remain for the time being a military zone with no local rights.

The nature of the Austrian monarchy changed appreciably with the accession of Francis Joseph. A cold, hard and ambitious young man, the new Emperor used the bureaucracy and the army to enforce his authority more than Francis I or Ferdinand's advisers had done. He sought the advice of the military—especially from his general aide-de-camp, Count Grünne—and tried to model the civil service on military lines. A new military police force was introduced. Austria remained a police state, as it had been in Metternich's time, but it was now a more efficient one. The bureaucracy, army and police all grew considerably in size, and in time produced great financial strain. Francis Joseph's government brought another change: it became increasingly clerical. The Concordat of 1855 gave the Church a stronger position in Austria than it had enjoyed since Maria Theresa's day.

The period 1849 to 1867 was one of trial and error so far as constitutions in Austria were concerned. The most notable constitutional reform of the period was the February Patent of 1861. The new *Reichsrath* created in 1861 was more like a parliament in size than its predecessors had been, but it was a conservative institution in the sense that it was elected indirectly by the local diets. No longer holding any provincial legislative functions, the local diets themselves were allowed to regulate only trivial local issues. The Hungarian Diet, no less than the others, became an insignificant local body, but there was one concession to the principle of dualism—all the delegates from Hungary in the *Reichsrath* were allowed to deliberate together over certain issues, while the non-Hungarian delegates could do the same over certain other issues. The *Reichsrath* had to be consulted before new taxes were levied, but in other respects it was not a powerful body. Old taxes never approved by the *Reichsrath* were still collected; the president and vice-president of the *Reichsrath* were appointed by the emperor; above all ministers were still responsible to the emperor rather than to the *Reichsrath*. The February Patent did not promise freedom of the press, and in other respects failed to give the guarantees needed by a liberal régime, but for a few years after 1861 Austria enjoyed a constitutional monarchy such as she had experienced before only during the few months of the 1848 revolution.

The early 1860s were years of reform also in Russia. If the emancipation of the serfs was the most spectacular reform of Alexander II, his reform of the legal system was the most successful. Previously there had been no clear distinction between the executive and judicial departments of government. The judicial system introduced in 1864 allowed for two branches: one administered by justices of the peace, the other by regular courts sitting under judges nominated from the legal profession by the czar. The justices of the peace were elected by the community and dealt with petty cases, often merely by persuading the disputants to accept a compromise settlement—much as solicitors might agree to settle a case out of court in the west. Immediately after 1864 justices of the peace acquired a high reputation for impartiality and good sense, and showed respect for the rights of the newly emancipated peasants. The regular courts dealt with more serious cases. They suffered more acutely than the lower courts from the shortage of trained lawyers, but they too were a striking improvement on the courts of Nicholas I.

Just as the dignity and independence of the serf were recognized by his emancipation and the new justice made available to him, so was his relationship to the *zemstvo* a more honourable one than had been his previous servitude to the landowner. The creation of the *zemstvos* was made a more conservative measure than had originally been intended by the narrowness of the regulations governing their elections, but even so they incorporated the electoral principle, which was thus introduced on a local and provincial level at a time when the introduction of such a principle in the central government appeared to the czar to be unthinkable. The *zemstvos* however had little independence of action. They were firmly subordinated to the Ministry of the Interior and so the ministry's officials and police could ignore or overrule any finding of the *zemstvo*. This meant that ultimately the *zemstvos* were not bodies of local government, except in so far as they administered school and hospital services, but rather organs of public opinion. And even the public opinion they expressed was of a very weighted kind. By a graded system of direct and indirect elections the single vote of a great proprietor was worth as much as several votes of urban merchants or numerous votes of peasants. The standard was purely according to material wealth, no longer according to title or social rank. It can then be said that the *zemstvos* were elected by the standards of a capitalist rather than a feudal society, though, once elected, they exerted the kind of communal authority which was still regarded with distrust by upholders of *laissez-faire* in the west.

The district or village *zemstvos* elected delegates to send to a provincial *zemstvo*. Secondary elections of this kind usually produce 'safer', or more conservative, upper assemblies, and in fact the provincial *zemstvos* had a still higher proportion of landowners than the district *zemstvos*. The administrative work of the *zemstvo* was carried out by a small committee of a president and one or two men elected by the whole assembly. The local officials of the czar's government could reject the president of the committee if they saw fit, and would anyhow use the *zemstvo's* executive committee for carrying out their own functions in such matters as recruiting, billeting or transporting the imperial troops. But the *zemstvo* executives performed their own local task of administration without great interference from the central government. They levied their own taxes, and employed their own teachers and doctors. In short they were more advanced local institutions than could be found in the richer countries of western Europe. The enlightened character of the *zemstvos* was, of course, often limited by the predominant role played on them by the nobility, and liberal Russian writers usually condemned them for this reason. The statute of 1870 introducing municipal assemblies, or *dumas*, spread the electoral system to the Russian towns. But here the control exerted over the assemblies by the Ministry of the Interior was still greater, and the independence of the police from the municipal *dumas* was more damaging to the reputation of those bodies.

The institutions created during the 1860s in Russia may have seemed inadequate to the intelligentsia, but they were at least never subsequently withdrawn. More important than the shortcomings of the reforms actually instituted was the glaring omission at the core of the régime: so long as no czar dared to grant a central constitution the essential condition for political stability was lacking. The contrast between the autocratic simplicity of Russia and the constitutional complications of the Habsburg Empire became still more marked after the establishment of the Dual Austro-Hungarian monarchy in 1867. Austria and Hungary could now have their own separate constitutions, though each had the same individual for monarch and shared the ministries of foreign affairs, war and finance. There was also an annual meeting of 'delegations'—an assembly consisting of sixty delegates sent from the Austrian parliament, and sixty from the Hungarian. At home the

Hungarians used their autonomy to restore the constitution of 1848, and for the rest of the century Budapest experienced considerable parliamentary vitality, in spite of the lack of any military or diplomatic independence.

The Turkish reform movement, or *Tanzimat*, was less concerned with the creation of governmental institutions than with the organization of the legal and educational systems. To reform law in the Ottoman Empire needed a revolutionary outlook. The existing laws were considered part of the faith of Islam, the revealed word of God, and even to suggest that they could be changed seemed blasphemous. The most that a Turkish government could safely do was to reinterpret or codify the sacred law, and even this could not traditionally be regarded as the legitimate function of a secular legislative body. Thus a new penal code in 1840 was radical for two reasons: because it declared all Ottoman subjects—Muslim and Christian alike—equal before the law, and so divorced law from religion and confirmed the principle contained in the sultan's Rescript of the Rose Chamber; and because it was prepared by a specially appointed committee without reference to the *Ulema*, the guardians of the Holy Law. The 1840 code was significant for the ideas it tacitly accepted rather than for its effectiveness. Reshid Pasha's Commercial Code of 1850 was to be more thoroughly acted upon, and suggested that there were whole spheres of human activity in which the *Ulema* could claim no interest. Other penal, commercial, maritime and agrarian codes, the work of Ali and Fuad Pashas, followed in the 1850s and 1860s. In the sphere of education the Turkish reformers were usually too ambitious. When a committee of seven men were appointed by the Porte in 1845 to report on the educational needs of the empire, they proposed the foundation of a ministry of education, a state university and a state system of primary and secondary schools. The ministry of education was created. The university, too, was duly founded, but building was halted almost as soon as it was started. By 1850 only six small state secondary schools were in existence. In the 1860s, however, the reform movement made at least one real achievement in the field of education. In 1868 the Imperial Lycée at Galatassaray was opened, and proceeded to teach both Muslim and Christian pupils in the French language. The school at Galatassaray played a large role in supplying a class of administrators familiar with western ideas and techniques. Of the reforms embraced by the *Tanzimat* those in education were the most successful. Eventually the new schools and colleges were to produce a new professional class, not all of whom were corrupt and many of whom were to be capable administrators. Judged by its immediate achievements the *Tanzimat* was clearly a failure. Judged by the task the reformers had undertaken and the ground on which they worked, their long-term effect was appreciable.

As the Christian Balkan states moved towards independence from the sultan they established constitutions of a defiantly western kind, usually with the help of the great powers. The Greek constitution of 1844 allowed for two small legislative houses. The lower chamber consisted of some eighty members, who were elected for only three years by universal manhood suffrage. The senate consisted of at least twenty-seven members who were nominated for life by the crown. Naturally it was assumed that the senate would act as the conservative element in the constitution, but in the event it was to lead the opposition against King Otto. Although it survived for twenty years, the constitution of 1844 did not bring political stability to Greece, though less because of any intrinsic weakness than because of the authoritarian attitude of Otto. The constitution of 1864 abolished the senate and enlarged the assembly, which was now to be elected for four years, still, of course, by universal manhood suffrage, and now by a secret ballot. It was to last for nearly half a century.

The principalities which became 'Rumania' in 1862 had a far less democratic constitution than Greece. But the Rumanians also looked to the west for their institutional patterns. The Rumanian nationalist movement was strongly influenced by French ideas. Exiles from the principalities had formed a Rumanian colony in France, and Bucharest tried to be a small-scale Paris. Even in face of the arrival of a Prussian prince in 1866, the Rumanians continued to look further to the west for inspiration. The constitution of 1866 was based on the Belgian Charter of 1831, and so introduced a moderately liberal, but not democratic, régime.

In Serbia the brutal tyranny of Milosh Obrenovich marked the first years of the period, but a constitution dragged from him in 1835 created an executive committee of six to limit the power of the prince, and a popular assembly to be elected annually. In this instance the great powers intervened against constitutionalism. Austria and Russia were both averse to a parliamentary régime so centrally placed in the Balkans. In 1838 the constitution was abrogated and replaced by an aristocratic régime, dominated by a senate of seventeen men appointed for life. For many years Serbia was to be fought over by the two rival dynasties, the Obrenovich and the Karageorgevich, with the latter supporting the idea of restoring the democratic régime of 1835, while the aristocratic senate remained usually the real power in the country. Not until 1869 did a more liberal constitution return.

As a province of the Ottoman Empire for the greater part of the period, Bulgaria could not have her own political institutions. After the Russo-Turkish War of 1877, Russian troops remained in occupation of the newly independent state, and even when the Congress of Berlin reversed the Russian settlement of the Balkans there was no practical alternative, for the time being, to leaving Bulgaria in Russian hands. But in the spring of 1879 Alexander of Battenberg was elected prince of Bulgaria. A German of twenty-two, without a political education, Alexander did not know how to work with the parliament which had been created earlier in 1879. Of all the Balkan states, Bulgaria in 1880 had less constitutional experience and fewer national traditions on which to build.

Taking them as a whole, however, the Balkan states which were born on the ruins of Turkey-in-Europe were precocious in their establishment of a political life. The small educated middle classes were determined to play a full part in ruling their country, and they quickly made greater opportunities for themselves than were available in the three great empires of eastern Europe. Deprived of a share in political life, the middle classes in both Austria and Russia had only one field of activity in which to earn a living—the civil service. Both countries had large and highly professional bureaucracies. The Austrian bureaucracy worked throughout the period with smoothness and efficiency, and was far less corrupt than the Russian. Disasters which overturned the political régime in Vienna—like those of 1859 and 1866—left the civil service untouched. Bureaucratic stability gave an air of unreality to the endless political crises and constitutional experiments. Russia had more than half a million civil servants, whose corruption was unequalled in western or central Europe. The lower grades of the service were wretchedly paid, and so had to take bribes to survive. It was generally assumed that officials would expect gifts of money for the performance of any bureaucratic function, and it would have been unthinkable for a peasant to protest against an extorted bribe. The most important ministries were those of the Interior and Finance. The minister of finance had wider powers than his counterparts in the west, because he was very largely responsible for directing trade and many of those industries which already existed. Alexander II's minister of finance, Reutern, modernized Russian finance by establishing a regular and public budget. He was followed by less competent ministers when he resigned in 1877 in protest against the extravagant policy of going to war with Turkey. Many administrative functions under Nicholas I were carried out by military authorities. The army organized the building of roads, forestry, mining and even education. Courts martial were far more active in Russia than in the west and performed functions which elsewhere in Europe would have been handled by the civil courts. The creation of the *zemstvos* in 1864 took much administrative work off the hands of the military authorities. There were now civilian bodies to control education, medical services and the buildings of roads. But the provincial governors, under the Ministry of the Interior, who limited the effectiveness of both the *zemstvos* and the urban *dumas*, had much the same power and responsibility under Alexander II as under Nicholas I.

If the Ottoman Empire had nothing approaching a civil service in the western sense, her army, which did a great deal of her administrative work, was not less efficient than the armies of the Austrian and Russian empires, and perhaps more successful. All three armies were recruited by primitive, unsystematic methods, for which the term 'conscription' seems misleading, and is used only for want of a better one. In all three armies, once the wretched soldier had been enlisted, his length of service was immensely long: fourteen years in Austria, until the reform of 1845 which reduced the period to eight years; twenty-five years in Russia under Nicholas I, until, under Alexander II, it was reduced first to sixteen, and then fifteen years; and twelve years in Turkey since Mahmoud II's Army Code of 1826. It is interesting to note from these figures that in 1830 the Turkish army had the most humane practice as regards length of service. The Austrian army throughout the period was too large for the economic capacity of the country. Her central position in Europe and her grave nationality problems within her own borders gave Austria's governments a sense of insecurity which involved her in excessive military expense. The effort of keeping her large armies mobilized during the Crimean War crippled Austria's finances. She emerged exhausted from a war in which she had remained neutral. Again in the Italian crisis of 1859 her army proved too large. The cost of keeping her army mobilized was again so great that she ended in May in blundering into a war from which she had nothing to gain and much to lose. In neither of the short wars against the great powers in which she was involved during the period—the wars of 1859 and 1866—did the Austrian army win a single victory. Against Piedmont alone, Radetsky had done well in 1848, and the Austrian fleet defeated a larger and

newer Italian fleet in 1866, but this was scant comfort for what had once
been a great military power.

The Russian army, too, was vast in size by nineteenth-century
standards. On the eve of the Crimean War it numbered some one-and-a-
half million, and cost 40 per cent of the national expenditure. Conscription was carried out by the crude process of levying serfs at irregular
intervals. The village communes were usually allowed to decide themselves which serfs should be sent, and decision was usually reached by
casting lots. But the landowners sometimes interfered and always
decided who should go from among their own domestic serfs. The
landowners could also threaten to send their serfs off to the army,
even when no levy was in progress. The frightful sentence of twenty-
five years' conscription was inevitably considered as a kind of civil
death. The village would never see the conscripted serfs again. After
three years their wives were allowed to remarry. The army into which
the poor peasant had been absorbed was, under Nicholas, the most
barbaric in Europe. There were endless floggings; sometimes a thousand blows were given, with thick birch rods. Such floggings, needless
to say, often ended in death. The humanizing effect of Alexander II's
reign was perhaps greater in the army than anywhere. In 1861 the czar
appointed the radical, D. A. Miliutin, to the War Ministry, where he
remained until the czar's death twenty years later. Miliutin abolished
the more brutal forms of corporal punishment in the army, as did the
Grand Duke Constantine, the minister of marine, for the navy. Miliutin
not only reduced the period of conscription, but improved the living
conditions for the soldiers. A minister of war or general who is more
humanitarian than his predecessors is invariably more efficient also,
and Miliutin was no exception. In view of the disastrous performance
of the army in the Crimean War, he reformed its organization and
introduced more modern weapons. He was not slow to copy the
Prussians in creating a general staff. One of Alexander's last genuine
reforms, a statute on military service in 1874, was the work of Miliutin.
It introduced an entirely new and modern system of conscription, by
which all young men of twenty became liable for service irrespective of
class or wealth. Those who would actually serve were selected by ballot,
would then be with the army for nine years, and then in reserve for a
further six. Again the influence of the Prussian army, which had just
astonished Europe, was felt.

The Austrian and Russian governments had considerable confidence
in the capabilities of their armies, but when war came their confidence

was usually shown to be misplaced. The Porte, on the other hand, rarely had confidence in the Turkish army, which usually surprised Europe by the tenacity of the resistance it offered to the enemy. Although an offer by Palmerston to send English officers to train the Turkish army was refused by Mahmoud II in 1834, the Turkish government was usually eager for western military advice. The next year, 1835, three English officers were in fact received in Constantinople as advisers to help reorganize the Turkish army, and Turkish cadets were sent to England to be trained at Woolwich. In 1838 the British government sent a naval mission to Turkey. But the British officers were not well received and the Turks on their side clearly gained little from the exchanges. In the same years—1835 to 1839—von Moltke, then only a lieutenant in the Prussian army, was in Turkey. He was joined by five other Prussian officers, but he too found life in Turkey unpleasant, because of the popular prejudice against the infidel. Turkey cannot be said to have gained much from direct western military advice in the nineteenth century. If the record of Turkish armies against the Russians in the wars of the century was a good one, it was mainly because of the sheer moral resistance of the Turkish soldiers and the genius of the generals, like Omar Pasha.

Nothing could conceal the fact that the three empires of eastern Europe were declining. The paralysis of the Habsburg government in the face of its constitutional problems, the unlimited corruption of the Russian bureaucracy and the financial incapacity of the Porte were symptoms of a general malaise. But even if the institutions of the three empires had been sound, they could not have withstood the great movements of thought and sentiment which characterize the nineteenth century—the nationalist movement which was already destroying the Ottoman Empire and would ultimately dismember the Habsburg monarchy, and the socialist movement which would one day overthrow the czar.

XII

Europe and the World

In the course of the nineteenth century Europeans completed the process of dominating the neighbouring continents of Asia and Africa. Vast areas previously inhabited by independent nomadic or primitive tribes were brought under European administration for the first time. Great decaying empires or principalities were either conquered outright, or, like China or Egypt, brought under the economic control of European powers. The process accelerated as the century went on, reaching its

BIBLIOGRAPHY. An eminent Indian historian has treated the subject of Europe in Asia—K. M. Panikkar, *Asia and Western Dominance* (London, 1959). Of Russian expansion into Asia and administration of the conquered territories a good study is Richard A. Pierce, *Russia and Central Asia, 1867–1917* (University of California, 1960). The literature on British rule in India is, of course, enormous, though much that was written before 1947 reads a little quaintly today. A recent introductory work which is up to date in its approach is W. H. Morland and Sir A. C. Chatterjee, *A Short History of India* (London, 1953). On the other hand a work which is dated in tone but very strong on administrative history is the *Cambridge History of India*, edited by E. J. Rapson (Cambridge, 1922–37). An elegantly written modern work, which yet considers the period very much from the British point of view, is P. Woodruff, *The Men who ruled India* (2 vols., London, 1953–54) and a scholarly study of the important years after the Mutiny is Thomas R. Metcalfe, *The Aftermath of Revolt. India, 1857–1870* (Princeton, 1965). A good survey of the Far East and of the European impact upon it in the period is Franz H. Michael and George E. Taylor, *The Far East in the Modern World* (Washington and London, 1956). A history by a Chinese historian which includes a wonderfully lucid and balanced account of China's relations with the European powers has recently been translated: Li Chien-Nung, *The Political History of China 1840–1928*, translated and edited by Ssu-Yu Teng and Jeremy Ingalls (Princeton, 1956). For British policy towards China during Palmerston's period an excellent monograph is W. C. Costin, *Great Britain and China 1833–1860* (Oxford, 1937), while a much more recent study of the opening up of Japan is W. G. Beasley, *The Modern History of Japan* (London, 1963). An authoritative work on French colonial history is the *Histoire des colonies françaises*, edited by G. Hanotaux and A. Martineau (6 vols., Paris, 1929–33). For the French conquest of Algeria there is now Claude Martin, *Histoire de l'Algérie*

culmination only in the years after 1880, but in the period 1830 to 1880
immense increases in European power were made. Only in the American
continents was Europe in retreat. In the half century before 1830 the
Spanish, Portuguese and British had been forced to abandon most of
their American empires, and in the half century after 1830 the South

française, 1830–1962 (Paris, 1963), which, in spite of its title, contains several
chapters of earlier history. Several short introductions to the history of Africa
have been published recently; one which deserves mention is D. L. Wiedner,
A History of Africa South of the Sahara (London, 1964). A great deal·has been
written on the European partition of Africa after 1880, but much less on the
period of African history covered by this book. From the literature on the
exploration of Africa, most of it, of course, written by geographers rather than
historians, one little book on Livingstone may be cited as an example—Jack
Simmons, *Livingstone and Africa* (London, 1955). West Africa has received
some very scholarly treatment in recent years, as West African countries have
one by one secured their independence. A good example is David Kimble, *A
Political History of Ghana, 1850–1928* (Oxford, 1963), but there are numerous
other works on both West and East Africa which must be left unmentioned. One
excellent brief study for whose mention space must be found is D. Fage, *Introduction to the History of West Africa* (Cambridge, 1959). On South Africa, the
Cambridge History of the British Empire, vol. VIII, edited by Eric A. Walker
(Cambridge, 1963) constitutes an impressive authority.

The best introduction to the history of Latin America for the period is provided by the chapter by R. A. Humphreys in the *New Cambridge Modern History*,
vol. X (Cambridge, 1960). Perhaps the most important factor for European relations with the young South American states was an economic one—the question
of European, and particularly British, investment in South American industries.
For this the key work is still Leland H. Jenks, *The Migration of British Capital to
1875* (London, 1927; latest, unrevised, edition, 1963). A definitive work has not
yet been written on the one major act of European intervention in the New
World in the period—Napoleon III's Mexican expedition—though the works
quoted for the Second Empire in chapter VIII, above, p. 165, are of course
relevant. For the diplomatic relations between the U.S.A. and the European
powers the standard study is S. F. Bemis, *A Diplomatic History of the United
States* (New York, 1947). H. C. Allen, *Great Britain and the United States: a
history of Anglo-American relations, 1783–1952* considers every aspect of the
special relationship between the two countries. A considerable literature, most
of it written by Americans, has gathered around the question of European
emigration to the U.S.A. Three works which are particularly relevant for this
period are: Robert Ernst, *Immigrant Life in New York City 1825–1863* (New
York, 1949); Oscar Handlin, *Boston's Immigrants, 1790–1865* (Harvard, 1941);
and W. S. Shepperson, *British Emigration to North America. Projects and
Opinions in the Early Victorian Period* (Oxford, 1957). An excellent introduction
to the history of Canada is Gerald S. Graham, *Canada. A Short History* (London,
1950), and a rather longer account is J. Bartlet Brebner, *Canada. A Modern
History* (Ann Arbor, 1960).

American nations painfully asserted their independence, while the U.S.A. grew to be a world power, in spite of the grim set-back of the civil war.

Asia

In Asia, the world's largest continent, a considerable power vacuum existed at the beginning of the nineteenth century, and into the vacuum the energetic European peoples were bound to expand. The European great power nearest to Asia was Russia, and it was the Russians who annexed the vastest areas of Asia during the period. The Russians had been on the offensive in Asia since the sixteenth century. They had reached the Ural mountains and the Caspian Sea before the end of the seventeenth. The region in which the greatest advances were made in the period 1830 to 1880 was to the south, in central Asia. This region was occupied partly by primitive, but settled, agricultural peoples. Most numerous of the nomadic peoples were the fierce Kazakhs, a race with some Turkish and some Mongol features. The Kazakhs, who may have numbered two and a half million in the 1860s, were Muslims, though not very strict Muslims: they had no mosques and their women did not wear veils. The Kirgiz, close relatives of the Kazakhs and living a similar nomadic life, probably numbered only 300,000 in the 1860s. The Turkmen were not more numerous, but some of them were settled farmers. The life of the nomadic peoples had changed very little in a thousand years, except that by the nineteenth century they had adopted the use of firearms for their habitual raids and blood feuds between clans. Some of the settled peoples of central Asia were more numerous than the nomads. The Uzbekhs, for example, probably numbered three and a half million in the 1860s. And among these settled peoples were those who could look back to a more civilized past, to the days of the 'golden journey to Samarkand'. But in the nineteenth century they were living in a primitive agricultural state, in mud huts often built in or near the ruined palaces of former civilizations. In terms of social organization even czarist Russia had something to offer to so backward an area.

Fresh advances were made in the reign of Nicholas I. In 1839 the Russians attacked the independent Muslim principality of Khiva, and in the 1840s and 1850s built forts deep in country outside the original Russian borders in this region. Whereas Russian expansion in the Balkans alarmed Austria as well as Britain, expansion in central Asia was of little concern to the continental powers of Europe. Only the British were alarmed at the advance of Russian forces towards India—

5. RUSSIAN EXPANSION INTO ASIA BEFORE 1880

alarmed, in fact, out of all proportion to the reality of the threat. British governments always failed to appreciate the immensity of distances in Asia and the impregnability of India's north-west frontier. But in the reign of Alexander II the Russian advance continued more rapidly. The czar and his chancellor, Gorchakov, were anxious not to antagonize Britain, but they were unable wholly to control those elements in Russia who were eager for expansion. In the remote parts of Russia's Asiatic empire were active local governors—men like Muraviev, who was governor of eastern Siberia from 1847 to 1861—and still more active military officers. The army realized the ease with which vast new imperial territories could be secured in central Asia. Thus, while expansion was not the determined policy of the government in St Petersburg, the officers on the spot could not be restrained from the kind of energetic action which was inevitably rewarded subsequently by promotion and military honours. The department dealing with Asia in the foreign ministry was also reluctant to be restrained by the cautious chancellor, and business men were eager to secure concessions for exploiting the mineral wealth of central Asia.

In the Far East the forward policy of Muraviev secured the founding of Vladivostock in 1860, and the still more dramatic policy of Ignatyev, the future minister in Constantinople, carved the Russian Maritime Province out of the Chinese empire in the regions of the rivers Amur and Ussuri. For this acquisition the approval of Alexander II had been obtained, as it had for the conquest of the Caucasus region from 1857 to 1864. Of more concern to Britain was the subsequent Russian advance southwards, along the eastern shore of the Caspian Sea, towards Persia. Gorchakov was opposed to this southwards advance, but could not prevent the establishment of a Trans-Caspian military district in 1874. Work was started on a Trans-Caspian railway in 1879. Yet farther to the east, earlier advances had been made. The capture of Tashkent in 1865 had been the work of a mere army colonel, Cherniaev, with no real authority from the czar. In 1866–67 the governor-generalship of Turkestan was formed from the conquests of the previous twenty years, the new post of governor-general being given to another military figure, General Kaufman. Under Kaufman, whose authority from the czar was real enough, expansion continued, Bokhara and Samarkand falling in 1868. As is so often the case with great military empires, czarist Russia was swelling to enormous proportions in what was to prove the last half century of her history.

The other large empire dominated by Europeans in Asia—India—

changed its character appreciably between 1830 and 1880. Before the eighteenth century, Europeans in India had been little more than modest traders. Whereas Russian expansion in Asia was a clear example of trade following the flag, European imperialism in India was the result of the flag following trade. The collapse of the Mogul Empire in the first half of the eighteenth century, and the resulting anarchy, had forced the European trading communities to pursue an imperial policy by the enlistment of native troops and military agreements with rival Indian princes. From these somewhat accidental origins the British empire in India had been built, under the authority of a mere chartered company —the East India Company. In the nineteenth century the bringing of European ideas of government, economics and culture to India was the work of the British, who showed in their performance of the task that strange mixture of blindness and selflessness, single-mindedness and rigid sense of duty which the Victorians showed in all their doings.

The East India Company was traditionally opposed to the establishment of British political control, and was concerned to limit its activities purely to trade. This had been particularly the case after the defeat of the French in the mid-eighteenth century, but with the rise of the Napoleonic empire, the British authorities, both in London and India, had decided with some reluctance that political supremacy was necessary. The new policy by which India was brought increasingly under the power of the British state, though still under the nominal authority of the East India Company, was quickly put into effect after 1815. In the Whig era of the 1830s, British political institutions, and education in English for the Indian populations, were introduced, largely at the promptings of the British radicals—Benthamites and Evangelicals alike. The radical Lord William Bentinck, first governor of India, enforced the new policy of westernization, which, if arrogant in its basic assumption, was introduced with caution and tact. In the 1840s, when railways were still a novelty in Europe, the British Indian government made preparations for the construction of a railway system in India. At the same time a vast scheme of irrigation for the Ganges Valley was inaugurated—a scheme of great economic significance for that densely populated area. Bentinck's successors—Auckland, Ellenborough, Hardinge and Dalhousie—were alike in their supreme self-confidence in the superiority of western civilization, and their determination to modernize the ancient and alien world into which their political careers had led them. But the self-confidence of the British in India was temporarily shaken by the suddenness and horror of the Indian Mutiny of 1857. Appalling atrocities were committed on both sides before the Mutiny was finally suppressed. In the past, British historians have dismissed the Mutiny as a reactionary and obscurantist movement by ignorant and superstitious Indian soldiers, while more recently Indian historians have depicted it as a national revolution. Neither representation contains the whole truth. The Mutiny was not limited to the army, but embraced peasant risings, and while the educated professional class of Indians gave no support to the Mutiny, it is also true that an element of national protest lay at the bottom of the movement. Whatever else it achieved the Mutiny made it clear that the political position of the East India Company was an anachronism. In 1858 the British government took over full and formal sovereignty and responsibility for the administration and laws of India. In doing so it also abandoned the attempt which had been made since the 1830s to westernize Indian culture in every respect. By declaring its religious neutrality, the British government recognized the massive failure of Christianity in India to secure converts from one much more ancient religion, Hinduism, or from the other more youthful and aggressive religion, Islam.

Territorially British possessions in Asia continued to expand in the period. In India itself the states of Nagpur and Oudh were annexed during the governor-generalship of Dalhousie, 1848–56. A series of wars with the Burmese led to the slow annexation of Burma, though the whole country did not become British until the 1880s. British possessions in southern Malaya had been united into the Straits settlements in 1826. From 1830 to 1867 the Straits settlements, including the young port of Singapore, which was to have so rich a future, were under British India, but in 1867 they were placed independently under the control of the Colonial Office.

The Far East

To the east, the great empire of China still tried to hold itself aloof from the European 'barbarians'. So far as the eighteenth century had been concerned the Chinese could make out a not unconvincing case for considering their empire more civilized than western Europe. While the historian of eighteenth-century Europe finds almost no census returns and few precise government statistics of any kind until the beginning of the nineteenth century, the historian of eighteenth-century China has at his disposal precise returns of population figures, acreage under cultivation and so on, at regular intervals throughout the century. Since the mid-seventeenth century China had enjoyed the settled rule of the

Manchu dynasty and a system of government administered by a merito-
cracy of scholar-gentry. But in the years immediately before 1830 the
Chinese administrative system declined in competence, the army in
particular becoming undisciplined and corrupt, though the Chinese
remained convinced that theirs was the central world civilization. China
was economically self-sufficient and the lack of contact with the west was
seen as a loss for the European 'barbarians' rather than for China herself.
In their vast sophisticated empire the Chinese felt no sense of isolation
from the west. It so happened, however, that in the very period when
Chinese institutions were falling into decay, Europe was being in-
vigorated and transformed by the industrial revolution and the ideas of
the French Revolution.

In Chinese history the period 1830 to 1880 is important precisely
because it witnessed the first major impact of industrialized Europe on
the ancient Manchu Empire. The period from the Opium War of 1839–
1842 to the Sino-Japanese War of 1894 was one in which the Chinese
authorities were forced to face the evidence of the greater material
power of Europe, with all the dangers to Chinese security and to the
Chinese economy which that power implied. The British victory over
the Chinese in the Opium War started the process of opening China to
western trade. By the Treaty of Nanking in 1842 China ceded the port
of Hong Kong to Britain, and whereas previously Canton had been the
only Chinese port open to British merchants, Shangai and three other
ports were now to be opened also. Later in 1842 the Treaty of Whampoa
granted France also certain commercial rights and promised toleration
of Catholics in China. Much as the Crimean War was to demonstrate the
weakness of the Russian imperial system to sections of Russian opinion,
so the Opium War showed for the first time the weaknesses of the
Manchu régime in China when exposed to the technological superiority
of Europe. And just as the pressure for reform in Russia and the
emancipation of the serfs was to some extent the result of defeat in
the Crimea, so did the defeat of the Chinese imperial forces lead to the
Taiping Rebellion of 1850–64. During the Taiping Rebellion, Britain,
this time allied with the French Second Empire, again made war on
China, and the resulting Anglo-French victories led to the Treaties of
Tien-tsin in 1858 and Peking in 1860, by which China was forced to
enter into diplomatic relations with the western powers on terms of
equality. The old claim that the Chinese emperor had a mandate from
heaven to rule the world and that the European sovereigns could only
present petitions to him was beginning to look untenable. In the Taiping

Rebellion the Chinese government used a few European officers and weapons, and international affairs began to be studied in China for the first time. But the small and superficial attempts at westernization were totally inadequate to resist subsequent aggression from industrialized Europe and Japan, or to prevent the disasters which overtook the Chinese Empire after 1880.

Beyond the southern borders of China the French started in the 1850s to build up their Indo-Chinese empire. Jesuit missionaries had been in the area since the seventeenth century, and it was partly to protect them, partly to obtain commercial concessions, that the French moved into Indo-China in the nineteenth century. Negotiations with the emperor of Annam having failed, Napoleon III's forces occupied Saigon in 1859, and eastern Cochin China in 1860. The French colony of Cochin China was founded in 1862, and a French protectorate in Cambodia in 1867. The whole apparatus of a centralized Napoleonic administration was subsequently transplanted in this remote corner of Asia.

The opening up of Japan in the nineteenth century was yet more sudden and violent than the opening up of China, and, like the latter, was caused partly by internal change, partly by external aggression. The sovereignty of the Japanese emperors had been purely nominal since the early seventeenth century. Real power lay with the Tokugawa family who, as members of the military caste, had assumed the title of *Shogun*. By 1830 the apparently feudal structure of Japanese society— the shogunate ruling over warrior and peasant classes—had in practice been modified by the growth of densely populated cities and a rich merchant class. Both the warrior class, or *samurai*, and the peasants were discontented. It required only the impact of the industrialized western world to bring revolution. The initial impact from outside came not from Europe, but from America. As soon as China, after the Opium War, had been forced to abandon her policy of commercial isolation, the western merchants turned their attentions also to Japan. Russia, and the U.S.A., which had recently acquired a Pacific coast, were the two powers which first showed an interest in the opening of Japan. An American squadron under Commodore Perry arrived off the coast of Japan in 1851, and a Russian squadron arrived from the Baltic in 1853. So completely lacking in modern weapons were the Japanese that the mere presence of foreign fleets was sufficient for the Americans—and subsequently the European powers, Britain, Russia, France and Holland—to secure commercial concessions. The shogunate accepted the policy of the opening of

Japan, but in so doing it forfeited popularity at home where hatred of the foreigner was growing. The long era of the Tokugawa shogunate ended in revolution in 1868, when a determined group of men seized power under the cloak of a restoration of the Meiji emperor to his former privileges. Japan was now firmly set on a policy of modernization and westernization—but westernization in order to secure independence from European or American political influence.

Australasia

Stretching south from Asia to Australia is the enormous group of islands of the East Indies. The Dutch empire of the East Indies had been founded as early as the seventeenth century, though New Guinea had been added to it as recently as 1828. Under the harsh régime of Dutch governors the East Indies were exploited with considerable ruthlessness for the economic advantage of Holland. In sharp contrast to the densely populated islands the great island continent of Australia was virtually deserted. After Europe herself Australia was to become the most European of the continents in human terms. When Australia was discovered by a European, the Dutchman Captain Jansz, in 1606, and first settled by Europeans, the British, in 1788, she was inhabited by comparatively few—perhaps 200,000—Stone Age people, whose way of life had probably not changed for countless thousands of years. Consequently the civilization which was built up in Australia in the nineteenth century was simply the result of strange geographical conditions playing upon an English community. The first settlement in 1788 was of 717 convicts at Port Jackson, where the city of Sydney was one day to be built. Over the years some 60,000 or 70,000 more convicts were to be transported to Australia from Britain, until in 1840 the practice was at last ended. By 1840 the convicts were already a small minority of the population. Six separate colonies were founded by settlers in Australia between 1825 and 1859, thereby making it almost certain that the whole island-continent would become British. The origins of New Zealand as a British colony differed from those of Australia. In New Zealand British sovereignty had been proclaimed in 1840, only after merchants and speculators had settled and quarrelled with the natives, the Maoris, who were more advanced than the Australian aborigines and so created a greater problem for the settlers. But the actual process of colonization in Australia and New Zealand was carried out in a systematic and scientific spirit in sharp contrast to British colonization elsewhere in the world. South Australia and colonies in North Island, New Zealand, and

at Canterbury and Otago in South Island, New Zealand, put into practice the ideas of Edward Gibbon Wakefield as they were later expounded
in his work, *A View of the Art of Colonization*, published in 1847. Wakefield saw colonies as the answer to overpopulation in Europe, and so
started a long tradition of thought on the subject.

Perhaps not surprisingly the rugged Australian colonists treated the
aborigines like animals, driving them away from their hunting grounds
and destroying their totem shrines. When the natives tried to return
they were hunted to death, as in the so-called 'battle' of Pinjarra in West
Australia in 1833. The British government did not recognize any rights
to land on the part of the aborigines, but it equally withheld approval of
bloody expeditions like that of the Pinjarra. The massacre of twenty-
eight innocuous natives at Myall Creek in New South Wales in 1838
encouraged the authorities to act: seven white men were found guilty
of murder and hanged. But massacres of the aborigines were not
permanently halted.

The British government did not long delay the grant of representative
home rule to the Australians, though they kept ultimate responsibility
in their own hands in London. The Australian Colonies Government
Act, passed in 1850 in Westminster, permitted the several colonies to
draw up their own constitution for local government. The extension of
this degree of trust to the colonists paid off, as each colony decided to
adopt the British model of a two-chamber legislature with an executive
government responsible to the legislature. Thus a uniform and purely
English-type régime emerged in Australia, and New Zealand followed
the same pattern in 1852.

Africa

Though so close to Europe, the continent of Africa had remained virtually unknown to Europeans throughout history, except for the southern
shore of the Mediterranean, the southernmost tip of the continent and
a few trading posts elsewhere on the coast. Although Europeans had for
several centuries before 1830 known the shape of the outline of Africa,
and had sailed around it, they had not penetrated to the interior. There
are simple geographical reasons for this. Africa has forbidding approaches
—few natural harbours, waterfalls or rapids near the mouths of the
rivers, deserts or malarial forests near the coast. The African peoples
had little to offer the European in trade and no rich cities for him to
plunder. The large exception to this pattern was provided, of course, by
Africa north of the Sahara. North Africa had seen many civilizations

since the beginning of history, and had been familiar to the ancient world. But the Sahara created a barrier more formidable than any ocean. Not until the period covered by this book did explorers penetrate into central Africa, and not until after 1880 was Africa fully partitioned among the European powers. But once Africa had been opened up by explorers, missionaries, and traders, the European governments moved in to annex, and speculators moved in to exploit, with astonishing rapidity.

The first movement of imperialism in Africa in the period was the French conquest of Algeria. From the early sixteenth to the nineteenth century the Algerian coastline was known to Europe as the home of the Barbary pirates. The decision taken at the Congress of Vienna to suppress the pirates by combined action had proved difficult to fulfil. Algiers was nominally part of the Ottoman Empire, but in fact ruled by one of the pirate chiefs who had assumed the title of Dey. In 1827 the Dey believed, with good reason, that the French consul was involved in dubious financial dealings in Algiers. In an angry interview the Dey struck the consul with his fan. In the eyes of the French the *coup d'éventail* was the final insult after a series of offences against French shipping, and an expedition was prepared by Charles X's government in the last weeks of its existence. Algiers was occupied by the French three weeks before the July Revolution in Paris in 1830. The Turks did not protest at the occupation of what was nominally Turkish territory. The British government merely insisted that French interests in Algeria should not spread to Tunisia or Morocco; the British were otherwise glad that the French could find an outlet for their energy outside Europe. But Louis-Philippe's forces could do little for the time being beyond occupying the city of Algiers and a few other points along the coast. Not until 1837 did they take the ancient city of Constantine. Meanwhile an Algerian nationalist leader emerged in the person of Abd el Kader, who fought brilliant guerrilla wars against the French throughout the 1830s. Not until 1847 did Abd el Kader surrender, having kept a French army occupied throughout the reign of Louis-Philippe. By 1848 the conquest at last appeared complete, and the revolutionary government in Paris organized Algeria into three departments represented in the French assembly in Paris. The step anticipated future developments, but under Napoleon III the generals in Algeria succeeded in reasserting their authority. Algeria was not yet conquered. Further campaigns had to be fought against the tribesmen in the interior throughout the life of the Second Empire, and not until 1879 was Algeria definitively placed under civil government. Meanwhile the economic development of the country was thorough and rapid. Roads were built and much land cultivated. The French started to settle on a large scale in the 1840s when it was clear that the government intended to conquer and pacify the whole country. By 1847 there were already 109,000 Europeans in Algeria, and Algiers doubled its population from 1841 to 1846.

The sultan of Morocco had given refuge and assistance to Abd el Kader in 1841, and so incurred the displeasure of France. A brief war was waged against Morocco in 1844, but the sultanate retained its independence from France until the twentieth century. Tunis, on the other hand, seemed a natural goal for colonizing activity after 1870 to two of the European powers: to Italy because of the briefness of the sea passage separating the African port from Sicily and because the only European colony in Tunis of any size was the Italian colony, and to France because Tunis bordered Algeria and formed part of the same geographical zone. French diplomats played a small role in the Congress of Berlin in 1878, but they secured one secret victory: Bismarck told them that he would look favourably on an eventual French annexation of Tunis, and even Salisbury promised France freedom of action in Tunis in return for her recognition of the British occupation of Cyprus. Bismarck believed that French activity in North Africa would antagonize both Italy and, ultimately, Britain, and so ensure the continued isolation of France in Europe. His policy was to work in his own time, but in the twentieth century France and Britain were to reach a sensible settlement of their aims in North Africa. When France annexed Tunis in 1881, she certainly antagonized Italy, though the rivalry, like all other rivalries over African issues, stopped short of war.

In the 1830s Egypt under Mehemet Ali became temporarily a strong maritime power in the Mediterranean, and so entered the main stream of European history. The diplomatic crises over Mehemet Ali's dramatic career are discussed elsewhere.[1] The French remained patrons of Egypt after the death of Mehemet Ali, and it was the French who designed and constructed the Suez Canal. But the Canal was used far more by British than French ships, and Britain soon acquired big financial shares in it. In 1876 the Egyptian government, which had remained in effect independent though in theory under the sovereignty of the Ottoman sultan, went bankrupt. The British and French governments decided to set up a dual financial control of the Egyptian government in order to protect the pecuniary interests of British and French shareholders. So started

[1] See above, pp. 155–7.

the sad last chapter of the story of Anglo-French intervention in Egypt, the story which had opened with the glamour and folly of Napoleon's campaign in 1798, and was to close with the miscalculations of the war of 1956.

Africa north of the Sahara was thus already to a great extent under the domination of Europeans by the 1880s. South of the Sahara the pattern was quite different. In the southern part of the great continent European governments showed little interest before the sudden post-1880 imperialist wave. Instead, European expansion was the work of solitary explorers. British governments before the 1870s showed no inclination to annex fresh territories, and in Africa were eager to relinquish the few colonial responsibilities they had acquired rather than to undertake new ones. But the exciting tales of the explorers roused public enthusiasm and prepared the way for the wave of imperialism which was to come.

First of the great explorers was Mungo Park, who in the last years of the eighteenth century had explored the Niger valley until his death by drowning on the Buesa Rapids in 1805. One of the most spectacular exploring achievements of the mid-nineteenth century was that of the German, Heinrich Barth, who from 1849 to 1853 covered immense distances by crossing the Sahara from Tripoli to the Niger and Lake Chad. But the man who captured the imagination of the British was the Scottish missionary, David Livingstone. Leaving England originally in 1840, Livingstone did not return for sixteen years. He went first to serve with the London Missionary Society in Bechuanaland, but soon quarrelled with his Boer colleagues and set out alone on a fantastic series of journeys into the interior of Africa. Between 1841 and 1853 he explored the Zambesi basin; in 1855 he discovered the Mosioatunya or Smoke-sounding Falls, which he renamed—a little insensitively perhaps—the Victoria Falls. Some impression of the public excitement caused by his discoveries, and of the spirit in Britain with regard to Africa, can be gained from the words with which Dr Andrew Buchanan persuaded the University of Glasgow to give Livingstone the honorary degree of LL.D. He had, declared Buchanan, 'made the most important advance ever yet made towards the civilization and Christianization of Africa'.[1] Livingstone had gone alone into the wholly unknown depths of Africa, had treated the Africans as fellow human beings, and had usually won their affection. He returned to Africa in 1858, discovered Lake Nyasa in 1859 and in the late 1860s disappeared in Tanganyika.

If Livingstone wanted to open up central Africa it was only in order

[1] *Livingstone's African Journal 1853–1856*, ed. by I. Schapera, vol. I, p. ix.

to destroy the slave trade and to spread Christianity. He had no thoughts of economic exploitation for its own sake, though he believed that European trade with the African on a fair basis would be for the good of all. The man whom the *New York Herald* in 1870 sent to find Livingstone saw Africa in quite a different light. Henry Morton Stanley, who had grown up in a Welsh workhouse, had stowed away on a ship to New Orleans, and subsequently made a successful career for himself as a journalist in New York. Crossing Africa from Zanzibar, Stanley found Livingstone at Ujiji on Lake Tanganyika in 1871. Livingstone died two years later, but Stanley's career in Africa was only just beginning. Impressed by the potential wealth to be drawn from Africa, Stanley returned to Europe to raise capital. He eventually secured the financial backing of Leopold II of Belgium, who had also been impressed by the possibility of exploiting the wealth of the Congo. Foreseeing a scramble for central Africa, Leopold called an international conference at Brussels in 1876 to draw up regulations for the exploration and colonization of Africa. The International African Association was founded at Brussels, with considerable sums from Leopold's private fortune invested in it, and branches in several countries. The name of the organization could not conceal the fact that it was a business concern run by Leopold himself, and having no connection with the Belgian state. In 1878 the two most ruthless men to interest themselves in Africa—Leopold and Stanley— joined forces, and when Stanley returned to Africa in 1879 it was to establish posts in the Congo Basin as an agent of the International African Association. Quick financial returns rather than the welfare of the natives were from the first the major object. The tragic subsequent history of the Congo owes much to the cynical manner in which it was first dominated by white men.

The early beginnings of the French and British empires in West Africa had already been made by 1830, and small extensions were made before 1880. At the most westerly point of the continent the French had been established in Senegal, on the mouth of the Niger, since the early seventeenth century. In the late 1870s they started to move up the Niger. British footholds existed in 1830 at Sierra Leone, the Gold Coast and Gambia. In 1847 Liberia, where a colony of freed American slaves had been settled, became an independent Republic and was quickly granted diplomatic recognition. The nucleus of what was to be Nigeria was formed in 1861, when the British signed treaties with native chiefs on the Lagos coast, where missionaries had been active for some fifteen years. But in West Africa, as in most other regions of the continent, the period of rapid and sudden colonizing activity was to come only after 1880.

In South Africa, on the other hand, Europeans had been settled for many decades. The Dutch had planted a calling-station at the Cape of Good Hope in 1652 for the benefit of their East Indies trade. The Cape Colony was occupied by the British during the Napoleonic wars, and formally annexed in 1814. For some years a disgruntled Dutch—or Boer—population lived under British rule. The abolition of slavery throughout the British Empire in 1834 still further exasperated the Boers, who believed that they were inadequately compensated for the slave labour of which they were deprived. Their reaction was to move away *en masse* to the north. By the Great Trek of 1835–37 some 10,000 Boer farmers moved across the Orange River, beyond the confines of the British colony. One group settled in what was to be called the Transvaal, and one group in Natal, where they fought a bloody war against the Zulus. Many Boers remained in the Cape Colony, but those who had resorted to what was in effect a tribal migration had reacted to a novel situation in a strangely African manner. When Natal was declared a British colony in 1843, many Boers again trekked to the north, to join their fellow-countrymen across the Vaal River.

Throughout the nineteenth century bitterness and warfare were to be recurring features of South African history—bitterness and occasional warfare between the British and the Boers, and wars of great cruelty between the Europeans and the African Bantu tribes—the Zulus and the Kaffirs. But so far as Europe was concerned these were remote wars fought by small colonial communities. The situation was only partly transformed when, in 1867, diamonds were discovered on the Orange River. The first rich industry in South Africa quickly developed; in 1871—when Bismarck was bringing the German Empire into existence, and Stanley was at last tracking down Livingstone in central Africa—the town of Kimberley was founded, and the British quietly annexed the diamond region, overcoming the vocal resistance of the Boers. Not until 1886 was the South African situation to be more radically transformed by the discovery of gold in the Transvaal. A situation acutely painful in its racial complexities was then to become one of grave crisis and major international concern. Of all the problems of Africa that in the south was to prove the most tragic and the most insoluble.

The total picture of European expansion into Africa, however, has its redeeming features. In the sixteenth, seventeenth and eighteenth centuries the Europeans—Portuguese, Dutch, British and French—had gone to both east and west coasts of Africa to secure slaves in native communities where slavery was already an established institution. In the nineteenth century, when the European nations at last abandoned slavery in their empires and outlawed the slave trade, they went to Africa for other reasons, some good, some bad. They went to Africa to preach the Christian gospel, to map unknown lands, to bring medicine and laws to the African, and to destroy both the slave trade and the cruel rituals of primitive societies; they went also for quick profits, cheap labour and a naive seeking for national prestige. No account of the opening of Africa can be complete unless it contains mention of both the good and the evil the European impact brought with it.

South and Central America

The story of the European impact on the American continents was reaching its last chapters in the nineteenth century. The American impact on Europe was soon to be of greater importance for the world. In the first quarter of the nineteenth century the mixed peoples of the Spanish and Portuguese empires in central and South America secured their independence, leaving in 1825 only the small colonies of British, French and Dutch Guiana to be ruled from across the Atlantic. By the end of 1830 revolutions against Spain, and against the heirs of Spain, had transformed Spanish America into eleven independent states—in South America: Colombia, Ecuador, Venezuela, Peru, Bolivia, Paraguay, Uruguay, Chile and the United Provinces of La Plata, which were to become Argentina; in central America: Mexico and the United Provinces of central America.

All these new states had become republics, but the one immense independent state which was heir to the Portuguese colony of Brazil took the form of a constitutional empire under a branch of the Portuguese dynasty of Braganza which was to survive throughout the period and until the creation of the Republic in 1889. Brazil inherited a degree of political stability from Portugal, in sharp contrast to the political inheritance left by Spain in South America. The movement against Pedro I of Brazil and his forced abdication in 1831 in favour of his five-year-old son, Pedro II, led to a more anarchical period under a regency until 1840, when the young king was proclaimed of age. But the period of the regency at least preserved the institution of the empire itself. The abdication of Pedro I had been important in a more fundamental sense; it had involved the passing of authority in Brazil from an emigrant Portuguese nobility to an American-born aristocracy. Pedro II's long reign was to last out the empire and he himself, an enlightened intellectual, was to live until 1891. The link between Brazil and Europe in the reign of Pedro II was mainly an economic one. British investors, in particular, preferred Brazil to the other South American states, partly because of its comparatively stable régime. In the middle years of the century the London Rothschilds provided considerable sums for the development of Brazil, and especially for the building of the railways. But relations with Britain were darkened by another factor: Brazil, unlike the other South American republics, was slow to abolish slavery—even slower than the U.S.A. Not until 1850 was even the slave trade outlawed in Brazil, and the attempts by British ships to stop the trade in the 1840s led to much friction.

Of the other South American states, Chile, too, had greater political stability than her neighbours, and close trade links with Britain. The rich nitrate industry depended heavily on British capital. Chile received immigrants from Europe, especially during the middle years of the century, when peasants arrived from the impoverished countryside of Germany. Peru and Bolivia, with their large American Indian populations, acute poverty, corrupt government and political instability, were less likely to attract European immigrants or capital.

Of much greater concern to the west European powers were the affairs of the United Provinces of the Rio de la Plata and their port of Buenos Aires, through which much foreign trade passed. In 1829 Juan Manuel de Rosas became governor of Buenos Aires, and in 1835 seized power as dictator of the United Provinces. He remained dictator until 1852, but his arrogant policies ensured that he would be surrounded by enemies, both within the Argentine provinces and outside. His bad treatment of French subjects in Buenos Aires led to a blockade of the city by the French in 1838. The French were allied with Uruguay which Rosas had tried to annex. The British too sympathized with Uruguay, and joined the blockade in 1845. The Anglo-French *entente*, which the governments of Guizot and Peel were in these years trying to cement, was thus operating against Rosas, but less effectively than was expected. The French and British were persuaded to lift the blockade without toppling Rosas from power. When he finally fell in 1852 it was as a result of internal rebellion rather than external pressure. Rosas went into exile in England, where he was allowed to spend the rest of his life in spite of the protests of radical M.P.s who believed that political asylum should be extended to revolutionaries but not to fallen dictators.

The constitution for the Argentine Confederation was drawn up after the fall of Rosas and after further years of fighting was finally accepted by the whole country in 1861. The constitution followed the pattern of that of the U.S.A. rather than any European model. After the troubles of the first half of the century Argentina enjoyed considerable economic development in the 1860s. The railways were built and immigration from Europe started. Again British investment played an important role, a large loan being negotiated with the House of Baring in 1866.

Meanwhile the emergence of a military despotism in neighbouring Paraguay led to the war of 1864–70, a war more terrible perhaps than any other between 1815 and 1914. Pathetically inadequate disputes over border issues encouraged the dictator of Paraguay, Francisco Solano López, to make war on a triple alliance of Argentina, Brazil and Uruguay. In the six years of bitter fighting more than half of the population of Paraguay, and some nine-tenths of her men, were exterminated. From this war of mass slaughter and destruction the European nations stood aside. Napoleon III was at first absorbed by his Mexican adventure and the rest of Europe was fully occupied by the German Question. The days were past when European powers would intervene in South America in time of crisis. The peoples of South America, with all their troubles and their poverty, were at least managing their own affairs.

The people of Mexico were also trying to manage their own affairs, but it was here, in the 1860s, that Napoleon III intervened on a large scale. The country had for many years been the battlefield for a struggle between the forces of the Church and the landowners on one side, and the anti-clericals and the working class on the other. The civil war was won in 1860 by the radical leader, Benito Juarez, who as president inherited a land disorganized and desperately impoverished by the fighting. In 1861 he suspended payments on foreign loans. France, Britain and Spain reacted by signing a treaty in London, by which they agreed to combine efforts for an intervention in Mexico for the specific and only object of securing the financial interests of their subjects. But Napoleon III had more ambitious plans than the British and Spanish governments. A group of Mexican exiles in Europe hoped to establish a monarchy in Mexico, sought the help of a great power, and found it in France. Almonte, an agent of the Mexican clerical party, captured the interest and sympathies of the Empress Eugénie.

Napoleon, pursued as always by the need to please the French Catholics, decided that the civil war in the U.S.A. provided an opportune moment for a major French intervention in Mexico. If a liberal Catholic prince could be established on a Mexican throne, the spread of 'Anglo-American barbarism' in North America could be halted. Napoleon had always been interested in central America: at the time of his imprisonment in Ham he had speculated on the possibility of cutting a canal in Nicaragua to connect the Atlantic and Pacific Oceans. He did not want to colonize Mexico for France, but merely to create a zone of political influence as a base for economic exploitation. The Anglo-Franco-Spanish expedition duly arrived in Mexico and occupied Vera Cruz in December 1861. At this point the French plan of restoration of a monarchy became evident, and both the British and Spanish governments protested that the Treaty of London had made no provision for such a restoration. In April 1862 the British and Spanish forces were withdrawn, leaving Napoleon a free hand, at least so long as the U.S.A. was immobilized by the civil war.

Napoleon had meanwhile settled on his choice for the Mexican throne: the Archduke Maximilian, brother of Francis Joseph. As governor of Lombardy Maximilian had acquired a reputation as a liberal and effective administrator. In June 1863 the French army entered Mexico City, an assembly of notables was called to prepare the way for the monarchy, and eventually in 1864 Maximilian assumed the title of emperor of Mexico. For two years Maximilian reigned in Mexico City, while Juarez maintained his authority both to the north and to the south. As soon as the American Civil War ended, in 1865, the government of the U.S.A. demanded the evacuation of the French army whose presence in Mexico ignored the Monroe Doctrine. In 1866 Napoleon began slowly to bring his troops back to Europe, where the growing strength and successes of Bismarck's Prussia were increasing the necessity of a large French army. By the spring of 1867 the last of Napoleon's troops had left Mexico, and Maximilian found himself without support. Even the Mexican clericals were disillusioned by his policy which had been too moderate for them. Maximilian's empress, the Belgian princess, Charlotte, was in Europe from the summer of 1866 on a desperate mission to secure help. But Napoleon had cut his losses, and could only advise Maximilian to do the same by escaping back to Europe. From a mistaken sense of loyalty to his followers in Mexico, Maximilian resisted to the end. Taken prisoner at Querétaro, he was executed by a firing squad on 19 June 1867. Juarez again became president of a Mexican Republic and for the remaining five years of his life stayed at the head of a reforming government. Even before the final tragedy of Maximilian's death, the Empress Charlotte had been going mad. She never again recovered her sanity. The prestige which Napoleon had lost by the Mexican affair was incalculable, while the absence of one fifth of his army from Europe during the crises of the Polish Revolt in 1863, the Schleswig-Holstein Question in 1864–1865, and the Seven Weeks War in 1866 permanently damaged his position.

A unilateral declaration of policy, having no validity in international law—the Monroe Doctrine—was to become increasingly important throughout the period as a controlling rule for relations between the European nations and the U.S.A. President Monroe's message to Congress in 1823 had contained the famous Doctrine, which stated in its most significant passage that 'the American continents' were 'not to be considered as subjects for future colonization by any European powers'. Intervention of European powers in the Americas would be considered 'the manifestation of an unfriendly disposition towards the United States'. For many years after 1823 the U.S.A. would have been unable to enforce the Monroe Doctrine alone. The British fleet dominated the Atlantic and British policy was therefore more decisive than American policy in discouraging the other European powers from intervention in the New World. The European powers regarded the Monroe Doctrine as an impertinence, and were eager to point out that it did not have the force of an international treaty. But by 1880 the U.S.A. had grown so strong that the Monroe Doctrine had become a very real factor in world affairs.

Early in the period the Monroe Doctrine became relevant in Anglo-American disputes over central America. The possibility of constructing a canal to connect the Atlantic and Pacific Oceans was one which interested both Britain, as the world's greatest sea power, and the U.S.A., especially after her acquisition of the western coastline as a result of the victorious war against Mexico from 1846 to 1848: there was virtually no overland connection between the East and California before the construction of a transcontinental railway in 1869. Besides her West Indian colonies Britain had for some years claimed a protectorate over the Indians of the so-called Mosquito Coast of Nicaragua and Honduras. In 1841 the British occupied the Bay Islands, off the coast of Honduras, and established a naval base farther north, at Belize. During the Mexican-American War of 1846–48 the British occupied the port of San Juan, farther south on the Mosquito Coast, and renamed it Greytown. These three steps, and especially the last, showed with what scant respect the British regarded the Monroe Doctrine in the 1840s. But as soon as the U.S.A. had freed her hands from the Mexican War, she pursued a policy

of strong diplomatic pressure to prevent Britain from dominating potential canal routes.

The two powers reached a compromise in the Clayton-Bulwer Treaty
of 1850. Palmerston had been reluctant, at this moment of European
crisis, to break completely with the U.S.A., and the American government was happy to neutralize central America. By the treaty both
powers agreed that any future canal would be free from the 'exclusive
control' of either of them, and would be a neutral waterway, without
fortifications on its banks, and that neither power would in future extend
her sovereignty into central America. For some years ill-tempered
argument continued as to whether the Clayton-Bulwer Treaty should be
interpreted retroactively and so oblige Britain to evacuate the Mosquito
Coast and Bay Islands. Eventually in 1859 the short-lived Tory government of Lord Derby in London decided that this miserable stretch of
malarial coast was not worth the continued enmity of the U.S.A., and the
territories were divided between Nicaragua and Honduras. In the event
the Panama Canal was not to be built until the twentieth century when
interpretations of the Clayton-Bulwer Treaty again, fifty years later, were
to be disputed.

North America

By the 1850s the U.S.A. was clearly becoming a force to be reckoned
with throughout the American continents, but with the outbreak of the
long and terrible civil war she was to be gravely weakened. From 1861
to 1865 the European powers had no United States of America to deal
with, but in her place two embattled states, the Federal Union of the
North and the Confederate States of the South, which had seceded and
regrouped under President Jefferson Davis. For the time being the
Monroe Doctrine could be forgotten.

When the North established a naval blockade of the South it at once
became clear that the war would have grave economic effects in Europe,
and especially in England. The cotton industries of Europe depended
very heavily for their raw cotton on the southern states of the U.S.A. By
far the largest cotton industry in the world was the one in Lancashire,
and whereas in the eighteenth century Britain had imported most of her
raw cotton from India, by 1860 72 per cent of it came from the southern
states of the U.S.A. The blockade of the South thus led to the acute
cotton famine in Lancashire with the resulting slump, unemployment
and widespread suffering. India was no longer able to provide even a
half of the needs of Lancashire, even when American competition was

removed. The much smaller French cotton industries also suffered, especially the largest of them, in Normandy. But Napoleon III was far more preoccupied with his Mexican project, which required the continuation of the American Civil War, than with the economic situation, which required its ending. The Confederacy hoped for European intervention in its favour, first in the form of pressure to stop the blockade, then in the form of friendly mediation. At least they hoped that the European powers would grant them recognition as an independent country. Jefferson Davis and his colleagues assumed that Britain and France would be bound to come to their aid because of the cotton famine, and the South was for this reason inclined to withhold cotton even when it was possible to break the blockade, which was by no means totally effective.

When Englishmen first heard of the differences between North and South in the U.S.A. they interpreted those differences as being simply a defence of the institution of slavery by the southern states and its rejection by the northern states. Thus *The Times* applauded Lincoln's election in 1861, declaring that he represented 'right' against 'wrong'. But when it became clear that the dispute was more immediately concerned with the right of a state to secede from the Union, opinion in Britain became confused and divided, and *The Times* decided after all that the South had a right to independence if it wanted it. Palmerston, as prime minister in England from 1859 until his death in 1865, had been sceptical of the idealistic nature of Lincoln's aims, and was inclined to sympathize with the struggle of the Confederacy as one for national independence. Palmerston certainly had an ulterior motive in hoping that the split between North and South would become permanent, and would so forever weaken a growing rival to British power, but he had no intention of intervening unless forced to do so by some issue of British prestige or vital concern. Gladstone, mainly because of the condition of Lancashire, tended to sympathize more overtly with the South, while Disraeli made no secret of his sympathy for the North. All Englishmen were aware of one danger: in the event of war against the North the defence of Canada might well prove a difficult proposition.

Both Britain and France, then, upheld a policy of neutrality, but the question of whether diplomatic recognition should be extended to the Confederacy remained. The reluctance of the two powers to recognize the South or even to protest at the blockade meant that their neutrality was working in favour of the North. But the situation appeared likely to change as a result of the *Trent* incident. In November 1861 the

Confederate States sent two agents, Mason and Slidell, aboard a British steamer, the *Trent*, across the Atlantic to negotiate with Britain and France. A Federal warship, the *San Jacinto*, intercepted the *Trent*, and removed Mason and Slidell. The Palmerston government protested strongly against the action, and seemed to threaten war against the North. Lincoln and his secretary of state, Seward, had not authorized the action of the captain of the *San Jacinto*, and were placed in an embarrassing position. Napoleon III united diplomatic efforts with the British, while the press on both sides of the Atlantic reflected or stimulated public rage. The Federal government was prudent enough to release Mason and Slidell, but in the midst of a war could not afford to antagonize their public further, and so were careful not to admit that the *San Jacinto* had acted wrongly in principle.

By the spring of 1862 the French government was more willing to intervene in favour of the South, either by forcefully breaking the blockade or at least giving diplomatic support to the South by mediating. But Palmerston was reluctant to abandon neutrality, in view of the attitude of the British public to slavery, and in spite of the cotton famine, and Napoleon at first would not act without Britain. Finally in January 1863 the French government offered its good offices to both sides, only to have a blunt refusal from the North. For the remainder of the war the likelihood of European intervention became increasingly remote.

In the eyes of many Europeans in the nineteenth century the U.S.A. was a new world to seek in times of trouble, if the fare could be raised for the journey. Most European emigrants to the U.S.A. in the period went from western and central, rather than from eastern or southern Europe. By far the largest single group were, of course, the Irish, but many emigrants came also from Germany, England, France, Switzerland, Scandinavia and the Low Countries. Many of the emigrants from the continental mainland of Europe were Jewish. There were many Jews among the great number of German immigrants, and the much smaller number of Poles were nearly all Jewish. By 1880 comparatively few Italians had arrived: the great Italian emigration was to follow soon after 1880. Over the period 1847–60 Irishmen arriving at New York alone numbered 1,107,034; in the same period 979,575 German-speaking emigrants landed at New York, 315,625 Englishmen, but not more than 100,000 of any other nationality. Irishmen accounted for nearly half the total.[1] Increase in emigration from Britain in the 1830s had already en-

[1] Robert Ernst, *Immigrant Life in New York City 1825–1863* (New York, 1949), p. 188.

couraged the British government to create a permanent emigration department in 1837, but by a coincidence in that year two events in North America—a financial collapse in the U.S.A., and rebellion in Canada—halted emigration westwards for the time being. After America had recovered from the slump of 1837-38 emigration figures quickly rose again reaching the proportions of a flood at the time of the Great Famine in Ireland,[1] and in the few years immediately afterwards. But even before the American Civil War figures had fallen off again during the period of prosperity in western Europe, and when the civil war started emigration somewhat naturally almost completely halted. The emigrants went to escape social distress—especially was this true of the Irish and Germans, many of the latter being artisans whose livelihood was endangered by the growth of large factories at home. Work could be found in America in the ambitious projects of canal, road and railway building. Jews tended to stay in New York or the larger cities, where, in the squalor, filth and vice of the tenements, they could at least enjoy religious freedom.

British North America, too, experienced a large influx of Europeans in the period, though a greater percentage of them came, of course, from the British Isles. Canada in 1830 was still regulated by the Act of 1791 which divided her into two provinces—that of Upper Canada, settled mainly by British colonists, and that of Lower Canada, the ancient French settlement which had been conquered by the British during the Seven Years War. Revolution broke out in both provinces for a complex of reasons, but taking the form of a movement of a majority in the elected assemblies against the imperial government as represented by the two governors. Far from being simply a rising of French settlers against a British authority, the rebellion was in fact more violent in Upper Canada under the popular leader, William Lyon Mackenzie, than in Quebec. The risings were put down, but the British government realized that the root of the grievances would have to be uncovered.

Lord Durham, a distinguished member of the Whig cabinet and a man who had played a prominent role in the fight for the Reform Act of 1832, was sent out as governor of the whole of Canada in 1838. 'Radical Jack', as Durham was called in England, hoped to be able to treat the rebels leniently, but quarrelled over the point with his government and resigned after being in Canada for only four or five months. But his short stay as governor produced a document of immense importance for the future not only of Canada but of the unborn British Commonwealth of

[1] See above, pp. 191-2.

Nations. His *Report on the Affairs of British North America* could be—
and was—applied to the other British colonies which had been settled
by Europeans. It recommended complete home rule by an elected and
responsible home government, with the imperial government retaining
control only over the drawing up of the constitution, foreign affairs, the
regulation of trade and disposal of land. Upper and Lower Canada were
to be integrated into a single colonial state. The Union Act of 1840
incorporated much of the Durham Report, but still did not introduce
responsible government in quite the sense that Durham, who had died
in 1839, had intended. The governor-general was still to remain responsible to the government in London rather than to the assembly in
Canada, though it was clear that he was intended to take into account
the wishes of the Canadian body when formulating his policy.

Fully responsible government was achieved in practice by Durham's
son-in-law, Lord Elgin, who, as governor-general from 1847 to 1853,
created the firm precedent that the executive sought the consent of the
native legislature on all Canadian issues. The two provinces of Nova
Scotia and New Brunswick, which had remained distinct from the province of United Canada, had been granted responsible government in
1847. Twenty years later the British North America Act created a confederation—the Dominion of Canada—out of Nova Scotia, New Brunswick and the two parts of United Canada—Quebec and Ontario. Meanwhile westward expansion over the Rocky Mountains had led to the
establishment of the colony of British Columbia in 1858, and the province of Manitoba was founded in 1870. The Dominion of Canada was
to become one of the largest countries on earth, and in so doing was to
face immense economic problems until she emerged in the twentieth
century as an important independent power. But already by 1880 the
constitutional basis had been firmly laid.

The British radicals, of whom Durham was a distinguished example,
were almost alone among Europeans in having speculated to any extent
on the nature of empire in the early and mid-nineteenth century.
Whether Benthamites, Evangelicals or, like Durham, on the left wing of
the aristocratic Whig group, the English radicals had at least taken time
to moralize about the virtues and dangers either of administering colonies
of European settlers, or of extending rule over other races. But on the
whole the statesmen and politicians of Europe in the period shared certain bland assumptions about imperialism, without troubling to argue a
case explicitly. They assumed without hesitation that their own particular blend of Christian morality, scientific knowledge and technical

proficiency would inevitably benefit other continents, whether those continents were inhabited by primitive and inarticulate tribes, fierce nomadic hunters, or decadent and declining empires. Some statesmen—Disraeli and Bismarck, for example—were, at least until the 1870s, extremely sceptical of the benefits to be gained by European nations themselves from indulging in overseas expansion, but they would certainly not have doubted that the non-European world would gain by increased contact with Europe. Napoleon III and Eugénie even believed that their own version of Catholic civilization would be a blessing for central America and would, by displaying its undoubted superiority, halt the advance of 'Anglo-American materialism'. But again their assumptions were based not upon an accurate knowledge of American society, or even on a careful analysis of de Tocqueville's writings on America, but simply on an inherent sense of pride in French cultural traditions.

The period 1830–80 thus differs from the post-1880 period in this absence of speculation and abstract argument on the theme of imperialism. The later age, the age of Pan-germanism and Cecil Rhodes, felt the need to justify itself in an excited and aggressive manner for spreading European systems and ideas. But in the mid-nineteenth century Europeans sent their armies and their merchants, their missionaries and their industrial products overseas without feeling the need to justify their action. In this, as in everything else, most Europeans of the period demonstrated a sublime self-confidence, a self-confidence which they had rarely felt before, and have never felt since.

XIII

Education, Scholarship and Religion

Respect for education had for long been a characteristic of the ruling classes of Europe, no matter what their political convictions or the constitutional régimes under which they lived. In Austria and Prussia in the age of Metternich a great deal of intellectual energy was lavished on academic work, energy which in Britain or France was spent on political speculation and parliamentary activity. Even in czarist Russia the government and the aristocracy had, since the days of Catherine the Great, regarded scholarship and literature with great reverence. Slowly in the course of the eighteenth-century Enlightenment the belief had emerged that everyone down to the poorest peasant should be provided with an education, at least to the level of literacy. In countries moving towards democracy, where an ever wider section of the population was

BIBLIOGRAPHY. The emergence of systems of universal education and the theorists who influenced them are studied in H. M. Pollard, *Pioneers of Popular Education 1760–1850* (London, 1956). Matthew Arnold's reports to parliamentary commissions are still a source of information and civilized comment on education in western Europe. Of these the most important—those made in 1859 on elementary education in France, Switzerland and Holland—have been published in book form under the title *Democratic Education*, edited by R. H. Soper (Ann Arbor, 1962), vol. II of the *Complete Prose Works of Matthew Arnold*. A detailed study of English education which is still a standard authority is J. W. Adamson, *English Education, 1789–1902* (Cambridge, 1930), while a more recent and very lucid, brief study of the period is contained in H. C. Barnard, *A Short History of English Education, 1760–1944* (London, 1947). A selection of documents and introductory discussion concerning the integration of the educational systems in Italy after 1861 is made by Giuseppe Talamo (editor), *La scuola dalla legge Casati alla inchiesta del 1864* (Milan, 1960), vol. VII of *L'organizzazione dello stato*, under the general direction of Alberto M. Ghisalberti and Alberto Caracciolo. Histories of science and individual sciences are, of course, numerous, though the nineteenth century has, surprisingly, been rather less well served than the seventeenth or eighteenth century. The last two chapters of C. Singer, *A Short History of Scientific Ideas to 1900* (Oxford, 1959) place the period in its securing representation in the political system, it became a matter of vital concern that the people should be educated. Opinion may have differed as to whether literacy should be a requisite for the vote, but most thinking people by the mid-nineteenth century agreed that if the vote had been granted, then at least literacy, and if possible a further stage of education, should quickly follow. The ruling representatives of the people were beginning to feel the need, as Robert Lowe put it, to 'educate their masters'. The nineteenth century is thus important in the history of education because it witnessed the development of systems of state education in most European countries.

In past ages education had been a responsibility of the Churches. Ecclesiastical educators—whether Catholic priests, Protestant ministers or Anglican parsons—had inevitably regarded the teaching process as including the imposition of a hard moral code by a severe discipline, but, in keeping with the growth of state education, in the nineteenth century a different approach developed. Education came to be regarded as having more to do with the enjoyment of life, and less with the avoidance of Hell. Rousseau's *Emile* had first suggested that the pupil should learn from a practical and enjoyable observation of nature, rather than from a severe literary discipline, and Johan Heinrich Pestalozzi (1745–1827) developed the idea far more fully both in theory and practice in Switzerland, early in the nineteenth century. Pestalozzi might almost have claimed to be the first man to make a scientific study of the process of learning and of teaching methods, and to realize that love rather than fear should be the compelling motivation for children at

broad context. W. M. Simon, *European Positivism in the Nineteenth Century* (Ithaca, 1963), is good on Comte and his influence. In 1959 the centenary of the publication of the *Origin of Species* brought forth a crop of writings on Darwin, of which one of the best was Gertrude Himmelfarb, *Darwin and the Darwinian Revolution* (London, 1959). Historians, like other professional groups, have written copiously on themselves and their craft. On this particular period G. P. Gooch, *History and Historians in the Nineteenth Century* (London, 1913) is one of the more thorough, if less pretentious, works. For the history of the Catholic Church there are two very readable works by a liberal Catholic historian, E. E. Y. Hales, *Revolution and Papacy, 1769–1846* (London, 1960) and *Pio Nono* (London, 1954); vol. xx, J. Leflon, *La crise révolutionnaire, 1789–1846* (Paris, 1949) and vol. xxi, R. Aubert, *Le pontificat de Pie IX, 1846–1878* (Paris, 1952), from the massive *Histoire de l'Eglise depuis ses origines jusqu'à nos jours*, edited by Augustin Fliche and Victor Martin, cover the period in some detail. The articles in Section I, 'Science, Religion and the Critical Mind', of *1859: Entering an Age of Crisis*, edited by Philip Appleman, William A. Madden and Michael Wolff (Bloomington, 1959), are all relevant to the main theme of the chapter.

school. Switzerland remained in the vanguard of educational development throughout the nineteenth century.

The French national system of education, like so much else in modern France, had originated in the first years of the reign of Napoleon I. By a single law of 1806 the whole system of universities, secondary and primary schools was planned, to be administered under the authority of the state. During the First Empire only one aspect of the projected system— the *lycées* or boarding schools for a small élite—had come into existence. For primary education Napoleon had fallen back upon special schools run by ancient Catholic orders, but supervised by local government bodies, and under the Restoration governments nothing was done to extend French education. When the July Monarchy came into existence Guizot was made minister of public instruction, and his work in this capacity was the most beneficial of his whole career. He found French elementary education in a deplorable state: an investigation carried out by some five hundred inspectors in 1833 reported that damp and unheated hovels served as schools, while tradesmen or drunken charlatans served as teachers. The contempt with which the priests regarded the lay teachers was only too often justified.

Guizot's solution was the Act of 1833, described by Matthew Arnold in his report to a British parliamentary commission twenty-six years later as 'the root of the present system of primary instruction in France'.[1] It preserved private education alongside state education, by permitting private establishments to operate without recognition by the Ministry of Public Instruction, but it created a sound basis for a public system. Every commune—the small local unit of administration—was to provide a school to which all boys of the area could go without paying a fee. Rich communes were to provide for their schools out of their own funds or taxes; where they could not afford to do so, the department would contribute; and when the department could not raise the money the Ministry of Public Instruction would obtain it by an annual vote in the Chamber. The schools were supervised by local boards containing some priests but a majority of laymen. Under the 1833 Act elementary education expanded considerably in France during the life of the July Monarchy. In the thirteen years from 1834 to 1847 the number of elementary schools for boys in France rose from 33,695 to 43,514. By 1849 over three and a half million children were going to elementary schools.[2]

[1] *Democratic Education*, edited by R. H. Soper (Ann Arbor, 1962), vol. II of the *Complete Prose Works of Matthew Arnold*, p. 67.

[2] *op. cit.*, p. 72.

Much less public money was made available for girls' schools, but in 1836 an ordinance extended the general provisions of the 1833 Act to girls.

The Second Republic in its early, left-wing phase planned a still greater extension of state education, and increased the salaries of the elementary school teachers, who had been desperately underpaid in Louis-Philippe's reign. But the trend was halted after the election of Louis-Napoleon as president. In 1850 a new minister of public instruction, the Catholic conservative, the Vicomte de Falloux, passed an Act which restored the influence of the Church, by making it easier for priests to become teachers, by giving the Church wide supervisory powers over all schools, and allowing many state schools to be replaced by Catholic ones. Falloux did not survive the *coup d'état* of 1851, but French education remained under the régime of the Falloux Act for the greater part of the life of the Second Empire. A change came only in 1863, when Napoleon III appointed as his minister of public instruction the quiet scholar, Victor Duruy. The choice was surprising since Duruy, the son of a worker in the Gobelins tapestry factory, was openly a republican. He started his period of office by writing to Napoleon recommending a really effective national system of elementary education for the final abolition of illiteracy and further expenditure on secondary education, especially by an increase of teachers' salaries. Duruy's proposal was accepted. Elementary education was made compulsory for the first time. In secondary education a wider and more modern curriculum was introduced. The development of secondary education in France had been more consistent than had that of primary education. Nearly 66,000 students were attending state secondary schools in 1866.[1] In the last years of the Second Empire the state spent large sums on increased teachers' salaries, and the creation of good school libraries. The Third Republic thus inherited an educational system which had recently been renovated, and which, since 1833, had, in Matthew Arnold's words, 'given to the lower classes, to the body of the common people, a self-respect, an enlargement of spirit, a consciousness of counting for something in their country's action, which has raised them in the scale of humanity'.[2]

In Prussia education was also organized by the state, through the

---

[1] British Parliamentary Papers. Reports of Commissioners, 1863, vol. VI, *General Reports of Assistant Commissioners Burgh Schools in Scotland, and Secondary Education in Foreign Countries*, p. 465.

[2] Matthew Arnold, *op. cit.*, p. 9.

provincial authorities, early in the nineteenth century. From the date of the creation of a Ministry of Public Instruction and Ecclesiastical Affairs in 1817 Prussian education evolved into an effective and modern system, influenced by the ideas and practice of Pestalozzi. In the German states as a whole a four-cornered fight developed for education, between the secular and ecclesiastical authorities, and the central and local ones. Everywhere in Germany the established Churches retained some control over education. Even in Hesse-Darmstadt, one of the most secular states so far as education was concerned, two out of every three seats on the district school board had to be filled by clergymen, and on the parish school board the chairman was always the local minister. In Würtemberg the same Lutheran establishment governed both the Church and the system of elementary education. In Prussia the state had a greater supervisory function than the Church, and the local officials who administered elementary education were responsible to two ministries— the Ministry of the Interior, and the Ministry of Public Instruction and Ecclesiastical Affairs.

In the mid-nineteenth century elementary education was compulsory for both sexes throughout Germany. In Saxony, Würtemberg, Bavaria and Baden children had to register for state schools. In other parts of Germany parents were obliged by law to send their children to school, but could send them to a private school, if they wished, without registering them under the state system. This was also the practice in Prussia until 1857, when the system was regularized and it was laid down that all children had to be registered for state schools. The rich dodged the 1857 law by paying fees for the district school, but in fact sending their children to any school they liked. If they thus retained a greater freedom of choice than the poor with regard to the education of their children— as the rich did everywhere in Europe—in Prussia they at least contributed to the costs of the national system. The age at which children were obliged by law to start school varied in different parts of Germany from five to eight years. In most German states they had to continue in school for as long as eight years, with the surprising result that in some parts of Germany the school-leaving age was no lower than that considered necessary in many civilized countries a century later.

On paper, then, the educational standards of nineteenth-century Germany appeared very high. But the question of education is always tied to that of social conditions. As child labour in the factories and pauperism were both increasing until about 1860,[1] children in the 1850s

[1] See above, p. 124.

in the industrial areas attended school less regularly. Especially was this the case in Berlin. The authorities in Saxony enforced school attendance more efficiently and evolved a system by which children went to school for part of the day, and worked for the remainder of the day. One teacher was employed for the whole day, teaching children on a shift system. Thus the wretched child of a cotton worker at Chemnitz[1] in 1859 was found to be working in the factory from 6 to 10 a.m., at school from 10 to 12, and in the factory again from 1 p.m. at least until 6 p.m., and often later.

For the education of her upper classes Prussia had, since 1819, evolved a system of secondary schools of high academic calibre. The so-called *Gymnasien*, of which fifty already existed in 1837, taught students aged from sixteen to nineteen. Religious instruction took up a great deal of time in the *Gymnasien*, but apart from this the curriculum was rather more varied than in the state secondary schools in France, and very much more varied than in the English public schools. It included philosophy, history (divided into 'sacred', 'profane' and Prussian), geography, arithmetic and geometry, and students were also taught to draw and play a musical instrument.

In Austria, too, educational standards were high. Auersperg's liberal ministry in 1869 brought in an important educational reform by introducing universal compulsory education for children from the ages of six to fourteen, and the scheme was thoroughly administered by the minister of education, Leopold von Hasner. It was much more advanced than the scheme introduced in England a year later. Since the days of Maria Theresa Austria's record in education had compared well with that of other countries. The Austrian provinces in Italy in the nineteenth century were probably the best educated part of the peninsula. In Lombardy alone in 1856 there were 4,427 elementary schools.[2] From 1856 to 1859 the Archduke Maximilian, who was governor of Lombardo-Venezia, still further extended the system of state schools, working with an Italian adviser on education, Cesare Cantù. In 1850 the Austrian authorities had altered the curricula of the state secondary schools in the Italian provinces by introducing a greater stress on the natural sciences at the expense of the classics and history. Though the motivation for the change was almost certainly political, its academic effects were perhaps in the long run beneficial.

In the kingdom of the Two Sicilies Ferdinand II's government depended increasingly on the priests for education after 1848. Archbishops

---

[1] Now Karl-Marx Stadt.   [2] Talamo, *op. cit.*, p. 14.

and bishops became the sole inspectors of schools and colleges of all kinds, and were alone responsible for nominating teachers to the primary schools. The most important secondary schools were run entirely by religious orders. In the Papal States Leo XII's bull *Quod divina sapientia* had placed education entirely in the hands of a clerical body in 1824, but during Pius IX's reforming phase, from 1846 to 1848, a Ministry of Public Instruction had been created, only to be discarded in 1848. After the pope's restoration in that year all teachers again had to secure a permit from the bishop of the diocese. But if a clerical régime over education was reasserted in 1849, some attempt to improve the schools continued. Private schools were rigidly supervised by the authorities, not only to ensure that they were orthodox in religion and politics, but also to maintain academic standards. However, schools run by religious orders remained the best in the Papal States. Elementary schools provided by the state—itself, of course, a clerical institution— were neglected, the elementary school teachers becoming increasingly impoverished after 1849. In the city of Rome in 1868 only 8,100 children between the ages of seven and fourteen went to school, out of a total of 11,261.[1] Leopold II's government in Tuscany was equally neglectful of elementary education, but provided a sound system of secondary education by a law of 1852, which obliged every commune with more than a thousand inhabitants to build and staff a free secondary school.

In Piedmont a Ministry of Public Instruction had been created in 1847, but, while Piedmontese education was more developed than that of Naples or the Papal States, it was less comprehensive than that of the Austrian provinces. During Cavour's premiership there were appreciable improvements, but it was in the brief period when Cavour was out of office, from July 1859 to January 1860, that the most sweeping measure was introduced, by La Marmora's government. It was not debated in parliament, as the king's government still held dictatorial powers, but was the special responsibility of the minister of public instruction, Count Gabrio Casati. It closely integrated all the schools and universities of Piedmont, and was extended to the rest of the kingdom of Italy in 1860 and 1861.

Although bitterly attacked by sectional and municipal interests, the Casati Law at least laid the foundations for an effective national system of education. The free elementary education which the communes were compelled to provide started a war on illiteracy: an illiteracy percentage of 78 in 1861 was reduced to 72 per cent by 1871. A national inquest on

[1] Talamo, *op. cit.*, p. 10.

education in 1864 revealed that elementary school teachers numbered 33,326, or one for every thirty-six pupils. In secondary education the Casati Law had aimed too high. The *licei*, or grammar schools for children in the last three years of their schooling, did not reach the advanced academic standards for which they had been intended, and the *scuole tecniche*, which concentrated on the sciences and so anticipated later developments elsewhere, were ill-attended. The weakness in Italian education was simply that the population did not use the state system fully. The very poor social conditions in the south made it impossible to enforce compulsory attendance at primary schools, with the result that the secondary schools also were starved of students. In the state secondary schools in 1864, 2,342 teachers were employed to teach only 24,492 children—an extravagantly good staff-student ratio.[1] Italian education had been in so primitive a condition in 1859 that the system which the Piedmontese government had tried to impose on the whole peninsula— a system based on that of France—had proved too ambitious. Even so, the state schools of the united kingdom of Italy were considerably better than any private ones, and a national framework had been designed for future development.

The most advanced educational systems in Europe were found in none of the larger nations but in the small, liberal states of Switzerland, Holland and Belgium. Matthew Arnold reported on the Swiss schools in 1859 that they were 'undoubtedly superior to the French schools', of which he had already written favourably, and that one canton—Aargau —'is said to possess the best primary schools in Europe'.[2] The influence of Pestalozzi had evidently been a very real one. In most Swiss cantons primary education had been made compulsory in the 1830s, and primary schools had been greatly improved and increased in number. As fully developed and civilized as the Swiss educational system was that in the Netherlands. A law of 1806 had laid the basis for state supervision of education, and all foreign observers from then onwards were surprised at the high standards maintained: hygienic schools, well trained teachers, the pupils industrious and happy; there was no corporal punishment and complete religious toleration. When Victor Cousin made a systematic investigation of all Dutch schools in 1836 he had nothing but praise for what he found. Belgium, too, had a strong tradition in education, a tradition inherited both from the Napoleonic and the Dutch periods.

---

[1] British Parliamentary Papers. Reports Commissioners, 1868, vol. VI, *Burgh Schools in Scotland and Secondary Education in Foreign Countries*, p. 529.
[2] *Democratic Education, op. cit.*, p. 31.

British education, on the other hand, suffered from a narrowly aristocratic attitude. If the English upper class was as well educated as that of any other in Europe, the rest of the population remained wretchedly ignorant and neglected. In education as in most other spheres the English have been reluctant to abolish old practices. Thus many types of schools had already accumulated by 1830, and when new educational institutions and ideas were slowly and reluctantly adopted, the old ones continued to exist alongside. For primary education the dame school played an important role throughout the greater part of the period, as it had already done for the previous century. The dame school was simply an establishment where a wholly unqualified woman kept a group of small children quiet while both parents went out to work. There was little pretence at such a school of teaching the children anything, although a small fee was charged, and the children of the poor were thus excluded.

For the children of the poor, charity schools had survived in England since the late seventeenth century. Charity schools were run by the parish, and their teachers—also for the most part without qualifications —had to be members of the Church of England. Their main preoccupation was in the teaching of the catechism, but some children certainly learned to read at charity schools. Sunday schools had originated rather later, during the early stages of the industrial revolution. They were intended particularly for children who worked in factories during the week, but they continued to serve a good purpose after child labour had been ended by legislation. Children at Sunday schools were taught to read in order that they might be able to read the Bible. They were not taught to write nor to do sums, as these talents were not needed for an elementary understanding of the Protestant religion. Employers who had never looked with sympathy on the charity schools which taught during the week, as such schools deprived industry of cheap labour, gave strong encouragement to Sunday schools. In the 1830s about one-and-a-half million children probably attended Sunday schools. No charge was made for the teaching; most teachers were unpaid volunteers; other costs were borne by the authorities of the Church of England and nonconformist groups who ran the schools.

For the greater part of the period the state in England was extremely reluctant to play any part in controlling education. All it was prepared to do for many years was to provide funds for the building of schools by private bodies. A committee of the Privy Council to deal with educational matters was set up in 1839 and placed in the hands of a reliable secretary, the dedicated Dr James Kay, better known by his subsequent titled name, Sir James Kay-Shuttleworth. Kay had high aims for generous state support of education. Most of them had to be abandoned in the face of religious prejudice and *laissez-faire* obsessions, but at least government inspectors were appointed from 1840 to demand certain standards from schools receiving state grants. In 1856 the committee of the Privy Council was replaced by a more workmanlike body, the Department of Education. Not until 1870, however, was anything approaching a national system of primary education created in England. The Education Act of 1870 was passed by Gladstone's liberal government and was the work of the Department of Education under the Quaker, W. E. Forster, a Yorkshire manufacturer with radical ideas. Forster's Act made it possible for the state to set up school boards in those areas inadequately served by primary schools. The boards were to be elected by ratepayers, many of whom had received their parliamentary vote only three years before. The boards could then found schools which they could finance partly from the local rates, partly from government grants, partly from school fees. Elementary education was still not to be free, but it was, at last, to be compulsory for children aged from five to twelve, and the school boards were given authority to accept children free if their parents were too poor to pay.

For Scotland, where the educational system had always retained its independence from that of England, an Education Act was passed in 1872. Private elementary education had on the whole preserved higher standards in Scotland than in England, and the Scottish Act of 1872 went a little further than the English Act of 1870, by making the leaving age thirteen rather than twelve for the public primary schools.

English children of the lower classes were thus at last provided for in 1870, if only to their twelfth year. The children of the upper classes had been given a rough and ready secondary education by the English public school for many decades before 1830. The most ancient and distinguished of the public schools had been founded originally for the teaching of 'grammar'—by which was meant the classics—to the sons of the poor. They had long since been monopolized by the rich for their own children, but the medieval character of physical hardship and a tough communal life remained. Only a few ancient grammar schools had retained their original charitable purpose. On the other hand some newer private schools, which aped the ancient ones, were of a very poor academic quality. A few private schools existed for the daughters of the rich, but their academic ambitions were much lower than those of the boys' schools. The great English public schools had been deteriorating in the half century before 1830. Violence among the boys seems to have been increasing. Brutal floggings by the masters were a symptom of declining discipline. But in 1830 the first steps of reform were being taken in one or two English public schools, and most impressively at Rugby. Dr Thomas Arnold, appointed headmaster in 1827, successfully introduced an atmosphere of Christian morality to Rugby. Though a puritan and a prig, Arnold at least succeeded in getting himself respected by the boys—no small achievement, as anyone who has been to an English public school can realize. More important, he taught the classics in such a way that they embraced history, philosophy and political science, instead of being an arid study in dead languages. More than anyone else, Arnold and his imitators were responsible for altering the character of the English ruling class, by giving them a more tight-lipped sense of moral duty and perhaps by depriving them of the extroverted appetites of a Fox, or even a Palmerston. The academic standards of the public schools, however, certainly improved, until Thomas Arnold's son, Matthew, could write of them in the 1860s as providing the best secondary education in Europe.

But only a tiny percentage of the population could be educated at the public and grammar schools. No universal system of secondary education was started in England before 1880, or indeed, until the twentieth century.

In eastern Europe little was done to remove illiteracy throughout the period, except that in Russia herself educational reform was associated with the establishment of the village *zemstvos* and urban councils or *dumas*.[1] These bodies virtually took over the bulk of the country's elementary education after 1865. At the accession of Alexander II in 1855 there had been less than 8,000 elementary schools in the whole of Russia. By 1880 in European Russia alone the number had reached 23,000, of which about 18,000 were the work of the *zemstvos*. There were only sixteen schools in St Petersburg in 1873, but by 1880, when the city *duma*'s educational expansion programme had taken effect, the number had risen to eighty-eight. The secularization of Russian education by the new local authorities continued the policy of Golovnin, who had already, as minister of education from 1861 to 1866, opposed the claims of the Orthodox Church to a monopoly of primary education.

If the schools of Europe multiplied and improved during the period,

[1] See above, pp. 278 and 291–3.

the universities also experienced a revival. The two great universities in the capitals of France and Prussia both originated in the Napoleonic period and vastly increased their scale from 1830 to 1880. The medieval University of Paris had been abolished by the revolution in 1793. In 1808 Napoleon had founded the imperial 'University of France', the first large secular, state-controlled university of the Christian era in Europe. Not only was it the heart of the provincial state universities of France, but it was also the headquarters of all the state schools of France, the centre of the whole educational system. The minister of public instruction was also the head of the University. The University of Berlin, founded in 1810, was to have an even more impressive academic record in the nineteenth century than the University of Paris. By 1866 Prussia had eight universities, all of them, like those of France, controlled by the state.

In the case of universities there is a greater political danger in any attempt by the state to abuse its controlling powers than in the case of schools. For the greater part of the life of the Second Empire, for example, the French universities were deprived of full liberty by the dictatorship. Fortoul, as minister of public instruction, obliged university teachers to take an oath of loyalty to the régime. Most complied, but those, like Michelet, the historian, who refused, lost their posts. Besides asserting the right to dismiss professors, a right not before claimed by the state, Napoleon III's ministers appointed the governing bodies of the universities. Perhaps even more sinister, though following a precedent set by Napoleon I, was the abolition of the courses in history and philosophy. But from 1867 Duruy, the new minister, did something to re-establish the independence of French universities.

In Italy all universities from the great University of Naples to humbler ones like those of Macerata and Cagliari were centralized under the new state after 1861. For a country with so low a literacy rate the scale of Italian university life was impressive. Already by 1866, before the acquisition of Venezia, there were fifteen universities in Italy. The subjects most commonly read in Italian universities were medicine and law, while in Germany literature and philosophy were more popular. Although the German universities maintained a literary and classical tradition, Germany was rich also in technical institutions. Already in the 1820s Karlsruhe, Dresden and Stuttgart had technical colleges. More than any other west European power Britain was neglecting technical education, in spite, or perhaps because, of her technological and industrial superiority. English schools and universities showed a quaint contempt for technical studies—a contempt for which Britain would pay a heavy price in the decades after 1880.

In universities as in schools the British practice was far more aristocratic than that of the other major countries of western and central Europe. Fairly reliable figures collected by Matthew Arnold in 1866 show that whereas in France one out of 1,900 of the population received some university instruction, one out of 2,200 did in Italy, and one out of 2,600 in Germany and German Austria, in England only one out of 5,800 was admitted. Presumably by 'England' Arnold intended to include Wales, but not Scotland, where the record was higher. The aim of the English university was to produce a small leadership élite, rather than a large professional or cultured class. Both the ancient universities of Oxford and Cambridge, limited to members of the Church of England, had suffered a long decline in the eighteenth century. Though they had continued to produce great scholars and great statesmen, their main function had been to allow rich young men to spend a few years in idleness. For a while Englishmen with a real concern that their sons should be educated sent them to Edinburgh rather than to Oxford or Cambridge. But in the course of the nineteenth century the two ancient English universities widened their curricula, tightened their examination systems and secured higher academic standards. At the same time they approximated more closely, perhaps, than any other universities in Europe, to Newman's ideal of a place where intelligent young men could read and converse at leisure about the important problems of life, without worrying too much about their careers, or the more mundane preoccupations of the world outside.

Meanwhile the University of London had been founded. Jeremy Bentham and a group of radicals had in 1828 sponsored University College as an undenominational establishment concentrating on the natural and social sciences, and medicine. From its very beginning the University of London was like those of Berlin and Paris rather than Oxford and Cambridge in one respect: it was non-residential and therefore cheap. In 1831 the religious balance in London was adjusted by the Anglican foundation of King's College. The two colleges could not yet grant degrees, but in 1836 a charter was granted to the 'University of London' allowing it to award degrees in arts, law and medicine. With the founding of other colleges and through its system of external degrees the University of London was to become an immense civilizing influence, at first throughout England, and then all over the world.

In eastern Europe university education was, of course, on a tiny scale compared with central or western Europe, but in Russia even under Nicholas I the universities expanded a little. The five genuine universities of Russia had only 2,002 students in 1836, but the figure had risen to 3,998 by 1848. The experience of the behaviour of the intellectuals of Europe in 1848, however, alarmed the czar, and the expansion of Russian universities was deliberately halted. The ability to choose their own staff was the extent of the autonomy of universities under Nicholas I, but at the start of Alexander II's reign more academic freedom was allowed. In 1863 Golovnin published a statute by which the universities could elect their own rectors. Inevitably any intellectual speculation in Russia was to acquire a revolutionary flavour.

The universities of Europe, whether controlled by the state, a Church or a private body, remained traditionalist in their curricula in one important respect: they were slow to accept the natural sciences as disciplines deserving equal respect with the classics, philosophy, history, theology or law. Only Berlin, where an Academy of Science had been attached to the university in 1809, and the new University of London, were honourable exceptions to the tendency. Yet the 'scientist', as a species distinct from the philosopher, was emerging in his own right in the first half of the nineteenth century. The identification of a new kind of truth—'positive' or 'scientific' truth—which he believed to be purer and more valid than other kinds of truth, was made by the Frenchman, Auguste Comte (1798–1857). Positive knowledge could be based only on observable phenomena. The fundamental idea of positivism, with its recognition of the value of the scientific method, was revolutionary and profound—too profound to have an immediate political significance. Unlike his early friend and associate, Saint-Simon, Comte influenced political thought only indirectly, through later writers and notably John Stuart Mill and Herbert Spencer.[1] But if Comte's basic idea was at once simple and seminal, the elaborate intellectual system which he constructed upon it was not wholly relevant. He believed that there had been three stages of civilization, the theological or imaginative stage, the metaphysical or abstract stage, and finally the positive or scientific stage. Comte treated scientists almost as a new priesthood, or, as T. H. Huxley later said, Comteism was 'Catholicism minus Christianity'. In a sense positivism was the most ambitious and optimistic of all the creeds founded in the nineteenth century, since Comte believed that human society itself could be investigated and regulated according to scientific

[1] See above, pp. 55–6.

method. He was thus the founder of sociology, which he regarded as the most complex and positive of the sciences.

While Comte was thus canonizing the inductive method, experimental science was, in fact, greatly increasing man's knowledge and control of his environment. Perhaps the most brilliant experimental scientist of the period, Michael Faraday (1791–1867), started his work in the field of chemistry, but then brought great advances in physics also. His discoveries in electromagnetics meant that when he died in 1867 the phenomenon of electricity had become more familiar to a growing body of physicists. The first use made of electricity was in the telegraph, which was developed in the 1850s, but by 1880 no practicable, cheap means of using electrical power for heating or lighting had been discovered. A Scotsman, James Clerk Maxwell (1831–79), continued Faraday's work in electromagnetism and thermodynamics, but Germany was the real home of the experimental scientists in the mid-nineteenth century. Faraday had done much of his work in Germany, in collaboration with Georg Simon Ohm (1787–1854), whose name was to be given to the unit of resistance in electricity. Robert Wilhelm von Bunsen (1811–1899), known to generations of school-children as the inventor of the Bunsen burner, is more important in the history of science for his work with his fellow Prussian physicist, Gustav Kirchhoff (1824–87), in spectrum analysis. Another German, Baron Justus von Liebig (1803–73), made considerable advances in organic chemistry, and applied chemical methods successfully to agriculture, and to the production of meat extracts. Finally, in mathematics, Karl Friedrich Gauss (1777–1855) had made fundamental contributions to integral calculus, and Bernhard Riemann (1826–66) had founded non-Euclidean geometry. In no previous period of comparable length had Germany contributed more to scientific speculation and knowledge.

But it was a Frenchman, Louis Pasteur (1822–95), whose discoveries were more immediately beneficent. Pasteur's studies in microbiology led him to the conviction that diseases are caused by germs, and so started a new era in the treatment of and protection from infections. His discoveries helped in the fight against phylloxera in the 1860s, and he evolved the process of 'pasteurization' for the conservation of wine and milk. In 1865, Joseph Lister, accepting Pasteur's germ theory of disease, used antiseptics in surgery for the first time. He sprayed the operating theatre with carbolic acid, and made surgery a far less hazardous business. After 1870 antiseptics were widely used.

None of these discoveries in physics, chemistry and biology had the same impact upon European society as was felt by Darwin's exposition of the theory of natural selection, a theory reached after long and minute observations in geology, botany and zoology. Charles Darwin had been born into a professional family in 1809. As a schoolboy and then a medical student at Edinburgh he was neither distinguished nor enthusiastic, his main enjoyment being the shooting of snipe. He went to Cambridge with the idea of preparing for the Church, but developed there a mild interest in zoology, botany and geology. Such was the unpromising beginning of a career which was to shatter man's deepest convictions as to the nature and origins of life on earth. In 1831 Darwin sailed as the naturalist on board the little ship *Beagle*, which was to spend five years surveying the coasts of South America. Even while the *Beagle* was crossing the Atlantic, Darwin was introduced to the concept of evolution by reading Charles Lyell's *Principles of Geology*. In the past, geologists had assumed that the structure of the surface of the earth was the result of the divine creation described in *Genesis*, subsequently modified by sudden cataclysms, one of which was the Flood. In recent years geologists had grown increasingly to doubt such an interpretation. Lyell's book, the first volume of which was published in 1830, explicitly, if undramatically, rejected the old theory of cataclysms and replaced it by a description of gradual movements of elevation and depression, movements which were still in progress. Here, then, was evolution in geological terms, though in his second volume of the *Principles of Geology*, published in 1832, Lyell was careful to point out that there was insufficient evidence to accept a theory of evolution so far as life on earth was concerned. It was precisely this evidence that Darwin, during the voyage of the *Beagle* and over the next quarter of a century, slowly accumulated.

Gentle, slow, self-effacing and amiable, Darwin did not conform to the stereotype of genius. For a man who was to create the greatest synthesis of scientific thought of the nineteenth century, he had surprisingly little relish for the construction of general theories. He much preferred the minute observation of plant and animal life, to which he brought an unsurpassed imaginative power and a good prose style, and from which he constructed a formidable body of indisputable fact. But so slow and reluctant was he to build hypotheses on his great collection of data—partly, it is true, because of ill-health—that the theory of natural selection was very nearly presented first to the world by another man. In 1857 Alfred Russell Wallace wrote to Darwin from the East

Indies, enclosing a paper containing a shortened form of something very like the theory of evolution by natural selection upon which Darwin had for so long meditated. From his observations in Malaya, and after not more than three years of speculation, Wallace had reached a position very close to Darwin's. If Darwin was to be recognized as the author of the theory of natural selection, it was partly because his work was the more thorough, but partly also merely because his reputation was already considerable and his contacts with influential scientists much stronger. Wallace, even more modest and generous than Darwin, merely became a disciple of the older man, and has been given, perhaps, less recognition by history than he deserves.

While Darwin was ill and mourning the death of a small daughter, and while Wallace was still in south-east Asia, a joint paper written by the two men was read to the Royal Society in 1858. The old belief that all existing plant and animal species had been separately created after successive cataclysms was shown to be no longer tenable, and the new concept of an evolution by natural selection and gradual adjustment to changing conditions was convincingly presented. Lyell, perhaps the most distinguished scientist in England, had already been convinced by Darwin, but the public for the moment heard only faint echoes of what had happened at the Royal Society. Darwin at once set to work to write a longer paper for the Linnean Society, and it was this second paper which grew into a small book and was published in 1859 under the title, *The Origin of Species*. Now at last the theory of natural selection reached a wider public.

Several theories of evolution had been published in learned journals in the past, and the new school of geologists already considered the earth to have lasted for about 100 million years. The professional world of science was thus partly prepared for Darwin's theory: striking evolutionary processes could more easily be imagined taking place over a period of 100 million years than in the short span which eighteenth-century scientists had imagined to be the life of the earth. But previous theories of evolution had been ignored by the public, and largely disregarded by the ecclesiastical and academic establishment. The *Origin of Species* now seemed to undermine the Judaic and Christian authorities by depicting man as part of the animal world. It offended, too, against Victorian pride and optimism by declaring that man had a common ancestry with some of the less attractive species of monkey. Only later was Darwin's theory to be interpreted as evidence of the grandeur and irrevocability of human progress. Its immediate effect was to start a bitter debate, first in English society, and then throughout Europe.

The German biologist, Ernst Heinrich Haeckel (1834–1919), a professor at the University of Jena, defended and popularized Darwinism in Germany. While still a boy Haeckel had reluctantly abandoned his faith during the intellectual turmoil of 1848. A young man of twenty-five when the *Origin* was published, he seized upon it as the justification for total war against religion and a defence of a materialist doctrine of progress. His approach and tone were far more aggressive than Darwin's and he was bitterly attacked by conservative and religious circles in Germany. Paradoxically his unpopularity was an advantage for Darwinism in Germany. Darwin's own mild and moderate approach to human and religious problems was cited approvingly against Haeckel. In England Darwin and his *alter ego*, T. H. Huxley, continued to refer to the 'Almighty', and even the 'Creator', though they could not believe in a personal God. Huxley gave the chilling definition of the 'Almighty' as 'the sum of the customs of matter'.

The son of a bank manager, Thomas Henry Huxley (1825–95) was a self-educated man in the sense that he had no formal schooling beyond the age of ten, but then read voraciously, until he became one of the best educated of Englishmen. He acquired his agnosticism and his respect for science while still very young, and long before he had heard of Darwin. He drifted into medicine, mainly because his two sisters had married doctors, and quickly distinguished himself. For his work in zoology he was elected a Fellow of the Royal Society at the age of twenty-five. More eloquent and dynamic than Darwin, Huxley started his career with more brilliance and promise. Yet after the publication of the *Origin*, Huxley tended increasingly to drown his own personality and career in the common defence of Darwinism. It was Huxley who coined the word 'agnostic', and fought the major battles in the press and on public platforms. Huxley's most important work, *Evidence of Man's Place in Nature*, published in 1863, and Darwin's own *Descent of Man*, published in 1871, turned the theory of natural selection into an orthodoxy among scientists, if not yet among other public figures. Herbert Spencer attempted to fit social and political development into the general pattern of evolution, and coined the phrase 'survival of the fittest', though Darwin continued to prefer 'natural selection', which was a more serviceable substantive in literary terms. Like George Eliot, John Morley and other Victorian agnostics, Darwin and Huxley were anxious to preserve public morality. Huxley argued at great length to prove that

Darwinism would be a greater ethical force than Christianity had ever been. He was as optimistic and correct in moral tone as any other Victorian:

> The more I know intimately the lives of other men (to say nothing of my own), the more obvious it is to me that the wicked does *not* flourish nor is the righteous punished . . . The ledger of the Almighty is strictly kept, and every one of us has the balance of his operations paid over to him at the end of every minute of his existence.[1]

The search for truth by scientific research could not be so harmful to public morality as the superstitions of the Churches had always been. Huxley had no doubt of the superiority of the scientific method, and confessed privately with cheerful arrogance that his two main pleasures lay in discovering scientific truth and 'jamming' it 'down the throats of fools'.[2]

The increased respect for the scientific method affected every corner of the intellectual life of Europe. Just as experiment was now the way in which the frontiers of physical science were advanced, so in history there was a conviction that progress depended on accurate scholarship. Germany took the lead with the influential series of chronicles and documents called the *Monumenta Germaniae Historica*, started in 1826 and still continuing. And just as Comte foresaw a growth of the 'social sciences' and Marx and Engels believed that their system of political thought was more 'scientific'—and therefore better—than previous systems, so did Leopold von Ranke (1795–1886) believe that he had founded a 'scientific' school of history in Germany. Ranke was the great forerunner of the legion of academic historians who were to base their monographs on thorough research into all the available sources. But Ranke did not limit himself to the claim that the scientific method should be used in historical research. He believed also that the interpretation and presentation of his material could be carried through 'scientifically' and impartially, and that the influence of his own background and convictions could be overcome by a scrupulous pursuit of objective truth. He declared that he was a historian first, and a Christian second. After his *History of the Papacy in the sixteenth and seventeenth century* had been published, he had an uneasy feeling that he had written more favourably of the Catholics than of the Protestants, and so decided that he would have to make the necessary small adjustment in writing his *History of Germany in the Age of Reformation*. He was evidently con-

---

[1] Quoted in William Irvine, *op. cit.*, p. 129.   [2] *ibid.*, p. 306.

founding impartiality with truth, but the fault was a less common one in Ranke's time than today. Most of his contemporaries were writing within a fixed tradition, if they were not overtly supporting a cause. And several of them, perhaps because of this, wrote more brilliantly than he did.

Jacob Burckhardt (1818–97), the Swiss historian who was invited to leave the University of Basel to succeed Ranke in his chair at Berlin, but declined, presented a more vivid and penetrating, if overdrawn, picture of Renaissance Italy, in his *Civilization of the Renaissance in Italy*, than Ranke had done of Reformation Germany. One of the few pessimists of the nineteenth century, Burckhardt had been disillusioned by the events of 1848, and was strongly opposed to ideas of progress and democracy. Although, like Ranke, he warned against the passing of moral judgments in historical writing, he practised the principle less consistently and his somewhat scanty work is for that reason more alive.

The two most influential English historians of the period—Macaulay and Carlyle—thought of their function in society as being quite other than 'scientific', though both were eminently sound in their methods of research. Thomas Babington Macaulay (1800–59) was more concerned with the literary expression of his narrative theme than with any pain-staking pursuit of objective truth. He hoped that his *History of England*, published from 1848 to 1855, would be read by a wide public, that, as he put it, the latest volume of his work would be on the bed-table of every lady of fashion. In this part of his ambition he had astonishing success: his work was one of the great best-sellers of the nineteenth century. Nor did he, like Ranke, underestimate or conceal his own political and religious convictions. His eulogies of the Reformation, the English Parliament, the 1688 Revolution and the 1832 Reform Act made him the high priest of Whiggism, and if the Whig tradition of history was limited in ideological terms and provincial in European terms, it was at least a clear-cut and uninhibited tradition.

Thomas Carlyle (1795–1881), an exact contemporary of Ranke, had an immense influence on most English writers, historical or otherwise, throughout the period. But his influence was a largely negative one, the influence of a prophet who warned against the encroaching evils of the nineteenth century—the evils of industrialism with its moral and physical ugliness, of science without religion, liberalism without strength of character, democracy without discipline or leadership. As a historian no less than as an essayist, Carlyle was always a preacher. In his histories he could handle detailed sources with skill, using them to evoke historical scenes and the atmosphere of the period with great power and conviction. He was perhaps at his best when dealing with a movement for which he felt contempt or his special blend of pity and irony, as in his *French Revolution*, published in 1837. In contrast with this rich canvas of human woe and folly, Carlyle's histories of his heroes, the *Life and Letters of Oliver Cromwell*, 1845, and the *History of Friedrich II*, 1858–65, seem less successful. But all his work is equally out of sympathy with the age of Comte and Darwin, an age which believed in progress and in itself.

Whether it is believed that historians can, or should even try to, be scientific and objective in every phase of their work, it is clear that Ranke succeeded in being less partial than any leading English or French historian of the period. Yet the successor to Ranke's chair at Berlin was Heinrich von Treitschke, whose political views have already been considered,[1] and whose historical work was no less slanted to a narrowly nationalist angle. Treitschke's interpretations could not possibly have been considered impartial, yet even he assumed the trappings and manners of the social scientist.

Meanwhile a Catholic historian in England was considering himself to be a scientist in a rather special sense: Lord Acton (1834–1902) believed that the role of the historian was no less than that of a moral scientist, an arbiter between the figures and movements of history. Having applied the disciplined methods of Ranke in the establishment of fact in history, Acton's historian then had to pass judgment on the great in history, making no allowance for *raison d'état*, or for loyalty to party or creed. On the contrary, the historian would do well to remember that 'power tends to corrupt and absolute power corrupts absolutely', that 'great men are almost always bad men'. However, the drawing up of universal moral standards for scientific application did not prove an easy task, and Acton's only explicit conclusion was that homicide should always be considered a crime. The Catholic historian who attempted to condone the instigation of murder by a renaissance pope, the Protestant historian who excused the instigation of murder by a Tudor monarch were equally at fault. They had reached the point where 'the negation of liberalism and the negation of Catholicism meet and keep high festival, and the end learns to justify the means'. In his role as moralizing judge of the actions of the past, the historian could thus make supreme use of the scientific method, in which Acton believed as fervently as T. H. Huxley. Unlike most Catholic thinkers, Acton felt himself in

[1] Above, pp. 48–50.

sympathy with science, progress, liberalism and the other nineteenth-century values. He believed that the Church must be reconciled with the modern world, and he perhaps exaggerated the ease with which such a reconciliation could be made.

The attitude of the Catholic Church to modern ideas always depends to some extent on the personality of the reigning pope. Pius VII, pope from 1800 to 1823, had at first shown some sympathy for the ideas of 1789, and had resisted Napoleon only over the issue of the Temporal Power. Pius VII believed that the Papal States were absolutely essential for the independence of the Church. His three undistinguished successors, before the election of Pius IX in 1846, inherited his fixed convictions on the Temporal Power, and in all other respects were far more conservative. Gregory XVI, elected pope on the eve of revolution in 1831, had a strong determination to resist any change in his own states, and to condemn any change outside. The papacy of the 1830s was thus not likely to receive with open arms the liberal movement of French Catholics which anticipated the Christian democracy of the twentieth century and was led by the brilliant abbot from Brittany, Felicité-Robert de Lamennais (1782–1854).

Yet the French liberal Catholics were passionately loyal to the papacy. For many decades there had been two conflicting Catholic traditions in France—the Gallican tradition, which recognized the pope's supremacy only in doctrinal and spiritual matters, and demanded that the organization and authority of the French Church should to a great extent be independent of Rome, and the Ultramontane tradition, which recognized the pope's authority in all things. When Napoleon I's Concordat had restored the Catholic hierarchy in France at the start of the century it had done so in an extravagantly Gallican form. Since then Gallicanism had remained on top in France and that very secular monarch Louis-Philippe showed no inclination to make concessions to the Ultramontanes. It was Lamennais who had the daring and imaginative concept of linking a new and purified form of Ultramontanism with the revolutionary traditions of liberty, equality and fraternity. In 1830 he founded L'Avenir, in whose columns he preached that the Church must take up the liberal doctrines of the nineteenth century and learn that the support of the peoples was worth more than the patronage of the princes. Charles de Montalembert, born in England in 1810, the son of an émigré, had learned to respect the liberalism of post-1832 England without ceasing to be a devout Catholic, and enthusiastically supported Lamennais. Another follower was Jean Baptiste Lacordaire, who had abandoned previous ideas of being a lawyer or an actor and had entered the priesthood, fired by Lamennais's vision of the renaissance of a free Catholic Church. The French bishops attacked Lamennais and his followers, and condemned *L'Avenir* for meddling in political and social questions in the name of Catholicism. Against the French bishops Lamennais decided to seek the help of Rome.

The most specific point at issue at that moment was the Polish Revolution, for which *L'Avenir* expressed passionate sympathy and for which Lamennais hoped to obtain the papal blessing. In December 1831 Lamennais, Montalembert and Lacordaire set out for Rome, but not until March 1832 did Gregory XVI grant them an audience. He then saw them for a quarter of an hour, spoke pleasantly on indifferent themes, but made no mention of Poland or the purpose of their mission. In August, after the three men had left Rome, the Papal Encyclical *Mirari Vos*, without mentioning Lamennais, denounced his ideas, singling out as mistaken the principles of freedom of conscience and freedom of the press. Lamennais tried to accept the verdict, and *L'Avenir* did not reappear, but he soon found that he was too heavily committed to the ideas of the French Revolution. He broke completely with the Church and welcomed the revolutions of 1848. He was elected to the assembly and remained a deputy until the *coup d'état* of 1851. Three years later he died, and was buried without Christian rites. The man who had foreseen the alliance with democracy which the Church was to make in the twentieth century had paid the price of anticipating the vagaries of Catholicism by over a century.

Montalembert and Lacordaire had sadly accepted the papal verdict in 1832. They tended to forget their liberalism and to turn their attention to a fight for the rights of the Church in France. They wanted to liberate both the Church and education from control by the Orleanist state. Montalembert had, unlike Lamennais, always regarded himself as an enemy of the ideas of 1789, and a spokesman for the parliamentary and monarchical principles of England. As a member of the House of Peers he had a permanent rostrum for preaching his doctrines, and the purchase of the journal *L'Univers* enabled him to keep alive the idea of a free Church in a free state. But by 1848 no measure limiting state control of education had been passed. After the revolution, Montalembert accepted the Republic, while hoping that the monarchy would be restored, and was elected to the assembly. He worked with Falloux in getting the Education Act of 1850 passed, and remained the most militantly Catholic figure in France.

The loss of Lamennais to the Church was more than counterbalanced in subsequent years by the conversions of prominent Anglicans to Catholicism. In the years following the 1832 Reform Act the Church of England passed through a period of unusual turmoil. The fear was current that the Whigs intended to disestablish the Church. The small group of men who founded the Oxford Movement were not in principle averse to disestablishment—since they themselves disapproved of secular control of the Church of England—but they were alarmed by the thought of the helpless position in which the Church would find itself after disestablishment, and its inevitable accompaniment, disendowment. The Oxford Movement originated at Oriel College in 1833, when a simple but zealous young clergyman, John Keble, had decided that the Anglican Church was in desperate need of spiritual revival and that in particular her ministers had forgotten that they possessed the true and only Apostolic Succession. A yet younger and more self-confident Oriel man, Hurrell Froude, joined forces with Keble, but a Common Room disturbance turned into a national movement only when the two men secured the alliance of a theologian and writer of genius, John Henry Newman (1801–90).

The most tangible aspect of the Oxford Movement was its attempt to stress the Catholic character of the Church of England, and to restore Catholic elements into its creed and ritual, without, of course, coming into communion with the mistaken See of Rome. Newman spread the doctrines of the Oxford Movement across England by editing a publication called *Tracts for the Times*. *Tract 90* declared that the Thirty-nine Articles which contained the basic doctrines of the Church of England had nothing in them directly contradictory to the teaching of the Roman Catholic Church—nothing to prevent the saying of the Mass or belief in Purgatory. Newman had now gone too far for the great majority of Anglicans. *Tract 90* was debated for four years, and then officially condemned by the University of Oxford. A few Anglicans had already followed the apparent logic of the Oxford Movement and entered the Roman Catholic Church, when, in 1845, Newman's own conversion to Rome was announced. It was a blow to the Church of England but much more of a blow to the Oxford Movement, which thereafter died as a positive force, though it survived as a High Church tradition in ritual.

The Catholic Church which Newman entered, and in which he was to be made a cardinal thirty-four long years later, was in 1845 on the eve of big events. The next year Pius IX was elected pope and a brief period of reform in the Papal States started, only to end in the revolution and reaction of 1848 and 1849.[1] The one point on which Pius IX refused to compromise was the Temporal Power, and this was an issue which was never to be solved in the nineteenth century. But in the early 1850s the pope had some notable triumphs. In 1850 he re-established the Catholic hierarchy in England, and in 1854 he proclaimed a dogma which had always been close to his heart—the dogma of the Immaculate Conception. After 1849 Pius IX tired of political issues, and busied himself increasingly in doctrinal matters. The policy of the Papal States was left in the hands of Cardinal Antonelli, the secretary of state, who, with his collection of jewels, illegitimate children, corruption and nepotism, resembled an Italian prelate of the fifteenth rather than the nineteenth century.

Meanwhile the *Risorgimento* was reaching its climax, and the question of the Temporal Power was becoming more insistent. A few liberal Catholics, and especially Acton and his former tutor, the German historian, Dr Ignaz von Döllinger, believed that the pope exaggerated the significance of the Temporal Power. Believing that it was doomed, they felt that there was a great danger in overestimating its necessity for the life of the Catholic Church. But Acton and Döllinger did not seek the personal approval of the pope for their beliefs—as Lamennais had done— since they knew that they would never obtain it. In the 1850s the Ultramontanes, who appealed directly to papal authority over the heads of their own national Catholic Churches, were all on the conservative wing of Catholicism. They wanted no flirtations with liberalism or modern ideas, and above all they wanted to preserve the Temporal Power. In England Acton fought a bitter campaign against the Ultramontanes as editor of a periodical called the *Rambler* from 1858 until 1861, when it was concluded and replaced by a more scholarly quarterly, the *Home and Foreign Review*, which Acton edited for the three years of its life. In 1861 Döllinger delivered in Munich a series of lectures which were subsequently published under the title *Church and Churches*. He proposed that the Temporal Power should be abolished and that the pope should take refuge in Germany for the time being; eventually the pope should be given sovereignty over a piece of territory smaller than the existing Papal States, but large enough to enable him to live freely without being the subject of another state. All such speculations were strongly condemned by the papacy, although the events of 1859 and 1860 had already deprived the pope of large portions of the Papal States.[2]

In 1864, on the tenth anniversary of the proclamation of the dogma

[1] See above, pp. 229–31.   [2] See above, pp. 235–8.

of the Immaculate Conception, Pius IX had a *Syllabus of Errors* published for the benefit of Catholic priests. It could be claimed that there was nothing new in the *Syllabus*: it was simply a compilation of errors already condemned in a large number of allocutions, bulls and encyclicals. But the effect of collecting together all those practices and beliefs of the modern world which the pope had condemned was impressive. Among the eighty propositions declared heretical were those that recommended the surrender of the Temporal Power, that recognized the right of the state to supervise education, that claimed freedom for the press, and, in the final proposition, that stated: 'The Roman Pontiff can and ought to reconcile himself to, and agree with, progress, liberalism, and modern civilization.' Not only, then, were progress and liberalism mistaken concepts, but it was a heresy to suppose that the pope could be reconciled to them. A few liberal Catholics and the whole non-Catholic world were shocked by the *Syllabus Errorum*. Odo Russell, the British representative in Rome, summed up the general feeling in a despatch to his uncle, Earl Russell, then foreign secretary. 'The Syllabus', he wrote, 'has either placed the Pope at the head of a vast ecclesiastical conspiracy against the principles which govern modern society, or it must put the Catholic clergy in opposition to the Vicar of Christ whom they are bound to obey.'[1] But Catholic priests showed no inclination to revolt. Most declared the *Syllabus* to be a useful guide, while the more moderate tried to explain it away.

It was already believed that the pope was preparing to declare the dogma of his own infallibility in *ex cathedra* pronouncements, and in 1867 the pope announced that a General Council of the Church would be convened to consider the question. No general council had been held since the Council of Trent in the sixteenth century. Most German and French bishops were glad of the opportunity of a council, but hoped that the dogma of papal infallibility would not result. Döllinger and other German ecclesiastical historians and theologians believed that the power of the papacy within the Church should be reduced rather than increased. The Council met in December 1869, in a transept of St Peter's, and did not break up until the summer of 1870. A considerable minority of bishops opposed the proclamation of the dogma, some of them because they believed that it was against the traditional teachings of the Church, others because they felt that the time was inopportune, even though the dogma itself was valid. But most of the minority preferred not to vote against the known wishes of Pius IX: all but two of them had left when

---

[1] *The Roman Question*, ed. Noel Blakiston (London, 1962), p. 303.

the vote was finally taken. The Pope was thus declared to be infallible in all *ex cathedra* utterances. In the intellectual anarchy of the nineteenth century it could be said in defence of the dogma that it gave to one large section of European society a sure spiritual authority. An elderly and distinguished Protestant—Guizot—used this argument in congratulating the pope on his achievement. But the greatest of Catholic scholars were convinced that the dogma ran counter to the spirit and history of the Church. Acton published an open letter to an anonymous German bishop, declaring that the Council had been a 'conspiracy against divine truth and law' and that the dogma was a 'soul-destroying error'.

Meanwhile the Temporal Power had come to an end with the occupation of Rome by the Italian army only two months after the end of the Council. The long-term results of the dramatic events which took place in Rome in 1870 were paradoxical: the proclamation of papal infallibility did not greatly alter the position of the pope in the Catholic world, while the loss of the Temporal Power greatly increased his spiritual authority.

After the Vatican Council Döllinger persisted in refusing to accept the new dogma; he wrote to the Archbishop of Munich firmly explaining his position, and three weeks later was excommunicated. Acton's resistance was no less firm, but the English historian took pains to indicate that he wished to remain in communion with the Church. He therefore suffered no greater penalty than that of having one of his articles denouncing the Council placed on the Index. Döllinger and other Germans who had been excommunicated—among then a few priests—reacted by publishing a statement, which they called the *Munich Declaration of Whitsuntide, 1871*, declaring in effect that they were the true repositories of the old Catholic faith and that the work of the Vatican Council had no legality. Thus began the Old Catholic movement, a movement in open schism with Rome. It encouraged Bismarck to embark upon his own war with the Catholic Church, the *Kulturkampf*, a struggle which did something to restore respect for Pius IX throughout Europe.[1] The old pope died in 1878, after a reign of thirty-two years. His successor, Leo XIII, was a more politic man with a stronger sense of the human needs of the nineteenth century. Bismarck seized the opportunity of ending the *Kulturkampf*, but a new struggle between Church and state was about to begin in the Third French Republic.

Elsewhere in Europe relations between Church and state were more peaceful. In Austria after the revolutions of 1848 and under the young

[1] For an account of the *Kulturkampf*, see above, pp. 223–4.

emperor, Francis Joseph, the Catholic Church gained a very strong position. The Concordat of 1855 gave the pope the right to correspond with Catholics in Austria and to publish his pronouncements without any sanction from the state, and all Catholic education was removed entirely from the control of the state and placed under the exclusive jurisdiction of the bishops. The Concordat in effect meant a reversal of traditional Austrian policy since the days of Joseph II, who had dramatically asserted the supremacy of the state over the Church.

In Russia the Orthodox Church was closely identified with the state, and exerted a strongly illiberal influence on the czar. In the principalities, too, the Orthodox Church had stood for legitimacy and the *status quo*, even when these included the sovereignty of a Muslim monarch, the Ottoman sultan. Elsewhere in European Turkey, however, the Orthodox Church was linked with nationalist movements, as it had been originally during the Greek Revolution. In Europe as a whole, and if the whole period of fifty years is considered, it is evident that there was an increasing separation of Church and state. Apart from some notable exceptions and occasional reactions, the predominant theme was the emergence of a strong secular state.

XIV

Literature and the Arts

European culture in the half-century after 1830 lay in the backwash of the Romantic movement. In poetry and music greater achievements had been made in the half-century before 1830, and in painting, sculpture and architecture much greater achievements were to be made in the half-century after 1880. In only one art form—the novel—was the nineteenth century supreme. Europeans of the mid-nineteenth century expressed themselves most happily in prose; they preferred, even in their poetry, the explicit statement to the poetic image; in their music, painting and sculpture they were often self-conscious and literary; their architecture usually showed an academic fascination for the styles of past ages. Only in the novel did the period prove to be—simultaneously in several parts of Europe—triumphantly creative.

BIBLIOGRAPHY. Histories of literatures are, of course, very numerous, and vary from the brief textbook written with some specific examination in mind to the huge compilations in many volumes and by many hands. Of the latter type, for French literature there is the *Histoire de la littérature française*, edited by J. Calvet, two volumes of which are relevant for the period: Pierre Moreau, *Le Romantisme* (Paris, 1932) and René Dumesnil, *Le Réalisme et le naturalisme* (Paris, 1955). Useful for quicker reference is Sir Henry Paul Harvey and Janet Ewing Heseltine, *The Oxford Companion to French Literature* (Oxford, 1959). For Italian literature there are the two volumes by Guido Mazzoni, *L'ottocento*, of the massive *Storia letteraria d'Italia* (Milan, 1934), or the rather more recent *Storia della letteratura italiana*, edited by Francesco Flora (Verona, 1948); vol. IV deals with the nineteenth century. A good survey of the English literature of the period is provided by the last three chapters of the famous work by Emile Legouis and Louis Cazamian, *A History of English Literature* (translation by W. D. MacInnes, London, 1926), while *From Dickens to Hardy*, edited by Boris Ford (London, 1958), vol. 6 of the *Pelican Guide to English Literature*, is an excellent collection of essays on the principal figures. W. E. Houghton, *The Victorian Frame of Mind 1830–1870* (Yale, 1957) is an important American work of mature scholarship. For German literature Roy Pascal, *The German Novel* (Manchester, 1956) is lucid and balanced. Janko Lavrin, *An Introduction to the Russian Novel* (London, 1942) is a sound survey, while Prince P. A. Kropotkin,

The most important phase of the Romantic movement in European poetry was already over by 1830. It had produced some of the most profound and richly introspective works ever written. The Romantic poets had escaped from the new industrial landscape and the wars of the Napoleonic period into their own souls; the novelists, on the other hand, had escaped to earlier ages, and had invented the historical novel. Sir Walter Scott (1771-1832) had found that a large reading public was eager to share in his escape. Scott himself died in the year of the Reform Act, but his novels continued to be widely read throughout the period, and not only in the British Isles. When they were written they helped their readers to forget the raw and ominous atmosphere of the years which followed the peace of 1815, but they paled to the complexion of mere adventure stories beside another historical novel written in the 1820s—Alessandro Manzoni's *I Promessi Sposi*. First published in three volumes between 1825 and 1827, *I Promessi Sposi* appeared in the definitive edition in which it has since been read only in 1840. Like all literary masterpieces it at once purified and enriched the language in which it was written. No other Italian novel of the nineteenth century was to reach Manzoni's single achievement. Other historical novelists— like the Tuscan, Ettore Guerrazzi (1804-73)—were immensely popular in their day, though their works—like Guerrazzi's *L'Assedio di Firenze*, published in 1836—often touched dismal depths of melodrama. Before

Russian Literature: Ideals and Realities (London, 1905) is an interesting commentary. For an introduction to the history of the music of the period the relevant portions of Alfred Einstein, *Geschichte der Musik* (Leipzig and Berlin, 1918, English translation by Eric Blom, London, 1938) is still as good as anything, while short biographies of the principal composers are provided by vol. 2, *After Beethoven to Wagner* (London, 1950), of *The Music Masters*, edited by A. L. Bacharach. The art of the period is studied in a full perspective in an American work, E. P. Richardson, *The Way of Western Art, 1776-1914* (Harvard, 1939), and in rather more detail by the Austrian, Fritz Novotny, *Painting and Sculpture in Europe 1780-1880* (Pelican History of Art, London, 1960), a book which, how-ever, excludes England from Europe, and pays disproportionate attention to German art. Possibly no group of artists have had more volumes of reproduc-tions lavished upon them than the Impressionists. The accompanying critical texts of these volumes are usually as worthless as the reproductions, but there are several notable exceptions. Among the best English publications are those from the Phaidon Press; *The French Impressionists* (London, 1952), with an introductory essay by Clive Bell, is an attractive example. As regards the archi-tecture of the period, Sir Kenneth Clark, *The Gothic Revival* (London, revised edition, 1949) is a delightful commentary on that phenomenon in England, while J. M. and Brian Chapman, *The Life and Times of Baron Haussmann* (London, 1957) gives a good account of Haussmann's rebuilding of Paris.

distinguishing himself as a political figure in the *Risorgimento*, Massimo d'Azeglio had been successful as a historical novelist, but to modern tastes his sensitive and urbane Memoirs, written in the last years of his life, are worth far more than his popular novels, *Ettore Fieramosca*, published in 1833, or *Niccolò dei Lapi*, published in 1841.

The sad fact must be admitted that no great literary renaissance accompanied the Italian *Risorgimento*, and the same is true of the unification of Germany. The quiet, conversational narrative of the novels of Wilhelm Raabe (1831–1910) is hardly the literary reflection of a great age. There was no German novelist with the universal significance of Manzoni, Tolstoy or Flaubert, but the reputation of one novelist of the period has experienced a revival. Theodore Fontane (1819–98), at first a chemist and then a journalist, took to the writing of poetry and novels only at the age of forty. The acute sensibility and psychological perception of his work have been fully recognized only in recent years. But Fontane's most successful novels came in the 1880s, and although he had shown enthusiasm for the German nationalist movement in his younger days, none of it entered his work.

Reaching a wider European public than Manzoni, Alexandre Dumas the elder (1803–70) also wrote historical romantic novels, but his *Les Trois Mousquetaires* (1844) and *Le Comte de Monte-Cristo* (1845) were eventually to find their proper level as children's classics. Dumas believed that his novels were not more important than his plays, which are now rarely performed, and the same is true of Victor Hugo (1802–1885). Perhaps the most comic feature of the French Romantics is their belief that their drama was of revolutionary significance. But Hugo's irrepressible imagination could not be limited to one literary form, it poured itself out in verse as well as novels and plays. The verbosity of the age is as clearly exemplified by the flood of words from the pen of Hugo as in the poetry of Tennyson or the speeches of Gladstone. Hugo's last and greatest novel, *Les Misérables*, written in 1862 in exile in the Channel Islands, emphatically displays all his qualities: his facility of verbal expression, his fluent power of narration, his lack of humour and his shallowness in the analysis of motive and character.

A contrast with Stendhal illustrates the superficial nature of Hugo's understanding of human motivation. Marie-Henri Beyle (1783–1842), who wrote under the pseudonym of 'Stendhal', was to have a greater influence on subsequent trends in French literature than Hugo, who represented at once the culmination and the conclusion of the Romantic movement in France. Stendhal anticipated a tradition in later French

writers—apparent equally in Balzac, Flaubert, Zola and Maupassant—
of an ironic approach to life: the author remains detached from his
work; he excludes not only sentimentality, but even any overt expression
of sympathy for his characters, even in the case of a character who is
autobiographical in origins. The non-involvement and mocking tone,
which became almost a convention in the best French novels after
Hugo, had few parallels in the great Russian or English novels. In
France it had the salutary effect of purging prose of rhetoric, and narrative of sentimentality; it substituted a cruel realism for the escapism of
the Romantics. Stendhal had too much psychological insight to take sides
between the protagonists of his novels; he analysed them each to the
point at which it was difficult any longer to judge them. In the same way
his novels were politically neutral. Although they dealt not with a remote
past, but with the world of his own youth, they gently satirized both the
nineteenth-century heirs of the *ancien régime*—the conservatives, priests
and petty princes—and also the self-styled 'liberals' and revolutionaries.
He poked fun at the escapism of the historical novelists. In the *Chartreuse de Parme* the hero, Fabrice del Ponzo, having compromised himself
with the authorities of post-1815 Italy by playing a part—however
ignominious—on the French side in the Waterloo campaign, is given
specific advice on how to clear his name: among other steps he must,
he is told, show a distaste for reading, especially anything written since
1720, except the novels of Walter Scott. Stendhal differed from his
Romantic contemporaries also in his contempt for rhetoric, for the
striking of postures, for what he called *l'emphase*, and for this reason both
heroes of his two great novels, *Le Rouge et le Noir* (1830) and *La Chartreuse de Parme* (1839), are essentially unheroic and have endearing
failings. Yet in other respects Stendhal was clearly part of the Romantic
movement, and his essay on *Racine and Shakespeare* was intended as a
manifesto of romanticism. In his respect for Shakespeare he was like
his contemporaries. Manzoni wrote more about Shakespeare than about
Dante, and Dumas said that, after God, Shakespeare had created most.

In England, William Makepeace Thackeray (1811–63) also professed
contempt for rhetoric and melodrama and deliberately wrote for a
modest middle class rather than for the rich or decadent aristocracy,
whom he satirized, or the gin-drinking lower orders. So unlike Stendhal
in many respects, Thackeray had one point of contact with him: both—
the Frenchman in *La Chartreuse de Parme* and the Englishman in
Vanity Fair (1848)—described the Waterloo campaign through the eyes
of individual soldiers who experienced only the utter confusion of

warfare. Both accounts have the note of complete authenticity which became increasingly the aim of the realist school of novelists, and which reached a culminating triumph in another battle scene—in Tolstoy's account of Borodino in *War and Peace*, where the horror of war is shown not as epic tragedy but as insane chaos.

A more impressive realist reaction against romanticism was the work of Honoré de Balzac (1799–1850). Unlike so many figures dealt with in this chapter, Balzac from the first was determined to earn a living from literature. Born at Tours, he went to a grim school, where he led a monastic life. Later, in his (and the century's) early twenties he imposed a similar régime on himself, by living in a garret in Paris on very slender means, rising at midnight to write and denying himself the pleasures enjoyed by his contemporaries. He soon discovered in himself an almost telepathic ability: by following workers around Paris he found that he could identify himself completely with them, to the point of feeling their heavy shoes on his own feet, and knowing their motivations and pre-occupations. His break with the Romantic tradition was thus not so much an intellectual decision as the discovery of a unique talent. He was struck by the fact that previous civilizations had left records of their political or military history, but little account of their social history, of the behaviour and thoughts of the bulk of the population. He decided that he would provide this account for nineteenth-century France, and the rich and wonderful series of novels which he called *La Comédie Humaine* was the result. Typical of Balzac's desire to reflect life with complete fidelity was the central role played in his novels by money. Writing under the July Monarchy Balzac knew only too well that hard cash was more omnipresent in life than the old themes of the Romantics—love, glory and death. Though he was himself a generous man, he could depict the obsessions of the miser, in *Eugénie Grandet* (1833), as convincingly as Molière had done. While Hugo wrote with too much facility, Balzac wrote with immense pain, endlessly correcting and polishing his paragraphs. He is a central figure of the age in the essentially prosaic nature of his genius. Like many of the realist novelists he had no feeling for poetry. Not only were his own attempts to write verse disastrous, but he had little critical sense as regards the poetry of others, and ultimately came to regard it as a primitive and artificial medium. He had no great respect for his immediate literary predecessors. If his work marked a break with the grand manner of the Romantics, he had no more respect for classical traditions. Gautier described how, on a visit to the Louvre, he failed to extract from Balzac any enthusiasm for the Vénus de Milo.

On the contrary, Balzac was more interested in a young Parisian woman —in the details of her dress and the movements of her facial expressions—than in the Venus. Balzac was pleased to observe that the young woman shared his distaste for the heavy waist of the goddess.

Balzac's realism anticipated Flaubert, Zola and, in painting, the Impressionists. Gustave Flaubert (1821–80) placed at the disposal of the novel the same meticulous observation of life and the same merciless honesty in depicting its pettinesses as Balzac did. But Flaubert was more concerned with the precise, photographic representation of people and objects and carried around permanently with him a notebook for the immediate recording of any detail which could be used in his novels. His greatest result, *Madame Bovary* (1857), was one of the three or four most perfect novels of the century, and Emma Bovary herself one of the most pathetic creations in the whole of literature. His prosecution in 1859 on the grounds that the novel was immoral was typical of the philistinism of the authorities of the Second Empire in its earlier and more dictatorial phase. Flaubert never repeated the achievement of *Madame Bovary*. *Salammbô* (1862) applied the same meticulous observation of scenery to a historical novel, which emerged as an indigestible epic, having all too much in common with the scripts of twentieth-century film extravaganzas.

The realistic novel reached its richest fulfilment in the work of Count Leo Tolstoy (1828–1910). In Russia the censorship was actually a stimulant to the production of the great novels, since they could express political and social ideas in a manner which appeared less revolutionary than straightforward political journalism would have done. Thus Nicolai Gogol, a history professor who turned to literature, could publish the most savage of all literary satires in his novel, *Dead Souls*, in 1842, while Ivan Turgenev could recommend the emancipation of the serfs in his *A Sportsman's Sketches* (1847–52), which was to be an influence on Alexander II. With Tolstoy the social message, important and insistent though it was, was transcended by the novelist's psychological insight and a creative power which far surpassed that of his predecessors among Russian novelists. A nobleman who had served as an officer in the Crimean War, and subsequently founded a school for children and adults, Tolstoy was deeply involved in the struggles and bitter problems of the Russia of his day. His involvement, expressed by his supreme literary craftsmanship, carried the realistic novel in *War and Peace* (1866) and *Anna Karenina* (1877) to a point of development beyond which it could go only with difficulty. Where the realism of Flaubert had been conveyed with a note of often cruel detachment, Tolstoy's novels were imbued with sympathy and benevolence, though never with sentimentality nor romanticism. After 1880 Tolstoy himself was to abandon the classical realism of his two greatest novels and to express a more mystical approach to life, as the result of a sudden and shattering crisis of conscience.

Tolstoy's near contemporary, Fedor Dostoevski (1821–81), has been contrasted with him by countless critics. If Tolstoy was deeply involved in the social problems of Russia, Dostoevski was a tragic victim of the cruelty of the czarist régime, and his art is a distilling from his own suffering. Condemned to death in 1849 for his connections with revolutionary circles in St Petersburg, Dostoevski was pardoned only at the last moment when he was already a broken man. Deportation to Siberia, exile and epilepsy completed his martyrdom. Consequently Dostoevski's finest novels, *Crime and Punishment* (1866), *The Idiot* (1868) and *The Brothers Karamazov* (1880), are written with a subjectivity more intense than that of any other novelist of the period. While the reader of *War and Peace* may feel that the characters are as real and familiar to him as any of his own friends or relatives, the reader of Dostoevski's novels comes to know the characters as he knows only himself. The realistic novel thus received an added dimension, and while on a superficial level it may seem a valid exercise of literary criticism to compare *The Idiot* with *Anna Karenina*, at a deeper level Dostoevski's novel is more comparable—however unfavourably—with *Hamlet*, *Faust*, or St Luke's Gospel.

In western Europe novels of social protest never reached this peak of literary achievement. The most they could do was to make careful observations of evil social conditions, sometimes in a philanthropic, sometimes in a satirical, spirit. The picture of English urban poverty given by Mrs Elizabeth Gaskell (1810–65) has already been noticed,[1] but it is significant that her most successful work, *Cranford*, which has the astringency almost of Jane Austen, is a study of the provincial middle class, while *Mary Barton* (1848), her epic novel of the Lancashire working class, combines a convincing realism with the sentimentalism of Dickens at his worst. If in France the two great realist novelists, Balzac and Flaubert, had been objective and satirical in their observation of society, a later generation of realists, of whom the most successful was Emile Zola (1840–92), were more emotionally identified with their human material. In the twenty novels which Zola wrote in the last twenty years

[1] See above, pp. 113–14.

of his life, he did for the Second Empire very much what Balzac had done for the July Monarchy, in that he gave a full and authentic picture of society. But while Balzac painted society with amused relish and penetrating wit, Zola's novels suggest a carefully controlled and never explicit anger. *L'Assommoir* (1877), the terrible chronicle of the *envachis-sement* of Gervaise, provided a grim indictment of the drunken society of the Parisian working class without a word of overt social criticism.

In England the most successful novelist of the period, Charles Dickens (1812–70), was, of course, concerned with social questions, though never with much consistency nor critical maturity. Dickens was less concerned with the industrial workers than with the lower middle class—clerks, or people, like domestic servants, who were in fact members of the working class yet acquired the social prejudices of the middle class by their close physical proximity to it. Dickens shows less sympathy for the ordinary worker than Zola or Mrs Gaskell, or even than Disraeli in *Sybil*. Yet if there is no proletarian zeal in Dickens there is certainly social protest of a kind. If he has little awareness of the lives of labourers he has great feeling for the lives of the poor, and especially for the children of the poor. As the son of a clerk who had been imprisoned for debt, Dickens knew poverty in his own childhood. But he was essentially an optimist, who was at his best in his humorous passages, and above all in *The Pickwick Papers*, which was serialized in 1836 and 1837, and in the long American novel, *Martin Chuzzlewit* (1843–44). His social satire was effective when, as in *Oliver Twist*, written in 1836 and 1837 at the same time as Pickwick, and the much later *Bleak House* (1852–53), it was sufficiently divorced from sentimentality. Many of his characters are two dimensional or amusing caricatures; some of his upper-middle-class characters are ludicrously lifeless; but at least two of his heroes—*David Copperfield* (1849–50) and Pip in *Great Expectations* (1860–61)—are as real and convincing as anyone in Tolstoy or Flaubert. Characteristic of his age and unhappy in its immense influence on later English romantic novelists was the embarrassing sentimentalism of Dickens—the senti-mentalism which marred *Dombey and Son* (1846–48), and which ruined *The Old Curiosity Shop* (1840–41), *A Christmas Carol* (1840–41) and *A Tale of Two Cities* (1859).

One aspect of the sentimentalism of the nineteenth-century novel is the virtuous, chaste and selfless heroine. Unhappily typical of the species is Lucia, the least convincing character in *I Promessi Sposi*, many of the heroines of Dickens, of course, and of the French romantic novels. Amelia Sedley in *Vanity Fair* would again be typical, were it not that

Thackeray himself scarcely seems to believe in her, and certainly has more sympathy for the amoral, brilliant and vital Becky Sharp. Women novelists, as would be expected, were less guilty of this particular fault. Thus when George Eliot (1819–80), perhaps the most accomplished woman novelist of the period in Europe, created an innocent and altruistic heroine in Dinah Shore for *Adam Bede* (1859), she felt that Dinah could be made credible only by being also a Methodist preacher. Nor, in spite of the author's own inexperience, is there anything sentimental in the heroine of Emily Brontë's *Wuthering Heights* (1847). The native passion and penetrating psychological insight of Emily Brontë's solitary masterpiece was to be repeated by a much more sophisticated novelist at the end of the period—by Thomas Hardy, whose *Far from the Madding Crowd* was published in 1874, and whose *Return of the Native* was published in 1878. With Hardy the realistic novel had taken a further twist in its attempt to analyse the human predicament.

The humour of the period—the humour of Balzac and of Dickens, and of the delightful, yet sad, Russian novel, *Oblomov*, by Ivan Goncharov (1812–91)—is more immediate in its appeal today than anything of earlier ages. Another literary form which was to suit the tastes of the twentieth century was evolved in the mid-nineteenth—the nonsense verse, or the nonsense story, exemplified in England by the limericks of Edward Lear (1812–88), and in Italy by the *Partenza del crociato* and other verses, by Giovanni Visconti-Venosta (1831–1906). Charles Lutwidge Dodgson (1832–98), writing under the name of Lewis Carroll, created the delightful *Alice's Adventures in Wonderland* in 1865, and *Through the Looking Glass* in 1871. In a surprisingly short time Alice was to become a central part of the Englishman's literary heritage, and to replace Cicero as a constant source of quotation in parliament.

One literary form, the short story, had barely come into its own by 1880. Prosper Mérimée (1803–70) had written the raw little sketch *Mateo Falcone* as early as 1829, and in some of the great novels there were embedded what were virtually short stories. The famous nun's story in *I Promessi Sposi* can certainly stand alone as a small gem of narrative, and the story of the bishop's candlesticks in *Les Misérables*, shamelessly sentimental as it is, has a unity of its own. Most of the Russian novelists also wrote shorter pieces of narrative, but these are usually brief sketches or latterday fables rather than complete short stories in the modern sense. Only with Guy de Maupassant (1850–93) was the modern form of the short story perfected, and his greatest works were not written until the 1880s.

The French Romantic writers of the July Monarchy believed that they were bringing a renaissance to the theatre. Hugo's *Hernani*, first performed in Paris in 1830, was execrated by the classicists and extravagantly lauded by the Romantics. Its presentation caused a minor riot. In retrospect it is difficult to see why so bad a play could have been regarded as being so significant. In drama the period 1830–80 is undeniably a bleak one. Not only is there no Shakespeare and no Racine; there is no Goldoni and no Sheridan. The poverty of good plays was partly— paradoxically—because greater crowds attended the theatre, and temporarily lowered tastes by a demand for sentimentality and vulgarity. Partly it was because brilliant writers who in earlier ages would have written for the theatre, in the nineteenth century wrote novels. If Balzac had lived a century or two earlier, he would probably have written satirical plays as successful as Molière's. Only towards the end of the period did the Norwegian dramatist, Henrik Ibsen (1826–1906), repudiate the sentimentalism of the Romantics. Ibsen's drama was mainly occupied with social and psychological problems, explicitly posed and discussed. His main theme was the struggle between the individual searching for truth, and the hypocrisy and conformism of bourgeois society. But his analysis of the struggle was by no means a straightforward or didactic one, and in the *Wild Duck* (1884) he seems almost to be on the side of hypocritical, conformist society. But although Ibsen had written his great poetic play *Peer Gynt* as early as 1867, his major and more characteristic works appeared in the 1880s and 1890s.

To say of an age that it is prosaic rather than poetic may seem a somewhat dangerous generalization, yet it is clear that the period 1830 to 1880 had no poets who were the equal of the great figures of the Romantic movement who died in the 1820s and 1830s. Goethe, although a critic of the doctrinaire Romantics, and in a sense a mediator in the conflict between classicism and romanticism, produced in *Faust* the greatest single literary achievement of the Romantic movement. But Goethe died in 1832. Not only were the next fifty years to produce no poetic drama to compare with *Faust*; they were to produce no poetic imagery to equal that of Keats, who died in 1821, no verse of the direct emotional appeal of Byron, who died in 1824, no sonnet with the sheer verbal beauty of *Alla Sera* of Foscolo, who died in 1827. Wordsworth lived on, a pale shadow of himself, until 1850, but all his verse of any significance was written before 1830.

The earlier Romantic poets of the nineteenth century were mainly concerned with introspection. A later generation was to turn again to external issues of politics or religion and to discuss in their verse the ideological conflicts of the day, but the most successful, and in literary terms the most revolutionary, of the Romantics were absorbed with the need, in Leopardi's words, 'esplorare il proprio petto'. Giacomo Leopardi (1798–1837) was himself, perhaps, the finest exponent of the introspective type of poet, whose verse was, in twentieth-century terms, simply a stream of consciousness. Whether Leopardi was—according to an earlier manner—addressing his thoughts and feelings in imagination to the moon, or the woman he loved, or a sparrow, or whether he was recording them—in a more modern and straightforward manner—only to himself, the effect of totally sincere introspection is not lost. Sick and hunchbacked, Leopardi lived withdrawn from most human society. The purity and sensibility of his poetry perfectly expressed the bitterness and almost intolerable sadness of his solitude, as in the short work, *A se stesso*:

> Or poserai per sempre,
> stanco mio cor. Perì l'inganno estremo,
> ch'eterno io mi credei. Perì. Ben sento,
> in noi di cari inganni,
> non che la speme, il desiderio è spento.[1]

The French Romantic poets, two of the most successful of whom were Alphonse de Lamartine (1790–1869) and Alfred de Musset (1810–57), were also more often than not introspective, concerned with their own loves and hates, memories and grief. If Musset was sometimes guilty of exaggerations and insincerities of which Leopardi would have been incapable, he sometimes wrote fine verse of great pathos. An English poet who deserves mention among the introspective Romantics is Emily Brontë, whose verse has, paradoxically, all the psychological maturity of her great novel. But not all of the Romantic poets whose work was so evidently introverted were so cut off from the world as Leopardi or Emily Brontë. Lamartine played a leading role in the February Revolution in Paris in 1848,[2] and was for a short while minister of foreign affairs under the Second Republic, and Heine played a prominent part in the movement of 'Young Germany'. Heinrich Heine (1797–1856), who spent much of his life in exile from Germany, added a new dimension of sharp irony to

---

[1] Now you will rest for ever, my tired heart. The last deception, which I believed eternal, has perished. It has perished. Well do I feel it—that in us not only the hope of dear illusions, but the desire for them is dead.

[2] See above, pp. 171–3.

the Romantic lyric poem. But it was an English poet, John Clare (1793–1864), who had been a farm labourer and, later, a penniless tramp, who asked the ultimate question in introspection. In the first line of his greatest work, Clare wrote: 'I am! yet what I am who cares, or knows?' In the England of Gladstone and Tennyson it is not surprising that these words should have been written in a mental asylum, the asylum in which Clare spent the last twenty-seven years of his life.

English poets, at least in the second half of the nineteenth century, more often looked outwards to the world beyond themselves, the world of intellectual debate and ideological conflict. The Italian *Risorgimento*, the Crimean War, the struggle between the Darwinians and the Churches, all inspired poetry which was to survive, though—as has already been suggested—the creations of the Italian and German nation states were accompanied by no poetry quite worthy of the occasion. Manzoni, the one major Italian poet who seemed likely to produce patriotic verse, experienced a conversion to devout Catholicism, and so produced instead religious verse. It was rather the English poets of late romanticism who celebrated the *Risorgimento,* and prominent among them was Algernon Swinburne (1837–1909), who dedicated his volume of verse, *Songs before Sunrise,* published in 1871, to Giuseppe Mazzini.

The English poet most completely in tune with his times, most fully occupied with contemporary issues, and therefore most brilliantly successful was Alfred Tennyson (1809–92), created a peer by Gladstone in 1883. In his early work Tennyson showed that he had quickly assimilated the technical achievements of the earlier Romantics, and especially of Keats, yet his work contrasted with theirs, and with that of his contemporaries in France, in that it was essentially extroverted. Even to express human emotions he tended to describe the external scene. Thus in his vast work, *In Memoriam,* written to purge himself of his grief on the death of his friend, Arthur Hallam, Tennyson wrote such lines as:

> He is not here: but far away
> The noise of life begins again,
> And ghastly thro' the drizzling rain,
> On the bald street breaks the blank day.

But the historical significance of *In Memoriam* lay in its attempt to work out a compromise between doubt and faith, apprehension and hope:

> Thou madest man, he knows not why,
> He thinks he was not made to die.

And the belief that 'somehow good will be the final goal of ill' was a sentiment to which de Tocqueville, Marx or T. H. Huxley could each in his own way subscribe, though Marx, if he ever read *In Memoriam*, must have felt that the 'somehow' was needlessly imprecise. Tennyson's technical virtuosity, combined with his somewhat incoherent discussion of contemporary intellectual issues identified him as 'a modern poet' to his Victorian readers. The other popular 'modern poet' of late nineteenth-century England, Robert Browning (1812–89), was also essentially an extrovert, in that his introspection was usually self-conscious and lacked the sincerity of a Leopardi. Browning's modernity depended upon his metric innovations and the colloquial nature of his verse, which gave him his reputation for obscurity. The religious doubts which Tennyson succeeded in dispelling—at least to his own satisfaction —by his ethical convictions, were arrogantly proclaimed by Swinburne, an atheist and republican, who yet wrote poetry in a controlled and regular metre. Swinburne's technical polish had the effect of blunting his blasphemies. His *Hymn of Man*, written when the Vatican Council was meeting in 1870, was intended to be a humanist denunciation of Christianity:

> By thy name that in hell-fire was written,
> > and burned at the point of thy sword,
> Thou art smitten, thou God, thou art smitten;
> > thy death is upon thee, O Lord.
> And the love-song of earth as thou diest resounds
> > through the wind of her wings—
> Glory to Man in the highest! for Man is
> > the master of things.

Queen Victoria was understandably shocked at such sentiments, but the radical nature of Swinburne's philosophy was partly concealed by the perfection of his metre.

So far as immediate political developments were concerned, both Browning and Swinburne were more excited by events in Italy than by the struggle of parties at Westminster. The major English poets did not immerse themselves in politics as did their contemporaries in France or Italy. No English poet in the period went into exile for political reasons, as did Hugo or Heine, partly because no English régime made exile necessary, but partly also because English politics did not sufficiently interest literary men. In Italy, on the other hand, the principal literary figure in the latter part of the period, the poet Giosué Carducci (1835–

1907), who led a classical reaction against decadent romanticism and the unhappy latterday influence of Manzoni, was elected a deputy in 1876, and in 1890 was to be made a senator. Carducci was perhaps the major literary product of the *Risorgimento*. An ardent republican as a young man, he adjusted himself to the monarchy after 1870, the anticlericalism of Victor Emmanuel's Italy making the adjustment easier. For Carducci, as for many poets at their more creative moments, a movement of ideas in the world outside was also a deeply personal experience. Nineteenth-century Europeans were particularly prone to crises of conscience brought on by some loss of convictions about the external, politico-social scene, rather than by any event in the individual's personal life or re-lationships. Such contrasting personalities as Robert Peel, Leo Tolstoy and John Stuart Mill are cases in point. Matthew Arnold's *Dover Beach*, a speculation on the growth of scepticism, and his only wholly successful poetic achievement, was at once a personal and a historical statement:

> The Sea of Faith
> Was once, too, at the full, and round earth's shore
> Lay like the folds of a bright girdle furl'd.
> But now I only hear
> Its melancholy, long, withdrawing roar
>
> . . .
>
> And we are here as on a darkling plain
> Swept with confused alarms of struggle and flight,
> Where ignorant armies clash by night.

One ultimate effect of the nineteenth-century Romantic poets was to kill the tradition of narrative verse, and to substitute for it the 'poet talking to himself' as the usual concept of poetry. But nineteenth-century poets themselves produced much narrative verse, though the novel rapidly became the more normal vehicle for story-telling. Alfred de Vigny (1797–1863) in *Le Cor* and *La Colère de Samson* wrote moving versions of the stories of Roland and of Samson and Delilah, and Tennyson's *Idylls of the King* was a more ambitious attempt to write a familiar legend in modern verse. As examples of strictly historical verse, Victor Hugo's two short impressions of the Retreat from Moscow, and Waterloo, incorporated into the single poem, *L'Expiation*, are unequalled in the period.

In 1857 a major revolution in the development of European literature was caused by the publication of a volume of lyric poems, *Les Fleurs du Mal*, by a virtually unknown writer, Charles Baudelaire (1821–67). The

brilliantly original and sensuous quality of the poems probably owed
much to Baudelaire's travels in the east. When he was a boy his stepfather had been appointed minister to Constantinople, under Louis-
Philippe. Young Charles already had plans for a literary career, and it
was to shake him out of this impracticable dream that his mother and
stepfather sent him on a long sea voyage—to India, Ceylon, Mauritius,
Madagascar. In so doing they had provided France's greatest lyric poet
of the nineteenth century with his most vivid source of imagery. *Les
Fleurs du Mal* was an astonishing first volume. From its opening poem,
Au lecteur, the last line of which, 'Hypocrite lecteur,—mon semblable,—
mon frère!' was a refreshing variation on the 'Gentle Reader' theme, it
was clear that the work had a new poetic integrity. It suffered the same
fate at the hands of the puritanical officials of the Second Empire as did
Flaubert's *Madame Bovary*, published in the same year, and *Les Fleurs
du Mal* subsequently had to be published in an expurgated version. Its
violent sensuality certainly had no precedent in the nineteenth century,
and it was linked with an equally violent anger at the inevitability of
death. Where Leopardi had considered the fleeting nature of life with
acute sadness, Baudelaire looked at it with savage bitterness and irony,
as in *L'Horloge*:

> Trois mille six cents fois par heure, la Seconde
> Chuchote: *Souviens-toi!*—Rapide avec sa voix
> D'insecte, Maintenant dit: Je suis Autrefois,
> Et j'ai pompé ta vie avec ma trompe immonde!

Baudelaire's verse has dated less than that of most poets who wrote
before 1914. His influence on the tone of French writing, both serious
and melodramatic, ever since, has clearly been immense. Two poets who
became known in the 1870s, Paul Verlaine (1844–96) and Arthur Rimbaud (1854–91), declared their debt to Baudelaire, though the dreamlike
quality and verbal simplicity of the verse of Verlaine contrasts sharply
with the brutal realism and vivid language of Baudelaire. Rimbaud,
rather than Verlaine, completed the revolution against French traditional poetic forms, a revolution begun by the Romantics.

In music as in poetry the period embraces the later phase of the
Romantic movement. The principal figure in the musical world of Paris
in 1830 was Louis Hector Berlioz (1803–69), who, as a young man of
twenty-seven, had already composed his *Symphonie Fantastique* and the
original version of *Faust*. Berlioz was as typical a Romantic as Hugo in his
love of Walter Scott and of Shakespeare, to whom he had been intro-

duced by performances of *Hamlet* and *Romeo and Juliet* by an English company in 1827, and in his striving for bigness, illustrated by his vast symphony, *Romeo and Juliet*, first performed in 1839, with an orchestra of 160 and a chorus of 98. In Italy in the early 1930s Berlioz had met Mendelssohn, and had formed a very high opinion of him—an opinion which was not reciprocated by the German composer. Jacob Ludwig Felix Mendelssohn (1805–47) was patronized by the European courts of his day: he was commissioned to write works for Frederick William IV —among them the incidental music for *A Midsummer Night's Dream*; he played the piano privately for Queen Victoria and Prince Albert; and the happiest years of his life were spent at Leipzig, where the king of Saxony provided him with the means to found the Music Conservatorium. The crowning achievement of Mendelssohn's career was the composition of the oratorio *Elijah*, from 1838 to 1845. The major passion of his life was the music of Bach, at a time when Bach was little known in Germany. Clearly he did not think of himself as a Romantic, yet in retrospect his work can be seen as a vital part of the Romantic movement. One of Mendelssohn's staff at the Leipzig Conservatorium was Robert Alexander Schumann (1810–56), a far more typical Romantic both in his life and his art. The piano music on which Schumann's reputation was made, and his four symphonies, are always lyrical and sometimes self-conscious and literary. Already in his twenties he suffered from acute depressions and melancholia. At the age of forty-four he tried to drown himself in the Rhine and spent the remaining two years of his life in a mental asylum. Many nineteenth-century artists suffered from neuroses which seemed an essential condition of their genius, but in the case of Schumann it seems probable that mental illness stunted and prematurely ended his work.

Music rather more readily than literature expressed nationalist sentiments in the nineteenth century. Most important of the composers whose work was inspired by the nationalist mystique, and in its turn stimulated patriotic fervour, was the Saxon, Richard Wagner (1813–83). Wagner's life was a breathless alternating of failure and success in his work, his financial dealings, and his marriages and love affairs. His tempestuous personality was attracted more forcefully by the theatre than the concert hall, and he chose as his supreme medium the opera. While Mendelssohn's great youthful enthusiasms were for Shakespeare and Bach, Wagner's were for Shakespeare and Beethoven, and he recorded in his autobiography that the most important experience of his life had been his first hearing of *Fidelio*. Wagner's own contribution to the history of músic and the theatre was his synthesis of his own dramatic poems and musical scores into powerful opera. At once his biggest and his greatest work was the cycle of four operas which he called collectively *The Ring*, and which told the Nibelungen legend. The poem of *The Ring* was completed in 1852, yet, after many interruptions, Wagner was still working on the music for *Götterdämmerung*, the last part of *The Ring*, when the German Empire was coming into existence. By then Wagner was appealing to the worst characteristics of the new Germany—its vulgarized mysticism and its absurd self-worship.

If Wagner reflected the spirit of German nationalism, Verdi reflected at least one aspect of the very different spirit of Italian nationalism. Verdi's operas contrived to be tragic and light-hearted at the same time —a paradox resulting, perhaps, from sudden personal tragedy occurring in the life of a basically happy man: when he was in his twenties, his young wife and only two children died within an interval of two years. The patriotic sentiments of Verdi's early operas, *I Lombardi*, first performed at La Scala in 1843, and *Ernani*, first performed in Venice in 1844, made him a popular figure in a political as well as a musical sense. His later operas, among them *Rigoletto* (1851), *Il Trovatore* (1853) and *La Traviata* (1853), gave him permanent popularity throughout the European world.

The second half of the period was dominated by the German composer, Johannes Brahms (1833–97), who, like Mendelssohn, was born in Hamburg, and who was a protégé of Schumann. The superiority of Brahms over all his immediate contemporaries could be claimed on the grounds that he never fell below an even standard of excellence, never descended to the facile or the insincere. He had a considerable range and could compose two sharply contrasting works in the same period, as in the case of his first two symphonies. Even more than most great creative artists, Brahms defies classification as a classicist or a romantic.

Just as the decadent Russia of the czars had produced two of the greatest novelists of the period and many writers of significance, so did eastern Europe as a whole produce a remarkable collection of composers. Frédéric François Chopin (1810–49), whose comparatively small-scale output was to have so great an influence on both serious and popular music, was a product of oppressed Poland, in the sense that his mother and upbringing were Polish, though his father was a Lorrainer. Among Russian composers of the period were Michael Ivanovitch Glinka (1804–1857), Alexander Porfyrevich Borodin (1833–87), Modeste Petrovitch Mussorgsky (1839–81), and Nicholas Andreavich Rimsky-Korsakov

(1844–1908) but the master of them all in the range of his often uneven work and the moving beauty of his melodies was Peter Ilitch Tchaikovsky (1840–93). If, however, Tchaikovsky's earlier work belongs to the age of Panslavism and the reign of Alexander II, with all its hopes and disappointments, the later work, including the famous Sixth Symphony with its neurotically sad slow movement, belongs to the post-1880 period.

In the plastic arts the period was a comparatively dismal one. Only in the 1870s was new life breathed into European painting, by the Impressionists. The general characteristics of nineteenth-century painting included its disorderly and fragmentary nature: there are no strong traditions or schools as there had been in previous centuries; artists were more individualist and to that extent less well integrated in society; they were often obsessed with the desire to reproduce nature in a purely uncreative way, so that just before the invention of photography many paintings already have the superficial effectiveness of unimaginative photographs. The fragmentation of artistic styles and the growing material and moral isolation of the artist were partly caused by the ideological confusion which followed the French Revolution, and partly by the lack of strong bodies who wished to patronize art, as the Church or the rich landed nobility had done in the past. The modern type of the lonely, suffering artist emerged—already exemplified by Blake, before the period started, and again, at the end of the period, by Van Gogh, who were the equivalent of Leopardi and Dostoevsky, or Schumann and Tchaikovsky, in the other art forms. Many artists in the early nineteenth century turned to landscape painting, looking back to Dutch models of the seventeenth century. They often painted deserted landscapes—like those of the German artist, Caspar David Friedrich (1774–1840)—landscapes viewed, as it were, from a position of great solitude, in much the same way as the poetry of Wordsworth had been written. The English contemporary of Friedrich, John Constable (1776–1837), painted warmer and more intimate landscapes than Friedrich's, but both were alike in their increasing concern for the suggesting of atmosphere and light, a concern which led to the later achievements of J. M. W. Turner (1775–1851), and, ultimately, to those of the Impressionists.

In a much older tradition was the work of Jean-Auguste-Dominique Ingres (1780–1867), a classicist who survived into a period when he was something of a curiosity, like Balzac's Cousin Pons, who still wore the fashions of the First Empire in the days of the July Monarchy. A student of David, Ingres had been already producing mature works in 1800, yet one of his most famous paintings, *The Turkish Bath*, now in the Louvre, was painted as late as 1860. Ingres was an accomplished draughtsman, concerned to give precise renderings of human and material details, but his portraits show something far beyond this—an acute psychological perception and a deep sympathy with the subject. In sharp contrast to the serenity of Ingres was the work of the central figure in Romantic painting in the first half of the period—Eugéne Delacroix (1798–1863). Like the Romantic novelists Delacroix escaped in his work from nineteenth-century France into earlier periods, fiction or mythology, or remote and exotic countries. A visit to Morocco in 1832 gave him a strong feeling for Africa, which inspired many of his paintings, as, for example, his studies of lions in violent action. Animals fighting or in dramatic movement were a favourite theme for Delacroix and were well suited to his dynamic, tortured style. He used colour in a less inhibited manner than his immediate predecessors or contemporaries, and in this he, too, prepared the way for the Impressionists.

In the spring of 1874 a remarkable group of artists collaborated in an exhibition in Paris, and were subsequently dubbed by a journalist *Impressionistes*. Among them were Claude Monet (1840–1920), Alfred Sisley (1839–99), Camille Pissarro (1830–1903), Paul Cézanne (1839–1906), Edgar Degas (1834–1917) and Auguste Renoir (1841–1919). Subsequently Edouard Manet (1832–83) was to be considered the leader of the group, though in 1874 he refused to be associated with them and did not take part in the exhibition. Manet alone among the Impressionists had been well known under the Second Empire. The sensation caused by the exhibition of his *Déjeuner sur l'herbe* in 1863 had contributed to his fame. But his social background and behaviour were more respectable than that of most of the others, who were happy to acknowledge his leadership, though in retrospect it is clear that he was by no means 'the finest artist of the group. The 1874 exhibition was a revolution in the history of painting, and like all cultural revolutions it was greeted by many conservative critics and most of the public with anger or derision. By the mid-twentieth century the work of the Impressionists, rendered stale by a million bad reproductions, was to be considered fitting decoration for girls' schools all over the Europeanized world. But in the 1870s their new techniques altered the whole flavour of painting. For the most part the Impressionists left their studios and painted in the open air. Their main concern was to paint light rather than mass, and for this purpose control and accentuation of colour were more important than draughtsmanship. They were essentially painters rather than designers, and abandoned all the old criteria of how pictures should be composed. They were neither literary nor intellectual but merely eager to suggest the abundant colour and beauty of their world.

Among the group who exhibited in 1874 Degas had little in common with the others, and Cézanne was to move far beyond Impressionism. Degas was always more concerned with line and composition, more of a classicist, than the others, while Cézanne was to become increasingly preoccupied with mass, with the suggestion of the three-dimensional world, and in his more mature works was already anticipating cubism. Of all the artists of the period Cézanne was to have most influence on the future. One great artist usually associated with the Impressionists, Vincent Van Gogh (1853-90), was younger than the others and did not exhibit with them in 1874. The most romantic of them all, Van Gogh surpassed them in his power of expression and vividness of imagination. While his mind deteriorated to madness and suicide, his creative genius reached a pitch unsurpassed in nineteenth-century painting.

The sculpture of the period was too often rhetorical, an unhappy influence from the baroque surviving longer in sculpture than in painting. Of the vast amount of lifeless sculpture which the twentieth century has inherited from the nineteenth two samples must suffice: the large work of François Rude (1784-1855) on the Arc de Triomphe, *The Departure of the Volunteers in 1792*—a ludicrous group of posturing figures, as heavy and humourless as the plays of Hugo or Dumas—erected in 1835-36; and the sad confusion of sculpture—the work of several hands—on the Albert Memorial, itself designed by Sir Gilbert Scott in 1872. Yet Rude was an honoured figure of the July Monarchy and contributed effectively to the creation of the Napoleonic Legend, while the Albert Memorial was immensely popular when its glittering gilt and shining marble were still new. Before the birth of the Impressionist movement the only living sculpture of the period was the work of isolated figures, working apart from any tradition, like the satirist Honoré Daumier (1808-79), whose cartoons and lithographs were, of course, far more numerous and better known than his sculpture, though the whole of his work has the same vitality and psychological perception. Daumier was the Balzac of art. He captured for posterity the precise moods, weaknesses and petty vices of the Parisians of his day, especially in his series of sketches from the law courts. Sculpture by Impressionist artists include the work of Degas and Auguste Rodin (1840-1917). Although he had not exhibited his sculpture by 1880, Degas had already started to work in the extra dimension, and was already showing the technical ability which was to be limited only by his growing blindness. Rodin's early works also expressed his genius quite fully—his pathos and drama which only rarely descended to rhetoric.

If the painting and sculpture of the period lacked a strong, central tradition of development, the architecture of the period was less fragmentary so far as schools of taste were concerned, but much more derivative. The nineteenth century failed to evolve its own architectural style, though some of the ideas which were to be adopted by twentieth-century architects can be traced to nineteenth-century theorists who, in other respects, were academic revivalists of the worst type. In every European country early in the period most buildings were constructed to neo-classical designs—inspired by either Greek, Roman or Renaissance models. Even in England, where the Gothic revival was to have most influence, the neo-classical styles of the Regency were frequently employed into the early Victorian period. In 1830 in London several elegant classical buildings were in course of construction, two of the most successful being the Athenaeum Club, designed by Decimus Burton (1800–81), and Carlton House Terrace, designed by John Nash (1752–1832). In Victoria's reign open battle was fought between upholders of the neo-classical and the neo-Gothic. The British Museum, with its large façade of Ionic pillars, designed by Sir Robert Smirke (1780–1867) was not completed until 1847, and a neo-Renaissance palace like Burlington House was built as late as 1866, to the designs of Charles Barry (1795–1860). But by this time the Goths were prevailing in England, though elsewhere in Europe, even where some tremors of the Gothic revival were experienced, most public and private building continued in classical traditions.

The Gothic style had never been completely abandoned in England. Even in the seventeenth and early eighteenth centuries leading architects who more normally worked in the idiom of Renaissance or baroque had occasionally experimented with versions of Gothic, though usually without much conviction. Then in the mid-eighteenth century had come the first phase of the Gothic revival, the phase usually associated with Horace Walpole's transformation of Strawberry Hill into a Gothic villa. But Strawberry Hill Gothic was a light-hearted development, a frivolity of eighteenth-century taste. The Victorian phase of the Gothic revival was the work of passionately religious men who saw architecture as a manifestation of public ethics. Chief of these was the eccentric and fanatic, Augustus Welby Pugin (1812–52), whose father had emigrated to England from France. Pugin was converted to Catholicism as a result of his passion for medieval architecture, thereby justifying the charge often made against the Gothic revival that it was Popish in sentiment. He designed many churches in a heavy, utterly lifeless and static neo-Gothic style, and wrote several tracts defending the Gothic revival and abusing its opponents with strong invective. Finally in 1852 he had a mental breakdown, and was confined in Bedlam, where he died shortly afterwards. Before his madness, however, he had become a highly respected and famous architect.

When he was still an unknown man, Pugin had played an important, though unrecognized, part in the building of the best known product of the Gothic revival—the new Palace of Westminster. When the old Houses of Parliament were burnt to the ground in 1834, a competition was held to decide the architect who would be entrusted with the task of replacing them. The competition was the major battle in the row between Goths and Classicists. It was won by Charles Barry, who usually designed classical buildings, but on this occasion had submitted plans for what was, at least in appearance, a richly Gothic palace. The basic plan of the new Palace of Westminster can, in fact, be interpreted as a classical one: its strikingly Gothic spirit comes from its pinnacles, ornamentation and details, which were entirely the work of Pugin. Officially merely the 'Superintendent of Wood-carving', Pugin, who had designed all the furniture and fittings, down to the umbrella stands and ink pots, had provided what is still the best known and best loved building in London with its strongly individual character.

If the Gothic revival did not deserve the devotion and burning enthusiasm of Pugin, it deserved still less the unbalanced genius of John Ruskin (1819–1900), whose imaginative, if rambling and contradictory, works of art criticism included an entire critique of nineteenth-century society. If on the one hand Ruskin praised the Gothic revival during the 1850s, on the other he was essentially a modern in his appreciation of two points: that architecture divorced from craftmanship and engineering is bound to be an arid art, and that materials should not be disguised, but their inherent qualities should be used and interpreted to the best aesthetic effect. Surrounded by the cheapness and ugliness of the speculative building of industrialized England, Ruskin reminded the nineteenth century of the medieval ideal which demanded that a man should approach his work in a spirit of dedication and joy.

The other countries of western Europe were nearly all to some extent influenced by the Gothic revival in England. In Germany the major product of the revival was the completion of Cologne cathedral between the years 1842 and 1871. During the reign of Ludwig II neo-Gothic and neo-Renaissance castles were built in equal profusion in Bavaria. Even Vienna shared in the Gothic revival, notably in the building of the Votivkirche, but on the whole both Austrian and Italian architecture tended to follow well worn classical traditions. In Holland there was one Gothic revivalist architect of real talent—Petrus Cuypers (1827–1921), a follower of the famous Frenchman, Viollet-le-Duc (1814–79). In 1845 a competition for the restoration of Notre-Dame was won by Viollet-le-Duc, who carried out his task all too thoroughly and ruthlessly. Four years later he performed an equal work of conscientious vandalism on the cathedral of Amiens. But in Viollet-le-Duc there was the same contradiction as in Pugin and Ruskin. While his attitude to the medieval architecture which he professed to love was absurdly academic and doctrinaire, he could show the kind of respect for materials which the twentieth-century architect was to show. The line from Viollet-le-Duc through Cuypers to modern architecture is a surprisingly direct one.

From the most important building project of nineteenth-century Europe—the transformation of Paris under the Second Empire—Viollet-le-Duc was deliberately excluded. In 1830 Paris was still within her ancient walls. The king lived in the Tuileries, the Louvre was already a museum, and already fourteen bridges—half the present number—crossed the Seine. But beyond the Champs-Elysées was open country. The Arc de Triomphe, on the edge of the city, was unfinished: started in 1809, it was not completed until 1836. In most respects Paris was still a medieval city with narrow streets and squalid, if picturesque, slums. Although Louis-Philippe's administrators cleared a few points here and there, the position was not radically changed until 1853, when Haussmann was appointed Prefect of the Seine. Georges Haussmann (1809–91) had secured his advance in the French bureaucracy by aggressive policies, and by his quick identification of his interests with those of the new régime after the *coup d'état* of 1851 and the proclamation of the empire in 1852. Always ambitious, clear-headed and self-confident, Haussmann was precisely the kind of tough, disinterested official Napoleon III needed to put through his large plan for the rebuilding of Paris. During Haussmann's prefectship eighty-five miles of new streets were built, including most of the long, broad, tree-lined boulevards which give Paris her character among European cities. The Bois de Boulogne was laid out as it is today, and a great new system of sewers was constructed. Overcoming strong vested interests, Haussmann demolished large areas of slums, and constructed a city which was at once modern and beautiful. He himself had neither architectural nor engineering experience, nor can it be said that he employed brilliant architects. The achievement was one of town planning, rather than of architecture, and as such was anachronistic. In other spheres, artistic or literary, the nineteenth century was an age of the individual, of the rebellious, independently minded, usually unhappy, artist or writer, who did not fit serenely into a tradition or convention, and who resented the complacency and optimism of society. Culturally it was an age of revolt and disintegration.

XV

Europe in 1880

Any period of fifty years or less must inevitably have been shaped by men who had grown up in a very different age and had themselves been influenced by events and ideas which were already remote. The period of European history covered by this book was, for example, considerably affected by the lives of Metternich—until his resignation in 1848, of Palmerston—until his death in 1865, and of Thiers—until his resignation from the presidency in 1873. Yet Metternich had grown up when Frederick the Great was king of Prussia, and the future Austrian chancellor was already a university student in 1789. Palmerston was a boy of nine when Pitt went to war with revolutionary France, and a member of parliament when the Treaty of Tilsit was signed. Thiers, whose policies made so firm a mark on the history of France throughout the period, could clearly remember the last years of the First Empire, and had himself published his *History of the French Revolution* before 1830. Metternich had grown to maturity while the ideas of the Enlightenment were still fresh, and both Palmerston and Thiers, in their different ways, had spent their most impressionable years under the shadow of the great Napoleon. In the same way the Europe of 1880 was the product of the ideas and developments of many decades.

The Third French Republic as it existed in 1880 was to some extent a synthesis of the several régimes which had ruled in Paris since 1789. It was without doubt a democracy, enshrining the two principles of universal manhood suffrage and ministerial responsibility to an elected assembly, two principles which could easily be traced to the Jacobins of 1793 and to the short-lived Second Republic of 1848–51, and which had been briefly restored during the last few months of the Second Empire. France in 1880 had a proud and efficient administrative system in the unbroken tradition established by the First Empire. Government was firmly centralized—a practice which could be traced again to the Jacobins and to Napoleon I. But coexistent with administrative efficiency was the

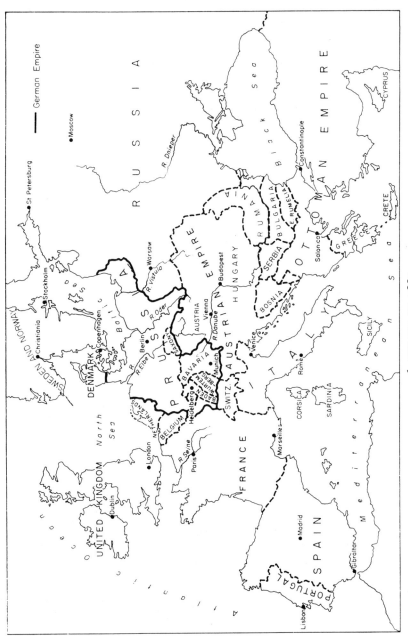

6. EUROPE IN 1880

German Empire

• Moscow

R U S S I A

CYPRUS

St Petersburg

R Dnieper

Black Sea

Constantinople

SWEDEN AND NORWAY

Stockholm

Christiania

Baltic Sea

Copenhagen

DENMARK

Berlin

R Elbe

R Oder

R Vistula

Warsaw

P R U S S I A

GALICIA

AUSTRIAN EMPIRE

AUSTRIA

Vienna

Budapest

HUNGARY

RUMANIA

BULGARIA

E RUMELIA

SERBIA

BOSNIA

OTTOMAN EMPIRE

Salonica

GREECE

CRETE

R Danube

BAVARIA

Munich

SAXONY

WÜRTEM-BERG

BADEN

Heidelberg

SWITZ.

ITALY

Venice

Rome

CORSICA

SARDINIA

SICILY

NETHER-LANDS

BELGIUM

London

Dublin

UNITED KINGDOM

North Sea

Atlantic Ocean

R Seine

Paris

FRANCE

Marseille

SPAIN

Madrid

PORTUGAL

Lisbon

Gibraltar

Mediterranean Sea

379

blight of political instability and public corruption—tendencies with which the July Monarchy had made France only too familiar. Finally the socialist movement, which had apparently been killed after the defeat of the Commune, was already in 1880 showing new signs of life. Since 1877 it had been safe to express socialist opinions again in France. A workers' movement called the *Fédération des Travailleurs Socialistes* was founded in 1879. In 1880 a Blanquist party, the *Parti Socialiste Révolutionnaire*, was founded; Blanquism could claim a clear line of descent from Babeuf and the hopes for a 'Republic of Equals' in 1797. In 1882 Jules Guesde founded a Marxist party, the *Parti Ouvrier Français*, the one French movement of the 1880s whose origins could not be traced to the Revolutionary or Napoleonic period, but lay outside France altogether.

In England in 1880 Gladstone replaced Disraeli as prime minister. It was a classic moment in the history of the British Parliament. The electoral pattern which has been called 'the swing of the pendulum' was operating more consistently than it had ever operated before or would ever do again. The richer urban working class had been given the vote by Disraeli in 1867, but in 1880 they had just voted for Gladstone, 'the People's William', who had given them, in the Midlothian campaigns, the first piece of modern electioneering. Forgetting the social reforms of the Conservatives, forgetting the 'peace with honour' which Disraeli had brought back from the Congress of Berlin as recently as 1878, the British electorate accepted Gladstone's argument that the Conservatives were greedy for more empire, and that such greed was not only immoral, it was also extravagant. Gladstone's success marked a temporary conversion of the enfranchised section of the working class to the doctrine which Cobden had preached—unsuccessfully—to the middle class in the 1840s and 1850s, the doctrine that no government should be allowed to spend money on foreign wars. That the British public soon forgot Gladstone's argument and accepted the necessity of his own particularly bloody intervention in Egypt in 1882 is not relevant to the significance of the Midlothian campaigns and the subsequent elections. The other part of Cobden's doctrine—the gospel of free trade—was no longer wholly acceptable in a world of rising tariffs, but Gladstone's victory at the polls showed that the new big electorate had inherited the mixture of high-mindedness and hypocrisy which had for long characterized the *laissez-faire* tradition, English radicalism, and the philistine middle class for which Matthew Arnold felt such contempt. On the other hand, England in 1880 was witnessing many improvements—the life of the worker was softening a little, education was at last becoming the concern of the state, political corruption was disappearing, a start was being made in the clearing of the slums, a great political leader was appealing directly to the people on questions of public policy, and if, in so doing, he over-simplified the issues, this was a price which had to be paid.

Britain in 1880 was strikingly isolated from Bismarck's Europe, or—as the British saw it—Bismarck's Europe was isolated from Britain, her wise institutions and her empire. For the rest of Europe the new Germany, with her large population and army, and her expanding industry, was the biggest fact of life in 1880. The German Empire was not, like the French Republic, a synthesis of past régimes. Rather was it a special creation of Bismarck, who had merely exploited movements of German nationalism and democracy, movements for which he had little sympathy. The German *Reichstag*, elected by universal male suffrage, but having little hold on the government, was only a sop from Bismarck to the traditions of the Frankfurt Parliament. The Second German Empire certainly owed something in terms of historical precedence to the Holy Roman Empire, but Bismarck saw the new Germany rather as an offshoot of the old Prussian state, with its mystique of royal authority, and its tradition of bureaucratic competence handed down from the days of Frederick the Great and Stein.

Italy, the other new nation state of western Europe, was in a mood of disillusionment in 1880, only twenty years after the culminating triumphs of the *Risorgimento*; and her chief political figure, Agostino Depretis, was no less disillusioned than his fellow countrymen, for all his personal success. In 1860, as a man of forty-seven, he had been an ardent follower of Garibaldi. In 1880 he was a skilful political manager and hardened cynic. But if Italy's parliamentary system was narrow and corrupt, she was at least accepted—however grudgingly—as a great power, she had no immediate enemies in Europe, and her political life was far from being stagnant.

Austria-Hungary in 1880 had not fully recovered the international prestige she had lost in 1859 and 1866, when she had been flung out of Italy and Germany. Unlike the Italian kingdom, the Habsburg monarchy had dangerous enemies—Russia and the rising nationalities of the Balkans. But also unlike Italy, Austria-Hungary had a close ally, and that the most powerful available—Bismarck's Germany. The Habsburgs had made their peace with the Hungarians, and it was a Hungarian foreign minister, Andrássy, who had arranged the treaty of 1879 with

Bismarck. Austria's institutions had never satisfied—and probably never could have satisfied—all her population, but at least they had averted violent revolution since 1849, and were to survive into the twentieth century. The principle of nationality, which had seemed to justify the creation of Italy and Germany, would ultimately, by the same facile logic, seem to justify the destruction of the Habsburg monarchy.

The sad and disappointing reign of Alexander II was in 1880 approaching its tragic end. The high hopes of his first years as czar had proved unjustified. The serfs had been emancipated in 1861, but complementary measures had not been taken. The Poles had lost what little autonomy they had possessed. Above all, no steps had been taken to provide Russia with a central constitution. Russia's attempt to champion the Panslavs in 1877 had been frustrated by the other powers. Apart from the conquest of some ancient cities and large tracts of central Asia, Alexander had little to his credit. By 1880 his police were becoming increasingly concerned at the revolutionary attitude of the intelligentsia. There was more unrest in Russia than there had been since 1825, and more political speculation than on any previous occasion.

Just as the ideas and the precedents which had helped to create the Europe of 1880 had a long ancestry, so were the aims and doctrines which were to shape the twentieth century already being formed in 1880. The democratic state in which private property and private enterprise were protected and sanctified had strong origins in the nineteenth century. In France it already existed in the Third Republic, with its principles of universal suffrage and parliamentary sovereignty. In England a steady advance towards universal suffrage was continuing, and a system of party politics was already being made more efficient and more mechanical. In Palmerston's day party organization had been a gentlemanly affair carried on in London clubs. With the growth of democracy more widespread organization, with stronger local units, were needed. For the Liberals Joseph Chamberlain created a national party organization of the modern type, firmly based on the agents in the constituencies. Disraeli had initiated, and Randolph Churchill was to complete, a similar process for the Conservatives. If Gladstone's Midlothian campaigns had foreshadowed the modern device of seeking an apparently precise electoral mandate for specific policies, Louis-Napoleon's presidential campaign as long ago as 1848 had illustrated some of the characteristics of twentieth-century electioneering methods. In Italy Depretis was employing political patronage of a kind suited to a modern democracy—promising, for example, special concessions for public works in a constituency whose member voted for him in parliament.

Twentieth-century fascist régimes might also have found precedents for their methods in the period before 1880—for example, in the ruthless competence of Louis-Napoleon's *coup d'état* of 1851, or in the existence of what was virtually a political police in the Russia of the czars. The racist basis of Nazism could trace its origins back beyond 1830 to some of the things Fichte and Hegel had written, and, in the period 1830 to 1880, to the ideas of Treitschke. The Prussian Junkers, exemplified in this by the greatest of them—Bismarck—had always disliked the Jews and the Poles, and regarded them as inferiors. The psychological sickness of antisemitism had been endemic in Europe for centuries, but the emergence of the concept of the nation state held a special danger for Jewish minorities, especially in central and eastern Europe.

A sure theoretical footing had already been prepared by 1880 for the socialist and communist movements of the twentieth century. The writings of Saint-Simon, Blanc and Proudhon had already been largely superseded in their influence by those of Marx. The first volume of *Das Kapital* had already influenced a generation of Marxists. Marx himself was to die in 1883, but the second and third volumes of his work were left in the safe hands of Engels, who published them in 1885 and 1894. One of Lenin's ideas, however, that of an élite group of revolutionary leaders, whose whole lives would be dedicated to the coming struggle for power, can be traced to Blanqui rather than to Marx, though it is a debt which Communist Russia has never acknowledged. Only two régimes in Europe had been recognizably socialist before 1880, and both had been revolutionary and ephemeral—the Second Republic in France from February to June 1848, and the Paris Commune for an even shorter period. But many socialist ideas had already been incorporated in otherwise capitalist countries: state-owned railway systems, social insurance schemes, government regulation and inspection of working conditions, state-controlled schools and universities. In nearly every European country at least one of these socialist elements had appeared by 1880.

The main note in the Europe of 1880, however, was a beginning of doubt—doubt which was not always silenced by aggressive self-assertion. It was not only that Darwinism had called in question the origins and purpose of mankind, and so his ultimate destiny. It was not even only the more immediate observation that the U.S.A. was becoming a formidable economic rival of the European powers, who were experiencing some—though not all—of the characteristics of a trade depression. It was also that in each country there seemed more reason for apprehension than there had in the recent past. In France and Italy the achievement of a degree of political democracy had brought mediocrity and corruption to public life. In Germany there was already fear of encirclement, a fear to be lulled only by vast armaments. In Britain the rate of economic growth had fallen behind that of at least two great rivals, and although the population continued to increase, the birth rate had started to fall. In Austria-Hungary no solution to the nationality problems had been found. In Russia it seemed increasingly unlikely that the czar's government could bring in political reforms, or cure its social ills. Almost everywhere the splendid hopes of the decades before 1870 had, in one way or another, been disappointed. Nowhere in Europe after 1880 could a poet have expressed quite the same triumphant self-confidence as the young Tennyson had once done in *Locksley Hall*:

> Not in vain the distance beacons. Forward, forward
>   let us range,
> Let the great world spin for ever down the ringing
>   grooves of change.
> Thro' the shadow of the globe we sweep into the younger day:
> Better fifty years of Europe than a cycle of Cathay.

Bibliographical Note

The books mentioned here are outline histories of Europe which could not be appropriately mentioned in the short bibliographies given at the start of each chapter. To place the period in a fuller context chronologically in a single volume, D. Thomson, *Europe since Napoleon* (London, 1957) is useful, while Charles Seignobos, *Histoire politique de l'Europe contemporaine 1814–1914* (2 vols., Paris, 1924) has never been wholly replaced as a straightforward and strikingly lucid political history. In the 'Rise of Modern Europe' series, edited by William L. Langer, two good volumes cover the second half of the period: R. C. Binkley, *Realism and Nationalism, 1852–1871* (New York, 1951), and C. J. H. Hayes, *A Generation of Materialism, 1871–1900* (New York, 1941), but until Professor Langer has published his own volume in the series there will remain a gap between 1832 and 1852. In the French series, 'Peuples et Civilisations', edited by L. Halphen and P. Sagnac, there are three volumes which are relevant to the period: G. Weill, *L'éveil des nationalités et le mouvement libéral 1815–1848* (Paris, 1930, revised edition 1955); Charles H. Pouthas, *Démocratie et capitalisme 1848–1860* (Paris, 1948); and H. Hauser, J. Maurain and P. Benaerts, *Du libéralisme à l'impérialisme 1860–1878* (Paris, 1939, revised edition 1952). A more recent French series in which each volume covers a longer period is 'Clio: Introduction aux études historiques', of which the relevant volume is J. Droz, L. Genet and J. Vidalenc, *L'époque contemporaine: I, Restorations et révolutions, 1815–1871* (Paris, 1953). A helpful recent bibliography is that prepared by Professor W. N. Medlicott for the Historical Association: *Modern European History 1789–1945. A Short Bibliography* (1961).

Index

INDEX

Bavaria, *continued*
1830, 209, 241; in 1866, 220; education in, 330; architecture in, 376
Bay Islands, 320
Bazaine, Marshal, 178, 222
Beaconsfield, Earl of, *see* Disraeli, Benjamin
Beagle, 341
Bechuanaland, 312
Beeton, Mrs, 131
Beirut, occupied by the British, 157
Belfort, 223
Belgium, 30–1, 95, chapter x; industrialization in, 68, 69; railways in, 74, 75, 77; machine industry in, 82; coal production in, 83, 256; joint stock companies in, 84; and the free trade movement, 97; and proposed customs union with France, 100–1; commercial policy, of 103; social conditions in, 119; trade unions in, 129; international aspects of the revolution, 154–5, 254–5; the constitution of 1831 in, 259–60, 294; guarantee of neutrality of, 262–3; education in, 333
Belinsky, Vissarion, 280, 281
Bentham, Jeremy, 42, 51–2, 53, 122, 199; and University College, London, 338
Bentinck, Lord William, 304
Berlin, population of, 85; Memorandum of (1876), 161; Congress of, 162, 273, 311, 380; the capital of Germany, 250; schools in, 331; university of, 337, 338, 339, 345, 346
Berlioz, Louis Hector, 368
Bernadotte, *see* Charles XIV, of Sweden
Berwick, 77
Besika Bay, 145
Bessarabia, 276
Bessemer, Henry, 80–2
Beust, Count Friedrich F. von, 9, 160, 272
Beyle, Marie-Henri, *see* Stendhal
Biarritz, 149
Birkbeck College, 81
Birmingham, 26, 77; growth of, 85, 190; during the Reform Bill crisis (1830–32), 182; after the 1832 Reform Act, 198
Birmingham Daily Post, 14
Bismarck, Prince Otto von, 3, 17, 18, 20, 42, 53, 82, 141, 325; and the Hohenzollern candidature, 5, 150–152; the memoirs of, 9; and the *Zollverein*, 99; adopts protectionist policy, 104, 249; and Austria, 1862–66, 148–9; and the Ems

telegram, 151; and the isolation of Austria in 1866, 158–9; and the isolation of France in 1870, 159; and the 'War in Sight' crisis (1875), 160; and the Eastern crisis of 1875–1878, 161–2; and the Dual Alliance with Austria (1879), 163; and the crisis over army reform in 1862, 217; his political beliefs, 218; and the Polish Revolution of 1863, 218–219, 279; and the Schleswig-Holstein question, 219; and the North German Confederation, 220, 246–247; and the Prussian liberals, 221, 225; and the foundation of the Empire, 222; and the *Kulturkampf*, 223–4, 352; and Tunis, 311; racialist tendencies of, 383
'Black Partition', 282
Blaenavon, 81
Blanc, Louis, 42, 58, 61, 102, 281; in 1848, 170, 171–2
Blanqui, Louis-Auguste, 170, 172–3, 380, 383; and the Commune, 178
Boers, 312, 314
Bohemia, 33, 91
Bois de Boulogne, 376
Bokhara, 303
Bolivia, 316
Bologna, revolution of 1831 in, 142, 226–7
Bolton, unemployment in, 114
Bordeaux, 84, 102; seat of French government (1870), 178
Bosnia, agriculture in, 92; Austrian ambitions in, 160; revolt of 1875 in, 161, 286; occupied by Austrians (1878), 163, 266
Boulogne, Louis-Napoleon's *coup d'état* at, 173
Bradford, growth of, 190
Brahms, Johannes, 370
Brazil, 315–16; and the war against Paraguay (1864–70), 317
Bremen, and the *Zollverein*, 99
Bright, John, 101; and the Anti-Corn Law League, 97, 184; opposes factory legislation, 125; and parliamentary reform, 187
Bristol, 79; living conditions in, 120; riots in (1830–31), 182; growth of, 190
Britain, *see* Great Britain
British Columbia, 324
British Guiana, 315
British Museum, 374
Brontë, Emily; as novelist, 362; as poet, 364
Browning, Robert, 366
Bruck, Baron von, 97, 99

388

Gold Coast, 313
Goncharov, Ivan, 362
Göransson, G. F., 80
Gorchakov, Prince Alexander, 9, 160,
218, 288; and reform of the Russian
diplomatic service, 139; and the
Italian crisis of 1859, 146, 147; and
the 'War in Sight' crisis of 1875, 160;
and the Eastern crisis of 1875–78,
161–3; and emancipation of the
serfs, 277; and Russian expansion
in Asia, 303
Goschen, George, 206
Gotha, 98
Gothic revival, 374–6
Graham, Sir James, 184, 185, 206
Gramont, Duc de, and the origins of
the Franco-Prussian war (1870),
150–1, 152, 177
Grand National Consolidated Trade
Union, 127
Granville, 2nd Earl, 159
Great Britain, chapter VIII; Parliament
in, 4–5, 7, 26, 198, 202; census in,
9; death rate in, 10, 116; social
conditions in, 10–11, 111–12, 113–
116, 120, 123; the press in, 13–14;
in 1830, 25–7; industrialization in,
27, 68, 70; railways in, 69, 73–5, 77,
78; canals in, 73; iron production
in, 79–80; steel production in, 80;
machine industry in, 82; textile
industry in, 82; coal-mining in, 83;
joint stock companies in, 84; growth
of cities in, 85; agriculture in, 88–9,
104; expansion of trade by, 94–5;
and the free trade movement, 95,
97, 104; and commercial treaties,
101; as the world's banker and
source of capital, 105; the Poor
Law of 1834 in, 111, 112, 130, 182,
183; truck system practised in,
117; public health in, 122; factory
legislation in, 124–6, 182; trade
unions in, 127–8, 189, 190; the life
of the middle class in, 131; the
Foreign Office and diplomatic
service of, 136–7; and the Polish
Revolution of 1830, 142; and the
Crimean War, 145, 186; and the
Italian war of 1859, 146, 147, 158;
and Mehemet Ali, 156–7; and the
Austro-Prussian war of 1866, 158,
187; and the Franco-Prussian war
of 1870, 158–9, 223; and the 'War
in Sight' crisis of 1875, 160; and
the Berlin Memorandum of 1876,
161; and the Bulgarian massacres
of 1876, 161, 162; occupation of
Cyprus by, 163; relations with

France of, 165–6, 194; 1832 Reform
Act in, 181–2, 183, 198–9, 204;
Repeal of the Corn Laws in, 184–5;
1867 Reform Act in, 188–9, 201–2;
education in, 189; introduction of a
secret ballot in, 201; administration
in, 204; and the army, 205–6; and
the navy, 206; and the Polish
Revolution of 1863, 218; and
Russian expansion in Central Asia,
301, 303; and the Indian Empire,
304–5; and China, 306; and the
Australian colony, 308, 309; and the
French in Algeria, 310; and Egypt,
311–12; and West Africa, 313; and
South Africa, 314; and investment
in South America, 316, 317; and
Rosas, 316; and Mexico, 317, 318;
and the Monroe Doctrine, 319;
and the American civil war, 320–2;
emigration to the U.S.A. from,
322–32; schools in, 334–6, 337;
universities in, 337; the novel in,
357, 360–2; in 1880, 380–1, 382
Great Eastern, 79
Great Exhibition of 1851 (in London),
185
Great Trek, 314
Great Western Railway, 78
Greece, 36, 155, 282–3; independence
of, 267; constitutions of 1844 and
1864 in, 294
Green, T. H., 42, 46, 56
Gregory XVI, Pope, 227, 347, 348
Greifenberg, 117
Grévy, Jules, 180
Grey, 2nd Earl, 181–3
Greytown, formerly called San Juan,
319
Grillparzer, Franz, 288
Grünne, Count, 290
Guerrazzi, Ettore, 355
Guesde, Jules, 380
Guizot, François, 15, 42, 52, 53;
commercial policy of, 100–1, 169;
and 1848, 170–1; and the British
entente, 194; and the *Sonderbund*,
259; and South America, 316; as
minister of public instruction, 328

Habsburg Monarchy, chapter XI;
the press in, 16; intervention in
Italy in 1821 by, 29–30; and the
German Confederation, 31; from
1815 to 1830, 33–4; and nationalism,
50, 268–70; revolutions of 1848 in,
51, 143, 268–70; industrialization
in, 71; railways in, 77; banks in, 85;
agriculture in, 91; and the free trade
movement, 97; and the *Zollverein*,

INDEX

Habsburg Monarchy, *continued*
98–9, 212; conditions of the peasants in, 110; diplomatic service in, 138, 139, 140; intervention in Italy in 1831 by, 142, 227; and the war with Sardinia (1848–49), 142, 230–2; and the war with France in 1859, 146–7, 158; and the Schleswig-Holstein question, 149, 219; and the war with Prussia in 1866, 149–50, 158, 239, 272; and the Mehemet Ali crisis (1840), 156; and the Crimean War, 157; and the Franco-Prussian war of 1870, 159; and the unsuccessful negotiations for an alliance with France and Italy before 1870, 159; and the 'War in Sight' crisis of 1875, 160; and the Eastern crisis of 1875–78, 162, 273; and the occupation of Bosnia and Herzegovina (1878), 163, 266, 273; and the Dual Alliance with Germany in 1879, 163, 225, 273; and the Erfurt Union, 215; the Bach system in, 271; and the establishment of the Dual Monarchy, 272–3, 292–3; censorship in, 286; the bureaucracy in, 295; the army in, 296; education in, 331, 353; and the Concordat of 1855, 353; in 1880, 381–2
Haeckel, Ernst Heinrich, 343
Hambach, nationalist festival at, 209
Hamburg; population of, 85; and the *Zollverein*, 99
Hammond, Edmund, later Lord, 137, 159
Hanover, 32; and the Middle German Commercial Union of 1828, 98; and the *Zollverein*, 99; in 1830, 209; annexed to Prussia (1866), 220
Hansemann, David, 16
Hardy, Thomas, 362
Hasner, Leopold von, 331
Hatt-i-Humayun, 286
Hatt-i-Sherif of Gulhané, 285, 286, 293
Haussmann, Baron Georges, 84, 376–7
Havas press agency, 17
Haynau, General, 270
Hegel, Georg Wilhelm Friedrich, 41, 44–6, 48, 49, 61, 62
Heidelberg, 213
Heine, Heinrich, 16, 366; as a poet, 364, 365
Hertslet, Sir Edward, 4
Herzegovina; Austrian ambitions in, 160; occupied by the Austrians (1878), 163, 266; revolt of 1875 in, 286

Herzen, Alexander, 280–1
Hesse-Cassel, 98; in 1830, 209; annexed to Prussia (1866), 220
Hesse-Darmstadt, 32; and customs union with Prussia, 97–8; in 1830, 241; education in, 330
Hirsch, Max, 129
Historians, 344–7
Holland, 30, 77, 100, chapter x; agriculture in, 93; and the free trade movement, 97; constitution of 1815 in, 260; constitutional reforms of 1848 in, 260–1; and the East Indies, 308; schools in, 333; architecture in, 376
Holstein, Baron Friedrich von, 6, 152
Home and Foreign Review, 350
Honduras, 319, 320
Hong Kong, 306
Hübner, Baron Joseph Alexander von, 7
Hugo, Victor; and the Second Empire, 176, 366; as a novelist, 356, 358, 362; as a dramatist, 363; as a poet, 367
Hungary, 33, chapter xi; agriculture in, 91, 92; free trade with the rest of the Empire in, 97; conditions of the peasants in, 110, 111; revolution of 1848 in, 269–70; and the Bach system, 271; and the establishment of the Dual Monarchy, 272, 292–3; the March Laws (1847) in, 289; in 1880, 381–2
Huskisson, William, 10, 27, 73; and free trade ideas, 95
Husrev Pasha, 287
Huxley, Thomas Henry, 339, 343–4

Ibrahim Pasha, 155
Ibsen, Henrik, 363
Ignatyev, Count Nicholas Pavlovitch, 160, 162, 163, 303
Il Corriere Italiano, 16
Illustrated London News, 14
Il Risorgimento (the newspaper), 233
Impressionists, 371–3
India, 145, 304–5, 320
Ingres, Jean-Auguste-Dominique, 371
International African Association, 313
International Workingmen's Association (First International), 64, 178
Ireland, 27, 69; nationalism in, 43, 191; agriculture in, 89–90; the Great Famine in, 89, 113, 184, 191–2; conditions of the peasants, 110, 112–13; and Gladstone's legislation, 189, 192; emigration to the U.S.A. from, 322, 323
Isabella, Queen of Spain, 150, 194, 196

34, 267; after 1815, 37, 38, 135; fall of, 142, 230, 269; and the annexation of Cracow, 143, 268; and Germany, 209, 212; and the Papacy, 227; and the *Sonderbund*, 259; and Swiss neutrality, 263

Metz, 222; annexed to Germany, 223

Mexico; Napoleon III's intervention in, 177, 317–18; and war with the U.S.A. (1846–48), 319

Mexico City, occupied by the French (1863), 318

Michael Obrenovich, Prince of Serbia, 284

Michelet, Jules, 337

Middle German Commercial Union of 1828, 98

Midhat Pasha, 286

Midlothian campaigns, 380, 382

Mikhailovsky, Nicholas Konstantinovich, 281

Milan, 77; revolution of 1848 in, 143, 229–30

Milan Obrenovich, King of Serbia, 284

Miliutin, D. A., 297

Mill, John Stuart, 42, 46, 48, 51, 53, 54, 140, 281, 367; political ideas of, 55–56; influence of Comte on, 339

Milosh Obrenovich, Prince of Serbia, 283–4, 294

Minghetti, Marco, 240, 249

Mirari Vos, 348

Modena, 29, 77; revolution of 1831 in, 142, 226, 227; Austrian occupation of, 145; and union with Sardinia, 235

Moltke, Count Helmuth Karl von, 220, 221–2, 251; in Turkey, 298

Monet, Claude, 372

Monroe Doctrine, 318, 319, 320

Montalembert, Charles de, 347, 348

Montenegro, 284; agriculture in, 92; war with Turkey in 1876, 161, 286; and the Treaty of San Stefano (1878), 162

Monumenta Germaniae Historica, 344

Moravia, 33; revolution of 1848 in, 269

Morley, John, 96, 343

Morning Post, 14

Morny, Duc de, 129

Morocco, 310, 311

Moscow, 78

Mosquito Coast, 319, 320

Motz, Friedrich von, 98–9

Music, 368–71

Musset, Alfred de, 364

Myall Creek, 309

Nagpur, 305

Nanking, Treaty of (1842), 306

Naples (the city), 75, 337; entered by Garibaldi (1860), 237

Naples, Kingdom of, *see* Two Sicilies, Kingdom of

Napoleon I, burial in the Invalides, 174

Napoleon III, 8, 77, 80, 84–5, 101, 102, 167, 325; personal diplomacy of, 3, 4; press policy of, 15; photographs of, 18; commercial policy of, 103; policy towards trade unions of, 129; and the origins of the Crimean War, 144, 145, 175; and the 1859 war with Austria, 145–7, 158, 176, 235; and the 1815 settlement, 148; and the Austro-Prussian war of 1866, 149, 158; and the 1870 war with Prussia, 151–2, 177, 222; and the presidential election in 1848, 173, 382; and the 'Napoleonic Legend', 174; and the *coup d'état* of 1851, 174, 383; and the clericals, 175; and Italian nationalism, 175–6, 234–5; and Rumanian nationalism, 176, 283; and the 'Liberal Empire', 176, 201; and the Mexican adventure, 177, 317–319; and the alliance with Britain, 194–5; and the use of plebiscites, 200; and the army, 205; and relations with Bismarck, 221; and the Roman question, 232, 239–40; and the annexation of Savoy and Nice, 236; and the Polish Revolution of 1863, 278–9; and Algeria, 310; and the American civil war, 321–2; and education, 329, 337

Nash, John, 374

Nassau; in 1830, 209; annexed to Prussia, 220

Natal, 314

National (French newspaper), 168

National Society (Società Nazionale), 235, 236, 237

National Workshops (in Paris in 1848), 130, 172, 173

Navarino, Battle of, 36, 155

Nemours, Duc de, 154

Nesselrode, Prince Karl Robert von, 9

Neuchâtel, 258, 259

New Brunswick, 324

Newcastle-upon-Tyne, 75, 82

New Guinea, 308

New Harmony, 127

New Lanark, 127

Newman, Cardinal John Henry, 338, 349

New York, 79, 322, 323

Peking, Treaty of (1860), 306
Pellico, Silvio, 30
'People's Freedom', 279, 281–2
Pepe, General, 231
Péreire, Emile, 75, 77, 84–5
Perry, Commodore, 307
Peru, 316
Peschiera, 230
Pestalozzi, John Heinrich, 327, 330
Piedmont, see Sardinia, Kingdom of
Pinjarra, 309
Pisacane, Carlo, 236
Pissarro, Camille, 372
Pius VII, Pope, 347
Pius VIII, Pope, 30, 226, 241
Pius IX, Pope, formerly Bishop of
    Imola, 238, 347; and the Kultur-
    kampf, 223–4, 352; from 1846 to
    1848, 229, 231, 349; restoration of
    (1849), 232; the 'prisoner of the
    Vatican', 240; and the Catholic
    hierarchy in Holland, 257; and
    education, 332; and the temporal
    power, 350; and the Syllabus of
    Errors, 351; and papal infalli-
    bility, 351–2; and the Concordat
    with Austria (1855), 353
Place, Francis, 183, 184
Plekhanov, George, 281, 282
Plevna, defence of, 162
Plombières, Pact of, 3, 146–7, 235
Poetry, 363–8
Poland, 64, 159, chapter XI; from
    1815 to 1830, 35; nationalism in, 43;
    industry in, 72; railways in, 78;
    revolution of 1830 in, 142, 154, 275,
    348; during the Crimean War, 175;
    revolution of 1863 in, 218–19, 278–9
Polignac, Prince Jules de, 25, 167
Populists, 281
Portarlington, 202
Portici, 75
Portugal, 27, 28, 142; and her former
    South American Empire, 315
Prague, Treaty of (1866), 220; revolu-
    tion of 1848 in, 269
Principalities of Moldavia and Wal-
    lachia, 36, 283; agriculture in, 92;
    invaded by Russia, 144; Orthodox
    Church in, 353
Prostitution, 132
Protocol of Paris (1856), on mediation,
    136
Proudhon, Pierre Joseph, 45, 60, 62,
    63, 64, 281; his influence in 1848,
    170
Prussia, chapter IX; and the German
    Confederation, 31; from 1815 to
    1830, 32–3; cotton industry in, 82;
    and the commercial treaty with

Austria (1853), 97; and the Zoll-
    verein, 97–9; and the commercial
    treaty with France (1862), 103;
    anti-truck laws passed in, 117;
    factory legislation in, 126; poor
    relief in, 130–1; brothels in, 132;
    diplomatic service in, 138, 139,
    140; during the Italian war of 1859,
    146, 158, 216; and the Schleswig-
    Holstein question, 149; and the
    1866 war with Austria, 149–50,
    158, 220; and the 1870 war with
    France, 150–2; and the Mehemet
    Ali crisis, 156–7; the army and
    general staff in, 205, 220–1, 251; the
    revolution of 1848 in, 213, 242, 243;
    and the crisis over army reform,
    216–17; and the Polish revolution
    of 1863, 219; and the Kulturkampf,
    223–4; and the Neuchâtel question,
    258, 259; education in, 329–30, 331,
    337
Pugin, Augustus Welby, 374–5, 376
Punch, 14

Quadrilateral, 230, 235
Quebec, 323, 324
Querétaro, 318

Raabe, Wilhelm, 356
Radetzky, General, 230, 231, 232, 269
Raiffeisen, Friedrich, 88
Railways, see under relevant country
Rambler, 350
Ranke, Leopold von, 48, 344–5, 346
Rattazzi, Urbano, 234; prime minister
    of Italy, 238; and the connubio with
    Cavour, 244
Redcliffe, Lord Stratford de, formerly
    Stratford Canning, 143
Reform Acts, see under Great Britain
Réforme, 171
'Reinsurance Treaty' of 1887, 163
Renoir, Auguste, 372
Reshid Pasha, 285, 286, 293
Reuter, Paul Julius, and the press
    agency, 17
Révolution, 168
Revolutions of 1830, 1848, etc., see
    under relevant countries
Revue des Deux Mondes, 15
Revue de Paris, 15
Rheinische Zeitung, 16
Ricardo, David, 52, 62, 95
Ricasoli, Baron Bettino; in Tuscany in
    1859, 235; prime minister of Italy,
    258
Richelieu, Duc de, 25
Riemann, Bernhard, 340
Rimbaud, Arthur, 368

in Holland, 333; in Great Britain, 334–6; in Russia, 336
Schopenhauer, Arthur, 46
Schumann, Robert Alexander, 369, 370
Schwarzenberg, Prince Felix von, 270–1, 289
Schwyz, and the *Sonderbund*, 258
Scotland; social conditions in, 113; Presbyterian revival in, 190; foundation of the Free Church of Scotland, 191; and the 1867 Reform Act, 201; education in, 335, 338
Scotsman, 14
Scott, Sir Gilbert, 137, 373
Scott, Sir Walter, 355, 357, 368
Sculpture, 373–4
Sebastopol, siege of, 276
Second Empire in France, *see under* France *or* Napoleon III
Second Republic in France, *see under* France
Sedan, 177, 222
Sedlnitzky, Count, 267
Séguins brothers, 74
Sella, Quintino, 249
Senegal, 313
September Convention (1864), 239
Seraing, 82
Serbia, 283–4, 294–5, agriculture in, 92; conditions of the peasants in, 110; war with Turkey in 1876, 161, 286; and the Treaty of San Stefano (1878), 162; independence of (1878), 267
Seven Weeks War, *see* Austro-Prussian war of 1866
Seymour, Sir Hamilton, 143–4
Shaftesbury, 7th Earl of, formerly Lord Ashley, 125–6
Shanghai, 306
Sheffield, 81; growth of, 85, 190; living conditions in, 119
Shuvalov, Count Peter, 160, 162, 163
Siberia, 109, 303
Sicily; conditions of the peasants in, 108; revolution of 1848 in, 229; occupied by Garibaldi in 1860, 237
Siemens, Friedrich, 81
Siemens, Werner von, 83
Sierra Leone, 313
Silesia, 85; conditions in, 117–18, 121, 124
Simon, Dr John, 122
Singapore, 305
Sisley, Alfred, 372
Slavery in the British Empire, abolition of, 182, 314; and the American civil war, 321, 322

Slavonia, 33
Smirke, Sir Robert, 374
Smith, Dr Southwood, 123
Société des Saisons, 172
Sofia, 163
Solferino, Battle of, 147, 235
Sonderbund, 258–9, 263
South America, 28, 38, 315; British and French investment in, 105
Spain, 27, 54, 195–7; from 1815 to 1830, 28; revolution of 1820 in, 29; agriculture in, 94; in Anglo-French relations, 194; and the Pope, 232; and her former South American empire, 315; and Mexico (1861), 317–18
Spencer, Herbert, 52, 96, 281; influence of Comte on, 339; and Darwinism, 343
Standard, 14
Stanley, Henry Morton, 313
Stanley, Lord, *see* Derby, Earl of
Steam-ships, 78, 79
Steel, production of cheap, 80–2
Stendhal (Marie-Henri Beyle), 356–7
Stephenson, George, 73, 75, 78
Stephenson, Robert, 75, 77
Stockton, 73, 75, 78
St Petersburg, 75, 78; schools in, 336
Straits Convention of 1841, 157
Straits Settlements (Southern Malaya), 305
Strasbourg; Louis-Napoleon's *coup d'état* at, 173; annexed to Germany, 223
Stuttgart, 215, 337
Südbahngesellschaft, 78
Suez Canal, 311
Sweden, 71
Swinburne, Algernon, 365, 366
Switzerland, 71, 77, 227, chapter x; and the free trade movement, 97; the 'era of regeneration' in, 258; and the *Sonderbund*, 259; in 1815, 261; the constitution of 1848 in, 261–2; introduction of the Referendum in, 262; guarantee of neutrality of, 262–3; factory legislation in, 264; emigration to the U.S.A. from, 322; education in, 327, 328, 333
Syllabus of Errors, 351
Syria, Mehemet Ali's conquest of, 155–7

Tahiti, 194
Taiping Rebellion, 306
Tamworth Manifesto, 13, 182
Tanganyika, 312
Tanganyika, Lake, 313

Prussia, 158; and Palmerston, 194; and Swinburne, 366
Victoria Falls, 312
Vienna, 77, 91; revolution of 1848 in, 268–9
Vienna Settlement of 1815, 36–7, 155; Annex XVII of (regulating diplomatic practice), 135; and the union of Holland and Belgium, 254; and the Swiss Confederation, 258, 263; infringed by Metternich in 1846, 268; and Poland, 278; and the Barbary pirates, 310
Vigny, Alfred de, 367
Villafranca, Peace of, 158, 235
Villèle, Comte de, 25
Viollet-le-Duc, Eugène Emmanuel, 376
Visconti-Venosta, Giovanni, 362
Vladivostock, 303
Vossische Zeitung, 16
Votivkirche (in Vienna), 376

Wagner, Richard, 369–70
Wakefield, Edward Gibbon, 309
Wales, social conditions in, 112
Walewski, Comte, 3, 200
Wallace, Alfred Russell, 341–2
'War in Sight' crisis of 1875, 160
Warrington, 201
Warsaw, 78; revolution of 1830 in, 275
Wellington, Duke of, 27, 73, 154, 181
Westminster, Palace of, 375
Westminster Review, 55
Weyerbusch, 88
Whampoa, Treaty of (1842), 306

Wiener Zeitung, 16
William IV, King of England and Hanover, 181, 183, 199, 209
William I, King of Prussia, and, after 1871, Emperor of Germany, 150–1, 152, 207, 215; becomes Prince Regent, 216; and the Schleswig-Holstein question, 219; and the North German Confederation, 220; proclaimed German Emperor, 222; and Bismarck, 247–8
William I, King of the Netherlands, 30, 154, 155, 254, and the Belgian revolution, 255, 256; abdication of, 257
William II, King of the Netherlands, 257; in 1848, 260–1
William III, King of the Netherlands, 257
Windischgrätz, Prince Alfred C. F. zu, 269, 270
Wiseman, Cardinal, 257
Wolff, Bernhard, and the press agency, 17
Wordsworth, William 363
Württemberg, 32; commercial policy of, 98; in 1830, 209, 241; in 1866, 220; education in, 330

Yorkshire, social conditions in, 117
'Young Italy', 227

Zola, Emile, 12, 120, 360–1
Zollverein, 70, 97–100, 103, 222, 248
Zug, in the *Sonderbund*, 258
Zulus, 314
Zurich, Peace of, 235